WELLINGTON'S WARS

WELLINGTON'S WARS

THE MAKING OF A MILITARY GENIUS

HUW J. DAVIES

YALE UNIVERSITY PRESS
NEW HAVEN AND LONDON

Published with assistance from the Annie Burr Lewis Fund

For information about this and other Yale University Press publications, please contact:
U.S. Office: sales.press@yale.edu www.yalebooks.com
Europe Office: sales@yaleup.co.uk www.yalebooks.co.uk

Set in Adobe Caslon by IDSUK (DataConnection) Ltd
Printed in Great Britain by TJ International Ltd, Padstow, Cornwall

Library of Congress Cataloging-in-Publication Data

Davies, Huw J. (Huw John), 1981
    Wellington's wars: the making of a military genius/Huw J. Davies.
        p. cm.
    Includes bibliographical references.
    ISBN 978-0-300-16417-6 (cl : alk. paper)
    1. Wellington, Arthur Wellesley, Duke of, 1769-1852—Military leadership.
2. Great Britain—History, Military—1789-1820. 3. Generals—Great Britain—
Biography. 4. Prime ministers—Great Britain—Biography. I. Title.
    DA68.12.W4D34 2012
    355.0092—dc23
    [B]
                                                                2011041773

A catalogue record for this book is available from the British Library.

10 9 8 7 6 5 4 3 2 1

Contents

Illustrations and Maps

Maps

Preface

A MILITARY GENIUS?

I begin to believe that the finger of God is upon me

Field Marshal Lord Wellington
Sorauren, 3 August 1813[1]

This book has its origins in a story about the Duke of Wellington that was told years after the Battle of Waterloo. In 1827, the Iron Duke was sitting for the famous portraitist, Sir Thomas Lawrence. Coincidentally, at the same time, former foreign secretary and Prime Minister George Canning was also sitting for Lawrence. Canning observed that on one occasion when he visited Lawrence a partially painted portrait of the Duke was visible in the studio. Wellington was seen to be holding in his hand a pocket watch. Behind him, scenes from the Battle of Waterloo were sketched out. A few days later, Canning returned for another sitting. The portrait of Wellington was still there, but in place of the watch, Wellington now held a large telescope. Canning asked Lawrence why he had felt the need to change his portrait. The answer speaks volumes not only about the Waterloo Campaign, but also about Wellington's character.

Wellington had asked why Lawrence depicted him with a watch, and when told that it was designed to show him waiting for the Prussians at Waterloo, Wellington was horrified. This alludes to one of the most controversial and hotly debated moments in British military history. Facing the French Army of 72,000 commanded by Napoleon Bonaparte, with 68,000 ill-trained, badly organised and multinational troops, Wellington chose a strong defensive position, one for which he had become famous, and waited to receive Napoleon's attack. Wellington had arranged with his Prussian ally, Field Marshal Gebhard von Blücher, for support later in the day. The Prussians were positioned some way to the east, and would not be able to come to Wellington's support until mid-afternoon on 18 June. Napoleon's attack on Wellington's defensive line was ferocious, and several times the Duke's forces nearly gave way. Two factors ultimately contributed to the French defeat. First, the French cavalry attacked too soon, and over-extended themselves, leaving the French infantry open to a British counterattack. Secondly, the timely, if late, arrival of the Prussians on the French right flank turned Napoleon's position and caused the general collapse of the French Army. Was the Prussian arrival key to victory at Waterloo or did they arrive in time to capitalise on a battle already won?

Wellington's reaction to Lawrence's portrait of him with a watch left few in doubt as to his opinion. 'That will never do!' the Duke is alleged to have exclaimed. 'I was not "waiting" for the Prussians at Waterloo. Put a telescope in my hand, if you please, but no watch.' Clearly, Wellington came to believe that the arrival of the Prussians played little part in his victory over Napoleon. But was this a reflection of his actual belief or merely a reflection of the image he sought to project of his victory? To hand any credit to the Prussians would be to undermine the decisive nature of his own victory. Worse, it undermined the political credibility of Britain's victory at Waterloo. This, for me, was the critical issue. Wellington was exercising his political generalship. Where had this aspect of his generalship come from, and how far did it dominate his military career and campaigns? Those are the basic questions that this book seeks to address.

Had he allowed Lawrence to depict him with a watch, a more accurate insight into Wellington's thought processes at Waterloo would have been revealed. Wellington agreed to fight at Waterloo only because Blücher promised his support. As such, the Prussians' arrival was an integral part of Wellington's battle plan. He knew he would face a tough ordeal against a superior, veteran force, commanded by a man who he believed accounted for an additional 10,000 men on the battlefield. The allies had a ramshackle coalition of British, Dutch, Belgian and German troops, some of them veterans, some new recruits, all of them under-trained. Wellington must have known that, on his own, he stood little chance of victory. The best he could do would be to stand on the defensive and wear down Napoleon's strength sufficiently so that when Blücher and his 50,000 troops arrived they would be able to strike the decisive blow. In this sense, Wellington was certainly waiting for the Prussians, and must have glanced more than once at his pocketwatch. 'Give me night, or give me Blücher,' as the Duke is alleged to have muttered as the battle appeared to be going Napoleon's way. This anecdote raised in my mind serious questions about Wellington, his skill as a general, and his motivations, both political and military. His military talents are on show in countless volumes, but his generalship is frequently dealt with as part of an isolated account of his campaigns in India, the Iberian Peninsula or at Waterloo. Can one really understand Wellington's generalship without understanding his career as a whole? Was the search for and maintenance of personal glory his only motivation in trying to hide the true impact of the timely arrival of the Prussians at Waterloo? Or was there another agenda? Taken as a whole, his military career from India through the Peninsular War and up to Waterloo suggests an alternative explanation. Wellington was a political general. Politics imbued his military experiences from his 'apprenticeship' in India. Indeed, the fact that Wellington effectively began his military career in India (setting aside a short deployment to the Low Countries, which taught him, famously, 'what one ought not to do') is significant. In India, the young Arthur Wellesley learned that Britain could not fight without allies, and that where there were allies, political problems were always nearby.

It was Karl von Clausewitz who remarked that 'war is nothing more than the continuation of politics by other means'.[2] Throughout his military career, Wellington encountered the turbulence created by the interaction of politics and war. From his earliest experiences of military operations, he was exposed to the frictions created by competing political and military objectives. 'Wars are not fought simply to defeat an enemy but to obtain political objects, and strategy must always be directed to the best means of obtaining these.'[3] If the ultimate British war aim between 1793 and 1815 was the defeat of France, it was certainly not the only one. These aims could not be achieved by Britain alone. A coalition of powers was necessary, while the means to pay for the war had also to be found. Out of this flowed several subsidiary war aims. If these aims did not match or, worse, conflicted with one another, then disaster was certain, unless a clear-sighted general was able to articulate a military strategy that prioritised these aims. Wellington encountered this problem throughout his career, from the ignominious retreat in the Low Countries, in December 1794, through the Peninsular War, to the final showdown with Napoleon at Waterloo. This inability to define a grand strategy was one of the major reasons why the war with Revolutionary and Napoleonic France lasted more than two decades. In India, Wellesley witnessed his elder brother, Richard, Lord Mornington, as Governor-General, manipulate the politics of the indigenous powers to engineer war in order to expand the British Empire. He observed how his brother, a skilled statesman, but overly ambitious and flawed, divided the native powers and subordinated them to a system of political authority in which Britain governed their economic and military power. Wellesley fought wars in India that were of his brother's making, and was intimately involved in the political process that resulted in, and ended, those wars. By his thirtieth year Arthur Wellesley had experienced the continuation of politics by means of war from the perspective of both the defeated and the victorious. India can therefore be said to be where Wellington served his military and political apprenticeship. This understanding of the political influences on military operations is key to understanding the Duke of Wellington's military success. But did it make him a military genius?

It was Clausewitz, again, who coined and defined the term 'military genius'. Such a person was a man with 'a very highly developed mental aptitude for a particular occupation', namely war. 'The essence of the military genius is that it does not consist in a single . . . gift' but in a combination of faculties and traits. Wellington, undoubtedly, possessed just such a combination. He had a 'special type of mind', a 'strong rather than a brilliant one', with 'a sensitive and discriminating judgement', which was able to 'scent out the truth'. He had the strength of character 'to keep [his] head at times of exceptional stress and violent emotion', allowing, for the most part, reason rather than fear or prejudice to define his decision-making. He also possessed the determination 'to stand like a rock' and act on belief despite uncertainty.[4] He was a strategic genius, able to translate frequently murky political objectives into clear-sighted military objectives and priorities. Falling out of this was his operational genius, coordinating the movements of divisions, corps and armies to achieve a decisive outcome that helped meet the obscure and contradictory political objectives that defined his strategy. But crucial to this was his tactical genius. His eye for terrain and his ability to out-think his enemies on countless occasions inspired his officers and men. He was also lucky: despite never shirking his duty to command from the front, and on many occasions exposing himself to enemy fire in order to direct a battle, he never suffered anything worse than a bruise. Taken together, these qualities merit the term 'military genius', but why was Wellington such a successful political general? The genius of Wellington's political generalship lies in the parts that make up the whole: the strategic approach; the clarity of his planning and orders; his use of intelligence; his decisive use of terrain; his recourse to deception and surprise; the trust in his subordinates and army; the limits to his objectives; his relationships, frequently stormy, with his allies;

and his ability, in the face of much resistance, to persuade his government to support his ideas, despite often unpleasant arguments. These skills were the product of his military career as a whole.

But inevitably, where there is genius, there are flaws. Wellington sometimes relied too much on his judgement and intuition, when they were contradicted by intelligence reports. On occasion, his decisions appeared dogmatic. When this happened, it is perhaps a mark of his military genius that he managed to extricate victory from the jaws of defeat. Furthermore, Wellington did not always display 'sensitive and discriminating judgement'. In India and Spain, he habitually misunderstood his enemies and his allies. Indian allies were viewed with distrust and suspicion, enemies with disdain. Arthur Wellesley, and his men, paid a heavy price for this misjudgement. When he got to Spain, he made the mistake of subconsciously equating his new with his former allies in India. As a result, he failed to understand the reasons behind Spain's resistance to Napoleon. This failure resulted in continuous stormy relations throughout the Peninsular War.

Ultimately, though, military success was the product of his political generalship. Wellington understood the muddy waters that surrounded Britain's strategic political objectives, and exercised his discretion in negotiating them. In India, he recognised the political requirement for expansion to ensure economic stability. In Spain, he realised that his first consideration must be the safety of his army. If he lost the army, the government lost the war. Faced with overwhelming French numbers in 1809, Wellington had no choice but to retreat and engage in a protracted war of attrition, leaving the Spaniards to the mercy of the French invaders. This was clearly not compatible with supporting his Spanish allies. With the French weakened, Wellington could shift from defence to offence. Throughout his operations, however, the first priority was the security of the British Army; the second was the liberation of Spain and the defeat of France. To some degree, then, the art of the political general was the art of prioritisation, but explaining to the Spaniards why their war of national survival was not the main British priority was no easy task. 'Everything in war is simple,' Clausewitz opined, 'but the simplest thing is difficult.'[5]

Likewise at Waterloo he recognised that Britain was fighting both to defeat Napoleon and to preserve the new European balance of power. Ironically, it was not only Napoleon, but also Wellington's allies the Prussians, who threatened this new order. They hoped to increase their power at the expense of France. The same political problems that had hampered the allied war effort at the beginning of the fight with France, when Wellington was a junior colonel, now threatened it at its

denouement, when he was a field marshal and a duke. Wellington therefore realised he needed to act to undermine the political legitimacy of his
allies at the same time as he was reliant on their military support in battle.
Such were the problems Wellington had to cope with in his military
career: a continuous act of balancing conflicting political priorities in
order to achieve military victory. The story of how he navigated this mine-
field is the real story of his military genius.

Inevitably, a book that concentrates on the development of a military
and political genius is not going to conform to the conventional parameters of a biography. This is no personal history of Wellington's life.
Where his family appear, for example, they do so because of the political
or military influences they had on Wellington's career. As an account of
the development of Wellington's political as well as military generalship,
the book concentrates heavily on his experiences in India. These were his
formative years as both a political and a military genius, and are therefore
deserving of considerable attention. Inevitably, as well, an account that
dispenses with the conventional 'man of destiny' argument – 'the finger of
God', the evidence suggests, was not on Wellington – and focuses on the
raw elements of Wellington's development will unearth some unsavoury
characteristics. The Duke of Wellington, then, who emerges from these
pages is a man full of contradictions. He was a hero to some, a villain to
others. For many, he was the man responsible for defeating Napoleon
Bonaparte, freeing Europe from the menace of Revolutionary France. He
was a man of extraordinary military talent and vision, who was ahead of
his time on the reform of pressing command issues such as intelligence
and logistics; his inspiring presence helped transform a bedraggled army
into the finest British fighting force for generations. For others, his hubris
meant he sought to discredit some and claim their achievements as his
own. Among his victims were fellow officers in his own army, members of
the government that tirelessly supported him, allies in Portugal and Spain,
and, of course, the Prussians at Waterloo, from whom he reputedly stole
victory. For fans of Napoleon, the name Wellington incites revulsion. To
them, he was a cautious general with no identifiable skill apart from an
excess of good luck – a Conservative (with a capital C), who though he
achieved considerable military success saw no need as a politician to
implement institutional reforms that had made that success possible. An
opponent of reform throughout his career, he can be held responsible for
the stagnation of military development in the nineteenth century that
ultimately led to the horrors of war at the beginning of the twentieth.
Fundamentally opposed to universal democracy, he was at once a hero and
a villain of the masses.

Wellington's own views are equally contradictory. His troops were the 'scum of the earth', but before Waterloo he commented, referring to a redcoat, 'it all depends on that article, whether we do the business or not. Give me enough,' he said, 'and I am sure.'[6] Similarly, he considered that he alone was fit to command. His generals, he argued, were 'really heroes when I am on the spot to direct them, but when I am obliged to quit them they are children'.[7] This comment was made in the wake of a close-fought action in which two of his most trusted generals had let him down. On other occasions, though, he was effusive about his generals' abilities. 'How would society get on without all my boys?' he asked in the wake of his victory in the Peninsula. So, depending on whether you think Wellington was a military genius, a man beloved of his men, a general of innate fighting skill and decision; if you think he was a miserable, intolerant and aloof villain; if you think he was cautious, or if you think he was aggressive, there is ample evidence from the Duke's own pen, lips and actions to support your case. The present volume is not going to come down on either side of this argument: Wellington was conflicted and a mass of contradictions. He was not the perfect military hero, as popular memory would have him. Alongside his many strengths, he had some intractable flaws. But amongst these contradictions, Wellington, throughout his military career, was an uncompromising, ruthless and brutal political operator. He understood the relationship between politics and war better, perhaps, than any of his peers. He found himself at the fault line of the two worlds of the politician and the soldier, and he navigated it with skill and precision; not without friction, but ultimately successfully. This understanding was the basis of his success and of his genius.

Researching and writing this book has been a genuine pleasure, made all the more so by the support and encouragement of friends, family and colleagues across three continents. I wrote my PhD at the University of Exeter, under the guidance and tuition of Professor Jeremy Black. His criticism of my work then, and support ever since, is the basis of my approach to historical enquiry. He will, I hope, recognise this book as the product of the original enormously ambitious research proposal I submitted about ten years ago. He wisely advised me to narrow my focus – to intelligence – but throughout my research for my PhD, I kept an eye out for material that would help me construct a much wider criticism of Wellington's generalship. This book, as with the PhD, would not have been possible without his scholarly wisdom. Professor Charles Esdaile examined my PhD and since then has been a good friend and critic of my ideas at conferences. His knowledge of the Peninsular War, and Spanish politics and society during it, is frankly unparalleled and, again, this book would not have been possible without his help. Others who have lent their thoughts and criticisms of my arguments over the years are Rory Muir, Randolf Cooper, Bruce Collins and the late, and much missed, Richard Holmes. To them, my thanks.

A word of thanks also to my friends and colleagues at the Joint Services Command and Staff College: in particular Niall Barr, Huw Bennett, Warren Chin, Jon Hill, Ashley Jackson, Rachael Kelly, Saul Kelly, Greg Kennedy, Ken Payne, Patrick Porter, Martin Robson and Chris Tripodi. Conversations over lunchtime seminars have often led to new and interesting avenues of enquiry. As well as this, the research I conducted in India would not have been possible without the generous financial support of the King's College Central Research Fund. I must also thank the students at the Staff College for their intellectually stimulating comments and contributions in relevant discussions; as also the organisers and participants of the various Staff Rides and Battlefield Tours to Spain and Portugal I have supported over the past few years. It is rare that one gets the opportunity to visit places of such importance to understanding Wellington's generalship, let alone to do so with serving military professionals who offered original and thoughtful suggestions to explain Wellington's actions.

The idea for the book would have remained just that without the enthusiastic encouragement of my editors at Yale, Heather McCallum and Rachael Lonsdale. Rachael's thorough comments on my original manuscript have undoubtedly made this a much better book. I must also thank the staff of libraries and archives from London to Lisbon and Durham to Delhi. In particular Professor Chris Woolgar and his staff at the Hartley Library in Southampton, keeper of the Wellington Papers, have been most helpful, as have the staff of the British Library, the National Archives in Kew, the National Army Museum in Chelsea, and the National Archives of India in New Delhi. It is with the permission of the Controller of Her Majesty's Stationary Office, that Crown copyright material is published from the Wellington Papers.

A special mention should be reserved for the group of American academics that I first met in 2008 at the Consortium on the Revolutionary Era, the Society for Military History and the International Congress on Military History: Barbara Cook, Llew Cook, Ed Cross, Lee Eysturlid, Paco de la Fuente, Jack Gill, Rick Herrera, Kenny Johnson, Kevin McCranie, Alex Mikaberidze, Josh Moon, Jim Sack, Rick Schneid, Ty Seidule, John Severn, Bruce Vandervort and Geoff Wawro. Their support, encouragement and friendship are extremely important to me. A special thanks to Mike Leggiere and Will Hay, whose exhaustive comments on my first draft manuscript proved transformative for the quality of both my writing and my argument. I owe them both a great deal. Needless to say, any errors that remain are mine alone.

Finally, none of this would have been possible without the support and encouragement of my family and friends. Pete Alborough, Victoria Eastwood, Dave Farmer and Tim Seward are immovable rocks of support and lifelong friends. Stephen Manning generously used a large portion of his air-miles to get me to Portugal for research (and battlefield tours). Abigail Locke and Jo Moss gave me a place to stay whilst I was researching in London and Southampton. I have to thank Susan Harvard and Sandra Smith (I know of no one else with more knowledge of Wellington's personal life, politics and humanity) for their tireless interrogations of my arguments and ideas. I owe my parents, Janet and John, my eternal gratitude and love for first suggesting I become a historian, when I thought the idea was complete madness, and then supporting me, when I realised it was all I wanted to do. Without them, this whole journey would not have been possible, let alone the book. Finally, it would not have been possible for me to research and write this book without the constant love and support of Elizabeth. This book is dedicated to her.

*   *   *

A brief note on names in the text. In 1798, Wellington's family name changed from Wesley to Wellesley. To avoid confusion, I have referred to Wellington as Wellesley until his elevation to a peerage in 1809, when I start calling him Wellington. After their father's death in 1781, Richard became the Second Earl of Mornington – an Irish title. In 1799, Mornington was given an Irish marquessate, and became Marquess Wellesley. However, to differentiate him from Wellesley, I continue to refer to him as Mornington throughout the chapters that focus on India.

CHAPTER I

An Introduction to War and Politics

ARTHUR WELLESLEY IN EUROPE AND INDIA, 1794–1799

Colonel Wellesley was missing, and the force under his command had been completely broken, repulsed and dispersed. . . They had stormed an entrenchment lined with the enemy's pikemen with lances at least twenty feet long, and for once the bayonet had proved ineffectual. The whole detachment was broken and then charged by the pikemen. . . The Colonel had been seen by some of the men making off. . . towards the encampment. . . He soon reached camp, and throwing himself on a table inside [the General's] dining marquee, burst into a violent passion of tears, exclaiming 'Oh, I'm ruined forever! I'm ruined forever! My God, I'm ruined forever! What shall I do? Where shall I go?'

Captain Ralph Bayly, 12th Regiment of Foot
Seringapatam, Mysore, India, 5 April 1799[1]

THIS was Arthur Wellesley's first real taste of battle, and it was a firm indication of the bitterness of war for an eighteenth-century soldier. Wellesley, a twenty-nine-year-old lieutenant-colonel, was in command of the 33rd Regiment of Foot. He had been ordered to capture a small wooded copse, known in south India as a tope. The British needed the tope if they were to stand a chance of successfully preparing siege works against Seringapatam, the island fortress that was also the capital of Tipu Sultan's Mysore. A British force numbering some 20,000 troops had arrived at the fortress two days earlier, after an arduous march that had seen countless lives lost in the inhospitable jungle that dominated Mysore. The Fourth Anglo-Mysore War had broken out after the renegade dictator, Tipu Sultan, had covertly sought assistance from the French, Britain's intractable European foe, in ousting Britain from the subcontinent.

Wellesley's attack on Sultanpetah Tope was badly coordinated. He had conducted no reconnaissance so knew nothing of the natural obstacles the enemy could use as a defence. The light from the campfires in his rear only served to make the darkness ahead of him more impenetrable. The failure of a bayonet charge on a ridge occupied by a line of enemy pikemen caused the attack to disintegrate. Unable to see where he was going, and quickly losing sight of his troops, Wellesley, injured in the knee by a spent musket ball,[2] panicked and fled back to the British encampment. The initial counterattack by Tipu's troops had caused the British soldiers to throw themselves to the ground. It was this that had resulted in the separation of Wellesley from the majority of his command.[3] He reportedly told his Commander-in-Chief, General Sir George Harris that his entire regiment had been wiped out, although other accounts suggest Harris had already gone to bed.[4] Whatever the situation, Wellesley certainly spent an uncomfortable night, at least until his second-in-command, Major Shea, returned with the main body of his regiment. Nevertheless, it did not look good for Wellesley.

The next morning, Harris asked his second-in-command, General David Baird, to lead a second assault on the tope, as the enemy troops there were hampering the position of the 12th Regiment which had successfully, although bloodily, taken a riverbank opposite the wood. Baird, however, insisted Wellesley be given a second opportunity. This was a clever move by Baird. He realised that unless Wellesley was given a chance to compensate for his failure the night before, the young colonel's career might very well have ended. This was unlikely to please the Governor-General, Wellesley's elder brother, Richard, Lord Mornington. But it cannot hide the fact that Wellesley had embarrassed himself. The operation was badly planned and mishandled. Only his closest friends appeared to forgo the temptation to gossip and complain of the distinctly light treatment he had received. It is unlikely that anybody else would have escaped censure. Of course, the following morning, with the scene of operations fully lit, Wellesley completely redeemed himself. The steady advance of the British troops caused Tipu's troops to retreat from the tope with virtually no resistance.

The incident was to leave a deep impression on Wellesley. From the outset, it was apparent that many in the army felt he had got off lightly. Bayly alleged that if 'any other officer in the army . . . [had] been guilty of similar dereliction from his duties of his profession, no earthly power could have prevented his dismissal from the Service'.[5] Undoubtedly, Wellesley's escape caused ill feeling, and it is not entirely certain whether this is unjust. The image Wellesley presents of himself in his correspondence, and from the comments and opinions of others, who may or may not have had an axe to grind, is of a pompous, arrogant, aloof individual, whose capacity for emotional intelligence was limited and sensitivity to the feelings of others virtually non-existent. Yet, to read historical accounts of Wellington's early career, one would think that he was centre stage during the planning and preparations and eventual execution of the Fourth Anglo-Mysore War. If all that were available were the published correspondence of Wellesley and Richard Wellesley, then this is an unsurprising conclusion. The correspondence of Harris and Baird mentions Wellesley's conduct, and both play down the glaring failure of 5 April, but these letters are to the Governor-General. Other accounts of the campaign speak differently. The few letters and diaries that survive barely mention Wellesley's actions. The most telling, perhaps, is that of Lieutenant-Colonel Barry Close,[6] who as Adjutant-General oversaw the planning and execution of the campaign. Wellesley is a marginal figure: a close friend, helpful, well informed, demonstrating skill and a capacity for clear-mindedness that was perhaps rare among his peers; but by no means the figure of authority and decision that appears in many later accounts.

But to say that Wellesley's career should have ended after the fiasco at Sultanpetah Tope is perhaps going a bit far. Baird, Wellesley's immediate superior, reportedly commented that he 'failed, not through the want of skill or bravery, but from circumstances'.[7] Nevertheless, it is hard to escape the conclusion that Wellesley eluded serious censure for this incident. Most seem convinced that his good fortune was the result of his family connection in the government. Neither Baird nor Harris was a fool, and neither wanted to antagonise the Governor-General unnecessarily.

The early years of Wellesley's military career, then, were not the glittering opening to predestined military glory. He displayed few of the characteristics that define a military genius. It was India that made Arthur Wellesley a military genius, and the lesson he learned at Sultanpetah Tope was one of many that the subcontinent would impart. To his brother, Wellesley wrote of his 'determination, when in my power, never to suffer an attack to be made by night upon an enemy who is prepared and strongly posted, and whose posts have not been reconnoitred by daylight'.[8] If he had learned the importance of thorough reconnaissance, the episode also left him with a bad case of damaged pride. For some historians, this led Wellesley to salvage his honour by attacking his enemies in India no matter the cost, turning him into an aggressive and unstable tactician.

*   *   *

The fiasco at Sultanpetah Tope came some twelve years into Wellesley's military career. After a brief stint at Eton, from where he was withdrawn when his father's death revealed the poor state of the family's finances, Wellesley was enrolled in the French Royal Academy of Equitation at Angers on 16 January 1786. A year later, Richard Wellesley, now head of the family as Lord Mornington, bought his younger brother a commission in the 73rd Highland Regiment. By September 1793, and having seen no active military service, Mornington had purchased three further promotions, and Arthur Wellesley was appointed Lieutenant-Colonel in the 33rd Regiment of Foot. Less than a year later, Wellesley was deployed in command of his regiment to the Low Countries. He arrived at Ostend at the height of summer in 1794, as the British Army was in headlong retreat following successive defeats at the hands of Revolutionary France.

The War of the First Coalition, as it became known, had a year earlier seemed so promising for the allied powers of Great Britain, Austria and Prussia. The ragtag armies of Revolutionary France were on the run, staring defeat in the face, and on the brink of losing the French capital, Paris. But the failure of the Great Powers generally to define a unified grand strategy to defeat Revolutionary France, and specifically the incompetence of the Duke of York, the commander of the British Army in the Low Countries, snatched defeat from the jaws of victory. In August 1793,

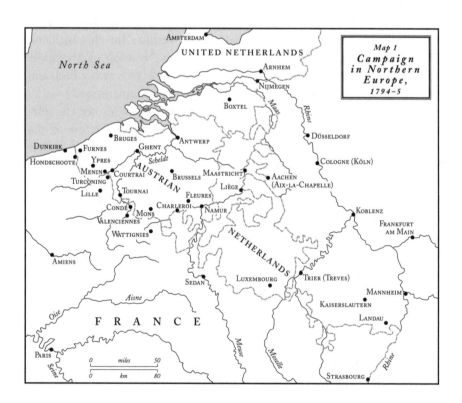

York had laid siege to Dunkirk, but had done so without siege guns. All he was able to do was blockade the town walls. The garrison called for back-up, and before the British siege train arrived, 45,000 French reinforcements marched on Dunkirk, forcing the 37,000 British troops to retreat into Belgium. Had the British and their allies, the Austrians and Prussians, decided to march on Paris together, there is little chance that the revolutionaries could have withstood the onslaught. But, in pursuing different political objectives, the allies gave the revolutionaries the time they needed to regroup and fight back. Failure to agree a unified grand strategy would blight the allied war effort for the next two decades.

The failure of the Dunkirk expedition literally and metaphorically opened the flood gates on the allied war effort against Revolutionary France. The mismanagement of the Dunkirk expedition mirrors that on a larger scale in the campaign as a whole: poor administration, communication and logistics. Worst of all, though, the operation suffered from poor intelligence. York was unaware of the best canal along which to transport the siege train once it arrived and he was completely unaware of the approach of the French reinforcements towards Dunkirk until the day before they attacked.

The entire allied line collapsed, and by October the British, Austrians and Prussians were retreating east through Belgium. In 1794, a massive French advance involving 207,000 troops fought and defeated the combined Austrian and British Armies at Tourcoing on 18 May. Worse was to follow. On 26 June, in an attempt to relieve the besieged city of Charleroi, an Austrian force of 54,000 attacked a French army of 70,000 at Fleurus. The French line held and counterattacked the Austrians. After this defeat, the Austrians fell back towards the Rhineland, breaking completely from the British. York, meanwhile, pressed by a second French advance, retreated towards the Dutch border, hoping to hold the British line at Antwerp and the Scheldt.

On the same day as the Austrians were defeated at Fleurus, Lieutenant-Colonel Arthur Wellesley arrived in Ostend in command of the 33rd. No sooner had he landed than he was forced to join the retreat, and the British fell back on strong defensive lines on the rivers Maas and Waal in the eastern Netherlands. The first line was outflanked when the French surprised and took the small but strategically vital village of Boxtel. It was here, on 15 September 1794, that Wellesley had his first experience under fire. Brief and trifling though it was, Wellesley and his regiment had to fight a delaying action to allow a beleaguered Guards regiment to extricate itself from heavy bombardment by a concealed line of enemy artillery, and a charge by a regiment of French cavalry. Despite facing an oncoming cavalry attack, the men under Wellesley's command held their fire. When the enemy was within range, Wellesley gave the order to fire, 'instantly throwing a few cool and well-directed volleys into the enemy's squadrons'.[9] The steadiness of his men, combined with the discipline of their firepower, halted the French cavalry and allowed the rest of the British force to retreat without incident.

Thereafter, the British fell back on Grave and Nijmegen, taking up strong defensive positions on the River Waal. York's position was undoubtedly good. The river was clearly the lynchpin of York's defence. In 1794, it would have been flowing at approximately 8 or 9 knots. Boats would take a great deal of time to cross, under fire from the opposite bank, and would end up about a mile downstream of their starting point. By 21 November York had fourteen regiments on the northern bank of the Waal, spanning seven or eight miles of its length. Wellesley and the 33rd were deployed at Tiel, seven miles west of Nijmegen, and twenty from Headquarters in Arnhem.[10]

Despite this seemingly unassailable position, it was the belief at Headquarters that the enemy planned 'to attempt the passage of the Waal'. For the 33rd, this meant that the men were 'all kept upon the alert'. From his location at Tiel, Wellesley believed 'it will turn out that they are going into Winter Quarters from Nijmegen, as I think it impossible for any troops (even the French) to keep the field in this severe weather'.[11] It was the severe weather that was to provide the route to victory for the French. On 5 December, a severe frost set in. Two days later, the river was glazed with a sheet of ice; on the 8th, and again on the 10th, the French attacked, but on both occasions they were repulsed. At the end of December they attacked again, this time in overwhelming force, puncturing the British defence in several places. On New Year's Eve, the British attempted a counterattack to capture a small fort at Tuil, four miles downstream from Tiel. The fort commanded the Waal for several miles in both directions, and if they gained this key French crossing point it should at least temporarily stem the French advance. Wellesley and the 33rd formed part of this offensive under the general command of Sir David Dundas. Rather than an explicit attempt to repel the French advance, it seems more likely to have been a delaying action to facilitate a general British withdrawal.

As a delaying tactic, the assault was successful. Dundas remained in Tuil until 4 January 1795, when it was evacuated, and the British fell back to the Rhine, some ten miles north of Nijmegen. This position was abandoned when the French managed to break through, cross the Rhine and station artillery on the Oosterbeek Heights. From there, they were able to threaten British Headquarters at Arnhem.[12] The third British defensive line was thus rendered untenable, and the army was again forced to retreat headlong to the River Ems. The allied campaign in the Low Countries was over. In March, the British contingent, which had fought valiantly on the continent for two years, was evacuated, broken and bruised, the 33rd Regiment of Foot and Arthur Wellesley among them.

The first practical military lesson Arthur Wellesley learned, then, was 'how one ought not to do it', and 'that', an ageing Duke of Wellington recalled in 1839, 'is always something'.[13] But this, despite Wellington's pronouncements years later, was not the only lesson. The campaign had also demonstrated the importance of the well-disciplined soldier. The capabilities of the British Army rested on the confidence and coherence of its regiments of infantry. A soldier unable to hold the line jeopardised the cohesion of his entire unit. At the same time, firepower held back until the last moment, when it was most effective, could have devastating effects on advancing enemy troops. What for many were simply instructions in a manual had been visibly demonstrated by the cohesion of the 33rd at Boxtel, compared with the disunity of the Guards. To Boxtel can be attributed Arthur Wellesley's understanding of the importance of the common soldier as the basic fighting unit of the British Army, of 'the mechanism and power of the individual soldier; then that of the company, a battalion and so on'.[14]

If Boxtel had demonstrated a positive, the campaign as a whole had also demonstrated a host of negatives. Wellesley had witnessed appalling command practices. 'I was on the Waal ... from October to January,' Wellington recalled, 'and during all that time I only saw once one general from the headquarters, which was old Sir David Dundas. We had letters from England, and I declare that those letters told us more of what was passing at headquarters than we learned from the headquarters themselves.'[15] Paralysis of command during the defence of the Waal had been noted by several sources. Dundas himself wrote repeatedly to Headquarters complaining of a lack of orders and direction.[16] The want of command was noticed at a basic level by the rank and file: lack of food, warm clothing and hospitals prompted the rapid spread of disease.[17] Perhaps dissatisfaction with the conduct of the campaign amongst both soldiers and officers would not have been so great if rumours of the frequent dinners and parties, of which extraordinary drunkenness was a distinct characteristic, had not filtered down from Headquarters. To make matters worse, the Duke of York enjoyed a barely civil relationship with his counterpart in the Dutch Army, the Prince of Orange. If the conduct of Britain's allies was poor, it was partially because the commanders of each force could not agree.

This state of affairs prompted one of Wellington's most famous maxims: 'the real reason why I succeeded in my own campaigns is because I was always on the spot – I saw everything, and did everything for myself.'[18] Certainly Wellington gained a reputation among his troops for being everywhere all the time, but it seems much more likely that his ability to engage in complex operations rested on his planning skills, acquired much later in India. In the Low Countries, York appears to have anticipated few of the setbacks he encountered, whether the result of enemy action, his own incompetence in command, or what Clausewitz later termed 'friction in war' – poor weather, technical failure, unexpected and debilitating illness.

Command difficulties were linked to the quality of officers in the British Army. Wellington later noted that although the men were good, the officers were more often than not of very bad quality. This resulted from the purchasing of commissions and promotions. Wellesley himself, of course, was a beneficiary of the system, but this masks the fact that men with limited experience, and even less professionalism, were put in positions of authority in the most severe of conditions. Over the next fifteen years, unsuited as he was to command, the Duke of York proved an adept administrator and began the process of reform in the British Army that was to produce the high-quality officers and troops that served Wellington in the Peninsula. Although he did not abolish the purchasing system (and indeed was forced to resign as Commander-in-Chief in 1809 because of a scandal over purchasing), he introduced uniform systems of training and drill, increased professionalism within the officer corps, and established the commissariat and ordnance on a war footing.[19]

The ill-fated expedition to the Low Countries provided numerous other lessons that would serve Wellesley in his future military career. If the command of the British Army left it beleaguered, there was little hope that Britain's continental allies would come to the rescue. But British ability to bring military power to bear rested on the support of her allies. Britain could not bring a large enough army to the field to defeat France without the support of at least one major continental power. This applied even in India, where after 1799 Britain became the dominant European force. Everywhere Britain fought on land successfully, she did so with the help of allies.[20] The campaign in the Low Countries was a good example of how not to manage an alliance-based military campaign. From the outset, strategic differences existed between Britain, Austria and Prussia. These manifested themselves quickly in the conduct of the campaigns. Britain's siege of Dunkirk, to the Austrians, came at the expense of a glorious march on Paris. The failure to take the fortress, weakly defended though it was, proved the turning point of the campaign.

If Anglo-Austrian cooperation before Dunkirk had been strained, it was virtually non-existent afterwards.

But it was towards the Dutch that the British were most indignant. York, with some reason, repeatedly blamed the Dutch for the failure of his plans, alternately calling them cowards and fools.[21] If York was too eager to blame the Dutch, his troops were also independently angry at their allies' shortcomings. After the evacuation of Nijmegen on 9 November, Corporal Brown of the Coldstream Guards remembered how, as 1,500 Dutch troops crossed a bridge of boats, 'the enemy having brought some guns to bear on the bridge, a random shot cut a rope, by which part of the bridge swung round to the enemy's side, and about 800 Dutch were taken prisoner'. According to Brown, 'the loss would not be great if they were all taken'.[22] Although he would not have realised it at the time, the campaign in the Low Countries gave Wellesley an important reference point for the problems resulting from poor relations with, and poor handling of, allied troops.

Associated with this were the difficulties the British encountered with the local population. The British retreat to Nijmegen had been precipitate and by the time they reached the Waal, the backbone of the British Army, its commissariat and supply, was starting to crumble. Starving troops fell upon the inhabitants of Nijmegen with ferocity. Support for the British among the Dutch populace was weak at best, but following the garrisoning of Nijmegen the atmosphere was one of barely concealed hostility. Corporal Brown, who was briefly part of Wellesley's brigade, noted how the army 'received in general but very indifferent treatment from the inhabitants, who by the bye ... are no friends to us, and give Old England but little thanks for expending her blood and treasure in defending them from the incursions of the [French], whom they would certainly make more welcome than us'.[23] It was with some reason that the populace were suspicious of the British. Setting aside Dutch sympathies for the French Revolutionaries aside, reports had arrived from other parts of the Low Countries of the barbarity of the British and Austrians. Stories of cellars pillaged, houses burnt to the ground and their inhabitants massacred, were rife by time the British arrived in Nijmegen.[24] Again, Wellesley would not have known it, but the problems caused by the indiscipline of British troops on foreign soil were to be a significant aspect of his future military career. The Low Countries campaign served to demonstrate this at first hand.

It was in the Low Countries that Wellesley gained an appreciation of rigorous command, vigorous discipline, good relations with allied armies and populations alike, and the importance of reliable logistics and intelligence, precisely because, on all these counts, the British Army had failed.

The withdrawal of the British force from the Low Countries in 1795 was a serious setback for Britain's strategy in the war against Revolutionary France. Prussia signed a separate peace treaty in April, and Holland and Spain changed sides. Efforts soon focused on establishing a new triple alliance between the British, Austrians and Russians, although the negotiations were fraught with difficulties. At the same time, new opportunities arose. The capture of French sugar islands in the West Indies, depriving the enemy of an important economic asset, became the main focus of British strategy, while other possibilities for military intervention in Europe revealed themselves: the Vendée revolt offered a chance to strike a blow in France itself, and naval support was quickly thrown into Royalist Toulon. Of the three options, only the West Indies was a military success, although at extreme cost as thousands of troops succumbed to yellow fever. The Vendée revolt was all but stamped out with brutal retribution against the revolutionaries, whilst in Toulon a Corsican artillery officer by the name of Buonaparte was able to deny the Royal Navy access to the port, demonstrating true military genius as he did so. Britain's Mediterranean strategy collapsed soon after, and in 1796 the Royal Navy was forced to withdraw past the Straits of Gibraltar into the Atlantic. Despite initial hopes that the war would be short, it was becoming clear that this conflict would be prolonged. Just how prolonged, was beyond anyone's imagination.

For Wellesley, meanwhile, the West Indies awaited. He and his regiment set sail in the autumn of 1795, but six weeks of gales prevented the completion of the voyage and Wellesley was spared the disease-infested campaigns on the sugar islands, returning to Cork in January 1796. The following April, the new destination of the 33rd was named: India. As Wellesley disembarked at Calcutta in February 1797, he could not have known the importance of this turn of events.

*   *   *

Wellesley arrived in India as Britain's relations with the native powers were reaching a critical juncture. He would have been well versed in the balance of power there, having spent the six-month voyage studying the political dynamics of the indigenous powers of the subcontinent. He knew that British intervention in India was based purely on economic gain. The majority of troops in the country were paid for by the East India Company, which effectively represented Britain's economic interests. The Crown was represented by the Governor-General, who commonly resided at Calcutta, but Britain's and the Company's colonies were divided into three administrative 'presidencies': Bengal (Calcutta), Bombay and Madras.

If Britain was a powerful economic force, it was not yet the dominant military and political power. The India Act of 1784 had intentionally imposed limits on British imperial expansion. Britain was in India for economic profit, and would bring European order to facilitate this, but she was not there for conquest. Conflict with any of the major native powers could take place only as the result of an aggressive act on their part; essentially the India Act outlined a policy of self-defence. The balance of power in India rested between three major native powers: Tipu Sultan of Mysore in the south; the Peshwa of the Maratha Confederacy, based in Poona, to the north; and the Nizam of Hyderabad, in the centre and to the east. Britain's relations with each varied along the scale between war and peace. Tipu had been at war with Britain once before (1789–92); his father Hyder Ali twice (1766–9 and 1780–4). Relations when Wellesley arrived were tense. There were rumours circulating that Tipu sought support from France and, although French power was on the wane in India, there would always be concern that Revolutionary France might seek to weaken the British position with the support of one or two Anglophobic native powers.

The Marathas were also a cause for concern, but their internal disunity prevented a coordinated attempt to undermine British power. Fractured and unstable, the Maratha Confederacy was a loose conglomerate of Indian princes nominally ruled from the city of Poona by the Peshwa, Baji Rao II. Between 1664 and 1680 the Maratha Confederacy had been established under the authority of a single figure, Shivaji, the son of a Maratha chieftain who had served in the armies of the Muslim kingdoms of the Deccan. After Shivaji's death, nominal leadership rested in the hands of the Peshwa, who represented the views of the united chieftains or *sirdars* and *jagirdars* of the Maratha Confederacy.[25] Constant military reform had maintained the superiority of the Maratha armies until the Battle of Panipat in January 1761 saw the Peshwa's army defeated by a joint Afghan/Indo-Muslim army. The Peshwa's central authority declined, and the Maratha *sirdars* gradually exerted their authority. From 1800, the most powerful was Daulatrao Sindhia, but also threatening the stability of the Poona government was Jaswant Rao Holkar, and Raghuji Bhonsla II. By the end of the eighteenth century, Britain and the East India Company were confronted with a disparate group of princely states that feared British encroachment, but competed with each other for influence. It was in Britain's interests to maintain this equilibrium, as, combined, the Maratha Confederacy could simultaneously threaten all three British presidencies in India.[26] Added to the mix was an innumerable quantity of less powerful chieftains, who continued to press for the authority of the

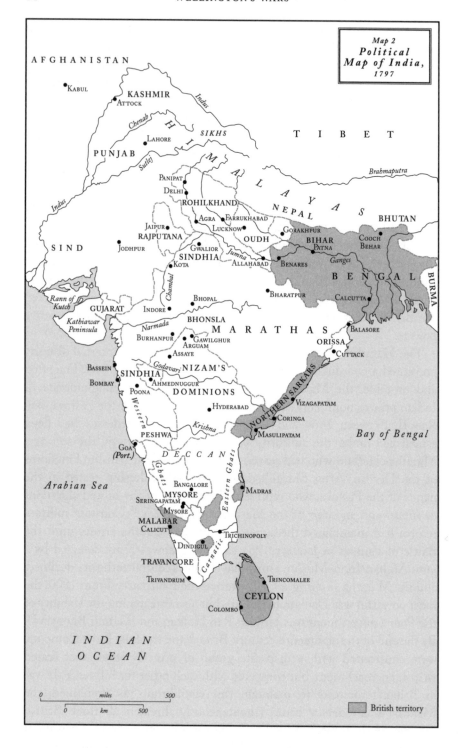

Map 2
*Political
Map of India,*
1797

AFGHANISTAN

Kabul

KASHMIR
Attock

Indus

Chenab

LAHORE

SIKHS

T I B E T

PUNJAB

Sutlej

H I M A L A Y A S

Brahmaputra

Indus

PANIPAT

DELHI

ROHILKHAND

NEPAL

BHUTAN

AGRA   FARRUKHABAD

JAIPUR

GORAKHPUR

COOCH
BEHAR

RAJPUTANA

LUCKNOW

OUDH

BIHAR

SIND

JODHPUR

GWALIOR

SINDHIA

Jumna

ALLAHABAD

PATNA

BENARES

Ganges

BENGAL

KOTA

BURMA

BHARATPUR

CALCUTTA

*Rann of
Kutch*

GUJARAT

INDORE

BHOPAL

Chambal

*Kathiawar
Peninsula*

BHONSLA

M A R A T H A S

ORISSA

BALASORE

Narmada

BURHANPUR

GAWILGHUR
ARGUAM

CUTTACK

Assaye

BASSEIN

SINDHIA

Godavari

NIZAM'S

AHMEDNUGGUR

BOMBAY

POONA

DOMINIONS

NORTHERN SARKARS

Western

HYDERABAD

VIZAGAPATAM

PESHWA

Krishna

CORINGA

MASULIPATAM

Bay of Bengal

GOA
(Port.)

Ghats

D E C C A N

Arabian Sea

Eastern Ghats

BANGALORE

MADRAS

MYSORE

SERINGAPATAM

MYSORE

MALABAR

CALICUT

TRICHINOPOLY

Carnatic

DINDIGUL

TRAVANCORE

TRIVANDRUM

TRINCOMALEE

CEYLON

COLOMBO

I N D I A N
O C E A N

| 0 | miles | 500 |
| 0 | km | 500 |

British territory

Peshwa. As well as making Maratha politics virtually impossible to comprehend, this internal rivalry weakened Maratha unity, and the unpredictability and inconsistency of the Confederacy's policies towards Britain seemingly increased the possibility of an unexpected attack.[27]

Representing the least threat was the Nizam, although the presence of French troops at Hyderabad was a cause for concern. Hyderabad was a waning military power, having suffered defeats at the hands of the Marathas (their neighbours to the north and west) in 1795. Consequently, the Nizam and his ministers sought support from European powers, namely the French and British. Shortly after Wellesley arrived in Calcutta, his elder brother was appointed Governor-General of India, although it would be some months before he arrived in Calcutta to take up his post. When he sailed, the youngest Wellesley, Henry, accompanied Mornington as his private secretary. Soon after Mornington arrived, a subsidiary alliance was concluded with the Nizam by which, in return for British support in defending Hyderabad's borders, the Nizam pledged exclusive allegiance to Britain, and promised to contribute a subsidiary force in any military operation in which the British became engaged. This system of subsidiary alliances was to become the bedrock of Mornington's vision for British India.

Recognising the threat posed by Mysore to the British position in Madras, Mornington was eager to bring Tipu Sultan to heel. He got his opportunity soon after he arrived, when news emerged that Tipu had sought a defensive and offensive alliance with the French. In reality, the threat posed by France to British India, even after Bonaparte's invasion of Egypt in 1798, was remote. 'The obstacles to the departure of any French force from Europe are obvious to everybody,' wrote Wellesley to his brother. Any invasion force would have to evade the British squadrons off the Cape and in the Indian Ocean.[28] Wellesley realised this, and Mornington realised this, but in London, the Secretary for War, Henry Dundas, concluded that Bonaparte's Egyptian expedition was a staging post for India. To contain the threat, Tipu had to be neutralised. Given the evidence, Dundas assumed that Tipu was 'making preparations to act hostilely against us' and therefore thought it would 'be more advisable not to wait for such an attack, but to take the most immediate and most decisive measures to carry our arms into our enemy's country'.[29] Dundas was advocating a pre-emptive attack, and Mornington would not stand in his way. He set about isolating Tipu by reaching agreements with the Nizam and the Marathas, while Wellesley sailed to Madras to join the preparations for war.

Once there, Wellesley became Mornington's unofficial military representative in South India, and was effectively the go-between for

Mornington on the one hand and General Sir George Harris, who was Commander-in-Chief of the Madras Army, on the other. Harris was more than happy to delegate to Wellesley and Lieutenant-Colonel Barry Close, the Adjutant-General, responsibility for planning and preparation. Having sailed to India carrying the exhaustive memoranda and reports of the commissary for the British campaign against Tipu in 1792, Wellesley was well versed in the transportation requirements of an army advancing into Mysore.[30] In this regard, Wellesley experienced at first hand the difficulty of balancing resources and requirements. 'It is impossible to carry on a war in India without Bullocks,' he wrote to Mornington in July 1798, 'and yet the expense of an establishment at all adequate to the purposes for which it is intended is so great that I cannot recommend one. You wish, however, to be in such a state as to be able to strike a blow at all times, and I know no means of making you so.'[31] Wellesley was not the only man devoting time to working out how to supply the army on its march into Mysore: he was a small cog in a large machine, which worked both inefficiently and, as shall be seen, ineffectively.[32]

Mornington ordered the Madras Army to begin its invasion of Mysore on 3 February 1799. Wellesley, meanwhile, had been given command of the Nizam's subsidiary force – some 16,000 troops, which, along with 900 British troops, formed one of the two invasion columns. The other, commanded by Baird, with Harris in overall command, consisted of 20,000 British soldiers and sepoys. The Mysore invasion began on 11 February. Accompanied by ten times as many camp-followers, bullock drivers and *brinjarries* (grain merchants), Wellesley's column occupied 18 square miles of ground.[33] From Vellore, the army marched to Rayakottai Ghat (pass), entering Mysore from the north-east. The marching was hard, the terrain composed mainly of thick jungle; conditions were hot and humid.

A month into the campaign, and the army was beginning to outpace its supplies. On 10 March, Harris noticed that

> our ... movement showed a very serious deficiency in the Bullock department, particularly in those attached to the Commissary General of Stores. The succeeding march of the 12th, although short and with an intermediate day of halt, marked this deficiency more strongly; crippled in our movements from this cause, our marches have been tedious though short; our halts have been frequent and our progress has been slow, unremitting attention to every species of arrangement by which the store department could be assisted or lightened, was indispensably necessary: some losses were daily sustained.[34]

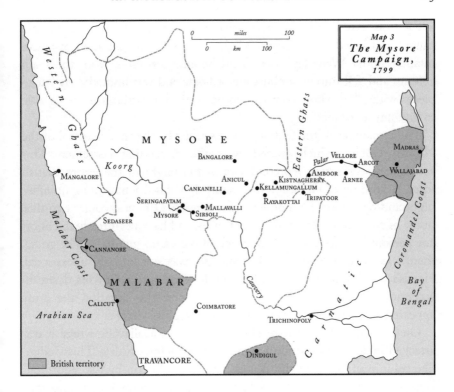

The logistical arrangements had been the responsibility of Wellesley and Close, although, as on previous campaigns, individual regiments had also been expected to organise supplies. But it appears their early confidence was somewhat misplaced. To be fair, the problems were not really Wellesley's fault. The army had marched too fast, and the British had consequently begun to experience supply difficulties. It was only when they reached Seringapatam that a detachment was sent to link with the supply columns. Yet, accounts of Wellesley's flawless planning need some revision. It is obvious that, despite his confidence, the arrangements he had helped make were not entirely adequate: this was partly the result of underestimation, but partly also caused by the nature of campaigning in India, where the distances covered meant armies frequently outstripped their supplies.

On top of this, Tipu had successfully executed a scorched earth policy. 'The towns and villages were in flames in every direction. Not one atom of forage or food could be procured; every tank or reservoir of water was impregnated with the poisonous milk-hedge, many horses and bullocks falling victims to the deleterious infusion.'[35] Mysore light cavalry also hampered the columns. Among other things, this restricted the quantity and quality of intelligence the invading army was able to collect. Scouts and patrols, as well as *harkarrahs* (native spies and runners) were commonly caught and killed by the Mysore light cavalry.[36] One battalion of native infantry under Wellesley's command became separated from the main column and 'fell into an ambuscade of horse and was immediately cut to pieces with [the] whole company in our sight but without us being able to give any assistance'.[37]

The remainder of the battalion was rescued by the timely arrival of the Nizam's cavalry, which chased away the marauding horsemen. This account, it seems, was representative of the plight of the entire British force. According to Wellesley, the enemy light cavalry had 'hung upon us, night and day, from the moment we entered his [Tipu's] country to this. Some of them have always had sight of us, and have been ready to cut off any persons venturing out of the reach of our camp-guards.'[38] The going, then, was extremely tough. This, though, was not entirely unexpected. Harris's complaints can, in part, be understood in light of his desire to accentuate the scale of his success: the worse the situation the army appeared to be in, the greater the magnitude of its victory.

On 27 March, the army reached the town of Mallavalli, where it was attacked by and successfully fought off the enemy cavalry. 'This wedge-like column of horse, at the nearest angle, was led on by two enormous elephants, having huge chains hanging on their proboscis, which they whirled about on both sides, a blow from which would have destroyed ten or twelve men at once,' recalled one participant.[39] Wellesley outflanked the enemy attack, while the Nizam's cavalry plugged a hole in the British line.[40] Wellesley's impact on proceedings has perhaps been slightly over-blown. Certainly his outflanking manoeuvre was important, but Harris had given the order, and in any event the British line, after it was re-inforced by the Nizam's cavalry, showed no sign of collapse. The most important role was probably that of the Nizam's cavalry, as it was the native horsemen who had closed the gap in time to prevent the charge of the enemy light cavalry from penetrating the British line.[41] Unsurprisingly, British accounts make little reference to the Nizam's subsidiary force and, when they do so, it is almost always a negative comment.[42] For Wellesley, though, the battle, and indeed the campaign, was Tipu's loss. 'If Tipu had had sense and spirit sufficient to use his cavalry and infantry as he might have done, I have no hesitation in saying that we should not now be here, and probably should not be out of the jungles near Bangalore.'[43]

The army reached the vicinity of Seringapatam early in April, arriving south-west of the fortress. Following the battle at Mallavalli, Harris had decided to march his army south of the River Cauvery. This was an inspired move. The detour had not been anticipated by Tipu so the army crossed unopposed on 29 and 30 March and, as the area had not been scorched, was able to replace the supplies which had fallen so far behind. The icing on the cake was information which suggested that the southern approach to Seringaptam was less well defended and the south-western walls of the fortress were in a worse state of repair than the north walls,[44] where Tipu had concentrated his defensive preparations.[45] On the evening of 3 April, Harris reconnoitred the three miles between the encampment and the fortress walls. On reaching the summit of a hill, Harris could see Seringapatam, and the land behind the fortress. Initially,

> There was only a few cavalry in sight; but suddenly a most terrific earthquake commenced; the plains in front were observed undulating like the waves of the sea, which magnificent motion continued for upwards of a minute. The view was really superb; an assemblage of 30,000 fighting men, 300,000 followers, 400 elephants, 1000 camels, with 150,000 bullocks.[46]

This was Tipu's army, still north of the Cauvery, retreating precipitately into Seringapatam. By the time the reconnaissance party returned to camp, Tipu had sent out a company of rocket men who were firing indiscriminately into the British lines. They were positioned in two sheltered and mutually supporting positions that gave them a direct line of fire into the British camp. An initial reconnaissance of these positions on 4 April had gone wrong, when the 12th Regiment got lost and attacked its own flank parties.[47] The decision was taken to clear these two positions on the evening of the 5th. Colonel Shaw of the 12th Regiment was tasked with clearing a dried riverbank, whilst Wellesley and the 33rd were given the job of clearing a thick wood to the left of the river bank. The night-time attack on Sultanpetah Tope was a shambles and Wellesley's initial failure to take the position, and his panicked behaviour afterwards, meant he was only given command of the reserve when a breach was finally established in Seringapatam's walls, a month later.

The fortress was stormed at one o'clock on 4 May, under the command of General Sir David Baird, Harris's second-in-command. The initial assault party, dubbed the 'Forlorn Hope' because of the small chance of survival, suffered badly. First they had to cross the river and many floundered on the unpredictable riverbed, the rest meeting stiff resistance in the breach itself.[48]

When Baird climbed through the breach he discovered a ditch and an inner wall that circumnavigated the fortress. Though in a state of disrepair, the wall still provided an extra and unexpected obstacle. Amid heavy fighting, the second wall was gained, and Baird pushed on into the fortress while a second detachment moved around the wall, to the northern gate, cutting off the defenders' avenue of retreat. At about three o'clock, the colours were planted on the ramparts of Seringapatam. The assault claimed the lives of 220 officers and soldiers (both European and sepoy), and 1,042 were injured.[49] Tipu Sultan had been killed in the assault.[50]

After it had fallen, Wellesley had moved into the fortress to attempt to restore order. It took two days to bring the marauding British troops under control and extinguish fires that had broken out across the city. At the end of it, Harris made Wellesley governor of Seringapatam; Wellesley delivered the news to Baird in a typically insensitive manner. He found Baird eating breakfast with his staff and reportedly said, 'General Baird, I am appointed to the command of Seringapatam, and here is the order of General Harris.' Shocked, Baird immediately rose and addressed his staff, 'Come, gentlemen, we have no longer any business here.' 'Oh, pray finish your breakfast,' Wellesley replied.[51] Many were astounded that Baird should be overlooked for a command that he so obviously deserved. Harris appointed Wellesley because he had exhibited excellent administrative skills during the preparations for the campaign, although Baird unquestionably had more military experience and was much more senior than Wellesley. Again, one cannot escape the suggestion that Harris was at least partly influenced by the knowledge that appointing Wellesley would please Mornington. Even Wellesley's friends perceived the hand of the Governor-General, although there is no evidence of this. Nevertheless, although well suited for the role, under the customs of the day Wellesley's preferment over Baird was unjustified. Indeed, two years later, when meeting the Duke of York, Harris was unable to provide an explanation for Wellesley's appointment.[52]

*   *   *

Four days earlier, Wellesley had turned thirty. There was nothing remarkable about his career so far. Although he enjoyed the good fortune of having an elder brother in a significant political position, which had brought him huge benefits in the last five years, in military terms Wellesley was apparently nothing special. Indeed, in his first major responsibility under pressure, he had panicked. This was not an auspicious opening to a military career.

What, though, had he learned from his experiences in India by 1799? In truth, the lessons he derived from the Mysore campaign were to define his approach to warfare. One of the cornerstones of Wellesley's claim to success in 1799 is his supposed role as architect of the logistics used by the British Army as it advanced against Seringapatam. Yet, this logistical system was not without its problems. The army frequently out-marched its supplies; there were too few bullocks (mainly because of attrition due to deaths from disease and surprise assaults by Tipu's light cavalry); and there were reports that camp followers starved to death during the month-long siege. Wellesley, however, escapes censure. It is also intriguing that someone with no real military expertise, no real experience of logistical planning and no real authority, bar his connection to the Governor-General, should be entrusted with the responsibility for the logistical preparation of the invasion of Mysore. A wider study of the minutes of the Military Board suggests that Wellesley was responsible, in concert with Lieutenant-Colonel Barry Close, the Adjutant General; Lieutenant-Colonel Sydenham, the Auditor General; and a host of captains and majors,[53] for laying the foundations of the army's supply system. He helped acquire the minimum number of bullocks necessary to make the march to Seringapatam feasible; he helped get the battering train to Vellore by early November 1798;[54] and he helped ensure that the army had access to the right amount of grain, a particularly important task considering that there was a general shortage of grain in Madras in late 1798.[55] He assisted in making a few pieces of the complex jigsaw puzzle that was an army's logistics, but he did not put that jigsaw puzzle together. Indeed, by mid-December, logistical preparations were still under way, and far from completion.[56] Wellesley could not be responsible for the final implementation of the logistical arrangements for the invasion of Mysore because he had already been put in command of the Nizam's subsidiary force.[57]

The failure of the army's supplies during its advance to Mysore was a cause for concern, but it was hardly unique to this war. Far from being a step-change in logistical planning, the 1799 campaign had many similarities with previous operations, including the ad hoc requisition of supplies by individual regiments, and last-minute gap-filling when shortages were discovered.[58] Wellesley readily acknowledged that the lack of bullock drivers was the 'great inconvenience' of the war. The problem was twofold: recruitment and retention. Not only did the British have problems finding enough drivers, but they could not afford to pay them when they did find them.

Previous assumptions that Wellesley was the architect of a successful supply train, and that this is somehow evidence of early military genius, need revision. He was not the sole architect of the army's logistics in 1799, and he therefore exhibited no instinctive understanding of it. Nevertheless, within a year of the capture of Seringapatam he demonstrated a propensity for detailed and innovative logistical planning. In order to achieve success in India, Wellesley argued, an entirely different approach to warfare was needed, one that was less dependent on supplies and more dependent on speed and manoeuvre:

> In the wars which we may expect in India in future, we must look to light and quick movements; and we ought always to be in that state to be able to strike a blow as soon as a war might become evidently necessary.[59]

This would take some refinement, but Wellesley had essentially conceived a radically different approach to warfare, and it bore a greater resemblance to the warfare practised by native Indian armies than it did to European approaches.[60] By necessity, 'Light and Quick' operations would be short-term deployments designed to achieve an effect quickly and decisively. Forced by the limitations of supply in a vast and hostile terrain, 'Light and Quick' operations would also be dependent on quality intelligence collection and analysis, swift decision, and highly mobile and lightly laden troops. The concept also called for aggressive and decisive action. When the enemy was located, it was to be attacked and defeated immediately. Here, then, was the aggression instilled by Wellesley's failure at Sultanpetah Tope. Over the next few years, Wellesley would add meat to the bones of this new concept; but although he thought 'Light and Quick' operations were the product of, and therefore restricted to, Indian warfare, it would turn out that his thoughts and ideas during his tenure at Seringapatam would be definitive later in his career as well.

*   *   *

Life as the military governor of Seringapatam was never mundane, but there were large amounts of trivial issues to deal with, from regional insurgencies to the remarriage of female Christian converts, to the number of pagodas a supply train needed.[61] Wellesley's role, from mid-1799 to mid-1800 at least, was the reconstruction and reconstitution of Seringapatam and Mysore, and of its forces in the wake of Tipu's demise. Tipu had enforced strict Islamic law on the Hindu-dominated Mysore. Support for the Sultan had been precarious at best, and the Hindu soldiers in Tipu's army were kept in line because Tipu kept their families as hostages in the villages outside Seringapatam.[62] Wellesley was responsible for dismantling Tipu's old army and reconstituting it under Hindu command. Many of the surviving troops, fearful of retribution from the British, fled Seringapatam. Wellesley's main preoccupation, then, was rebuilding the defences of the city. This is not to underestimate the challenge such a role presented, as his time as governor of Seringapatam provided a wealth of administrative experience.

The conquest of Mysore presented a number of political problems. Mornington had to work out how to divide the newly conquered territory. If Mysore was to be annexed, then the Nizam would have to be rewarded, and, to avoid unpleasant recriminations from Poona, the Peshwa would have to be given a share of territory as well. Instead, it was determined to restore the old Hindu dynasty, deposed by Tipu's father, Hyder Ali, decades earlier, to Seringapatam under the terms of a subsidiary alliance. This allowed the British to compensate the Nizam without making any specific promises to the Peshwa, who was told he would get some territory, but deserved none. Barry Close, who had been appointed Resident to the newly restored Maharaja at Seringapatam, was put in charge of negotiations for the subsidiary alliance, and for identifying the new boundary between Mysore and the expanded territories of the Nizam and Peshwa. Representing the Maharaja, who was just six years old, was one of Tipu's former lieutenants, Purnea, who had approached the British after the fall of Seringapatam and offered to help restore order.

The negotiations were lengthy, finally reaching fruition at the end of March 1800.[63] Although the Nizam went away happy, relations with the Marathas were less pleasant, and effectively the negotiations only put a lid on increasing tensions. Wellesley himself viewed conflict with the Marathas as inevitable, but thought immediate provocation unwise. He advised Mornington that Britain and the East India Company should not annex territory in Mysore so as to provide a border between Britain and the Marathas. 'It is impossible to alter the nature of the Marathas; they will plunder their neighbours, be they ever so powerful.'[64] The Marathas became an ongoing problem for the British.

In reality, though, Wellesley figured marginally in the negotiations with the Nizam and the Peshwa. In other areas as well, he remained a marginal figure. There was a series of rebellions and disturbances on the Malabar Coast, but as governor Wellesley was responsible only for the administration of the army. Indeed, it seemed his career was to be that of a distinguished administrator. Several historians have pointed out that at this juncture Wellesley would have made an excellent quartermaster.[65] Other colonels, such as James Stevenson, conducted military operations; detachments were sent out to quell the disturbances usually in the most brutal of fashions.[66] Wellesley was eventually given overall command of the army in Mysore after Harris left to return to Britain in September.

Between then and November, Wellesley took to the field himself, moving north to the border between Mysore and the Maratha Confederacy. Here a series of uncoordinated rebellions was finding support from the Marathas, and a strong military movement was necessary to exert British authority. One suspects the Marathas, never serious in their intentions, were testing British resolve. They melted away as Wellesley moved north. In the meantime, Wellesley worked with Purnea to establish British authority in northern Mysore, and did so with some success. The relationship he developed with Purnea was to serve him beneficially in the difficult year ahead, and seems to have been based on mutual respect.[67] As he returned to Seringapatam, Wellesley's correspondence reflects the intense interest he took in terrain. He was clearly expecting trouble in the region and he did not miss the opportunity to learn as much about it as possible.

In the summer of 1799, rumours of a new threat began to emerge. A bandit, whose name was reported as Dhoondiah Vagh, was said to be launching raiding parties into Mysore, capturing small strongholds and spreading dissent on the borders with the Maratha Confederacy, and appealing to rebellious *killedars* (fortress governors) who resented the British occupation. British attempts to destroy him constantly failed.[68] Wellesley was not involved in the initial attempts to attack Dhoondiah. Harris himself led a campaign against the freebooter, but the latter dispersed his ramshackle force. Then the true nature of his identity emerged. Dhoondiah was not just any rebellious native trying his luck against the British. He had been a prisoner of Tipu Sultan and escaped from Seringapatam when the British batteries blew a hole in the prison wall. Upon his escape, Dhoondiah began coordinating various disparate rebellions, while he drew military strength primarily from the troops who had fled Seringapatam after the British attack. Dhoondiah Vagh had effectively replaced Tipu. This was a military problem with Seringapatam at its heart, and Wellesley, as military governor of Seringapatam, was responsible for that problem. Who would have thought that a criminal with a poorly trained, disparate and unlikely collection of Hindu and Muslim troops, would be the making of Arthur Wellesley?

CHAPTER 2

Command Apprenticeship
THE CAMPAIGN AGAINST DHOONDIAH VAGH, 1800

Get powers if possible to treat with all the principal people who border upon the country intended to be attacked, find out how far your success would coincide with their interest or not, for you really reap great advantage by knowing these particulars, by deceiving those whose interest is against you and getting the assistance of those who wish well to the affair on which you are employed.

Anonymous
Calcutta, India, 1780[1]

THROUGHOUT the spring and summer of 1800, Colonel Arthur Wellesley faced the greatest challenge of his life so far. The previous summer, an individual, going only by the name Dhoondiah Vagh, had begun organising and shaping the disparate and small-scale rebellions against the newly imposed authority of the British in Mysore. The officers and men of the British East India Company were used to sudden outbreaks of violence in isolated regions throughout India. For them, it was the natural reaction of the previously lawless inhabitants to the imposition of order and control. Small-scale rebellions were commonplace, and treated with a ruthlessness and rapidity designed to demonstrate the force and will of British arms. Dhoondiah Vagh was treated in much the same fashion. Before his departure for England, Sir George Harris himself conducted a punitive expedition to northern Mysore, at its ill-defined border with the Maratha Confederacy, in order to put down the rebellion. By the autumn of 1799, it seemed as if Dhoondiah had indeed been defeated, another insignificant challenger to the omnipotence of British arms.

But in early 1800, Dhoondiah returned stronger and more organised than the previous year. In the months in which he had seemingly been inactive, it appears he had been establishing a reputation throughout the region, and in so doing developing a mythical status that was as attractive of support as were his actions against the British. There were rumours, for example, that Dhoondiah was the son of Tipu Sultan, and this swiftly got Wellesley's attention.[2] In early February 1800, Dhoondiah had been considered nothing more than a bandit, and little attention was devoted to him, but within ten days, Wellesley learned that Dhoondiah had been joined by between seven and eight thousand men, and was marching toward Chittledroog with the intention of plundering the region.[3] Wellesley found 'all these rumours of men being raised in the country ... very extraordinary, and they deserve the attention of this government. This story about Dhoondiah has come to me now through three different channels, and they appear to be distinct from each other.'[4] A single individual, who started out as a bandit with a small gang, had, with the help of a grand rumour about his heritage, turned that gang into an army several thousand strong, highly mobile and flexible. He benefited from popular support and increasing strength and represented a growing political, military and economic threat to British government in India. By May, Wellesley pointed out that 'Dhoondiah's name is being used wherever there is unrest, therefore it is necessary for the government to get the better of him'.[5]

As well as representing a significant military threat, if the rumours about his strength and support proved accurate, Dhoondiah Vagh also posed a significant political and economic threat. Conducting an inquiry into the origins of Dhoondiah's insurgency, following his defeat, Mornington identified the threat as fourfold. Politically, Dhoondiah sought to destabilise British rule by generating support for and engaging in a widespread uprising. Military stability was threatened by the occupation and destruction of fortresses critical to the maintenance of lines of supply and communication. The rich and prosperous region of Bednore was particularly targeted for lightning strike operations intended to undermine British economic stability in the region. Finally, Dhoondiah sought to undermine all three by actively seeking support from the Marathas.[6] Reports that Dhoondiah had been engaged in secret negotiations with Daulutrao Sindhia Maharaja of Gwalior and one of the major *sirdars* or chieftains in the Maratha Confederacy, were received as early as February. Similar reports suggested that Dhoondiah also sought to denude the British of cavalry by bribing the Nizam of Hyderabad's horsemen, and persuading them to join his cause.[7]

Adopting their usual military strong-arm response to such threats, the British initially sent out columns of redcoats to engage in punitive raids on villages thought to be sympathetic to Dhoondiah. But such measures proved both ineffective and counterproductive.[8] The redcoats, sent out to 'restore tranquillity' in rebellious localities, usually by the wanton torching of villages and stealing of livestock, tried to instil in the inhabitants an 'apprehension of their own safety'.[9] Such measures failed to stop the attacks, undermined British moral authority and increased native support for Dhoondiah. This was partly because the insurgents were not fixed in certain areas as previous rebellions had been, and were able to melt away to the safety of the border regions of the Maratha Confederacy, for example. Such was the situation encountered by Lieutenant-Colonel J. Montressor, an officer commanding a punitive expedition against the fortress and town of Arrakerry and its surrounding villages. After setting the villages alight, the British force pursued a body of irregular troops, but 'they retired into narrow pathways where I did not think it advisable to pursue them and on my directing my troops to return, they [the enemy] rallied with such spirit that I was occasionally obliged to charge them from the rear'.[10]

The actions of what had previously been a suspected ragtag band of freebooters showed a clear understanding of British counterinsurgency tactics, and evidently demonstrated the greatest threat to British interests since Mysore had fallen under British control the previous year. The rebels did not give up the fight when their villages were destroyed, and instead melted away into the jungle. In so doing they preserved their strength to continue to harass British troops, and, more importantly, British economic interests in the region. Such a situation was, and is, a classic characteristic of an insurgency – attacking at the weakest point, and refusing to fight a battle on conventional terms.

If the British were willing to commit enough troops, they could hunt down and eradicate the insurgents, but even in the early days of the British Empire, military power and conquest were recognised as the most unwieldy of Britain's tools of authority. Punitive military action against Dhoondiah, and all the collateral damage such action caused, served to alienate rather than subjugate the population. Overuse of the military would eventually ruin Britain's moral credibility. The military, after all, although the guarantor of British political and economic authority in India, was a very small European force: '30,000 strangers', as Wellesley later termed them.[11] British power in reality rested on its political and economic credibility. Mornington was extending this with his subsidiary alliance system. But a coordinated rebellion against British authority would be unstoppable. The British had to be seen as invincible, but fair. As such, it was 'particularly desirable for a government, so constituted as the Company's, never to enter upon any particular object, the probable result of which should not be greatly in favour of success'.[12] In other words, Britain's moral force and reputation would be disgraced upon its first defeat, and military operations should only be entered into when success could be virtually guaranteed.[13]

At the same time, however, Dhoondiah had to be defeated militarily, and until he was he would continue to be identified as a figurehead of anti-British rule, to whom those with even the slightest grievance would pledge their support. But unless the flow of political and military support to Dhoondiah from local chieftains and rajahs could be stemmed, Wellesley was unlikely to be able to defeat the insurgent militarily. The political primacy of the campaign against Dhoondiah was thus established. In order to defeat Dhoondiah militarily, the British had first to isolate him politically.

As ever, though, politics in India was far from straightforward. Mornington's wider policy in India included bringing the Marathas into a subsidiary alliance with the British. He appreciated that the Marathas were unlikely to acquiesce without a fight to what effectively amounted to British control of their economy and external relations. Expecting a war with the Maratha Confederacy in the near future, Mornington therefore prohibited any formal political or military alliance between the British in Mysore and the Maratha Confederacy specifically aimed at defeating Dhoondiah's insurgency.[14] This significantly hamstrung Wellesley, who recognised that Dhoondiah was using Maratha territory as a base for his marauding attacks on British troops and supply lines.[15] Unable to form a direct alliance, Wellesley nevertheless had to come to some sort of informal agreement with the Marathas in order to ensure they did not offer Dhoondiah support and that they would allow a British force to pursue Dhoondiah into Maratha territory.[16] Yet Wellesley had nothing tangible to offer the Marathas in return for their compliance. Similarly, military operations could only take place with the support of the local Indian chief-tains of the towns and villages inside Mysore territory, through which Dhoondiah operated. Without political agreement throughout Mysore, and indeed beyond, on the need to destroy Dhoondiah's force, reliable intelligence on the latter could not be guaranteed. Furthermore, Wellesley had little chance of operating successfully unless his supplies and transpor-tation could be guaranteed.[17] Political, and by extension moral, support was crucial to success on every level.

Wellesley therefore had to achieve political success on four separate fronts if he was to set the conditions to achieve military success against Dhoondiah.

First, he needed political agreement that recognised Dhoondiah as a threat not only to the British but within individual localities and on a regional level. Secondly, he had to ensure political support for his military actions, without committing Britain or the East India Company to an alliance with the Marathas. Thirdly, Wellesley needed political support to guarantee an accurate, reliable and timely supply of intelligence on his enemy, crucial in defeating any insurgency. Finally, Wellesley realised that he had to work to transform latent political support into active military cooperation in order to guarantee supply lines and transportation equipment.

On the first front, that of agreeing with local chieftains that Dhoondiah represented a universal threat, Wellesley apparently adopted an approach typical of the British in India – that of assuming the automatic superiority of the British cause. In so doing, Wellesley, initially at least, naively assumed that anyone with political authority in India would pledge support to the British by default, since Dhoondiah represented a threat to all forms of government, not just British. And, by and large, this strategy succeeded in suborning most political authorities to the British plan to destroy Dhoondiah, at least in theory. In reality, the situation was not so clear-cut. Individuals who had initially pledged support to the operations to destroy Dhoondiah when they were first pressed to do so by Wellesley failed to demonstrate such commitment when it was actually required. In many cases, political and military incompetence disguised the true nature of various chieftains' reluctance to participate in military action against Dhoondiah.

On one occasion, Wellesley accused an uncooperative chieftain of treachery. While preparing his military plans at Hurihur (a town near a ford on the River Tungabhadra), Wellesley became increasingly irate at the intransigence of the locals despite having received the political support of the town's *amildar* (manager or organiser). In this case, a small fortress guarding the far bank of the river was abandoned and allowed to fall into the hands of the enemy without any resistance. At the time, the British were just six miles away, and well within reach of garrisoning it themselves.[18]

Evidently, a certain portion of this diatribe can be attributed to what was to become one of Wellesley's greatest foibles: his constant attempts to apportion blame elsewhere. Nevertheless, a certain level of political commitment was lacking in the *amildar* of Hurihur, as he would not maintain control of an important fortress that, in Dhoondiah's hands, now presented an extra obstacle to Wellesley's military plans. Nor was this an isolated example. The *amildar* of Chitradurga, upon whom Wellesley relied for logistical support, also failed on a number of occasions to live up to his promises. He failed, for example, to stock the magazines for the army, which significantly undermined Wellesley's preparations,[19] and then, when the army was finally ready to advance, there was a lack of boats to cross the Tungabhadra, something that predictably infuriated Wellesley.[20]

Although a certain amount of blame can be placed on the incompetent shoulders of his allies, Wellesley must bear some responsibility for the inconveniences and 'unpleasant consequences' that affected his attempts to gain political support for his campaigns against Dhoondiah. Wellesley overestimated his political authority. By assuming he had the unqualified political support of the local chieftains he failed to understand the wider political situation. In effect, the local chieftains were being forced to make a choice between British rule by proxy, and an insurgency which, to all intents and purposes, sought to rid Mysore of the British presence. No wonder, then, that faced with nothing in return for their support, local chieftains, and *amildars*, should prove somewhat lackadaisical in the prosecution of their allotted tasks. On the surface, Wellesley had, by late May and early June, acquired the support of the chieftains of the towns and villages through which his force would be operating. In reality, when it came to the crunch, latent political support did not automatically translate into active military support.

However, the critical political agreement would be with the Marathas. Not only was Dhoondiah attempting to draw support from the weaker Maratha *jagirdars* (landlords) whose territory bordered that of Mysore,[21] but he was using their territory, which the British could not enter without causing major diplomatic difficulties, as a base of operations.[22] Wellesley, then, had to negotiate an agreement with the Marathas to allow him to enter their territory, and, with their support, hunt and destroy a force of 40,000 well-armed insurgents. He had nothing to offer the Marathas in return for their acceding to such an agreement.[23] As if this were not complicated enough, Wellesley was about to enter the intricate labyrinth that was Maratha politics. Negotiations were always going to be difficult, but in the event they were extraordinarily complicated, and proved a useful harbinger of the problems Wellesley would encounter when war eventually broke out with the Marathas in 1803.

In the first instance, Wellesley had to seek permission to enter Maratha territory from the Peshwa, although at this point his authority was nominal. Conducting negotiations in Poona on Wellesley's behalf was the British Resident, William Palmer. Despite some initial obfuscation, the Peshwa agreed to allow the British into Maratha territory.[24] In reality, the negotiations with the Peshwa were merely for show, and it was the *sirdar* Sindhia's opinion that appeared to count. Initially, the latter was extremely sceptical about the need for a British military operation, observing 'that there was no necessity for its passing into the Maratha territories in pursuit of Dhoondiah Vagh, as he [Sindhia] had appointed a strong detachment of his own troops (and which was to be reinforced by those of the Rajah of Kolapore) to attack and reduce the force of Dhoondiah'. Having chased the insurgent out of Mysore, Sindhia 'requested that the British army might be directed to remain on its own frontier'.[25] Wellesley, though, did not trust that Sindhia would come good on his word and destroy Dhoondiah. Rather, he suspected Sindhia would strive to use Dhoondiah as a weapon to keep the British weak and on the defensive in Mysore.

Palmer speculated that Sindhia had other ulterior motives for the decision to prevent the British from entering Confederacy territory. Uniting the not inconsiderable forces of the Rajah of Kolapore and Dhoondiah Punt Goklah would easily defeat Dhoondiah, but Palmer suspected that there was a power play at work, in which Sindhia did not want the British involved.[26] The political reality was much more complicated, and Wellesley found his negotiations hampered by the internal problems and frictions inherently associated with the declining status of a once unified power. Sindhia, it appears, was supporting the Rajah and Goklah in their attempts to seize territory from Ball Kishen Bhow, the established *jagirdar* and favoured British proxy on the Mysore border.[27] Dhoondiah Vagh's insurgency was performing the inestimable service of weakening the authority of the latter, while providing a convenient opportunity for the Rajah and Goklah to send in a force ostensibly to attack the insurgent but in reality seeking to seize new territory.[28]

For Wellesley, the problem was acute. In late July, he was unsure whom he could rely on and who was his enemy. Intelligence suggested that the Rajah had sent a force not to resist Dhoondiah, but to support him.[29] On top of this, Wellesley had already approached Ball Kishen Bhow with a view to restoring his authority when the insurgency was defeated. Having failed to gain concrete support from the Maratha capital, Poona, Wellesley had turned to direct intervention. In mid-June, he had written to Ball Kishen Bhow attempting to secure access to Maratha territory.[30] By the end of July, however, Wellesley had realised that simply restoring the authority of Ball Kishen Bhow would not be sufficient to prevent future instability in the border region between Mysore and the Maratha Confederacy. Indeed, he had gone as far as to recognise that, for the Marathas, Dhoondiah's insurgency was not a major problem, whilst the Rajah of Kolapore and Goklah saw the insurgency as a solution to their problems.[31] In this political environment, the British were merely collateral damage in a civil dispute internal to the Maratha Confederacy. But, as he had earlier remarked, the British position in Mysore was at stake, and he was obliged to act to end the threat.[32]

For Wellesley, the simplest way to stop Dhoondiah's insurgency was to deprive it of its means of support:

> It is clear that Doondiah's power and success are to be attributed to the quarrels between the Chiefs on the frontier, principally between Bhow and the Rajah and their extreme weakness in consequence of their contests. I propose then to endeavour to reconcile the Rajah of Kolapore, whose *vakil* [emissary] is on his way to my camp, with [the Bhow], and I have written to Lieutenant Colonel Palmer to request that, as the Bhow's family have . . . possession of the Savanore and Darwar Countries, they may be given over to them entirely as the sole *jagirdars* and *zemindars* [landowners] under the government of Poonah. I hope to succeed in these objects with the assistance of Lieutenant Colonel Palmer, if his Lordship [the Governor-General] should approve of them, without pledging His government to anything, and if they are obtained, we may hope that such a force, as Dhoondiah has, will not again be assembled in this country.[33]

Mornington, though, did not approve.

> The plan proposed by you for uniting the Rajah of Kolapore with [Ball Kishen Bhow] appears to contain the best immediate security against future disturbances in your quarter; but the governor . . . has not the means of judging how far it may be consistent with the actual state of affairs at Poona; His Lordship therefore deemed it expedient that you should strictly avoid committing the British Government on any point connected with that arrangement . . .[34]

The best means Wellesley had at his disposal to gain Maratha support for a military campaign against Dhoondiah's insurgency was expressly forbidden by the Governor-General. This was on the ostensible grounds that it might conflict with the policy of the Poona government (which it would because of Sindhia's support for the Rajah of Kolapore, whilst the Peshwa supported the Bhow). In reality, however, Wellesley's plan threatened to restore stability to the fractured south of the Confederacy. Sindhia, who was expressly seeking to undermine the Peshwa, might be moved to intervene directly in Poona. The British, who officially supported the Peshwa, would then be drawn into a conflict against Sindhia, much earlier than expected. So, not only was Wellesley forced to seek agreements with Marathas he knew he would soon probably be fighting a war against, but political imperatives rendered the best solution to the present crisis impossible.

In the event, the intrigues of Sindhia, the Rajah of Kolapore and Goklah came to naught, when Goklah was killed in a surprise battle against Dhoondiah on 3 July.[35] This event appeared to galvanise Maratha resistance to Dhoondiah, who was now viewed as a major threat. Wellesley had nothing to offer but his goodwill. In this regard, political support was closely linked to military success, and was time sensitive. He could gain tacit political support, but this would solidify only when he achieved a measure of military success against Dhoondiah. Wellesley gained valuable experience of dealing with slippery allies, which was to stand him in good stead later in his career. Added to these problems of trust was the unrelenting pressure of time. Wellesley himself noted 'how true it is that in military operations time is everything'.[36] Military success would have to be delivered swiftly, or the tacit political support of the local chieftains and the Marathas would vanish. If Wellesley did not act quickly and decisively, and allowed Dhoondiah 'to hold out at all, he will certainly receive support against us from the great body of Marathas'.[37] Nevertheless, although Sindhia was never completely trusted not to engage the British directly in battle, he declared that all his troops had been ordered to attack Dhoondiah.[38] Once this tentative agreement was in place, the momentum of military operations against Dhoondiah would become unstoppable.

* * *

While political negotiations were under way, Wellesley orchestrated a concurrent intelligence-gathering operation. Intelligence was collected both on the enemy and on the local terrain. Topographical intelligence was perhaps relatively simple to acquire, provided the personnel sent to map the terrain were reliable and sufficiently qualified to make judgements on distance and accessibility. Military intelligence collection and analysis were altogether more complex. Having very limited experience of this, Wellesley would inevitably find it a trial and error process, but he was acutely aware that he could not pursue Dhoondiah if he did not know where he was or if he could not form some sort of picture of his modus operandi.

Wellesley needed to know the composition, strength, morale and fighting ability of the force that Dhoondiah had assembled. So varied and unreliable were the rumours that this information could only be obtained direct from source. Under the coordination of Lieutenant-Colonel Barry

Close, who acted very much as Wellesley's chief of staff, sepoys were sent to infiltrate Dhoondiah's camp. This was quite a significant undertaking. Sepoys from the 11th Native Regiment of Madras conducted two intelligence operations, and another three were conducted by *harkarrahs*, indigenous spies specifically paid by the British.

Some sepoys managed just two days in Dhoondiah's camp before their identities began to be suspected by other camp members. Nevertheless, they were able to provide intelligence on the strength of Dhoondiah's force and, to a certain degree, on Dhoondiah's intentions. Of particular significance was the fact that Dhoondiah's force never stayed longer than two days at any one site, making it difficult to track. With the main portion of the force directed against small fortresses, Dhoondiah's intention, it seemed, was to cut the British communication between Mysore and Madras. Dhoondiah never announced his intention to move, or where he was moving to, until the night before departure, and only he and his 'inner circle' were privy to his longer-term plans, making it very difficult for a low-level and temporary spy to gain any credible long-term intelligence. Tactically, however, the sepoys were able to report very accurately on the strength of Dhoondiah's force. On 11 April, it numbered 15,000 horse, 5,000 infantry, 6,000 *peons* (Indian light infantry or militia), a 'vast store of *brinjarries*' (grain merchants whose services were retained to fill magazines), 'two small guns and one elephant'. Crucially, however, this force might increase by between 25 and 1,000 men a day, as the disaffected flocked to Dhoondiah's cause.[39]

The sepoys also discovered that Dhoondiah's approach was to 'annoy without openly attacking the British troops'.[40] He also began raiding several towns at once, creating panic and confusion amongst the inhabitants. This presented Wellesley with contradictory and confusing information, and prevented positive identification of Dhoondiah's main camp after the sepoys had left it.[41] So long as Dhoondiah stuck to such tactics, Wellesley would find it very difficult to bring him to battle.

A second duo of sepoys who infiltrated Dhoondiah's camp discovered that Dhoondiah was collecting his entire force to march to meet Goklah, one of the three Maratha chieftains (along with Sindhia and the Rajah of Kolapore) who were trying to use Dhoondiah to overthrow the local Maratha *sirdar*, Ball Kishen Bhow.[42] Wellesley was at this time unaware of Goklah's true intentions regarding Dhoondiah, and for a time it looked as if Goklah was collecting his force to fight Dhoondiah.[43] Goklah sent his *vakil* to Dhoondiah's camp,[44] but Dhoondiah did not want to become subservient to another warlord, and instead he attacked and destroyed Goklah's force on 3 July. The latter was killed by Dhoondiah himself, who then proceeded to rub 'his body over with [Goklah's] blood'[45] in what appears to have been an attempt to reinforce the mythical status that Dhoondiah had been creating for himself throughout the year.

Despite these setbacks, the intelligence operations did provide some rays of hope for Wellesley as he planned his military campaign. There was, for example, considerable information on the composition of Dhoondiah's force. Although it now amounted to more than 50,000 troops, the majority of these, some 30,000, were irregular light cavalry, which posed a limited threat to well-formed infantry and artillery.[46] If this element of Dhoondiah's force could be dispersed or prevented from fighting, Wellesley could instead target the heart of the enemy force – the relatively small number of infantry. Moreover, Dhoondiah's victory over Goklah helped to create the conditions for such a scenario. The battle on 3 July had essentially been a conventional affair, with Goklah's force engaged in a pitched battle against Dhoondiah's force.[47] Details of the battle are vague, and it is unclear to what extent the main fighting elements were infantry or cavalry. What is clear is that Goklah underestimated his enemy, and did not engage his full strength in the battle, which was fought on Dhoondiah's terms. Dhoondiah became convinced after this battle that his army was a capable fighting force and should abandon its irregular guerrilla-style approach in favour of more direct action against British troops. Wellesley had every intention of offering Dhoondiah just such an opportunity to fight. While the political negotiations and intelligence operations had been under way, Wellesley had been devising a radically different approach to war-fighting in India – a concept he called 'Light and Quick Operations'.

By June 1800, Wellesley's force was ready to take the field. The intention was for his army to advance rapidly, unencumbered by a large supply train. Wellesley divided his force into two main columns, one under his command, and the other under Colonel James Stevenson. Supporting columns were commanded by Colonels Bowser and Maclean. A small force of *pindaris* (Indian light cavalry) provided a third column of pursuit,[48] which would be augmented by Maratha cavalry once Goklah's death persuaded Sindhia to support Wellesley unconditionally. Wellesley envisaged a lightning strike against Dhoondiah's force, rolling up his outlying positions and forcing him to battle. Born of an understanding of how difficult it was to bring an insurgency to conventional battle, the plan was heavily reliant on near perfect intelligence, which, despite the system Wellesley had quickly organised, was not forthcoming until the end of June. Furthermore, the risks associated with leaving behind the majority of his supplies were huge. If the plan faltered, and Dhoondiah was not brought to battle, then Wellesley and Stevenson would need to retreat from the newly captured territory to resupply themselves, or their army would starve. In the first instance, this is almost exactly what happened.

Before operations could begin in earnest, Wellesley needed to cross the River Werdah; even though he was only a day later than planned, the river had flooded and could only be crossed in boats, but these, although previously promised by local chieftains, were not forthcoming. Instead, Wellesley had to stop and begin the time-consuming and laborious process of building a bridge, exhausting his supply of grain in the ten-day wait.[49] Fearful of being outflanked, Wellesley sent detachments to help secure the country behind him. As a result, Wellesley was not ready to proceed again until 30 June, by which time Dhoondiah had escaped further north.

Wellesley now realised that he initially needed to move ahead slowly, securing the country as he advanced. He remained unsure of Dhoondiah's precise location or intentions and there was still the possibility that he might double back and attack the British from behind. Instead, the British would first advance methodically, relying on local supplies.[50] Wellesley's finessed concept of operations envisaged the achievement of three separate aims. First, as the British advanced, this time slowly but decisively, the territory they occupied was to be cleared of insurgent forces. Secondly, to ensure the captured territory did not fall back into the hands of rebellious forces once the British continued their advance, redoubts were to be built and garrisons were to be established, consolidating British control and starving Dhoondiah of sanctuary. Thirdly, Dhoondiah's movements were to be closely followed, a task that became easier as his options decreased with growing British success. Once Wellesley was sure of his enemy's location, 'Light and Quick' operations were to be instituted again, striking against the insurgent rapidly, causing surprise and forcing a conventional battle on Wellesley's terms.

The British forces Wellesley had with him in the field were not strong enough to garrison captured territory as well as lead a counterinsurgency campaign, so Wellesley relied on the support of the local Maratha *jagirdars*. This was perhaps the first stumbling block in Wellesley's new concept of operations, as, typically, the native force 'were so slow in their motions to take possession of the fort of Manowly, that the enemy re-occupied it on the night of the 31 July'. Inconveniences such as this aside, the benefits of the new plan soon became apparent. For the remainder of the campaign, Wellesley 'enjoyed the greatest of all blessings for Troops, a quiet rear, and a secure communication with our own country, and I am anxious to a degree that it should not be disturbed for any trifling object'.[51] As the success of this tactic started to take effect, Wellesley began clearing enemy territory of rebels and consolidating it with native forces.[52]

As the British force advanced, Wellesley became reliant on a continuous supply of intelligence on the whereabouts of Dhoondiah himself. He believed that if Dhoondiah could be captured or killed the insurgency would crumble, and he began sending officers and *harkarrahs* on intelligence-gathering missions, specifically to locate Dhoondiah's encampments. Unfortunately, the intelligence was nearly always two days out of date by the time Wellesley received it.[53] On 11 July, however, Wellesley received information that Dhoondiah was moving to attack him,[54] so he elected to seize Savanore earlier than expected, to provide a place of security for his baggage while he engaged Dhoondiah. What at first appeared to be a conventional action actually turned out to be a subtle adaptation of tactics on Dhoondiah's part. Dhoondiah began taunting the British, and on more than one occasion Wellesley 'dashed' at his opponent, leaving his rear and flanks overly exposed and resulting in no success, when it emerged Dhoondiah had already hightailed it to a different area. This tactic had two effects. First, it led Wellesley on several wild-goose chases, which resulted in a drop in morale. Secondly, it gave Dhoondiah the opportunity to examine his opponents' abilities. Although Wellesley was slowly reasserting control, Dhoondiah was still able to learn the British routine and plan of action. This demonstrates a reasonably complex understanding of the military situation, and certainly one which Wellesley had underestimated. Wellesley is not to blame for these events. His plan remained sound; the problem was judging when Dhoondiah was bluffing and leading the British force astray.

These clever tactics aside, the British were now pursuing a fairly sensible counterinsurgency campaign, one that was already starving Dhoondiah of support, and would eventually starve his troops of food. If Wellesley could avoid being drawn into a conventional battle, in a weakened state, on Dhoondiah's terms, as Goklah had been at the beginning of July, then the insurgency would eventually start to lose strength. Rather than pursuing wild-goose chases, Wellesley diverted more effort to securing the territory he was advancing through. In order to do this, the British had to wrest several reinforced strongholds from Dhoondiah's control. The first of these was Savanore, captured on 10 July. The next, the larger fortress of Koondgul, was stormed on the evening of 14 July. This success reaped more strategic benefits. As the British began to reassert military authority across the region, political support started to re-emerge. Wellesley noted following the fall of Koondgul that he had re-established his 'superiority in the opinions of my own people, of [Dhoondiah] and of the country'.[55] He continued the consolidation of military and, with it, political authority by capturing the insurgent stronghold of Dummul on the morning of 26 July.[56] Moreover, Wellesley's decision to appoint the former governor of Dummul, a Maratha, to oversee the reconstruction of both Dummul and Koondgul played well in Poona.[57]

Following Goklah's death, Sindhia arrived in late July to take command of the Maratha cavalry that had survived the battle and remained loyal to the Marathas. The minor chieftains and *jagirdars* were suspicious of Sindhia's intentions, and rightly so. His real intention in taking command of Goklah's force was to ensure that the British withdrew once Dhoondiah was defeated. Free of British interference, Sindhia would be able to reinforce his power base and challenge the authority of the Peshwa in Poona. The political wrangling was postponed so that he could focus on destroying Dhoondiah, but the British, including Wellesley, were concerned that a hostile Maratha Confederacy would quickly replace the insurgent, as a new, and much more worrying, foe. The military success of Wellesley's concept of operations must take some credit for keeping the Marathas in line, at least until Dhoondiah was defeated.

On 31 July, following the capture of a fourth insurgent stronghold, Gudduck, Wellesley struck a highly successful blow against Dhoondiah's force. Responding to intelligence that Dhoondiah was encamped on the River Malprabha, near the stronghold of Manowly, Wellesley formed a lightning assault, which was to include Bowser's column. Arriving on the banks of the river, Wellesley found a sizeable portion of the insurgents' supplies, but not the man himself. The force guarding the supplies, numbering 5,000, was attacked and destroyed, with most drowning as they fled into the fast-flowing waters.[58] In the long term, the attack was decisive, since it materially undermined Dhoondiah's source of supplies, and therefore threatened the main bargaining chip with which he maintained his force – a guaranteed supply of food and water and payment. But the pursuit of the insurgents was to last another month, and Wellesley can be criticised for striking too fast, when intelligence of Dhoondiah's presence had not been verified. On the other hand, he was well aware of the difficulty of bringing an insurgent to battle, and could not waste the opportunity to strike against an encampment. Wellesley's entire concept of operations was rooted in 'Light and Quick' movements, and if he had waited for verified intelligence he might have lost the opportunity altogether and, with it, the initiative he had worked so hard to gain.

The victory, partial as it was, continued to improve British political authority in the region, and the remaining month and ten days it took to track and defeat Dhoondiah can be seen as the final phase of the campaign, and was certainly the embodiment of 'Light and Quick' operations. Previously non-existent, support now came flooding in from local chieftains, suddenly and 'sincerely desirous of being on the best terms with' the British.[59] Politically, the campaign objectives had been achieved. British political and military authority in the region had been reasserted and arguably the insurgency, starved of support and supplies, could have been left to wither on the vine. Dhoondiah, however, was much too dangerous to be left alone. 'Dhoondiah or somebody else will certainly return as soon as we withdraw to our own country,' wrote Wellesley.[60]

Continued stability depended on Dhoondiah's defeat. Not only would the message be sent that rebellion in any form would not be tolerated, but successive insurgencies might be discouraged. Wellesley therefore instituted a plan of operations that was decidedly risky for a force of the size he had. Dividing his force, Wellesley planned to 'sweep along the whole line from Darwar to the River, and Dhoondiah must either go into the Jungles, or he must go to the southward of Darwar into the open country. If he goes into the Jungles, we shall easily come up with his rear, if he takes to the plain I shall cross upon him with my detachment.'[61] Dhoondiah could pursue one of two options, and Wellesley was prepared for both. In the event, the rebel fled into the jungles.

The continuing reverses Dhoondiah was suffering began to take a toll on his support, and intelligence reports indicated that desertions were rampant, with miscellaneous groups of bandits breaking away from the main force, and caches of arms being found in various villages in Dhoondiah's wake. Eager that a new insurgency should not form around any stragglers, Wellesley dispatched small parties to destroy the groups.[62] Despite the ferocity of his pursuit, Wellesley was unable to stop Dhoondiah from escaping across the Malprabha at the end of August – a second opportunity to bring the insurgent to battle apparently lost.[63]

Nevertheless, the British and Maratha force continued to sweep forward, preventing the possibility of being outflanked. Eventually, amid rumours that Dhoondiah was preparing to cross the Tungabadra, back into Mysore, Wellesley struck with lightning speed on 10 September, and cornered the insurgent at Conaghul. Any chance of escape was removed when Stevenson's column swept down from the north, effectively encircling Dhoondiah's force. The ensuing events were less a battle and more a rout:

[Dhoondiah] had not heard of my being near him ... He however drew up in a remarkably strong position when he saw me, and his people, which I think to have been 5000 in number, stood with apparent firmness. I charged them with the 19th and 25th Dragoons, and the 1st and 2nd Regiments of Native Cavalry, and drove them till they dispersed, and were scattered over all parts of the country.[64]

Dhoondiah was killed in the action; his body was found later in the day, and brought into the British camp tied to the barrel of a cannon.[65] British losses were slight, early estimates accounting for 'some horses, one man of the 25th [Dragoons] killed and a few wounded'.[66] With the death of the insurgent, British military and political authority were restored. The campaign had been highly successful, despite the fact that Dhoondiah had seemingly escaped so many times. Unsurprisingly, these instances were played down. British authority had taken a severe knock with the development of an organised insurgency. In documenting its defeat, there seemed little need to highlight every wild-goose chase.

*　　*　　*

Wellesley's first independent command had been a total success. On paper, he had successfully destroyed a force of much greater strength (some 40,000, compared to Wellesley's 8,000), and had gone some way, although not completely, to restoring his sullied reputation after the disaster at Sultanpetah Tope. Moreover, Wellesley's concept of operations, 'Light and Quick', had proven highly effective against Indian warriors. This was perhaps because it was such a break with previous British approaches to warfare, and resembled much more closely the predatory style of the indigenous forces. There had been few logistical difficulties, and those that did occur were relatively minor. The 'Light and Quick' concept had been entirely reliant on the political and military support of a host of minor allies among the landowners and chieftains of the border region between Mysore and the Maratha Confederacy. It was a reliance which Wellesley acknowledged shortly after Dhoondiah's defeat: 'They [the allies] are of use in protecting my rear, my baggage, and my camp. If I had not had them, my cavalry would have been much distressed . . .'[67] Most importantly, though, bearing in mind this was his first command, Wellesley had experienced at first hand the political machinations of a foreign power. He had also learned that political imperatives and caveats trumped military objectives. It would have been far easier, and less costly, to help stabilise the Maratha Confederacy in an effort to bring to bear the full power of the Marathas against Dhoondiah's insurgency. But such a settlement ran contrary to Lord Mornington's political assumptions about the Maratha Confederacy. He estimated, however controversially, that the Confederacy represented a major threat to the British position in India, and expressly forbade any alliance or agreement that sought to strengthen its power before British forces were strong enough to resist it militarily. Arthur Wellesley learned a very valuable lesson in his campaign against Dhoondiah Vagh: if the military solution contradicts political imperatives, find a different military solution. It was the most valuable and accurate experience of the campaign and one that he would carry with him for the rest of his military career.

Wellesley also learned a few inappropriate lessons. His very first engagement in India, the skirmish at Sultanpetah Tope outside Seringapatam, had imbued him with an aggressive tendency that remains at odds with the persona with which he was labelled later in his career. The fiasco had saddled Wellesley with an undesirable reputation, of a commander unwilling to take risks. His resolution to adopt the 'Light and Quick' approach to warfare was the natural result of such an experience. The success of the campaign fought against Dhoondiah Vagh had only cemented these conclusions. In Wellesley's opinion, military success in India depended on tactical aggression:[68] a swift response to intelligence of a nearby enemy force, fixing that force in place, and destroying it with relentless, and ultimately decisive, attacks, led by well-trained European-led infantry. This would break an Indian enemy's will to fight. Success depended on surprise, determination, aggression and, above all, a resolution never to retire in the face of a native enemy. In adopting these principles, Wellesley had unconsciously adopted tactics that were more reminiscent of Indian than of European warfare. They were conclusions drawn partly from Wellesley's personal desire to prove his command capability under pressure, partly from the outstanding success of his campaign against Dhoondiah Vagh, and partly from his erroneous assumptions about the nature of Maratha warfare.[69] In planning the campaign against the Maratha Confederacy in the spring and summer of 1803, Wellesley made a classic mistake: he planned the last war.

CHAPTER 3

Learning the Wrong Lessons

WAR WITH THE MARATHAS, 1801–1803

My fingers itch to begin.

Colonel Arthur Wellesley
Dummel, India, 27 September 1800[1]

IN the wake of the defeat of Dhoondiah Vagh, Wellesley's political education continued apace. After the ringside view of the diplomatic prelude to war with Mysore, his role in the arrangement of political affairs at Seringapatam following Tipu Sultan's death, and the detailed and multi-faceted negotiations preceding the counterinsurgency against Dhoondiah, over the next three years Wellesley would be thrust to the forefront of national diplomacy as his brother invested him with the authority to reach a settlement with the Marathas. In part, this demonstrates Mornington's trust in his brother, in part, it represents the lack of trust Mornington had in the abilities of others, but most of all it shows Mornington's ultimate desire for war with the Marathas.

Wellesley's nuanced perception of the viability of an open conflict with the Marathas, expressed privately to his friends,[2] has induced some of his biographers to conclude that he was resistant to war.[3] This is a preposterous conclusion to arrive at. Not only was Wellesley desperate to reverse his suboptimal reputation for battlefield success, but the notion that a military officer seeking a reputation upon which he could build a career would seek to avoid hostilities is wholly ridiculous.[4] At the same time, Wellesley realised that a reputation gained in an illegal war was no reputation at all, so he sought, above all, to ensure that any war with the Marathas, when it came, was just. His letters and memoranda between 1800 and

1803 were, therefore, attempts to ensure that his brother did not engage in illegal conflicts.

Initially, Wellesley thought that the British had grounds to go to war with the Marathas as soon as Dhoondiah Vagh had been defeated. Following the insurgent's demise, Wellesley remained with his force well inside Maratha territory, in case a war with Sindhia became inevitable. At this point, the British were trying to persuade the Peshwa to sign a subsidiary alliance. Sindhia had used the campaign against Dhoondiah to position forces in the south to apply pressure on the Peshwa to prevent such an alliance. If the Peshwa signed, it was expected that Sindhia would move to occupy Poona and depose the Peshwa. At the height of the crisis, Wellesley expected on a daily basis that Sindhia's forces would attack him. And he relished the opportunity to prove himself capable.[5] In the event, the Peshwa refused to sign a treaty with the British, succumbing to the pressure placed on him by Sindhia, and the prospect of war receded. Without any reasonable grounds, Wellesley could not support a conflict. 'The refusal of the Marathas to accede to our terms of closer alliance cannot be deemed an attack,' wrote Wellesley to James Kirkpatrick, British Resident at Hyderabad, in November, 'and I have not heard of any circumstances in their late conduct which can be deemed one. Hostility then on our part might be thought a breach of the laws for the government of this empire.'[6]

Soon after, Wellesley was appointed to command a standing force based at Trincomalee, designed to be a reactive strike force. The command presented interesting administrative and management issues, as well as plenty of scope for reputation-making. Shortly after this, however, the British government decided to attack French-held Egypt from both the Mediterranean and the Red Sea. The Trincomalee force was the ideal choice for the Red Sea expedition, but, as it was to cooperate with General Sir Ralph Abercromby, who would command the Mediterranean wing, a more senior officer than Wellesley would have to be appointed to its command. The man selected was General Sir David Baird, whom Wellesley had unceremoniously upstaged at Seringapatam in 1799. Hearing unofficially that he was to lose his command, Wellesley unwisely sailed from Trincomalee to Bombay in the hope of outpacing Baird. On his arrival, any plans of military glory Wellesley had were thwarted when he contracted a severe case of the Malabar Itch. Wellesley angrily blamed his brother for the loss of his new command. 'I am of the opinion,' he wrote to Mornington, 'that under the command of ... [Baird] I shall be as useless to the army as I should be if I were to return to Mysore.'[7] But it was to Mysore that Wellesley reluctantly returned for the next eighteen months, 'with a pleasure more than equal to the regret which [he] had on quitting it'.[8] The comment was disingenuous. His arrogant and spiteful attitude contributed to a lengthy cool period between the two brothers, as Wellesley had had his heart set on an independent command. The notion that he was happy to return to the monotony and obscurity of Seringapatam is patently absurd.

Back in southern India, Wellesley oversaw courts martial, arbitrated in petty land disputes, administered the province, and continued to suppress minor rebellions on the western fringes of Mysore. In reality, Wellesley resented his continued governorship of Mysore. He had understood the necessity of establishing British authority in the region quickly and efficiently, but now viewed his position as a dead-end role, ill suited to a military officer. He also had grave concerns about the nature of Britain's government in Mysore. It was the almost continuous difficulties the British faced on the peripheries of their control that worried Wellesley: 'The extension of our territory and influence has been greater than our means,' he wrote to his friend Thomas Munro: 'we have added to the number and description of our enemies ... wherever we spread ourselves ... at the same time that, by the extension of our territory, our means of supporting our government, and of defending ourselves, are proportionately decreased.'[9] Nevertheless, in the course of two years, Wellesley improved the productivity, security and efficiency of Mysore. He was able to fashion a well-trained sepoy detachment, which was to benefit from a surplus of cattle, bullocks for supply trains and the fertile agriculture and plentiful resources of the province.[10] On 29 April 1802, Wellesley was rewarded with promotion to Major-General. But his concern about the over-extension of British power would prove remarkably prescient.

*   *   *

A state of intermittent civil war had existed within the Maratha Confederacy since the middle of 1799. Until then, a strong chief, Nana Fadnavis, had recognised that internecine warfare only weakened Maratha power, and had supported a strong central authority: the Peshwa. In 1800, Nana died, and the fragile peace between the Peshwa and the various contending chiefs collapsed. Baji Rao II, a weak and unpleasant man, was the Peshwa, but he was challenged by Sindhia, Maharaja of Gwalior, by Jaswant Rao Holkar, whose base was Indore, and by the Bhonsla Raja of Berar, whose territories were in the south and east of the Maratha Confederacy.[11] The main fighting took place between Holkar and Sindhia, with the latter inflicting several heavy defeats on the former. By October 1801, Baji Rao, anxious that Sindhia was negotiating covertly with Bhonsla to usurp his authority, secretly approached the British to reopen the negotiations for a defensive alliance that had stalled in 1800. The new negotiations faltered almost instantly when Mornington demanded more territory from the Peshwa than he was willing to part with. At the same time, Sindhia and Bhonsla tried to restrict Baji Rao's independence by insisting that any negotiations with the British could take place only with their consent.

The relationship between the Peshwa and Sindhia was complicated. Clearly the two did not trust each other and often conspired against one another. This was never more obvious than when Sindhia pressurised the Peshwa in 1800 and 1801. Yet Sindhia's campaigns against Holkar between 1799 and 1801 were in support of the Peshwa. When it was in their mutual interest, the two supported each other. Such was the case in the autumn of 1801.

In April 1801, Baji Rao had executed Holkar's brother, prompting Holkar to swear to take revenge. Consequently, the Peshwa confiscated Holkar's *jaghire*, or territory, on 29 October 1801. A civil war then broke out, in which Holkar achieved unexpected and repeated success against forces sent against him by both Sindhia and the Peshwa. This culminated in a battle outside Poona on 8 October 1802. Holkar once more prevailed, leaving the Maratha capital unprotected. As Holkar's force neared Poona, the Peshwa again turned to the British for assistance.

If Mornington had been truly determined to avoid war with the Marathas he would not have supported the Peshwa. Baji Rao was known to be weak and double-dealing. Wellesley had called him unsteady and duplicitous when negotiating with him in 1800.[12] Lieutenant-Colonel William Palmer, the British Resident at Poona, believed that 'nothing short of imminent and certain destruction will induce him [Baji Rao] to make concessions'.[13] It was clear that Baji Rao was an unstable leader whose term as Peshwa would be short. Stability and security would be more likely if the British supported one of his challengers or, better still, just left the Marathas alone. But Mornington seemed determined on finding order where there was none, and instructed Barry Close, Palmer's successor in Poona, to negotiate with the Peshwa.[14] The negotiations began in July 1802 but had reached no conclusions by mid-October, because the Peshwa wanted to establish an alliance with the British, despite refusing any concessions in return.[15]

In the event, Palmer's prediction was right. Holkar arrived outside Poona on 24 October. The Peshwa offered considerable concessions to Holkar, including the lawful restoration of his *jaghire*. Holkar, wise to the Peshwa's duplicitous ways, refused any accommodation and won a decisive victory over the Peshwa's forces at Hadapsar on the 25th. Anticipating the defeat, Baji Rao signed an ill-defined treaty of defensive alliance with the British, the details to be worked out later.[16] Soon after, the Peshwa fled

Poona, seeking asylum with the British at Bassein. It was another two months before Close was able to hammer out a definitive alliance. The Treaty of Bassein was signed on 31 December 1802.[17]

War only became inevitable because Mornington chose to make it so. He did not have to accept the Peshwa's agreement, but did so as it allowed Britain to intervene legally in Maratha politics in Poona. If Mornington had wanted to ensure the Marathas remained politically disunited, he could have maintained relations at arm's length. Such a course would have meant that the Maratha Confederacy posed virtually no threat to the British. 'It is possible that the disunion of [Sindhia and Holkar] may be more advantageous to us than any arrangement we could make with the Peshwa,' wrote Wellesley, 'and that we ought not to interfere in such a manner as to induce them to unite.'[18]

But such a course would not extend British influence. Furthermore, in the mid- to long term, if one of the stronger chiefs, such as Sindhia or Holkar, succeeded in the struggle and forcibly unified the Confederacy, the British might face a much more challenging threat than they did in 1802–3. On this subject, Wellesley's opinion appeared to differ, depending on the recipient of his letters. To his old friend, Major John 'Boy' Malcolm, his thoughts on the subject appeared balanced. To his brother he wrote much more forcefully, suggesting the inevitability of war.[19] 'We are ready and the supposed enemy are not, and every day's delay after this time is an unnecessary increase of expense to us, and an advantage to them.'[20]

This was hardly the voice of someone who opposed war. Events, as they turned out, proved Wellesley correct. By striking first and fast, the British did so before any meaningful resistance could be gathered.[21] After receiving the initial agreement signed by the Peshwa on 25 October, Mornington immediately gave orders to begin assembling a detachment of 7,000 troops on the banks of the River Tungabadra,[22] ready to march into Maratha territory, defeat Holkar if he resisted, relieve Poona and restore the Peshwa.[23]

Wellesley was informed on 9 November 1802 that the Governor-General was preparing to order a detachment of Company troops to relieve Poona. He received the dispatch on the 12th, and the same day wrote immediately stating his suitability for the appointment to its command. Such a moment was not a time for modesty. 'Independent of the experience I have of the country, the principal *Sirdars* are acquainted with me, and I have kept up a communication with them ever since I was there before. This will be of great consequence in our operations,' he wrote to Mornington.[24] Wellesley was appointed to the command the following March.[25]

Unlike the campaign against Dhoondiah, the advance on Poona was a much more extended march into enemy territory. Outside the domains of the southern *jagirdars*, the British could not expect a friendly reception, and would therefore have to rely on their own supplies. As with the campaign against Dhoondiah, new supply depots would be established, as the army marched.[26] Although the British were never without a supply train, the distance to the nearest depot would always remain comparatively short. Wellesley would not be able to operate along the same highly manoeuvrable lines he had in 1800, but the mobility of his army was still relatively good. Critical to the success of this approach was the establishment of friendly relations with the southern *jagirdars*, who would be allowed to trade freely in the British camps. 'We shall enjoy advantages nearly as extensive as we should supposing that the countries were in our own hands, without spending time, money, and lives to conquer them',[27] Wellesley explained.

However, this simply stated principle was hard to achieve in reality. Wellesley employed a variety of tactics to gain local support. The chief problem was the familiar divisions within the southern *jagirdars*. 'Since the year 1800, when I was in this country before,' wrote Wellesley, 'it has been one continual contest for power and plunder between the different chiefs who have armies under their command.'[28] Reconciling the majority of these chiefs to the support of the Peshwa, and, by extension, the British, was difficult but not impossible. In the first instance, Wellesley informed hostile *jagirdars* 'who were under the Peshwa's displeasure' that 'a promise of ... British influence [would be] exerted to restore them to the confidence of their sovereign', if they supported Wellesley's advance to Poona.[29] Still more seemed to be persuaded by the efforts made by the British to enforce order as they marched through the country. 'The march of a British force through this distracted country,' wrote Malcolm in early April 1803, 'has had the happy effect of reconciling its contending chiefs, and of giving confidence to its oppressed inhabitants.'[30]

By the beginning of April 1803, Wellesley had 'prevailed on all [the] chiefs to cease their contests for the present and to join this detachment with the troops which would otherwise be employed in the plunder of the country or in the prosecution of their private quarrels, and to cooperate with me in the service of the Peshwa'.[31] Wellesley was exaggerating slightly – Malcolm later on wrote that 'we have not been joined by all the *Sirdars* who were expected ... [but] we have not required their assistance'.[32] The army was nevertheless well supplied by local inhabitants who supported the Peshwa's restoration,[33] although the closer the army drew to Poona, the poorer the countryside became.[34] As the British

advanced further into Maratha territory, leaving behind the friendly territories of the southern *jagirdars*, the anticipated hostile reception nearer
Poona failed to materialise.

On 16 April, however, Wellesley received the disturbing news that
Holkar had instructed his deputy, Amrit Rao, to burn Poona as the British
column closed in.[35] Worried for the safety of his family, and afraid of the
wider repercussions that the destruction of Poona would have on his
support, the Peshwa urged Wellesley to 'detach a detail ... to make a
forced march to Poona, and use all possible means for the protection ...
of the city from being ruined by fire'.[36] On the evening of 19 April,
detaching his cavalry from the infantry,[37] Wellesley force-marched some
60 miles in thirty-two hours. The march encountered few problems – the
heat and the hardness of the roads damaged some of the gun carriages[38]
– and Amrit Rao fled Poona on the morning of 20 April when he heard
of the speed of the British approach.[39] The forced march proved decisive,
helping reaffirm the British commitment to the restoration of the Peshwa.
Although Wellesley found Poona deserted, Malcolm hoped that the city
would soon recover. 'We ... have probably saved the city from destruction
by fire, or, at all events, from promiscuous plunder,' he observed. 'I have
not a doubt of its being restored in a few days to a state of as much tranquillity as it has ever enjoyed.'[40]

Certainly, the consequences for the British position in the Maratha
Confederacy if Poona had burned would have been irreparable. The
damage done by Holkar's army during its occupation of Poona had been
severe enough. Wellesley concluded that war had been inevitable. He
argued that Holkar's occupation of Poona was unsustainable, and that in
his search for supplies he would have attacked first the Nizam's territory
and eventually British possessions as well. Britain would be on the defensive – an undesirable position in India politically – and forced to retaliate
when unprepared and with her own resources depleted by the invasion.
Better for the British to strike now pre-emptively, and remove the threat
from the Company's territories, than wait for the war to come to them.[41]

The Peshwa returned to Poona in early May, and the tricky business
of persuading Sindhia and Bhonsla to accept the terms of the subsidiary
alliance with Britain now began.[42] Initially, Wellesley, Malcolm and Close
were confident of success.[43] Sindhia and Bhonsla's *vakils* believed that
they would each contribute one third of the territory ceded as part of the
Treaty of Bassein by the Peshwa to the British, with the Peshwa himself
ceding the remaining third. This, unsurprisingly, proved to be a wildly
optimistic assessment. Although in theory they accepted the treaty,[44] in
practice, both Sindhia and Bhonsla appeared to be preparing for war. Both

had mobilised their forces, numbering 52,700 troops, mainly composed of cavalry according to Lieutenant-Colonel John Collins the British Resident formerly at Sindhia's court. Collins also noted that the Maratha force had moved to a threatening position on Hyderabad's border.[45] This provocation ostensibly caused Wellesley and Malcolm to despair, but this was merely false morality. Both Wellesley and Malcolm (the latter in particular) were, and would continue to be, the instruments of British aggrandisement on the subcontinent.

If Sindhia and Bhonsla rejected the alliance with the British, it was because they recognised the true nature of the British policy of expansionism that had begun in 1799. Holkar, too, had recognised the threat. After capturing Poona and upon hearing of the agreements with the British, Holkar argued that 'Baji Rao has destroyed the Maratha Power. He has taken money from the English, and given them territory. In the [course of] time they will seize the whole, as they have done in Mysore ... Should the English, uniting with Baji Rao, ascend, Sindhia and I should accommodate our difference, and jointly oppose the British troops.'[46] Unfortunately for the Marathas, such a combination of force seemed remote.

For the British, meanwhile, Poona had acquired a new level of strategic significance. Retreating from Poona would invite aggression against the Nizam, and possibly against the Company's territories,[47] so the British would maintain their position. If the other *sirdars* did not agree and chose to challenge the British, then the latter would defend that position. And for the British in India, the best form of defence was offence. Wellesley became fearful that his brother had once more overstepped the mark. 'The greater experience I gain of Maratha affairs,' he wrote privately to Malcolm, 'the more convinced I am that we have been mistaken entirely regarding the constitution of the Maratha empire. In fact, the Peshwa never had exclusive power in the state.' Wellesley was slamming the stable door after the horse had bolted. 'Even supposing that by withdrawing we could stop the hostilities, which I doubt,' he wrote to Malcolm, 'we should only defer them to a period at which probably we should be less prepared than we are at the present moment.'[48] And to Collins he argued that 'to withdraw from the alliance with the Peshwa ... would give reason to our enemies to suppose that we wanted confidence in ourselves and that their menaces had had their effect and their hope of advantage from the war would be increased'.[49] To be seen retreating before a native Indian enemy would invite further aggression. The British could not back down: to do so would jeopardise the political and military edifice upon which British power was built.

By July, an impasse had been reached whereby neither side wished to be seen to be the aggressor. Wellesley had marched with his army near to Sindhia's territory, ostensibly to secure Hyderabad in the event that the elderly Nizam died,[50] but in reality in anticipation of war.[51] And so the procrastination continued. The slowness of the decision-making arose in part because Mornington remained in Calcutta and each new development had to be referred to him. In late June, Mornington decided that this had to be stopped. 'It is ... necessary during the present crisis,' he wrote to Wellesley, 'to unite the general direction and control of all political and military affairs in Hindustan and the Deccan under a distinct local authority ...'

> Your approved ability, zeal, temper, activity, and judgement, combined with your extensive local experience, your established influence, and high reputation among the Maratha Chiefs and States, and your intimate knowledge of my views and sentiments concerning British interests in the Maratha Empire, have determined me to vest these important and arduous powers in your hands.[52]

In reality, these new powers were merely a cipher, a thinly veiled green light for war to begin. In a secret dispatch the following day, Wellesley was instructed to issue an ultimatum to Sindhia, asking for a precise declaration of his intentions. If Sindhia's intentions were not sufficiently conciliatory – which they were almost certainly unlikely to be – then Mornington instructed Wellesley to engage 'in the most active operations' against Sindhia and Bhonsla, and to 'proceed to the utmost extremity which appears to you to promise success, without admitting pacific negotiation, until the power of the opposing chief shall have been completely destroyed'.[53] It is clear from his correspondence with Malcolm and Close that Wellesley expected to be given fairly limited British objectives in any war with Sindhia: the establishment of a strong British detachment at Poona, enforcing the security of the Company's territories in the south was a legitimate enough reason for a brief war to reinforce British military superiority.

But the secret dispatch outlined a much more ambitious agenda. It dismissed the notion that this was anything but a war of British aggrandisement, and demonstrated how accurate Holkar was in his initial concerns about the British alliance with the Peshwa. In essence, Mornington wanted to reduce the Maratha power to a rump. In the west, Sindhia was to surrender Gujarat and all his coastal possessions, and in the east, Bhonsla was expected to surrender the remaining stretch of coast that linked the Calcutta and Madras presidencies. Mornington also wanted to annex the majority of Sindhia's northern territories, including Delhi, Agra and lands to the banks of the Jumna and Ganges. The result would be uninterrupted British dominion of the lands up to Oudh, and the complete excommunication of the Marathas from the Sikhs in the Punjab.[54] Moreover, this would give the East India Company direct access to the ailing Mughal Empire, with all the political benefits such a relationship offered. Economically, the British would also gain control of the fertile and rich Jumna–Ganges Doab. In this sense, then, whilst Wellesley's theatre in the Deccan was the main trigger for the war, the main objective was in Hindustan.[55] This would require a second front. From his instructions it can be seen that Mornington considered war both inevitable and crucial to continued British prosperity on the subcontinent.

Whether they signed or not, though, was immaterial. Neither Sindhia nor Bhonsla could be trusted. 'Unless, therefore, Sindhia shall have afforded full satisfaction and security in your judgement, you will pursue him across the Nerbudda, if you should deem that movement advisable for the purpose of reducing his means of mischief,' Mornington instructed Wellesley. Meanwhile, 'the retreat of Bhonsla ... to any place situated within ... [his] territories, or elsewhere, will not exclusively amount to a sufficient degree of satisfaction and security, after the recent proofs which the confederacy has disclosed of determined hostility and arrogant ambition.'[56] Unsurprisingly, Sindhia and Bhonsla refused the British terms. On 6 August, Wellesley wrote to Sindhia informing him that he had offered 'peace on terms of equality ... you have chosen war and are responsible for all consequences'.[57]

The war which began on 6 August 1803 saw the British launch a two-front campaign, with Wellesley commanding in the Deccan, and the Commander-in-Chief, General Sir Gerard Lake commanding in Hindustan, attacking Sindhia's territories from the north and focusing on Delhi. What, though, of Holkar, whose actions had initiated the descent into war between the British and Sindhia and Bhonsla? Wellesley, Malcolm and Close clearly expected a war to begin with Holkar as well. The Treaty of Bassein had been signed in order to oust him from Poona; it seemed unrealistic that he could now be persuaded to accept the original terms of that treaty. Once again, internal Maratha divisions intervened to prevent a united campaign against the British. As Holkar had been considered the main, and most likely, enemy, Wellesley and Close had directed most of their intelligence collection efforts in his direction. In June, news was received of Holkar's retreat northwards 'leaving behind everybody that could not keep up with him'. This persuaded

Wellesley to conclude, correctly, that this looked 'very like a breakup of the confederacy...'[58]

This was good news for the British, who would have been tested by a unification of the three major Maratha *sirdars*. Such a confederacy might have persuaded others who were currently ambivalent or supportive of the British to join, and might even have enticed the Peshwa to renege on the Treaty of Bassein. Wellesley would have been pleased with this result, increasingly concerned, as he was, that the British and Company armies were overstretching their capabilities.

On the face of it, for Wellesley, the powers granted him by Mornington were an extremely gratifying testimony to his political skill, and an extraordinary development in civil–military relations. In reality, the powers – in so far as they could be utilised to avoid war – were meaningless. Mornington only granted political authority to a military officer because he had already concluded war was inevitable. What is more, he embraced that prospect, and relished it. And despite his protestations about the difficulties of the British position in the Maratha Confederacy, Wellesley embraced and relished the prospect of war as well. His comments on the strategic significance of Poona, the requirement to undermine the Maratha *sirdars'* power before it grew too great, and the wider need to establish British military superiority in south India testify to this conclusion. At the same time, however, Wellesley was aware of the limits of British expansionism, and evidently felt that the more he learned about Maratha politics, the more he realised that his brother had started an unstoppable chain reaction of events which might escalate beyond what the British sought or planned for.

The over-extension of political objectives and ambitions without the military means of achieving them was another important lesson for Wellesley, who would encounter similar political over-extension later in his career. The difficulty for a general in such circumstances was balancing political objectives with military reality, and doing so without appearing insubordinate, unsuccessful, incompetent, or all three. In 1803, with such ambitious political aspirations, Wellesley knew that the war with Sindhia and Bhonsla would have to be won quickly and decisively. But, as with the political machinations leading to war, in the actual fighting, Sindhia would prove to be full of surprises.

*   *   *

The story of the Deccan campaign of the Second Anglo-Maratha War is one of intelligence failure. This was not a collection failure; information that would have led to accurate assumptions about Maratha military strength and techniques was available for anyone to see. This was a failure of analysis and interpretation and the person ultimately responsible was Arthur Wellesley. Until the Battle of Assaye on 23 September 1803, nearly every assumption Wellesley made was inaccurate. The fact that Wellesley managed to turn defeat into victory at that battle is testament not to the success of his planning capabilities – because on nearly all counts his plans disintegrated – but to his extraordinary skill as a battlefield general.

Wellesley's first key assumption was that any war against the Marathas would resemble the campaign against Dhoondiah Vagh. 'The experience which has been acquired in the late contest,' wrote Wellesley confidently shortly after defeating Dhoondiah, 'of the seasons, the nature of the country, its roads, its produce, and its means of defence, will be of use . . .'[59] Wellesley therefore planned to use an adaptation of his 'Light and Quick' concept of operations. He could not expect to advance far into enemy territory, win over the population and immediately start living off the produce of those lands. Such an approach would alienate the locals, assuming they were supportive in the first place.[60] A supply train would be needed, but a forward supply depot was desirable to make that train as small as possible, and further resupply a relatively easy task.[61] Wellesley's Army of the Deccan would not be as 'light' as the detachment he used against Dhoondiah, but it would be markedly more efficient than the army that had marched to Seringapatam in 1799.

The initial target, then, was the large fortress of Ahmednagar, to the north-east of Poona. After the capture of Ahmednagar, Wellesley's Deccan army could advance swiftly and decisively, with secure supply lines, in an intelligence-led operation against Sindhia's and Bhonsla's forces, wherever they might be. Accurate and reliable intelligence was obviously the key to success. The main problem Wellesley envisaged was actually going to be bringing the Marathas to battle. 'The Maratha army is principally composed of cavalry,' he wrote in an 1801 Memorandum on operations in Maratha territory, 'and their plan of operations against a British army would be to endeavour to cut off its communications with its rear, and impede the junction of its supplies from the Mysore country.'[62] This approach to warfare he termed 'predatory horse'. 'The Marathas have long boasted that they would carry on a predatory war against us,' he opined. But 'they will find that mode of warfare not very practicable at the present moment, and at all events supposing that they can carry their designs into execution, . . . they cannot expect much success from them. A system of predatory war must have some foundation in strength of some kind or other.'[63]

Wellesley's force therefore needed to be able to strike quickly and decisively against a Maratha force whenever his intelligence sources located one. In this regard, he appears to have expected a rerun of the several lightning strikes he made on Dhoondiah's force in August and September 1800. In making this assumption about the Maratha 'way of war', Wellesley was committing his first, and probably most egregious, mistake. Predatory light cavalry, or *pindaris*, and the style of warfare they practised – known as *bargi-giri*[64] – were one of a selection of different approaches to mounted warfare adopted by the Marathas since the seventeenth century, and this approach was generally used in combination with infantry and artillery.

Assuming that the Marathas' preferred arm was light and irregular cavalry might not have been so bad if Wellesley had not also discounted their abilities in other arms, notably in infantry, artillery and engineers. Despite his extensive reading on the political and military nature of India during his voyage to the subcontinent in 1797, Wellesley had apparently overlooked several accounts of the impressive capabilities and training of the Maratha infantry soldier.[65] Instead, he probably paid more attention to the accounts of the behaviour of the Maratha infantry in the Third Anglo-Mysore War, which suggested they would be unreliable on the battlefield. During this war, the Maratha infantry had supposedly been 'composed of . . . despicable poor wretches of the lowest caste, uniform in nothing but the bad state of their muskets, none of which are either clean or complete; and few are provided with either ammunition or accoutrements'.[66] In battle, meanwhile, the infantry performed worse than even the low expectations such a description encouraged. 'Part of the Maratha infantry charged at times, when they saw the enemy appearing to give way, but were always beat back . . . in such disorder as greatly increased the difficulty in forming and leading our sepoys.'[67]

This helps explain Wellesley's conclusions regarding the Maratha infantry, but it was not the only intelligence available. In late July, Wellesley received from Collins detailed intelligence of Sindhia's force. Collins reported that Sindhia's cavalry outnumbered his infantry by more than two to one, and also pointed out that Sindhia had upwards of 7,700 European-trained and commanded infantry.[68] Of course, bearing in mind Wellesley's premature conclusions about the nature of the Maratha infantry, it is easy to see why he might discount the strength of these forces on paper, but he was overlooking their training as well as their numbers. Sindhia had retained the services of several European officers in order to improve the training of his infantry battalions, thus bringing them into line with the troops of other indigenous powers such as those

Map 4
The Deccan Campaign,
August–December 1803

of the Nizam, who had been employing British, French, Dutch and German officers since the 1790s. European drill practices also theoretically gave Sindhia a distinct advantage over his opponents within the Maratha Confederacy. Indeed, a Frenchman, General Perron, commanded Sindhia's army whilst the Hanoverian officer, Colonel Pohlman, commanded his elite infantry brigade.

In late August, Wellesley met Collins personally near Aurangabad. Neither soldier impressed the other. Wellesley appeared aloof and arrogant to Collins, who thought him too young to command an army. To Wellesley, meanwhile, Collins's overt flamboyance, his penchant for outdated eighteenth-century fashions and gaudy jewellery, undermined his credibility. Nevertheless, during the course of that meeting, Collins warned Wellesley that the Maratha infantry was not to be underestimated. 'I tell you, General, as to their cavalry ..., you may ride over them wherever you meet them, but their infantry and guns will astonish you.' On the return trip from Collins's camp, Wellesley and his staff joked about the eccentric appearance of 'little King Collins'. As a result, his warnings went unheeded.[69] In reality, Collins, an experienced veteran of Indian military affairs, was a highly reliable source, and Wellesley would rue his failure to listen to him, 'little realising how true his words would prove'.[70]

Wellesley was displaying classic signs of cognitive dissonance, a modern term used militarily to describe a scenario where a decision-maker prefers a predefined scenario to the alternative, and probably less pleasant, scenario suggested by intelligence. Wellesley compounded matters by keeping 'the intelligence department ... to himself', and not listening to the advice of more objective subordinates. 'I have long since learned to supply abundance of ifs, in the most positive stories,' wrote Mountstuart Elphinstone, Wellesley's head of intelligence, in early September.[71] Elphinstone, though, was in the minority. Wellesley surrounded himself with few objective staff officers. Captain Ralph Blakiston, for example, had deeply flawed perceptions about intelligence collection. This required 'no great art', he argued: 'plenty of gold is all that is necessary there, and all the world over'.[72] Wellesley would later learn that paying for intelligence was a sure way of getting the information he wanted, but not necessarily reliable information.

There were also other factors in Wellesley's repeated intelligence failures. Having expected the main enemy to be Holkar, *harkarrahs* were repeatedly sent to his camp, most reporting the irregular nature of his cavalry and the apparent lack of organisation, training or drill in his infantry forces.[73] *Harkarrahs* who were sent to Sindhia's camp appear to have paid particular attention to the nature, strength and condition of the

Maratha cavalry, but the intelligence provided by these sources was of patchy reliability.[74] As Blakiston observed, 'the difficulty of obtaining correct information in a strange part of India can be estimated by those only who are well acquainted with the character of the natives. It is their policy to hold every fact they possess, even though it cost them nothing to give it; and to deceive you by means in their power, even when they can themselves derive no apparent benefit from so doing.'[75] Blakiston was falling foul of the cultural nuances of south India. Information was treated as a commodity, and therefore worth something. It could be traded and bargained, but never given away. The fact was that the political machinations under way in this part of India meant that everybody, no matter how insignificant, was a stakeholder in the outcome of the conflict. Many of the individuals whom Blakiston encountered might well have wanted Sindhia and Bhonsla to be defeated, but they also had a concern in who or what replaced them, and the British were not necessarily the best option. Information therefore provided a means of attempting to influence the outcome of the conflict.

Blakiston was not alone. Elphinstone himself felt out of his depth. He had replaced Malcolm – who had fallen ill – at the last minute, taking over on 10 August. He immediately admitted that he was in 'the old predicament, *"nec quid agam scio"* – I don't know what to do'.[76] He had no control over the intelligence department, and this he attributed largely to the fact that he inherited a prefabricated intelligence system from Malcolm. He realised too late that he should have established a new network geared to the needs of the army, as he understood them. Malcolm had been an intelligence officer when the army was preparing to go to war, when intelligence collection would have been focused on finding out the strengths of the enemy army, and the political intentions of Sindhia and Bhonsla. An army at war required much more precise information on the location and intentions of an enemy force. Instead, Elphinstone wasted valuable time trying, and failing, to understand Malcolm's networks, only for them to be largely useless. 'I think, if anyone in this line were to apply, he might improve the intelligence,' he wrote despondently in October, 'but I had some people given to me, and a way shown to me, and so fell into the habit of jogtrottery, the great foe of improvement.'[77] Moreover, Elphinstone had other problems: he was not a Marathi speaker. 'My stock of [Marathi] is really too small,' he later admitted. 'I cannot readily understand all that is said to me, much less say all that I ought to express. I mean in talking to Marathas, which is my common employment.'[78] Elphinstone was clearly too inexperienced – only twenty-four years old – for the position of intelligence chief.

On top of these problems, it also appears that Sindhia was deliberately supplying Wellesley with disinformation. The *harkarrahs* employed by the British in the Deccan were brought with them from the south. As they were of different ethnic origin to those that served in the Maratha army, they were easily identifiable to Sindhia's men.[79] Sindhia intercepted *harkarrahs* sent by Collins into his camp,[80] and also publicly boasted of the 'predatory war' the Marathas intended to wage against the British.[81] This was supported by information from 'all the *harkarrahs*, who came in from [Sindhia's] camp [that] said he ... was on the predatory ... and that his marches would be long and rapid'.[82] Sindhia was suggesting that he would pursue a cavalry-based predatory form of warfare, specifically attacking Wellesley's supply lines and raiding the Nizam's territory, purposely to force the British into making a mistake. In the event, his deception plan worked perfectly.

It was not until much later in the campaign that Wellesley and Elphinstone realised they needed to employ local *harkarrahs*, although Wellesley felt he could not trust them.[83] That said, it did not seem to matter where the *harkarrahs* were from; they were generally unreliable and problematic. Elphinstone was constantly complaining that his *harkarrahs* were poorly trained, getting captured, bringing back false information or deserting.[84] Later, Elphinstone needed Close to send 'five pair of *harkarrahs*, as one of those who came before has been taken, and four have run away'.[85] Wellesley also perceived the *harkarrahs* to be unreliable. 'These *harkarrahs* are not to be believed: they never bring any intelligence that is worth hearing, and when they circulate their false reports they do infinite mischief to our cause.'[86] This was a serious hindrance. Wellesley's entire concept of operations was dependent on timely and reliable intelligence, but as the campaign progressed, it became obvious from Elphinstone's forthright letter of 11 September that Wellesley and his staff had no idea where their enemy was. 'Where [the enemy] are now I am not certain,' he wrote. 'They cannot be far off ... maybe ... forty miles from [Peepulgaon]. But I think I heard it repeated by a native intelligencer to the General today that they had marched to Amber. Amber, I am told, is ... four, [or] ... six or seven [miles] from this.'[87]

Sindhia also engaged in a proactive counterintelligence campaign. On 10 September, a reconnaissance party of 100 native cavalry was attacked by 250 *pindaris*. At the same time, 250 Mysore horsemen were attacked, and some of them relieved – embarrassingly – of their mounts.[88] 'One of my *harkarrahs* has reported that he saw an action between our infantry and the enemy's cavalry yesterday morning, in which there was much firing of cannon, and the latter were driven off.' Although with hindsight it is clear this was an elaborate, and successful, attempt to mask his infantry force, this only confirmed for Wellesley the poor nature of Sindhia's army. 'I suspect,' he wrote in the same letter, 'that [Sindhia's] cavalry are very bad and very useless.'[89]

Through a combination of intelligence failure, incompetence, misinformation, cognitive dissonance and cultural arrogance, Wellesley determined that his enemy was composed mainly of irregular light cavalry and poorly trained infantry; that it was badly commanded and likely to pursue a predatory form of warfare designed to maximise the opportunity for plunder, while avoiding conventional battle at all costs. Even once the campaign was under way, little seemed to contradict these assumptions. In theory, and according to Wellesley's plan for the campaign, well-trained intelligence collectors would track the enemy force, its movements restricted by the natural obstacles provided by terrain, and eventually force it to accept battle (for the British would attack whenever and wherever they found the Maratha army concentrated). It was then expected to capitulate swiftly in the face of sustained British aggression, superior infantry tactics and firepower, supported by artillery. What Wellesley actually faced was a well-trained and European-commanded infantry force with a significant cavalry component, and a surprisingly large artillery battery, which was adept at manoeuvring in the testing terrain of the Deccan. Sindhia deliberately perpetuated the myth of predatory warfare in order, he hoped, to force Wellesley to offer battle when the British were divided and weak, and the Marathas concentrated and strong. Through a combination of factors, all of which can be traced to the misidentification of lessons arising from his experiences so far in India, Arthur Wellesley was about to march his army straight into a trap.

*　　*　　*

When war broke out on 6 August, Wellesley was well placed to capture a strategically valuable prize, having advanced to within a few miles of the fortress of Ahmednagar on 4 June. Not only did it offer a forward supply base for sustained operations in Sindhia's territory, but capturing it would deprive Sindhia of the valuable resources still inside. To capture Ahmednagar, a nearby small village or *pettah*, which was surrounded by an 18-foot-high wall, would have to be captured first. On the evening of 10 August, an attempt was made to storm the *pettah*. 'The ladders were speedily planted, and the assault made,' recalled one observer, 'but each man as he ascended, fell, hurled from the top of the wall. This unequal struggle lasted about ten minutes, when [we] desisted, with the loss of about fifteen killed, and fifty wounded.'[90] There was no ledge behind the wall upon which the storming party could alight. An attempt had to be made on one of the more strongly defended bastions, but once this was successful, the storming party got inside the village and opened the gates, allowing the rest of the force to enter. A battery was established and fire opened on the fortress itself. On 12 August, having gone unpaid by Sindhia, and with nothing to gain by continuing the fight, the garrison of the fortress capitulated.

Thereafter, Wellesley and his second-in-command, Colonel James Stevenson, moved north towards Aurangabad in two columns, operating separately but in communication with one another. The concept of operations clearly resembled the 'Light and Quick' approach of 1800. Elphinstone supposed 'there will be hard marching in the Dhoondiah style'. Wellesley kept his officers on notice to leave the baggage, because as soon as intelligence indicated the position of Sindhia's troops he would make a dash to confront and defeat them.[91] Indeed, Elphinstone remarked on how lightly the officers of the army travelled. 'They do not talk in camp of the comfort of being snug and compact, with a fine small tent, easily pitched, and nice light baggage, that soon comes up,' he wrote on 22 August. 'They have neither the comforts of a Bengal army, nor do they rough it like the Ducks.'[92]

'Light and Quick' operations were, however, dependent on intelligence for success, and in this environment intelligence was hard to come by. The nature of the terrain made communications difficult, and Wellesley and Stevenson were frequently unaware of each other's movements and actions. Wellesley was subsequently criticised for his decision to separate his forces,[93] but this was a perfectly logical extension of the 'Light and Quick' concept, bearing in mind the intelligence at his disposal and the conclusions he had arrived at. Nevertheless, it seems this played straight into Sindhia's and Bhonsla's hands. 'We made several marches and counter-marches, owing, I believe, to the movements of a large body of cavalry which Sindhia . . . had detached to manoeuvre on our rear, in order to favour the advance of a large body of infantry and guns which were then in full march from the Deccan,' observed Blakiston. 'In a part of their object they seem to have succeeded; for while we were endeavouring to counteract the movements of their cavalry, their infantry and artillery were enabled to ascend the Adjuntee pass.'[94]

Close was later to observe that Sindhia had deliberately drawn Stevenson's column off with the threat of light cavalry assaults on his baggage train and communications. 'Stevenson opposed him by corresponding movements, but [Sindhia] stole a march on the Colonel and came through the Pass unnoticed.'[95] In this way, the campaign proceeded through late August and into September, with the army chasing nothing but shadows through a barren and desolate landscape.

On 21 September, Wellesley and Stevenson rendezvoused at Budnapur. As intelligence indicated that the Marathas were some 16 miles away, Wellesley opted once more to separate his army, sending Stevenson north-west while he went north-east. This he argued was because both columns could not use the same route, and since the Marathas were so far away, it would be better to engage in a pincer movement.[96] Despite the criticism directed at Wellesley, it is difficult to fault his logic, based as it was on his imperfect assumptions about Maratha fighting techniques, and poor intelligence as to their location. Blakiston believed that 'had [Wellesley] then possessed the experience he afterwards obtained of the discipline of Sindhia's infantry, and of the efficiency of his artillery, or had he relied sufficiently on the information given him by Colonel Collins, I much doubt whether he would have ventured on so hazardous a step'.[97] But Wellesley was right when he said both columns would not be able to utilise the same route; the road Wellesley took was, in places, little more than a path. He planned to attack the Maratha Army on 24 September, but on the 22nd Elphinstone received intelligence that indicated the British were 'within sixteen miles, at farthest, of Sindhia ... with all his horse, from 16,000 to 20,000, two brigades ... and forty pieces of cannon'. All seemed set for a battle, as Wellesley had planned, but Elphinstone remained sceptical. 'Even *they* [Sindhia] talk of fighting on Saturday, and this is Thursday. But who knows what a native will do; perhaps they will give us the slip and get to the southward.'[98]

Note the emphasis placed here by Elphinstone on the strength of the Maratha horse, and also the expectation, shared by Wellesley, that the Marathas would try to escape. This helps explain Wellesley's decision to attack the Maratha Army at Assaye as soon as he became aware of its presence, and not to wait for Stevenson's column to arrive in support. Captain James Welsh, a staff officer in General Lake's army, reinforces this argument by afterwards reporting that two captured horsemen had informed Wellesley 'that the cavalry were actually preparing to move'.[99] Blakiston also believed Wellesley wanted to surprise Sindhia:

The truth is, I believe, that [Wellesley] had obtained information on which he thought he could rely, that ... the confederate sovereigns had come to the resolution of retiring ... and conceiving, I suppose, that either division of his army was capable of coping with the enemy's force when in retreat, he determined, by a rapid movement on each flank, to prevent the possibility of their gaining any of the passes in the range of hills ...[100]

Wellesley decided to attack on the 23rd, even though he had marched his force some 21 miles in the previous twenty-four hours and they were undoubtedly exhausted.[101]

Once in a position to reconnoitre the enemy, Wellesley found the combined Maratha Army drawn in a strong defensive position running west to east on the opposite bank of the River Kaitna. The Maratha infantry numbered over 10,000, with an additional 40,000 light horse and *pindaris*. One 6,000-man brigade of the Maratha infantry was commanded by the Hanoverian officer Pohlman with a further 2,500 troops commanded by the Dutchman John James Dupont. The British numbered just 1,300 European and 2,000 Indian infantry, and 1,200 cavalry, 4,500 in total. The enemy numbers were unsurprising – Wellesley had been warned by Collins that the Maratha infantry was over 7,000 strong – but for Wellesley it was not numbers that mattered, but their quality. Even though the Maratha infantry outnumbered the British force by more than three to one, Wellesley was confident that they were no match for his own highly trained infantry. The next few hours were to prove him brutally wrong in this assumption.

Behind the Maratha position ran the River Juah. The two rivers combined one and a half miles to the left of the Maratha line. The Maratha infantry occupied this small *doab*, whilst the cavalry were on the other side of the Juah. The Marathas were not expecting battle that day, and their heavy artillery bullocks were grazing. Wellesley's decision to attack was a complete surprise, and prevented up to a third of the Maratha firepower from being used in the ensuing battle.[102]

Nevertheless, the Marathas would be able to bring into action in short order much of their lighter weaponry, precluding the possibility of a direct river crossing in the Maratha front. Wellesley therefore chose to cross the river between Waroor and Peepulgaon, not just because the proximity of the two hamlets on opposite sides of the Kaitna meant that there would obviously be a ford between the two, but because the mud walls of the hamlets would provide visual cover from Sindhia's artillery. Also, by crossing at the far left of Sindhia's line, Wellesley hoped to outflank and turn the Maratha position.

The Marathas began firing ranging shots as the troops crossed, one of which decapitated Wellesley's aide-de-camp. With the body trapped in the saddle, the horse panicked and 'kicked and plunged, and dashed the poor man's brains in our faces, to our no small danger and annoyance'.[103] Despite this, the army was able to cross in a little over two hours and form up in two lines of infantry, with the fork of the Rivers Juah and Kaitna in their rear. In the meantime, the Marathas were hastily redeploying their line, transforming their infantry from a line running parallel with the Kaitna into two hinged lines. One ran perpendicular to the rivers, and directly in Wellesley's front, and the other, at right angles to the first, ran parallel with the Juah. The hinge of the two lines was at the village of Assaye, which straddled the Juah on the far left of Sindhia's line. Blakiston observed that the Maratha infantry were performing this 'manoeuvre ... in the most steady manner possible ... for each battalion came up into the new alignment in line, the whole body thus executing a kind of echelon movement on a large scale'. It was a complicated manoeuvre that could only be performed successfully by well-trained infantry. If they were capable of this, then presumably they were also disciplined fighters. When Blakiston reported this change of position to Wellesley he 'found that, not supposing the enemy to be capable of such a manoeuvre in the face of an attacking force, [Wellesley] had, in conformity with his original intention of attacking them in flank, already formed the infantry in two lines'.[104]

What must have gone through Wellesley's mind on hearing this extraordinary news? If Sindhia's infantry were able to redeploy their forces quickly and successfully, then all of his assumptions about the nature of his enemy had been false; the Maratha infantry would not break and flee at the first British shot. Collins was right. Sindhia's infantry had astonished Wellesley. His outflanking manoeuvre had failed. As the Maratha infantry line formed, a heavy cannonade opened on Wellesley's army. Under intense pressure, and in the midst of the action himself, Wellesley ordered the redeployment of his own infantry from two lines into one, with the British 78th and 74th Regiments on either flank, and the native infantry in the centre. So furious, though, was the bombardment from the Maratha artillery that he ordered an immediate advance to capture the guns. The second line of infantry was ordered to redeploy during this advance.[105]

There was nothing else Wellesley could have done in the circumstances. Unless he advanced immediately, the centre of his line, where most of the fire was directed, was in danger of collapsing. This was a desperate moment, but there was one thing that Wellesley did not do, and this probably decided the battle. Under intense bombardment from an artillery battery that he had thought did not exist, facing well-trained infantry that challenged his perceptions about Maratha warfare, and with his own life and those of his men in great jeopardy, Arthur Wellesley did not panic.

Elphinstone recalled that it became imperative to advance and take the Maratha guns, which were now firing devastating canister and chain shot.[106] Wellesley was in the thick of the action, a characteristic for which he would become famous. Indeed, at Assaye, he had one horse shot under him and another piked.[107] The right-hand side of Wellesley's line, consisting mainly of the 74th Regiment of Foot, advanced in considerable confusion. Wellesley had ordered his right to advance to the perimeter of the village of Assaye, but the 74th advanced into Assaye, where it suffered terrible losses. As a result, rather than moving forward in one line, Wellesley's infantry splintered into two lines once more, with the left, led by the 78th, advancing on the Maratha artillery, and the right, led by the 74th, bogged down in Assaye.

At this point, a Maratha counterattack at Assaye gave 'no quarter to any of our wounded, only cutting and shooting them as they came up with them'.[108] Wellesley was forced to deploy the 19th Dragoons to rescue the remains of the 74th. He was reluctant to use his cavalry so early, as he would be unable to pursue the enemy when they were defeated or cover his own retreat, if he was defeated, but there was little option. If the Marathas were allowed to regain Assaye, then Wellesley's line could be outflanked. The charge was costly but effective, pushing the Marathas out of Assaye.

Meanwhile, the sepoys bore the main brunt of the artillery bombardments. 'In the space of less than a mile, 100 guns, worked with skill and rapidity, vomited forth death into our feeble ranks,' recalled Blakiston. 'It cannot then be a matter of surprise if in many cases, the sepoys should have taken advantage of any irregularities in the ground to shelter themselves from the deadly shower.'[109] At a time of racial intolerance for the perceived cowardly behaviour of sepoys in the face of severe enemy fire, Blakiston's reflection on the ingenuity of the indigenous troops is unusual, and it was an opinion he shared with Wellesley. In the years and battles that followed Assaye, a classic hallmark of Wellesley's choice of battlefield was the reverse slope, which helped protect his men from artillery assaults that preceded infantry attacks.

Eventually, the infantry overwhelmed the Maratha gunners, many of whom were 'bayoneted in the act of loading their pieces'.[110] Moving on to the second line of guns, Wellesley's infantry found themselves under fire from behind, as the Maratha gunners 'pretended to be dead [and] turned the guns we had taken upon us, which obliged us to return and again to drive them from them'.[111] This 'ungentlemanly' action contributed to the opinion many British officers had that indigenous Indian warfare was conducted dishonourably. Despite this delay, Wellesley's infantry advance continued, pushing the Marathas back on their second line, on the River Juah, while the cavalry charge on the right helped to rout the Maratha force.

Despite overwhelming odds, through dogged determination Wellesley's force had defeated the Marathas. Among the survivors, the dominant view

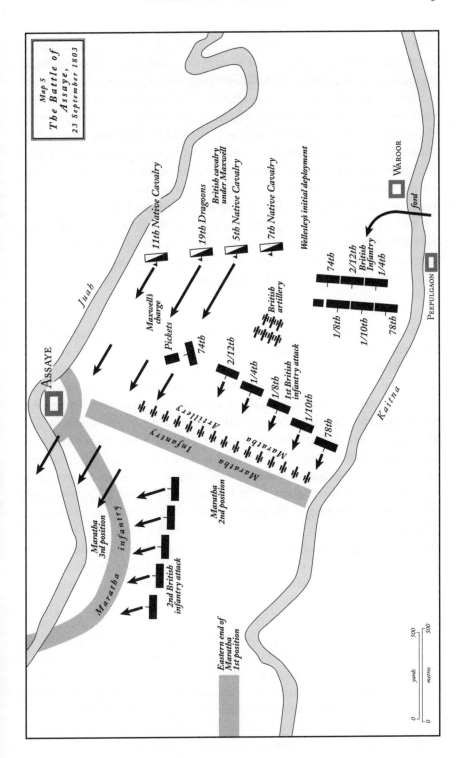

Map 5
The Battle of
Assaye,
23 September 1803

was that Assaye had been 'the bloodiest battle ever fought in India'.[112] The cost of the battle had been high: 428 British (European and sepoy) lay dead; 1,138 wounded out of a total of 4,500. Maratha losses were reported as approaching 6,000, although this was unconfirmed, and would certainly have included non-combatants.[113] Wellesley's men were too exhausted to pursue the fleeing Marathas, and turned their attentions to the wounded who lay strewn on the battlefield.[114] Wellesley was visibly shaken by the ordeal of the battle, and by the losses his men had suffered. He spent that night 'not in "the pride & circumstance of glorious war" but on the ground close to an officer whose leg was shot off and within five yards of a dead officer'.[115] The impact on his approach to warfare would be massive. Elphinstone captured the mood when he wrote of 'a Roman Emperor who said he liked the smell of a dead enemy. If he did he was singular in his taste. We are horribly perfumed with such a smell as he liked, but I would rather smell a living enemy.'[116]

*   *   *

Although Wellesley's battlefield prowess at Assaye was admirable, the fact remained that he had been caught unawares by the strength and skill of the Maratha infantry. 'It may be now seen . . . that Sindhia never meant to pursue a predatory mode of warfare,' commented Close when he received news of Assaye. 'In passing through the ghat with his cavalry, circulating the reports which he did, and running to the south of our troops, his real design was to draw off our attention from the ghats by making us tenacious of Hyderabad and of Poona, and afford leisure to his numerous infantries and cumbrous train to come uninterrupted and unnoticed through the ghats.'[117] It had become startlingly apparent that Wellesley had misjudged his enemy. Assaye had therefore badly shaken Wellesley's confidence. He was in command of a force that had been specially configured to engage an enemy that did not exist in the manner he had anticipated. In the weeks after Assaye, Wellesley decided that 'it is . . . peculiarly incumbent on me to act with caution'.[118] Close agreed, noting that

> Sindhia's army, in general, is not equal to the ancient hardy mode of Maratha predatory warfare, that the main part of his troops have adopted entirely the European style of carrying on war, and that, consequently, although his army may comparatively be powerful, it must yet be more tangible and more liable to defeat by the British troops than if it were composed principally of the thrifty hardy cavalry which originally raised the Marathas into a commanding nation.[119]

The Marathas had adopted European tactics, whilst the British had adopted South Asian tactics. Wellesley now had to decide whether he should abandon the 'Light and Quick' concept. Here, as well, there was a risk. In the wake of their defeat at Assaye, the Marathas might also conclude that they had adopted the wrong tactics, and revert once more to 'predatory' warfare. For a while after Assaye, it seemed that this might be the case. At the beginning of October, news arrived that Sindhia and Bhonsla had separated,[120] and were not in agreement on what strategy to pursue against Wellesley. Sindhia, with his strong infantry brigades, wanted to confront Wellesley in a conventional battle, whilst Bhonsla had preferred the use of predatory horse.[121] Now, with Sindhia weakened after his pummelling at Assaye, and with news that the two had separated their forces, Wellesley decided to adopt a political strategy and try and reach a separate peace with Sindhia, thus fracturing the fragile alliance between the two Maratha *sirdars*.

By mid-November, then, Wellesley was negotiating with Sindhia's *vakils*,[122] whilst intelligence indicated that Sindhia's position as *sirdar* was under threat due to significant disaffection within his camp.[123] As usual, however, negotiations with Sindhia did not progress simply, and Wellesley once again found it difficult to trust the information he was receiving about Sindhia's intentions. Sindhia had 'many people about him who will engage . . . to prevent any negotiation from taking place'.[124] The terms of any suspension of hostilities required Sindhia to agree to all of Britain's war aims, and withdraw his own force out of the Deccan. For Wellesley, an armistice with Sindhia was a necessity. 'It is not in my power to do anything more against [Sindhia],' he wrote. 'It is impossible to expect to make any impression upon this army unless by following it for a great length of time and distance.'[125]

The arrangements for an armistice were reached on 23 November, after Wellesley refused to negotiate on the terms of the cessation of hostilities.[126] However, characteristically, Sindhia failed to withdraw his force, and on the 29th Wellesley found it encamped at the village of Arguam with Bhonsla's infantry. As at Assaye, Wellesley decided to attack immediately, despite requests not to do so by Sindhia's *vakils*. In failing to withdraw, Sindhia had violated the terms of the armistice with the British.

Meanwhile, Wellesley had adopted a different strategy against Bhonsla, which emphasised targeting and destroying his military strength. Bhonsla's military power rested on a chain of fortresses from Burhanpur to Gawilghur. Target these, and the British would 'destroy all the power and influence of Bhonsla and deprive him of the means of supporting an army'.[127] On 15 October, Burhanpur surrendered without a fight, and six days later, Asirghar

surrendered after just a one-hour bombardment.[128] Stevenson, who had led
both attacks, was now eager for an immediate attack on Gawilghur, but
Wellesley hesitated, unsure whether to believe reports that Bhonsla's predatory horse were moving south to attack his rear.

Then, on 6 November, Wellesley received intelligence that Bhonsla was
'flying to the eastward as fast as he can along the Godavari ... This movement relieves us from all apprehension of his attacking the territories
of the Nizam or the Peshwa and immediately sets at liberty Colonel
Stevenson's corps.' Wellesley was now confident that his rear was not at
risk from an attack by Bhonsla's predatory horse. This would allow the
British to concentrate on their march into Berar, and eventually on
assaulting the seat of Bhonsla's power at Gawilghur. 'I think it very
possible,' wrote Wellesley gleefully, 'that four armies may be in that
country in a few days which will be delightful to [Bhonsla].'[129]

At Arguam, as Wellesley's army neared the combined Maratha Army, a
vakil from Bhonsla approached. He asked 'Whether, if [Wellesley] came
up with their army, he would attack them?' Wellesley replied, 'Most
undoubtedly.'[130] By early afternoon, Wellesley's army, still marching in two
columns, came within sight of the Maratha Army. Blakiston noted that the
enemy, consisting mainly of Bhonsla's infantry, 'were drawn up in a plain
about three miles in ... front, without showing any disposition to retire',
but apparently offering battle. 'This was a piece of braggadocio which the
General could not stand',[131] and he decided to attack immediately.[132] After
the bloodbath of Assaye, it is perhaps surprising that Wellesley elected to
engage in a second head-on attack, but the reality was that, unlike at
Assaye, there was nothing to stop him doing so. He had with him his
entire army, and, although it was late in the day, not attacking meant
risking the Marathas escaping. The enemy army was drawn up in a single
line, composed of Bhonsla's infantry, numbering between seven and ten
thousand, on a plain in front of the village of Argaum, with forty or fifty
supporting pieces of artillery in their front.[133] On their right was Sindhia's
cavalry, and on the left, Bhonsla's. Behind Bhonsla's infantry, and destined
to play no part in the coming battle, were the remains of Sindhia's infantry.

In order to enter the battlefield, Wellesley's army would need to file past
another small village called Sirsoni. The 'galloper guns' – six-pounder guns
that usually accompanied the cavalry, but that, owing to a shortage of
horses, were, on 29 November, drawn by oxen – entered the field first.
'Scarcely had the leading platoon gained the end of the village, when
the enemy opened at once all their guns on it, from the distance of about
1000 yards, and being well directed, most of the shot took effect in the
head of the column.'[134]

It was an ambush. Bhonsla had deliberately enticed Wellesley to attack him. By forcing Wellesley to use a bottleneck in the form of the narrow road past Sirsoni, Bhonsla had been able to pre-register his guns on the village to immediate and devastating effect. And immediate and devastating it was. The bullocks turned and charged head-on the advancing infantry. Some were crushed under their own guns. 'Dreading perhaps a second Assaye ... the troops coming up in the rear ... became alarmed. A panic seized them; and two battalions of sepoys, with the infantry pickets, actually turned tail, and hastened to seek shelter behind the village.'[135] Observing this, Wellesley rode up to the panicking men and formed them up again behind the village, before personally leading them back on to the battlefield to the position they were originally intended to take. Wellesley was typically immodest. 'If I had not been there,' he wrote after the battle, 'I am convinced we should have lost the day.'[136]

Wellesley then ordered them to lie down, reducing their chances of being hit by the Maratha artillery and preventing them from running again. This was not the first time such a tactic had been used by the British,[137] but it was the first time Wellesley had used it deliberately, and it would not be the last. Nevertheless, Wellesley expressed some regret about this incident in the aftermath of the battle. 'If we had had daylight an hour more, not a man would have escaped ... But as it was, so much time elapsed before I could form [the panicked sepoys] again, that we had not daylight enough for everything that we should certainly have performed.'[138]

Those who were first on to the battlefield had some time to wait before the remains of the army, including Stevenson's column, could take up their positions, during which time they were exposed to the Maratha artillery bombardment. Eventually, by late afternoon, 'we were ordered to leave our guns and advance ... It was a splendid sight to see such a line advancing, as on a field-day; but the pause when the enemy's guns ceased firing, and they advanced in front of them, was an awful one.'[139] The Marathas targeted the 74th and 78th Regiments, but were heavily beaten – 600 killed and wounded, according to Welsh, with eight standards captured. A second advance of 5,000 enemy infantry, hoping to take advantage of the initial attack by outflanking the British line, was also beaten back. Two enemy cavalry charges were halted by steady and sustained musketry. Wellesley then sent in the cavalry, who 'followed the enemy for some miles, cutting down about three thousand of the fugitives'.[140] The following day, Elphinstone visited the battlefield and 'counted twenty-nine guns, three of which were of iron. In one part of the line, where the 74th and 78th charged, the ground is covered with dead.'[141]

Argaum had been a major tactical success. Despite the initial surprise of the accuracy of the Maratha artillery fire, Wellesley's force had successfully formed, then advanced, before routing the enemy in another infantry battle. Bhonsla's force was all but destroyed, and no longer capable of fighting a conventional battle against the British. Seeing the writing on the wall, Sindhia agreed to the terms of the armistice of 23 November, and withdrew his force. Wellesley and Stevenson pressed on to Gawilghur, where they arrived in the first week of December.

Gawilghur was impregnable from the south, perched, as it was, atop a steep cliff. From the north it was more approachable, but the fortress here was double-walled. Taking Gawilghur was not going to be an easy task. The difficulty would be increased by the design of the fort, which was asymmetrical and followed the contours of the hill on which it was built, using these natural features as part of its defence. Wellesley once more divided his army into two columns. The first, under Stevenson, advanced north through the hills to circle the fortress and approach from the north, where an attack could more easily be made. Wellesley, meanwhile, would approach from the south in what he later described as a feint. Stevenson led the main assault on the fortress, and given the man's more recent experience of sieges, and the extensive preparations he had undertaken after the capture of Asirghar in mid-October, this seems a reasonably sensible decision.[142] But previous sieges in the Deccan had ended with the garrison accepting payment in return for handing over the fort to the British. In this case, a full-scale assault was necessary, as Bhonsla's men had concluded that if they could not escape, then they would fight to the death. In preparation, they killed their wives by slitting their throats.[143]

At the northern face, Stevenson erected two batteries that opened fire on the 13th, and had created a practicable breach by the evening of 14 December, but only in the outer walls. The inner fort would need to be taken by escalade. The storming party on the northern side was commanded by Colonel Kenny and consisted of two companies of the 94th Regiment and a native regiment, with the rest of the 94th in support and two brigades in reserve. From the south, Wellesley orchestrated two diversionary assaults, one under Colonel Wallace consisting of the 74th Regiment and five companies of the 78th, and one, to attack the north-western gate, under Colonel Chalmers and consisting of the other five companies of the 78th, and No. 1 Battalion, 8th Regiment.[144]

The attack began at ten o'clock on the morning of 15 December. With fire support from the two brass twelve-pounders and the howitzers, Kenny's men gained the breach and forced their way into the outer fortress. Knowing that Chalmers was attacking from the north-west, they made their way to that gate. The garrison of the outer fortress had planned to use this as their escape route, 'not supposing [the British] would take the trouble to go so far round to guard the road'. Caught in a two-pronged assault, the garrison was killed to a man. An unnamed officer in Chalmers's storming party recorded the horrific sight inside the gate: 'I stepped over dead bodies to get in ... and when I was in had to walk many paces over them. I am certain that there could not be less than one hundred dead and dying of enemy close to the gate.'[145]

Once inside, Captain Campbell, who had assumed command after Kenny was injured, scouted for a suitable place to scale the inner wall. He led the light infantry of the 94th in the escalade, and quickly broke open the gate for the remainder of the storming party to take the inner fortress.[146] The assault was astoundingly successful, and no doubt the result of Stevenson's extensive preparations. Hand-to-hand fighting inside the fortress had been intense, but British casualties were minimal – just 126. Maratha losses were estimated to be as high as 4,000, while captured with the fortress were 52 pieces of artillery, 150 wall guns and 2,000 Company muskets.[147]

* * *

The defeats suffered by the Marathas at Argaum, Gawilghur and Delhi in November and December 1803 dealt a crippling blow to Maratha power in South Asia. But Mornington was not satisfied that only two out of three chieftains had been subdued. In early 1804, he set his sights on the final defeat of Holkar as well. Such a policy, in Wellesley's view, over-extended British power. The British had defeated or co-opted no less than five previously independent political entities since Mornington had become Governor-General. Wellesley himself had been involved in the subjugation of three of them. The focus should now have been on reinforcing that success, as there were 'increased causes of discontent, [and] diminished sources of profit' which might combine and produce a rebellion against British rule. In this atmosphere, 'intriguing, discontented and rebellious' supporters of the defeated powers could threaten the British position. 'Nothing can keep these people in order excepting the Company's arms,' Wellesley argued in late 1804, but 'the Company's arms cannot be everywhere'.[148]

By opposing Mornington's policy of war against Holkar, Wellesley precipitated the resurfacing of the tensions that had boiled over in 1801 after the Trincomalee fiasco. The brothers did not disagree on the same scale as then, but Mornington felt let down by Wellesley, whose political recommendations in the wake of the defeat of Sindhia had also fallen wide of the mark. The armistice Wellesley had agreed with Sindhia in November 1803 set the foundations on which the peace negotiations, conducted principally by John Malcolm in January 1804, would be built. Wellesley had, however, failed to specify precise geographical boundaries of the British annexations of Sindhia's territories. In particular, Wellesley failed to guarantee the surrender of Gwalior – Sindhia's capital and a fortress that controlled the navigation of the Jumna – to the British. Mornington was anxious that the Marathas be denied the ability to influence the political or military economy of the Jumna, which formed part of the lucrative Ganges *doab*. Wellesley was embarrassed by the oversight, and it was difficult for him to escape the suggestion that he had been duped by Sindhia's *vakils*.

His solution was that the peace treaty should include a formal defensive alliance between the Company and Sindhia, a modification of the subsidiary alliances with Hyderabad, Mysore and Oudh. This would allow Sindhia to remain in Gwalior, whilst securing the navigation of the Jumna for the British. 'Under the circumstance of his having agreed to the treaty of defensive alliance,' he argued, 'this measure cannot be deemed a dangerous one.'[149] Although this solved the problem in the short term, it did not guarantee the security in the Ganges *doab* that Mornington thought he had obtained in the victory over Sindhia. Allied to the British Sindhia might now be, but he had shown himself untrustworthy in the past, and there was every possibility that he would renege on his promises when the time seemed ripe. Had Wellesley contrived to force Sindhia out of Gwalior, the British position would be undeniably secure. As it was, there would always be some question over the security of the *doab* as long as Sindhia continued in Gwalior. For Mornington, Wellesley was at least partly to blame for this unsatisfactory outcome.

If Wellesley's failure to secure Gwalior for the Company was the most glaring of his errors in the post-war settlement, it was, in fact, the least of his mistakes. As with other subsidiary alliances, a joint force of Company and indigenous troops would be positioned within Sindhia's territory. Wellesley had cogent reasons to disagree with this course of action. A carbon copy of the subsidiary alliances with Hyderabad, Oudh and Mysore was not suitable for the Marathas, Wellesley argued, because of the nature of the Maratha armies. Since the end of the war with Sindhia, his army had gone unpaid. Composed principally of *pindaris* (the infantry component had largely been destroyed in the war), who usually derived their income from plunder, the fact that they were unpaid meant that they had resorted to plundering the fertile region of the Ganges *doab*, and also as far south as Hyderabad. The army itself, regardless of Sindhia's relations with the Company, was now a security threat to the British. Wellesley argued that with no regular source of income, 'they will join any chief who will profess an intention to lead them to plunder'.[150] The most likely contender would be Holkar, who was an increasing threat to the British.[151] Bizarrely, then, Wellesley argued that the British should not post a Company subsidiary force inside Sindhia's territory. Instead the British should pay to reconstitute Sindhia's own army. If it was well paid, then it would not need to plunder in order to sustain itself, and would no longer represent a threat to other Company territories. 'The peace must introduce new modes of acting and thinking upon every subject,' Wellesley argued.[152]

These ideas were coherent and based on an appreciation of what motivated the main Maratha fighting force. But they missed the point of the subsidiary alliance. The troops sent by the Company were not just for the defence of the Company's new ally, but were intended to exert pressure on that ally. Without Company troops deployed to Gwalior itself, the British were showing a sign of weakness, and this would be a problem when Mornington chose to pursue a war against Holkar.

For Mornington, who was facing increasing pressure from the Company's Court of Directors and from Whitehall to rein in his expansionist policy, the temptation to clean up the last messy remnants of Maratha independence, in the form of Holkar, was too great to ignore. Holkar had shown growing animosity towards the British in the wake of Sindhia's defeat, taking the opportunity of Sindhia's lack of defences to engage in private plunder.[153] Wellesley, confident though he was of British victory in any campaign against Holkar, would have nothing to do with it. He perceived Holkar to be nothing more than a 'freebooter', and easily beatable. Bearing in mind the shock he had experienced when confronted with the true nature of Sindhia's army at Assaye, it seems strange that Wellesley should make another, equally erroneous generalisation. Nevertheless, he advised restraint until the defensive alliance was concluded with Sindhia. Anything else would encourage Sindhia to see which way the wind was blowing before taking sides.[154]

As it was, Sindhia became a significant player in the British preparations for war. Mornington's initial approach was to ensure that Sindhia, who had been engaged in an ongoing civil conflict with Holkar, bore the burden of the war. But in so doing, the British made Sindhia the arbiter of power in the Deccan. As should have been expected from such a conniving individual, Sindhia procrastinated and, as Wellesley had predicted, refused to pledge support to either the British or Holkar. In part, this was Wellesley's fault. A British subsidiary force in Gwalior would now have been most useful to pressure Sindhia into toeing the British line.[155]

From his own position, Wellesley was reluctant to engage in another campaign in the Deccan, which was 'entirely exhausted by having been the seat of the operations of the late war, and by having been plundered for years'. On top of this 'a scarcity of rain in the last season ... has produced a famine, for which the army must feel the consequences'.[156] In order to fight Holkar, who had the advantage of defence in depth, the British would have to leave behind the fertile lands of Mysore, but, without a friendly source of food and water in the Deccan, the army would be reliant once again on lengthy supply lines. There was the danger of over-extension and the consequent requirement for retreat, and the associated loss of face such a move would bring. In short, the British were in danger of repeating the mistakes that had befallen the army that had marched on Mysore in 1799. Wellesley's solution included no logistical miracle-working. Rather, he simply refused to get involved.

Militarily, if not politically, Wellesley was proved correct. Mornington sent a British detachment to attack Holkar in the summer of 1804, under the command of Lieutenant-Colonel William Monson, but it over-extended itself and blundered into enemy territory with no supplies or support. A precipitous retreat ensued, which appalled Wellesley. 'Monson's disasters are really the greatest and most disgraceful to our military character of any that have ever occurred.'[157] Privately, Wellesley believed Monson should have attacked Holkar without hesitation, as he had done against Sindhia at Assaye and Bhonsla at Argaum, 'and he would probably have put an end to the war'.[158] This lends weight to the argument that Wellesley believed that tactical victory rested on swift and decisive action in the face of a defending army.

The war with Holkar started badly, and only got worse for the British, with the Commander-in-Chief, General Lake, being unable to repeat his successes of the previous year. The war ended in stalemate, with no decisive victory for the British. In its absence, Holkar could claim victory simply by dint of his survival. Mornington's political conquest of India fell at the final hurdle and, despite accomplishing much, he faced recall by Whitehall, which had succumbed to the disapprobation of the Court of Directors. Wellesley, no doubt much to Mornington's chagrin, had predicted this course of events. 'I consider the renewal of war to be the greatest misfortune that could occur,' Wellesley wrote to his elder brother before the war with Holkar had begun. 'In the eyes of those who are to judge of your conduct, it would efface the glory of the last war and of your whole administration.' The war in Europe had rendered it impossible for ministers in Whitehall to take 'an enlarged view of the present state of affairs in India. Everything has been so much altered within these last five years that I doubt very much whether there is any man in England who understands our present situation.'[159]

Wellesley's recommendation had been that Mornington jump before he was pushed. In Whitehall, the ministers were 'guilty of a breach of faith. They promised you their support, and now they refuse to give it.' In Wellesley's view, Mornington could not stay to see through the realisation of all his plans for India. 'I would recommend that you should fix a time in which you might possibly complete everything, and on no account whatever ought you to stay beyond that time.'[160] But Mornington did not take Wellesley's advice, and tried to complete his dream of British paramountcy. Following the failure of the war against Holkar, he resolved to resign, but was beaten to it by the government, who had already ordered his recall and sent out his replacement, the elderly veteran of empire, Lord Cornwallis. The appointment of the latter was, to Wellesley's mind, 'intended as a mark of disapprobation'.[161] Richard Wellesley left India in the summer of 1805, four months after Wellesley had also embarked for England.

*   *   *

Rather than a flowering military genius, the Wellesley of the Deccan campaign was manifestly incompetent in the organisation of his intelligence collection; and arrogant to the point of imbecility in the analysis of that intelligence and in his interpretation of the nature of his enemy. From these errors stemmed most of the problems that Wellesley encountered in 1803. Despite these errors, he still won. Perhaps this was to be Wellesley's greatest redeeming feature. Another man might well have assumed that he got it right, and that that explains his repeated victories against the Marathas. Wellesley did not make that mistake. When he left India, he considered himself to have 'understood as much of military matters as I ever have done ...'[162] In other words, he was acknowledging that his military understanding was badly lacking, and that he had learned from his mistakes.

The most important of these lessons was on use and misuse of intelligence. In the wake of the intelligence failures that blighted his campaign, Wellesley wrote a detailed memorandum that captured his experiences, but also explained how he would improve and adapt the system. During the 1803 campaign 'three distinct departments for intelligence were formed in camp', but, in future, when intelligence arrived at one, it should then be 'compared with that brought in ... from other quarters', allowing a 'tolerably accurate opinion' to be 'formed of the facts

reported'. Multiple source cross-referencing like this would help weed out
inaccurate and fabricated intelligence, as would rewarding *harkarrahs*
highly, 'particularly when they brought any intelligence on which operations could be founded', whilst those who 'brought any which was known
to be false' were 'punished and turned out of the service'. Besides this, a
network of informants was maintained 'to find out the reports of the
country, and everything which could throw light upon the enemy's
designs'.[163] There were clearly a number of suggestions from Elphinstone,
who thought there were 'many improbable things in our system'.[164] This
memorandum would prove a useful template for the organisation of
intelligence collection in the Peninsular War, suggesting, as it did, methods
for multiple collection techniques, and cross-referencing to ensure information was reliable. However, it did not identify the key failing in 1803
– Wellesley's erroneous assumptions – and provided no suggestions for the
mitigation of cognitive dissonance. Wellesley would continue to balance
his own judgement and intuition against intelligence.

On the surface, there was also a marked difference between Wellesley's
tactics in India and his tactics in the Iberian Peninsula. The former is
marked by overt aggression and recklessness, the latter by caution and an
emphasis on defensive warfare. Apart from the empirical problems –
Wellington only fought two defensive battles after 1812, in the Pyrenees
and at Waterloo – this argument is much more complicated. Did Assaye
really convince Wellesley to be less reckless and aggressive? Or was his
cautious approach in Europe a natural predisposition which existed in
India but was momentarily conquered by a desire to prove himself in battle
and wash away the embarrassment of the disaster at Sultanpetah Tope?
Did Wellesley pursue an Indian doctrine based on racial stereotypes, which
determined that a European should never retire in the face of a native force
because of the moral imperative to appear invincible?[165] Was the counter
to this a European doctrine that respected the military power of more
symmetric opponents, such as the French? In reality, Wellesley did not
have an Indian or a European approach to warfare. Careful analysis of his
'way of war' in the Peninsula reveals stark similarities with his 'way of war'
in India. The two are one and the same, and are presented here on a sliding
evolutionary scale, for what he developed in India in 1800, he continued to
use, in new and more developed ways, in Spain thirteen years later. Rather
than proving the superiority of Western tactics, this suggests that by
adapting to and developing a response to Indian tactics Wellesley was
transferring those tactics back to Europe. Wellesley's time in India might
be at an end, but his political and military experiences there would have a
profound impact on the rest of his military career.

In the final analysis, then, what was it that determined British victory over the Marathas in 1803? Had Western infantry tactics proven superior to those of the Marathas? This seems unlikely: it was Wellesley's dogged determination in attacking against the odds that had shocked and confounded his enemies, not the superiority of his troops or tactics, or their or his bravery. Rather, the Marathas were stunned by Wellesley's recklessness. Of course, this was not just a product of Wellesley's perceptions of warfare in India and specifically against the Marathas, but also of his personal circumstances at the time. Before the Battle of Assaye, Wellesley was painfully aware that he had yet to prove himself capable on the battlefield, and he was convinced he was facing an inferior enemy, whose infantry would be woefully inadequate against the European training and drill that the British used. Now view this from the perspective of the Marathas. On 23 September, they were attacked by a force that they outnumbered nearly three to one, like for like (infantry versus infantry), but in total by more than ten to one. Then, two months later, they were attacked again by the same force with slightly less favourable odds, but still in a position of numerical superiority. To the Marathas, Wellesley appeared willing to risk more and lose more than they were.[166] To both Sindhia and Bhonsla, it was the sheer force of Wellesley's determination to win that secured victory at both Assaye and Argaum. Wellesley's intelligence failings, his arrogance and inappropriate assumptions about Maratha military training, and his own failings as a warrior previously in his career, all played into this narrative.

Unquestionably, though, the hard lessons Arthur Wellesley learned in his campaign against the Marathas provided the key foundations of the military genius that was to emerge in the Iberian Peninsula. His political acumen in dealing with unwieldy allies would prove useful training for his command of the Spanish and Portuguese in the Peninsula, not to mention for how to deal with the conflicting strategies of his own government. On his return to England in September 1805, Wellesley discovered just how unimportant the Indian subcontinent was in London. With the exception of a year of peace between 1802 and 1803, Britain had been at war with France continuously since 1793. Napoleon Bonaparte had just been crowned Emperor of the French, and was embarking on a campaign that within two years would see French influence extend from Madrid to Moscow. Britain, meanwhile, was growing increasingly isolated. Political wrangling had paralysed strategic decision-making, and there was no coherent strategy against France. This was a political crisis that was to beset the British war effort until 1808, and one in the middle of which Wellesley soon found himself.

CHAPTER 4

From India to the Peninsula

1804–1808

The security of Europe is essential to the security of the British Empire. We cannot separate them.

Lord Grenville, Foreign Secretary, 1791–1801[1]

ARTHUR Wellesley returned to England in September 1805 to find a country, indeed a world, transformed. A war had raged between France and Britain for more than a decade and, although Britain was on the brink of naval supremacy, Napoleonic France was likewise on the brink of continental supremacy. All things considered, Britain was losing, and the government had no idea what strategy to pursue, or how to implement one when a decision was reached. Wellesley was no bystander in this great strategic game. His hard-won reputation, combined with his brother's fall from grace, led to his taking on a central role in a crisis that very nearly saw Britain politically, if not militarily, defeated by Napoleon. When Wellesley returned from India in early September 1805, he was braced for a prolonged political battle defending his brother's reputation. But he was to realise very quickly that the attention of the government, and the public, was focused not on India, but almost exclusively on the war with France. Wellesley duly arranged to meet Lord Castlereagh, Secretary of State for War and the Colonies, in order to defend his brother's administration of India. He was kept waiting for nearly an hour outside Castlereagh's office, in the company of a very famous, short naval officer with one arm and one eye. There is precisely nothing noteworthy or important about this happenstance. Nevertheless, every biographer of Nelson and Wellington has felt compelled to comment on it, but it is instructive on one issue.

Vice Admiral Lord Nelson was waiting to receive his instructions from Castlereagh to sail to Cadiz to prevent the Spanish fleet from sailing to support the French and therefore from launching an attack on British possessions in the West Indies, or possibly, even, launching an invasion of mainland Britain. Nelson obviously did not know who Wellesley was, and treated him as he did all those he met and did not know, particularly army officers: as if he were an idiot. 'He entered at once into conversation with me, if I can call it conversation, for it was almost all on his side, and all about himself, and, really, in a style so vain and silly as to surprise and almost disgust me.'[2]

Wellesley clearly said something to Nelson to indicate his impatience, and that he was, in fact, not an idiot, but a *some-body*. Nelson briefly left the room, during which it is supposed that he found out who Wellesley was, and returned to engage in a far more satisfactory conversation about British strategy. Nelson expressed a hope that Wellesley would soon be assigned to attack the French in Sardinia.[3] Wellesley was surprised. 'He talked ... with a good sense, and a knowledge of subjects both at home and abroad, that surprised me equally and more agreeably than the first part of our interview ...'[4]

The conversation gave Wellesley a small taste of the difficulties he and his brothers were to face in the next two years in resolving the question hanging over Mornington's reputation. Nelson, it seems, had not asked about India. And the reality was that with a war against a seemingly unstoppable military power in France, led by a first-class military genius in the form of Napoleon Bonaparte, getting anybody to care about or discuss Indian politics in public would be near impossible. The government had to deal with a foundering strategy, and the prospect that this war was rapidly turning into a war of national survival. In such an atmosphere, Indian matters were a stick to beat the government with, but not something which the government could expend much time defending. Wellesley quickly realised this, and attempted to prepare his brother. 'The real truth,' he wrote in late December 1805, 'is that the public mind cannot be brought to attend to an Indian subject.'[5]

Mornington arrived in Dover in January 1806, to a frosty reception from his family, and promptly entered the political wilderness. Wellesley, meanwhile, had entered Parliament with a seat for Rye, Sussex on April Fool's Day 1806. Thus he would be well situated to defend his brother publicly. Around the same time, Wellesley proposed to Kitty Pakenham. Wellesley had first met Kitty in 1792. Although physically and intellectually attracted to one another, when Wellesley proposed, the Pakenham family rejected him out of hand. The precarious state of Wellesley's finances and the relatively low social position of the family rendered Wellesley an unsuitable match. Wellesley's success in India had changed all that, and he was now considered a highly eligible bachelor. On returning from India, he had been persuaded to renew his proposal without seeing Kitty. Some argue this was a matter of principle: Wellesley was duty-bound to renew the offer of marriage now that his social circumstances had improved. The reality was arguably somewhat baser. Wellesley had lost in 1793. It might have been a different battle to the ones he had become used to in India, but it was a battle nevertheless, and he needed to account for it.[6] The renewal of the proposal was a way of atoning for his failure in 1793, and was based on his memories of Kitty Pakenham that were ten years out of date. It was, therefore, a mistake. The spark that had attracted him to her in the first place was long since extinguished. On 10 April, they were married, but just four days later, Wellesley returned to London and his new career in Parliament, where his time would be partly taken up in defending his brother. The marriage, sadly, was not to be a happy one. More pressing matters were soon presenting themselves, however. Wellesley was acting as strategic advisor to the government on how best to prosecute the war against France.

*　*　*

In June 1806, an unauthorised expedition led by the naval officer Sir Home Popham attacked and captured Buenos Aires, a Spanish colony.[7] This offered a new opportunity of maritime economic expansion at the expense of Spain, a French ally. Wellesley was asked to provide strategic advice on how best to exploit this potentially lucrative new avenue of trade. He thus found himself in the midst of discussions that resulted in the beginning of a shift from a maritime economic strategy to a more focused military strategy aimed at defeating Napoleon. The culmination of this strategic transition was the pre-emptive strike on Copenhagen in 1807 and a prolonged expeditionary operation in the Iberian Peninsula that began in 1808. Instead of direct attacks on Napoleon's power, this new strategy sought to play the long game. It would deprive Napoleon of the key resources he needed to fight and win wars in Europe, and was the only way a maritime power like Britain could precipitate the defeat of a military power like France. After experiencing the impact of over-extension and profligate spending in India, Wellesley understood better than most that Britain could only defeat Napoleon if she consolidated her resources and outlasted him. Wellesley helped articulate a strategy that reflected the key tenets of Britain's power: maritime trade, and a balance of power in Europe to reduce the threat to this trade.

Britain was a maritime power – she derived her principal strength and power from trading on and across the world's oceans and seas. 'British naval power ensured that Britain gained . . . wealth and her opponents lost it, and this was vital to the ability of the British state to finance its actions in peace and war.'[8] During the French Revolutionary and Napoleonic Wars, Britain pursued a maritime economic strategy. Wherever Britain's maritime security was threatened, Britain would fight to defend it. There were three major interdependent maritime strategic interests in Europe – the Low Countries, the Mediterranean, and the Baltic. Britain would be compelled to go to war if the security of any one of them was jeopardised.

The Low Countries of Europe – Holland and Belgium – formed the major maritime interest, and any violation of the sovereignty of this territory would almost certainly result in the British taking military action. If an aggressive power occupied the Low Countries, and with it the ports of Antwerp and Flushing, then that power was in a position to threaten Britain's maritime capability. This was because, unlike France's Channel ports at Boulogne and Cherbourg, or her western port at Brest, or the northern German ports in the Baltic, Antwerp offered easy access to the Channel, based on prevailing winds and currents. From Antwerp, then, British domination of the Channel and her North Atlantic trading routes could be challenged. Worse, the Dutch ports offered direct access to Essex, Kent and the Thames estuary, and were therefore the best ports from which to launch an invasion of England in the age of sail. So, when France invaded the Low Countries in 1793, Britain acted militarily to deprive France of this territory. She failed, and for the next twenty years French power dominated the Low Countries, posing a constant threat to British maritime security. The problem, though, for British policy-makers was not just how to get France out of the Low Countries, but what and who would replace her. Britain needed an independent friendly state in the Low Countries, and this objective entwined Britain in the wider continental dynamic.

The Mediterranean was strategically less significant than the Low Countries – Britain had, in fact, withdrawn from the sea in 1796 – but maritime control was deemed a vital aspect of colonial defence. With free rein in the Mediterranean, France might plausibly occupy Egypt, and from there pose a threat to India. It was to offset this threat that the British re-entered the Mediterranean in 1798, only narrowly failing to intercept Bonaparte's invasion force bound for Aboukir Bay in Egypt.[9] Within the Mediterranean dynamic, the main military responsibility was blockading the southern French port of Toulon. To facilitate this, and to offer the warships on blockading duty a base for revictualling and repair, both Malta and Gibraltar had to be maintained as British dependencies. It was over the independence of Malta that the short-lived Peace of Amiens (1802–3) – the brief interlude between the Revolutionary War and the Napoleonic Wars – fell apart. Britain refused to evacuate Malta, expecting that such a move would result in the French moving in shortly after. Malta had a major strategic shortcoming: it was unable to feed itself. Therefore, a British presence on Sicily in order to supply Malta – as well as to threaten southern Italy – was necessary. This resulted in what Hall refers to as a strategic 'chain reaction: to guard against unwelcome French expansion in the Mediterranean required a squadron to blockade Toulon and other harbours used by the enemy. To facilitate this naval presence required Malta's retention as a naval base, while to feed and protect Malta involved the securing of Sicily.'[10]

The third maritime strategic interest was a friendly and open Baltic. This became especially problematic after Napoleon overran Prussia in 1806 – meaning that a substantial portion of the Baltic coastline was in enemy hands for the first time. Britain relied on Baltic oak, and was especially reliant on Russia for other vital materials for shipbuilding. The Baltic was Britain's main avenue of communication with Sweden and Russia, and closing it would cripple British military planning, and significantly increase the diplomatic strength of France. On top of this, Whitehall remained concerned about the naval power of the various Baltic nations. The belief that the Danish fleet was about to be taken by Napoleon prompted a pre-emptive assault on Copenhagen in August 1807.

The stability of Europe was critical to British maritime economic security. The military strategy that Britain adopted would have to be sufficiently broad to achieve and secure these three important interests. Throughout the French Revolutionary and Napoleonic Wars, there was a range of options available to ministers in Whitehall. British strategy did not evolve from one approach to the next as failure and stumbling blocks were encountered. Rather, the British opted to utilise a range of approaches in parallel. At one time or another, it could be argued that the British preferred one military strategy over another, but until Napoleon was defeated, all options remained on the table. For a brief moment, and not for the first or last time in the history of Britain's wars in Europe, a strategy of isolation was considered, but such a strategy overlooked Britain's reliance on a European balance of power, which was the only way to guarantee the independence of the Low Countries and the freedom of the Mediterranean and the Baltic Seas, and hence secure British maritime security. Grenville and Pitt, the architects of Britain's strategy in Europe between 1793 and 1803, recognised this.[11]

The most common approach adopted by the British government throughout the Revolutionary and Napoleonic Wars was coalition-building. If Britain was to achieve her aims on the continent, then she would have to do so in alliance with the other Great Powers, Austria, Russia and Prussia. They had wildly different and contradictory aims and objectives, not all of which were of interest to Britain. But differences between any of the Great Powers, as well as between the Great Powers and Britain, could split any coalition, particularly when one power was heavily defeated by Napoleon. Broadly speaking, but by no means comprehensively, there were five areas of friction which the French could exploit to undermine any continental alliance. As the war progressed they increased or decreased in relative importance, but, to a lesser or greater extent, they all jeopardised the coalitions which British ministers expended a great deal of time, energy and treasure on building. They were the sovereignty of the Low Countries (a question primarily concerning Austria and Britain); the question of the division of Poland (a concern for Austria, Prussia and Russia); the sovereignty of the Italian States (a serious issue for Austria); the independence of the smaller German states such as Westphalia and Saxony (a concern of all the Great Powers); and the relations between the Russian, the Austrian and the Ottoman Empires, the last of which was beginning its long and terminal decline.

It was apparent to the British by the end of the first coalition that only a unified allied war effort that focused solely on the defeat of France, and left other, lesser, political decisions for the peace negotiations, would be successful against Revolutionary France, and particularly against Napoleon.[12] Even before the collapse of the coalition, Lord Grenville, then Foreign Secretary, had grasped the reasons behind its inevitable failure. 'The ill success of the last campaign,' he wrote at the end of 1794, 'arose from the want of concert between the European powers.'[13] Grenville knew that individual national armies operating as part of a coalition had to serve a 'single master-plan', and this could only be determined by previously defined political aims. But building such an alliance proved near impossible. What precisely did a defeated France mean? Forcing the Revolutionary government, and then Napoleon, to accept the pre-war boundaries? Or did defeat mean the defeat of the Revolution, the overthrow of that government, and, after 1804, the removal of Napoleon and the restoration of the Bourbon monarchy? Britain, whose Conservative government existed as part of a parliamentary monarchy, hated the ideals of the Revolution and quickly recognised that neither the Revolutionary government nor Napoleon could be adequately contained behind France's pre-war borders.[14]

Regime change quickly became the major British objective in the wars against France, but others powers, such as Austria, envisaged living with Revolutionary or Napoleonic France. So long as this difference of opinion existed, Napoleon might be able to sue for a separate peace with each member of the coalition. Grenville achieved some success in 1798–9, having espoused a 'strategy of overthrow' and convinced the Russians and the Austrians that only the restoration of the Bourbons to the throne of France would secure European peace. The military effort, mainly on the part of Austria (an Anglo-Russian assault on Den Helder in Holland turned into a fiasco), which benefited from unified political objectives, achieved some success against the French but eventually over-extended its supply lines, just as France fell back on defensive strength in depth. Austria suggested an operational pause, in order to allow the allies time to regroup and invade France, but Britain and Russia, sensing blood, forced an immediate attack. Outnumbered and outclassed, the allies were overrun, and with Austria wavering anyway, the coalition collapsed.[15] It would take time to invade France, and this gave Napoleon a strong hand when it came to a negotiating position. He could split the coalitions against him by offering favourable terms to one participant as the momentum of any allied advance simmered out. All the while, he was in a position to regroup and strengthen his own forces, just as his enemies were at their weakest and most vulnerable.

The obstacles to a successful continental coalition were, therefore, many and varied. Internal political divisions always made alliance negotiations difficult and time-consuming, whilst the cracks between the allies could be cleverly exploited by Napoleon. In the event that a coalition was created and did not fragment, deciding on unified political objectives, the fate of France and the likely shape of post-war Europe would pose an almost insurmountable hurdle. Thereafter, the not insignificant challenge of defeating Napoleon in battle awaited. Unsurprisingly, then, the coalitions of the Great Powers against France proved extremely fragile. As they repeatedly collapsed, Britain was forced to use different strategies in the war against Napoleon.

Britain tried to guard against the fracturing of her alliances by heavily subsidising the allied war effort. In 1799, £2 million was set aside to finance the formation of the Second Coalition.[16] Subsidies alone were not enough, however, and the British on several occasions deployed forces to the continent in an effort to bolster the continental campaign, by either diverting French resources, or providing military support to the main effort. Thus, the British deployed to the Low Countries in 1794–5, and in 1799. An expedition sailed for the Low Countries in the autumn of 1805 (in which Wellesley commanded a brigade) but the defeat of the Austrians at Ulm in October, and both the Austrians and the Russians at Austerlitz in November, rendered the expedition pointless and it never disembarked. In 1809 another attempt was made to take Antwerp from a base established on the island of Walcheren in the Scheldt estuary. The expedition was a disaster, with momentum quickly running out, and the force languished on malaria-infested Walcheren for months before finally being evacuated. Further deployments were made in 1814 and, obviously, in 1815. Other expeditions were launched to Italy in 1806; to the Dardanelles in 1807; to Stralsund on the Prussian coast in 1807; and Egypt in 1801 and 1807.[17] Of these expeditions, all were to areas of vital strategic concern to the British, whether it was defence of the homeland, or defence of the empire. Only three, though, were successful: Egypt in 1801, and the Low Countries in 1814 and 1815.[18]

Although she was an overwhelming naval and maritime power, Britain had a small army, so it was pointless for the British to fight Napoleon alone. Nevertheless, there were repeated occasions throughout the war when Britain found herself alone in the fight. During these periods, the British could only implement a strategy that would deprive the French of resources while increasing British strength. In the 1790s, this translated into colonial campaigns in the West and East Indies, but the strategy was abandoned on the outbreak of the war against Napoleon in 1803 because of the spiralling cost of war in India, and the extreme loss of life encountered in the West Indies: an estimated 100,000 British soldiers fell victim to disease.

Despite this, Britain could not escape criticism from her potential continental allies. To the Great Powers, it looked at the time as if Britain was taking advantage of the war in Europe to extend her empire. Whispers of 'Perfidious Albion' damaged Britain's diplomatic weight in the various negotiations for continental coalitions. But Britain's empire was, in part, responsible for her economic durability,[19] along with the development of a domestic taxation infrastructure, throughout the Napoleonic Wars.[20] Yet in spite of the distrust of the Great Powers, Britain engaged in a surprisingly small amount of colonial expansion. What expansionism took place was specifically aimed at depriving France or her allies of colonial resources that might threaten Britain's maritime dominance. In 1805, for example, the British attacked and captured the Cape of Good Hope, with a force of 6,500 men.[21] It was this force that went on to capture Buenos Aires under Sir Home Popham in 1806. The government in London stopped short of condemning the attack on Buenos Aires, and sent a follow-up expedition to the River Plate to reinforce the troops that had originally captured the city. Brigadier-General Sir Samuel Auchmuty was given the command of 5,000 men, and attacked and captured the walled city of Montevideo.

Since the collapse of the third coalition in 1806, Napoleon had effectively excluded Britain from the continent. The capture of Buenos Aires offered the possibility for the British to open up and exploit the trading potential in the Spanish colonies of South America. Some members of the cabinet even ruminated that the exploitation of South American trade might be an adequate replacement for the trade lost by Britain's likely exclusion from the Mediterranean, whilst also fatally undermining in the long term Napoleon's grip on power.[22] This was a vast overestimation of the commercial and strategic value of the South American economy, but the British government diverted considerable time and energy into developing a strategic plan for the exploitation of the New World.

Wellesley was brought in as a military advisor – a not unrealistic prospect despite his relatively junior rank: Wellesley's political connections, his military experience in India, and his reputation for careful planning meant he was an ideal choice to advise the government on its military policy, particularly towards a new imperial venture.[23] Keen to exploit the initial military success at Buenos Aires, the Ministry of All the Talents, led by Grenville, touted a number of increasingly hare-brained plans for South America. The most audacious of these was a plan to launch a coordinated attack from both the east, exploiting the foothold in Buenos Aires and opening a new front in Mexico, and the west, launching from India and attacking via Manila.[24]

Wellesley, who had planned an abortive assault on Manila in 1798, immediately discounted this plan. Weather conditions alone would render the coordination of two simultaneous attacks impossible.[25] Instead, Wellesley planned consecutive assaults on the east coast, the west coast and finally Manila, taking advantage of more appropriate weather for amphibious assaults.[26] He based this assessment on an intelligence source in South America, a commercial trader who had provided useful information to Grenville when the latter was Foreign Secretary.[27] Based on this, rather than Manila, Jamaica – already a British possession – would be a better option as a staging post for the operation. Wellesley suggested that a corps of 12,000 troops be collected at Jamaica in order to launch an attack on Mexico in December. An additional 3,500 troops from India would arrive as reinforcements in February.[28]

Such planning was completely pointless, however, because in January 1807 news was received that the British force in Buenos Aires had been attacked and forced to capitulate the previous August. The government should have abandoned its plans as there was clearly little support for a British military campaign in South America. Wellesley thought that the British 'ought not to rely entirely upon the accounts which we have received of the inefficiency of the Spanish military establishments in America'.[29] However, too much time, money and effort had been invested in the campaign. Such were the problems associated with planning a military operation on the other side of the planet in the early nineteenth century.[30] Wellesley thought it would still be possible to attack Mexico successfully, but 'the gain which Great Britain will derive from the possession of this colony, under present circumstances, will not compensate for the loss which may be sustained'.[31] Whatever was decided for the rest of the continent, the government was compelled to send a relief expedition to rescue the prisoners who had surrendered in August, but this too ran into difficulties and was forced to withdraw completely from Buenos Aires in July 1807.[32]

Meanwhile, the Talents Ministry collapsed in March 1807, and a new Tory administration took office under the Duke of Portland, with Wellesley's allies Castlereagh and Canning back in the War and Foreign Offices. Castlereagh considered a military strategy in South America to be ill-founded and concentrated instead on developing a maritime trading strategy, establishing a friendly government in South America rather than trying to enforce British rule there.[33] Canning, on the other hand, preferred concluding a separate peace with Spain.

Napoleon's invasion of Portugal in the autumn of 1807 – and his subsequent subjugation of Spain – rendered this avenue moot, but it did raise the possibility that Napoleon might be able to extend his authority to South America, something that would be disastrous for the British. In an effort to protect its sovereignty, the Portuguese royal family fled Lisbon for Rio de Janeiro. This offered yet another new prospect for the British in South America. Castlereagh suggested sending 8,000 men to recapture Montevideo and Buenos Aires in order to secure the Portuguese in Brazil, prevent French exploitation of Spanish colonial resources, and establish a British trading presence in the major sea ports of South America.[34] Wellesley, in his continued capacity as strategic advisor, agreed. In his view, British policy should be directed at establishing a military presence in support of the Portuguese in Brazil in either Buenos Aires or Mexico. Rather than direct military conquest, the British could only aim to stir up revolutionary independence movements. Such a move would considerably reduce the cost – in terms of troops and money – of opening the South American market to British trade.[35] Wellesley once more engaged in detailed planning for amphibious assaults on Mexico and modern day

Venezuela. The latter offered the greatest opportunity for success, and was also the area of South America that was most ripe, according to intelligence, for revolutionary insurrection against Spanish rule.[36] A force of 8,000 troops was assembled at Cork in Ireland to sail to the West Indies in preparation for the campaign.

In the event, the British strategy of maritime economic expansion in South America fell victim to events in Europe. Efforts to open up the market in Brazil would continue through to 1810, but the forced abdication of Charles IV, the King of Spain, and then his son Ferdinand VII in favour of Napoleon's elder brother Joseph, set in motion a rebellion against French rule that was to define the final years of the war against Napoleon, and rendered any sort of anti-Spanish campaign in South America politically impossible. The revolt in Spain opened a new avenue for British military engagement on the continent, and the troops originally destined for the South Atlantic would now be diverted to Portugal.[37] The Iberian Peninsula was not an area of vital strategic importance to Britain, but, over the next seven years, it became the area of Britain's greatest military commitment to the war against Napoleon. British intervention in Spain and Portugal therefore reflected the adoption of a new strategy.

This was an extension of the fourth and final key strategy that the British government pursued during the Revolutionary and Napoleonic Wars. With no allies on the continent, and limited means of colonial expansion, British ministers turned to the use of small-scale military raids designed specifically to deny the French access to key resources required to succeed in a war against Britain. Typically this translated into coastal raiding, and swift military strikes against French ports where invasion flotillas were being built. Although these efforts often resulted in limited success, this did not prevent the British from trying. By and large, these operations were small affairs, designed to have minimal effect on British military capability and to be easily planned and executed but to have a major – if temporary – effect on French capabilities.

Thus, between 1804 and 1809, amphibious raids intended to capture or destroy French warships were considered for Ferrol, Cadiz, Toulon, the Texel, Cronstadt, Vigo, Port Mahon and Cherbourg. Invasion flotillas were the targets during raids against Dieppe, Granville and Calais in September 1803, whilst Boulogne was the repeated focus of British attacks in March, April, October and November 1804, and November 1805.[38] The most astonishing example of this strategy was the decision to launch a pre-emptive attack against Copenhagen, to capture the Danish fleet and prevent it falling into Napoleon's hands, an operation in which Wellesley participated.

News of Napoleon's defeat of the Russians at Friedland reached London on 30 June 1807, and the Portland ministry tensed in anticipation of the collapse of the Third Coalition. Napoleon was now able to create and enforce the Continental System. He closed most European ports to British trade. Aware that Britain's obstinate determination to remain in the war stemmed from concerns for her financial security, Napoleon decided to focus his effort on what Clausewitz would later describe as Britain's 'centre of gravity': her economy.

Meanwhile, a British agent allegedly present at the signing of the Treaty of Tilsit between France and Russia (but more likely told of the details after the event) reported Napoleon's intention to force the Danish government to relinquish its not inconsiderable fleet to French command.[39] Canning argued convincingly that a pre-emptive strike was necessary to prevent the Danish fleet falling into French hands, if the Danish government did not willingly surrender the fleet to the English.[40]

On 26 July, Admiral Gambier sailed with instructions to try to bring the Danes to terms by diplomatic means. On the 30th, 18,000 troops, including Wellesley, who was appointed to command the reserve, sailed to join Earl Cathcart, the British military commander. Diplomacy failed, and the British Army disembarked and invested Copenhagen between 16 and 24 August. On the 18th, Wellesley defeated an attempt to relieve the city at Kjøge. Here Wellesley once more demonstrated his flexibility and dexterity under pressure, swiftly manoeuvring key elements of his infantry and cavalry into position to fend off what was a spirited Danish attack.[41] On 2 September, the bombardment of Copenhagen began. The densely populated city quickly caught fire, and many civilian casualties were sustained. The bombardment lasted three days before the government capitulated, sparing the city the terror of a British assault, and the ensuing pillage and other horrors allowed by the laws of war. On the 7th, the Danish surrendered their fleet and the British agreed to withdraw in six weeks. Fifteen ships of the line were captured, four of which were later integrated into the Royal Navy.

The operation was a complete success. The British had managed to deny Napoleon access to significant naval resources, and had established their control of the Baltic for the rest of the war: the attack also served as a useful deterrent to the other Baltic powers. Russia and Sweden were anxious to avoid hostility with Britain at sea.[42] But the British were widely vilified for the pre-emptive action – such a move was a propaganda gift to Napoleon – and there was even discontent within the British military over the action. Captain Charles Paget questioned whether it 'would be justifiable without any previous hostile act on their part, to take their fleet from them [the Danes], on the plea of it being a means ultimately of Bonaparte to execute his plan of invasion?'[43] In the event, however, it appears Canning's intelligence was right. Soon after the expedition had sailed, Canning received information which appeared to confirm that the French were '*actually* about to do that act of hostility [invade or coerce the Danes], the possibility of which formed the groundwork of my Baltic plan'.[44]

The Copenhagen expedition marked a significant change in British strategy. Britain was now fighting a war of national survival, and it was recognised that the threat from France was not going to be dealt with in a single campaign. Britain, having been forced to fight a long war since 1793, now began fighting a long war on her own terms. Gone was the determination to defeat Napoleon outright. Instead, Britain would adopt a strategy that would deprive Napoleon of the resources he needed to fight the British: manpower, materiel and ships. This was a long game; a death by a thousand cuts. But it was also a classic containment strategy. Napoleon's power would be curtailed, diverted and, wherever possible, drained. Whenever a new opportunity to attack the French emerged, it would be taken.

This was the primary justification for the intervention in the Peninsula. Although the Peninsular War offered Britain the opportunity to fight French forces directly, this was not, and could not be, the primary motivation for intervention. The war would not be won in Spain: there was no evidence that prolonged engagement in Spain and Portugal would lead to wider success against the French. The main benefit of a British military deployment to Iberia was the opportunity it offered to undermine Napoleon's access to key resources.

As long as Iberia remained outside Napoleonic control, Britain could ensure that the French did not have unrestricted access to Spanish and Portuguese ports or the ships in them. In the early years, as well, the campaign offered an agreeable drain on Napoleon's manpower resources and prevented him exploiting the Spanish colonies in South America. Most importantly, the Peninsular deployments acted as a defensive war. If France was fighting Britain in Spain, she was not fighting Britain elsewhere – be it in northern Europe or in other areas that endangered colonial possessions. But aside from this, Spain and Portugal were not major strategic concerns. In fighting the French in the Peninsula, the British were effectively containing Napoleon's power, providing breathing space until a new coalition of Great Powers could be assembled to wage war against him in central Europe: the only theatre where Napoleon could be defeated decisively. In this regard, then, the deployment was not considered the 'main effort' in the war against France. Other opportunities for denuding Napoleon of naval and military resources would be taken wherever and whenever they arose. The scene was set for ongoing military battles between Britain and France, and for political battles between the British Army and the British government, during the Peninsular War. The main protagonist in both was Arthur Wellesley.

* * *

In June 1808, Wellesley was in Cork, with a force of 10,000 troops, awaiting deployment to Venezuela.[45] The Commander-in-Chief, the Duke of York, informed him on 14 June that instead he was now destined for the Iberian Peninsula, 'to be employed on a particular service'.[46] Wellesley was to land on the Portuguese coast and act to liberate Lisbon, which had fallen to French forces in the autumn of 1807. Napoleon's decision to invade and partition Portugal, and then subjugate Spain, deposing the Bourbon monarchy in Madrid in favour of his brother Joseph, was the product of a combination of strategic factors. Key here is Napoleon's Continental System, which in 1807 extended across Europe with the exception of Portuguese ports. Foiled in Denmark, Napoleon sought to undermine British power either by forcing the Portuguese regency to accept French terms and declare war on Britain, or by invading Portugal and deposing the monarchy. On 19 July 1807, Napoleon instructed his Foreign Minister Talleyrand to order Portugal to close its ports to British trade, arrest all British subjects in Portugal and confiscate all British property in the country. The failure of the Portuguese to acquiesce to all of Napoleon's demands gave the French emperor the pretext he needed to order the invasion force he had prepared in the south of France – the First Corps of Observation of the Gironde under General Jean Andoche Junot – to begin its march through Spain to the Portuguese frontier.

Since the Portuguese government recognised the inevitability of French domination they agreed to Napoleon's demands, seeking only a guarantee of the Bragança dynasty. Napoleon would not back down, however, and ordered Junot to accelerate his march, fearful that the British would send an army to defend Lisbon. Junot's army, bedraggled after a forced march through inhospitable terrain in appalling weather conditions, entered Lisbon on 30 November 1807. Their victory was muted, however, by the sight of the Portuguese fleet, supported by the Royal Navy, escaping the Tagus estuary at the last moment, transporting the Portuguese royal family, the Treasury and the majority of Lisbon's political elite to Brazil.

Spain, meanwhile, had supported the French invasion of Portugal, but the Spanish first minister, Manuel de Godoy, had for the last few years been working to extricate Spain from its alliance with France – an alliance that had seen Spanish power devastated in the war with Britain, both militarily at the Battle of Trafalgar, and economically, her ports blockaded by the Royal Navy, and her vital supply line with the colonies in South America cut. In 1806, as Napoleon went to war against Prussia, Godoy saw an opportunity to break with France, but the overwhelming French victory at Jena-Auerstadt in October that year, and the resultant dismemberment of the Prussian state, caused Godoy to backtrack. He claimed the mobilisation of Spanish forces had been against Britain rather than France, but Napoleon smelled a rat. He remained convinced that administrative, economic and military incompetence within the Spanish state were preventing her from benefiting from the untold wealth that the South American colonies were providing. All that was needed was the strong hand of France, and Spain would be restored to her previous imperial glory, with France, of course, being the primary beneficiary.

Three corps were assembled in south-western France in preparation for military intervention in Spain. Initially, at least, it seemed to Napoleon that what was required was a wholesale reordering of the Spanish government, leaving the Bourbon dynasty on the throne. But infighting between the King, Charles IV, and his son Ferdinand, resulting in the eventual forced abdication of the former in favour of the latter, convinced Napoleon that the Bourbons would have to go. The 60,000 French troops waiting on the border were ordered into Spain, ostensibly in support of the invasion of Portugal, and to guard against a British counterattack from Gibraltar. Marshal Joachim Murat was appointed on 20 February 1808 to command them and began a gradual approach to Madrid. Charles and Ferdinand sought Napoleon's mediation in order to settle their dispute and were both invited to Bayonne. There, Napoleon finally revealed his hand. On 5 May 1808, both were forced to concede the throne of Spain to Napoleon, who offered it to his older brother Joseph. Napoleon had apparently subjugated the Peninsula in one fell swoop. He was warned by his security chief, Fouché, that Spain might yet prove a difficult nut to crack. 'The rabble', Napoleon believed, would only require 'a few cannon shots [to] disperse them'.[47] Events were to prove this analysis to be devastatingly inaccurate.

Already Spain was in revolt. Fearful that the monarchy was about to be usurped, a large and rowdy crowd gathered outside the royal palace at Aranjuez on 2 May. Murat sought to disperse the crowd and, in the process, ten Spaniards were killed in a volley of musket fire. The crowd dispersed, but word quickly spread through Madrid of the French brutality, and bands of lightly armed civilians started to coalesce throughout the city. At the end of the day, and after a series of skirmishes with French troops, 300 Spaniards lay dead, and a further 200 were executed overnight. The French suffered 31 dead and 114 wounded. This was the famous *dos de mayo*, and news of the rebellion against the French quickly spread throughout Spain's regions. Over the next few weeks and months, a large-scale rebellion broke out. *La guerrilla* had begun.

The insurrection was overwhelmingly regional, with little national cohesion or overall strategy. In some ways this was a weakness, but in others it proved a strength. Napoleon would have to subjugate the whole of Spain to defeat *la guerrilla*. Underestimating the determination, if not the military ability, of their opponents, the French spread themselves too thinly throughout Spain. Where irregular resistance was encountered, the French almost invariably received a bloody nose, as at Valencia and Saragossa. The unexpectedly hardy resistance of the Spaniards shocked the French, but Napoleon appeared to refuse to accept the reality of the situation. Where French forces encountered regular Spanish armies, they met with higher levels of success. Any pretence, though, that the French were on course for the subjugation of the Peninsula was dispelled on 19 July, when the Spaniards, under the command of General Francisco Castaños, captured 17,000 and killed 2,200 French troops under General Pierre Dupont at the Battle of Bailèn in Andalusia. In any event, Bailèn had two effects. It convinced the Spanish that they were capable of defeating the French without any significant political or military reform, thus lulling them into a false sense of security; while it also prompted Napoleon to march to the Peninsula at the head of massive reinforcements, consisting of elite French troops.

In this atmosphere, delegates from Asturias arrived in England seeking assistance from the British government, and Britain enthusiastically delivered. Within two months of the outbreak of the rebellion, Britain had sent over 30 guns, 12,000 swords, large amounts of ammunition and $500,000 in gold bullion.[48] Spain, however, did not want military intervention, despite the British government offering armed support. For a foothold on the continent, Britain would have to look to Portugal. Spurred on by news of French brutality in Lisbon, and of the rebellion in Spain, similar nationalist movements developed in northern Portugal. A new government coalesced around rebel leaders in Oporto, and it was from there that the British received requests for assistance. An immediate military response was also possible. Sir Brent Spencer commanded a division of 5,000 troops in Gibraltar that had been earmarked for, but denied service in, Madrid, and the government decided to bolster this force with Wellesley's 10,000 troops based in Cork.

Early intelligence indicated that Junot's force in Lisbon was small, perhaps 4,000 troops, but then it emerged that it was several times larger.[49] An additional 15,000 troops would have to be sent by the British;[50] Wellesley was too junior to command a larger force. Castlereagh reluctantly informed him he was to be superseded by Sir Hew Dalrymple and Sir Harry Burrard once the reinforcements arrived. The appointments were not unreasonable. Wellesley was a newly promoted Lieutenant-General and number 105 on the seniority list. The Duke of York, the Commander-in-Chief, could not contemplate such a junior general commanding a force of some 30,000 troops, by far the largest army Britain had committed to Europe for decades. Dalrymple, as governor of Gibraltar, had become intimately acquainted with Spanish affairs, and although he was not an experienced operational commander his second-in-command, Burrard, made up for this shortcoming, albeit the latter had a reputation for caution.

Nevertheless, Wellesley took his supersession as a personal insult, and was to remain bitter about it for years to come. 'They removed me because they thought very little of anyone who had served in India,' Wellington complained many years later to his friend John Croker. 'An Indian victory,' he suggested, 'was ... actually a cause of suspicion.'[51] At the time, Wellesley's response to Castlereagh, his closest friend in the cabinet, was icy. 'All that I can say on the subject is, whether I am to command the army or not, or am to quit it, I shall do my best to insure its success ... You may depend on me ... I shall not hurry the operations, or commence them one moment sooner than they ought to be commenced, in order that I may acquire the credit of the success.'[52] Castlereagh, nevertheless, tacitly suggested he should press on with the operations in the small amount of time available before the arrival of Dalrymple and Burrard, and it appears Wellesley had every intention of doing so. 'I hope that I shall have beaten Junot before any of them arrive,' Wellesley wrote privately to the Duke of Richmond, 'and then the government can do as they please with me.'[53]

He arrived at Corunna on 20 July, ahead of his force, before sailing on to Oporto. He was advised both by the Junta in Corunna and Oporto not to attack Lisbon directly, and he agreed. 'I should have no doubt of success ... if I were once ashore,' he wrote to Castlereagh, 'but to effect a landing in front of an enemy is always difficult, and I shall be inclined to land at a distance from Lisbon.'[54] He therefore decided to disembark his army in Mondego Bay on 1 August.

From the outset, Wellesley encountered logistical difficulties. The commissariat had not procured enough horses or oxen in advance.

Wellesley was faced with a shortage of suitable pack animals the moment he landed at Figueiras. 'I have had the greatest difficulty in organising my commissariat for the march, and the department is very incompetent,' he wrote in frustration to Castlereagh: 'the people who manage it are incapable of managing anything outside of a counting house.' As a result, Wellesley had to march without one third of his dragoons and one of his artillery batteries.[55]

Supplies were not just a problem for the British. Within days of his arrival, the Portuguese general Bernardino Freire pressed Wellesley for supplies for his troops. Wellesley was shocked, writing sarcastically to Castlereagh that 'it was a proposition of a novel nature to require an army landing from its ships not only to supply its own consumption of bread, but likewise that of the army of the state to whose assistance it had been sent'.[56] Worse was to come. Wellesley was informed by the British liaison with the Portuguese, Colonel Nicholas Trant, that Freire intended to operate in support, but independently, of the British. Rather than joining Wellesley as the British marched south, Freire proposed to take an inland route to Santarem, where more supplies were reportedly available, with the possible objective of cutting off the French retreat from Lisbon.

Wellesley was furious at the plan, describing it as 'useless and ... crudely digested'. 'Freire will have to justify himself with the existing government of Portugal,' he continued melodramatically, 'with his Prince, and with the world, for having omitted to stand forward upon this interesting occasion, and for having refused to send me the assistance.'[57] Just days into the campaign, and Wellesley was already encountering problems with his new allies.

On top of this, he suffered from a dearth of reliable information.[58] Efforts were immediately made to establish an intelligence network. Officers across the army were tasked with gaining informants within the local population. Others, the soon to be famous 'intelligence officers', went in search of tactical information themselves.[59] Thus, within a week of disembarking in Portugal, Wellesley had encountered the four main problems, aside from the French, which were to dog him for the whole war: political interference from London, which had resulted in the immediate loss of his command; logistical difficulties; testing relations with his allies; and unreliable and uncertain intelligence.

Having spent a week readying his army of 14,000 (Spencer's 5,000 men had arrived on the 6th), Wellesley marched south on 7 August. The march was arduous, in the searing summer heat, 'over an uninterrupted plain of white sand, hot enough almost to have dressed a beefsteak, into which we sank ankle deep at every step'.[60] The first shots exchanged between the

French and British were at Obidos on 14 August. Wellesley determined that the village was critical to future operations, and ordered it occupied.[61] The French occupiers retreated with no resistance, but troops of the 95th Rifles pushed on too far, found themselves almost surrounded by far larger numbers of French troops, and had to fall back under heavy fire. Three days later, the British attacked a delaying force of 6,000 troops under the command of General Delaborde, in the village of Roliça. Delaborde had originally occupied Roliça, but on the British approach he abandoned it for strong positions on several steep hills and escarpments overlooking the village. Wellesley divided his force into three columns, the right sent to outflank the enemy, the left to guard against suspected reinforcements from the east, and the centre to attack the village and heights head-on.[62] Steep, but navigable pathways, etched by streams and rivulets, were eventually found, allowing the British to gain the heights. Delaborde was forced to retreat, but the action had cost 500 casualties to the French 700.

Hearing that the further reinforcements under Brigadier-General Acland had arrived, Wellesley now marched to the coastal village of Vimeiro, 12 miles to the south-west. Reaching the village on the evening of 20 August, he was also advised that Sir Harry Burrard had arrived. In a meeting with Burrard aboard the *Brazen*, Wellesley learned that his superior was unhappy with the plan to march on Lisbon, but intended to spend one more night before disembarking and taking command of the army. Then, early on the morning of 21 August, Wellesley was brought news that the French were approaching in strength. He ordered his staff to prepare for battle, making as little commotion as possible. Whether this was to deceive the French or Burrard is unclear.[63]

At eight o'clock, 'a cloud of dust was observed' on the horizon.[64] Junot had marched from Lisbon with the intention of intercepting Wellesley, and with the British cornered on the coast, a significant opportunity to defeat them seemed to be in the offing. Wellesley, however, had occupied a strong position on the heights around Vimeiro. Junot, outnumbered though he was, split his force, sending two brigades under Solignac and Brennier to the east to try and encircle Wellesley's position. Wellesley responded by sending two brigades to counter the French move.

Junot himself attacked Wellesley's centre in Vimeiro with two divisions. On reaching the British line, the divisions separated into columns, which attacked the British at several points simultaneously. The French encountered sharp resistance from 95th Rifles, and the 50th, 52nd and 97th Regiments who were covered by the hedges and vines. A heavy firefight erupted. 'In spite of the deadly fire which several hundred riflemen kept up on them,' recalled one participant, the French 'continued to press forward with great determination, until the old 50th regiment received them with a destructive volley, following it instantly with a most brilliant and decisive charge with the bayonet, which broke and sent back' the startled French forces.[65] Junot's initial attack on Wellesley's centre was eventually terminated by the charge of the cavalry reserve from the valley below, and a second attack by the French divisional general, Kellerman, was beaten off outside Vimeiro in a desperate fight.

On the British left, no sooner had the two British brigades arrived than Solignac, who had been separated from Brennier by the rough terrain, attacked. Only when further reinforcements came up, charging with fixed bayonets, did the French attack collapse, leaving six guns in British hands. A further attack by Brennier from the ravine briefly recaptured the guns, but another bayonet charge forced the French back into the ravine.[66] With Junot in retreat, the British began a pursuit. But an order arrived to desist, not from Wellesley, but from Burrard.

Wellesley was furious. Burrard had actually arrived mid-battle, but had allowed Wellesley to continue in command. With the French attack defeated, however, Burrard felt that a general pursuit would over-extend the British position and make it vulnerable to a counterattack. He was wrong. An immediate pursuit might have destroyed Junot's force. 'Sir Harry, now is your chance,' Wellesley was overheard shouting at Burrard. 'The French are completely beaten; we have a large body of troops that have not yet been in action.' If the British pursued Junot now, 'we shall be in Lisbon in three days!'[67]

Burrard's hesitation, however, gave the French the opportunity to regroup. 'It must be borne in mind,' wrote one observer, years later, 'that every minute, nay, every second, was of the last importance to us, if the enemy was to be followed up after his defeat, and the passes gained before he could reach them.' Only one day later, the French were able to 'protract the contest for a length of time', having by 'then had possession of all the defensible positions between us and Lisbon'.[68] Wellesley was altogether more vehement, directly criticising Dalrymple, who had arrived on the 22nd. 'We are going to Hell by another road,' he wrote to his brother and confidant, William Wellesley-Pole: 'The French are fortifying trenches ... and we shall have to conquer them again ... [Dalrymple] has no plan, or even an idea of a plan, nor do I believe he knows the meaning of the word plan.'[69]

Small wonder, then, that given these obstacles, the cautious and inexperienced Dalrymple, and the cautious and dim-witted Burrard, would accept terms of capitulation offered by Junot. The two generals, along with Wellesley, signed the notorious Convention of Cintra on 30 August.

Under the terms of the Convention, in return for the French evacuation of Lisbon, the British would ferry Junot's army – all 20,900 troops – with its weapons and 'personal property' (loot) to France. Wellesley, anticipating the unpleasant political fallout the Convention would generate in Britain, immediately began reinforcing his position. 'Although my name is affixed to this instrument,' he wrote to Castlereagh, 'I beg that you will not believe that I negotiated it, that I approve of it, or that I had any hand in wording it.'[70]

The reaction of the press in London was vitriolic. Wellesley was their main target. 'If the Wellesley family must be employed,' ranted the *Morning Chronicle*, 'let it henceforth be in regulating the Dublin Police or guarding the residence of the Irish Clergy!'[71] Dalrymple and Burrard were recalled to London to account for their actions, and Wellesley voluntarily left Portugal to answer the same questions, and because he felt he could not continue in any other position in an army that he had once commanded. Sir John Moore had arrived with a further 20,000 troops from Sweden, and was also senior to Wellesley. At a Court of Inquiry, Wellesley publicly stated that he abided by the general terms of the Convention – allowing the French to evacuate Portugal – but that he disagreed with the specific terms, although he 'did not think it proper to refuse to sign the paper on account of my disagreement on the details'.[72] On 22 December, the Court of Inquiry reached its inevitable decision that all three generals were blameless, but only Wellesley escaped with his reputation largely unscathed, and for this he had to be grateful to Castlereagh and Canning, both of whom had rallied to his defence. The same could not be said of Dalrymple and Burrard, who received such faint praise as to be permanently damned.

* * *

In any event, the miserable affair was soon overshadowed by the near destruction of the British Army and the death of Moore at Corunna. Against his better judgement, and after much procrastination, Moore was pressured by both the Spanish and British governments to march into Spain to act in support of the Spanish defence of Madrid after Joseph's retreat earlier in the year. In doing so, he was falling between two conflicting British strategic priorities, namely supporting the new Spanish allies, and not risking his army. Aware that he had to advance to justify the British deployment to Spain, he was also aware that to do so carried enormous risk. He therefore marched his army north-east of Madrid. Despite achieving early success against Soult's cavalry at Sahagun on 21 December, he soon faced encirclement by Napoleon himself, in command of far superior forces. Madrid had fallen to a concerted French drive, with some 200,000 reinforcements, through the Somosierra Pass on 30 November, and the French Emperor was now able to turn his attention to eliminating the British threat.

On 23 December, Moore ordered a precipitate and devastating retreat to Corunna on the north-west tip of Spain. The retreat did much to sour Anglo-Spanish relations, as the British Army collided with the remnants of a Spanish force. Discipline disintegrated, and redcoats began pillaging the villages through which they marched and committing all manner of atrocities on the population. The town of Bembibre, for example, 'exhibited all the appearance of a place lately stormed and pillaged. Every door and window was broken, every lock and fastening forced',[73] whilst another village was completely gutted by fire, 'the wretched inhabitants ... sitting amidst the trifling articles of property they had been able to seize from the flames, contemplating the ruins of their homes in silent despair'.[74] The army finally reached Corunna on 12 January 1809, hotly pursued by Soult, Napoleon having given up the pursuit to return to Paris and prepare for war against Austria. On 16 January, Moore was fatally wounded while directing reserves in a defensive battle which allowed the majority of the British Army to embark on British transports in Corunna harbour. The campaign had cost the British Army in the Peninsula a fifth of its strength. Worse was the loss of huge numbers of guns, ammunition, gunpowder and stores, not to mention the heartbreaking slaughter of the cavalry's horses.

What had the campaign achieved? It is perhaps too much to say that Moore's actions saved Andalusia and Portugal from a decisive invasion by Napoleon, thereby preventing the French from gaining a swift victory and extinguishing the spark of insurrection before it had a chance to catch proper hold. However, it is fair to say that the French advance was stalled, and that Moore had given the Spanish valuable breathing space. The British Army had been saved, although in a parlous state, and could be reconstituted and sent back to Lisbon, or elsewhere, depending on the strategic prerogatives of the government.

In the wake of Corunna, the British government seemed paralysed by indecision. The horrors of war were for the first time made startlingly apparent to the public when the tattered remnants of Moore's army disembarked at Portsmouth and Plymouth. 'Now indeed the miseries of war have been brought home to our doors,' wailed *The Times*.[75] The wisdom of the war in the Peninsula was publicly questioned, both in Parliament and the press. At the same time, Canning, displeased with the direction war policy had taken within the cabinet, and particularly resentful of Castlereagh, whom he perceived to be at the centre of indecision, began plotting a major reshuffle. Finally, the cabinet was distracted by a scandal involving the Duke of York (Commander-in-Chief) and his mistress Mary Ann Clarke, who was accused of selling promotions. York was soon replaced by Sir David Dundas, but the scandal rumbled on, and the cabinet failed to arrive at a suitable strategic response to Corunna for some months.

Before them were three options: evacuate the Peninsula entirely (there were still 16,000 troops in Lisbon under Lieutenant-General Sir John Cradock); move the troops in Lisbon and redeploy them to a more useful strategic location in the Peninsula, such as Cadiz or Gibraltar; or – and it must be noted that there was considerable lack of enthusiasm for this option – reinforce Lisbon and prepare for the inevitable French invasion. The second option was almost instantly removed from contention by the refusal of the Spanish government to countenance the deployment of any British troops to Cadiz. The competition, then, was between evacuation and reinforcement, and into the political fray, once more, stepped Sir Arthur Wellesley.

CHAPTER 5

The Search for a Strategy

THE DEFENCE OF PORTUGAL, 1809–1810

I have always been of the opinion that Portugal might be defended, whatever might be the result of the contest in Spain.

Lieutenant-General Sir Arthur Wellesley
London, Great Britain, 7 March 1809[1]

IN March 1809, Lieutenant-General Sir Arthur Wellesley penned a memorandum explaining how Portugal could be defended, and how Britain might be able to draw Napoleonic France into a prolonged war of attrition.[2] The British government welcomed the plan as a viable escape route from a strategic dilemma which had paralysed decision-making since the beginning of the year: namely, whether or not to withdraw from Spain and Portugal altogether. This is all the more surprising considering the lack of detail and evidence that Wellesley presented. He advocated the restoration of the Portuguese Army, and the reinforcement of the British contingent in Lisbon, but nowhere did he explain what it was about Portugal that made it so defensible, or did he present any definitive assessment of how long Britain's commitment to Spain and Portugal would last. He spoke in superlatives: the contest will 'eventually' be decisive; the ultimate benefit will outweigh the 'expense incurred'.

He implied that the campaign would be cheap, effective and successful. And, fortunately for Wellesley, the Portuguese and the Spanish – and possibly for Europe – the British government bought it. In reality, the next two years would see Wellesley seek government support for a defensive strategy that was based on a planned retreat of the British Army from Spain and most of Portugal before the overwhelming might of the French Army.

It was a strategy that offered no foreseeable successful conclusion, and that relied on the British Army cocooning itself in Lisbon, safely supplied from the sea by the Royal Navy while the French Army stripped bare the rest of Portugal, in the process devastating the Portuguese economy; and leaving Spain to face the wrath of Napoleon's forces alone. There was little – a couple of battlefield victories aside – in the next two years that the British government could call cheap, effective or successful. Despite Wellesley's close association with senior members of the government – his brother, once more, among them – convincing them to support his strategy would be almost as difficult as the fight against the French itself.

Wellesley not only believed that Lisbon was a valuable strategic position, useful as a base of operations in Spain, but that it was the only strategic position which the British could afford to defend. His view was that Lisbon would be cheap to defend, but expensive for France to capture. In addition, the British could reconstitute the Portuguese Army, making the officer corps and staff British, and institute a vigorous programme of training and drill. A core 'Anglo-Portuguese' Army would therefore be ready quickly and effectively to take to the field against the French. In total, Wellesley estimated, this would cost the government no more than £1 million on top of the war expenditure to which it was already committed. It was nothing, Wellesley argued, compared to the long-term gains the British would make in repulsing the French in Iberia. In essence, Wellesley was arguing that for a minimal expenditure of men and materiel, the British could inflict a humiliating and costly war of attrition on the French.[3]

Wellesley's case was aided by the arrival of a secret diplomatic dispatch from Vienna, announcing the Austrian intention to declare war on France later in the year. To do so, Austria requested an immediate subsidy of £2.5 million, followed by an additional £5 million per year to sustain the war. Such a request was impossible to meet even at the best of times, especially since the total sought was more than Britain had spent on subsidising all continental alliances thus far. Austria also requested that a second front be opened. Britain was therefore able to refuse to pay the subsidy, and to demonstrate her continental military commitment by pointing to her ongoing military deployment in Iberia.[4]

Wellesley had the emphatic support of Castlereagh, and of Canning, who was extremely enthusiastic about continuing the war in the Peninsula. There were, however, significant opponents of hostilities, not least of them William Huskisson, the Chancellor of the Exchequer. In August 1809, he wrote a damning memorandum of the strategy the government had now developed against Napoleon. In his view, a protracted war in

Spain and Portugal would cost the British government £6 million a year, a figure far in excess of the £1 million Wellesley had estimated. With no income from foreign sources, the British government would be forced to increase personal taxation, which he felt the British people would be unwilling to pay. He estimated that to finance a protracted war, the government would require an immediate loan of £22.5 million, the interest on which alone was approximated to be £1.35 million a year. The problem stemmed from Napoleon's Continental System. Unless the British started using their military resources to secure other forms of income, most likely from the New World, then the British economy would be devastated.

The alternative Huskisson favoured was a rapprochement with France, which would bring to an end the continental embargo on British goods. 'Many burdens and obstacles, both in Parliament and the country, would be softened by a system of rapprochement,' Huskisson argued. He saw no reason to begin a protracted offensive war against Napoleon, when previous strategists, notably Pitt, had opted for a defensive war. Huskisson's position reflected his lack of strategic understanding. Pitt had presided over three of the most expensive and offensive military campaigns in British history, and had been forced on the defensive only by the lack of strategic options in Europe. Nevertheless, Huskisson's memorandum reflects the degree to which Britain was in dire straits economically between 1806 and 1809. Britain, Huskisson argued, 'ought to confine its exertion to the maintenance of maritime superiority and to the defence of its empire abroad, not engage in a costly war in the Peninsula'.[5] The British should limit themselves to short-term continental operations, specifically designed to support an allied military campaign, just as the Walcheren Campaign, well under way by August 1809, was intended to do. As such, the memorandum was to have major implications for Wellesley's future operations in Spain, because Huskisson limited the amount of money available to Wellesley to pay his troops and for supplies, instead diverting resources to other military operations.

After much wrangling, however, in early April 1809 an additional 20,000 troops were earmarked for the Peninsula, and Wellesley was appointed to the command of the army at Lisbon. General John Cradock, who had commanded in Lisbon over the winter of 1808–9, was appointed to command the British garrison at Gibraltar.[6] However, the government's strategic priorities remained unclear. Castlereagh informed Wellesley that 'the defence of Portugal you will consider as the first and immediate object of your attention', whilst the government left it to 'your judgement to decide, when your army shall be advanced on the frontier of Portugal, how your efforts can best be combined with the Spanish as well as the Portuguese troops in support of the common cause'.[7] The following day, though, Castlereagh contradicted this instruction by informing Wellesley that he 'should not enter upon a campaign in Spain without the express authority of [the] government'.[8] These conflicting instructions reflected the tensions within the government over balancing the need to achieve decisive results against France whilst taking no undue risks with the safety of the British Army: objectives which, at the moment at least, were incompatible. Wellesley arrived in Portugal on 22 April, and assumed command from Cradock on the 25th. Before he could implement his plans for the defence of Portugal, or, indeed, come to a conclusion about his confusing instructions regarding Spain, Wellesley first had to deal with the threat posed by Marshal Soult, who had occupied Oporto the previous month.

* * *

Prior to his departure from the Peninsula in January 1809, Napoleon had left instructions that Soult and Marshal Claude Victor-Perrin were responsible for the conquest of Portugal. In Napoleon's mind, now that the northern half of Spain had been effectively subjugated, it should take only until the summer to conquer the remainder of the Peninsula. Napoleon was being wildly optimistic. Soult was supposed to have arrived in Lisbon by 10 February. In fact, he was not ready to cross the frontier until the 13th, and, finding his way blocked by a strong fortress on the Portuguese border at Tuy, it was 9 March before he actually crossed into Portugal, taking with him a meagre and badly supplied force of 22,000 troops. That said, the resistance he was to encounter was even more meagre.

As they marched, Soult's army was constantly harassed, but successfully saw off a challenge posed by 12,000 troops under General Francisco Silveira, and then by a mixture of 20,000 regular and irregular troops at Braga on 20 March. This latter force was in complete disarray following the murder of its commander, Bernardino Freire, and disintegrated soon after the initial French attack. The way was now open for Soult to enter Oporto. With no government in control, few defensive arrangements were made, and as the French army marched into the city, mass panic ensued, in which hundreds died in a stampede down the steep streets to the River Douro, still more drowning as the only pontoon bridge across the river collapsed. At the end of the day, 800 men, women and children lay dead on the streets of Oporto, or were washed by the river into the Atlantic. Those who remained endured the torments of pillage and rape at the hands of the French soldiery. Soult, though, could go no further. Harassed

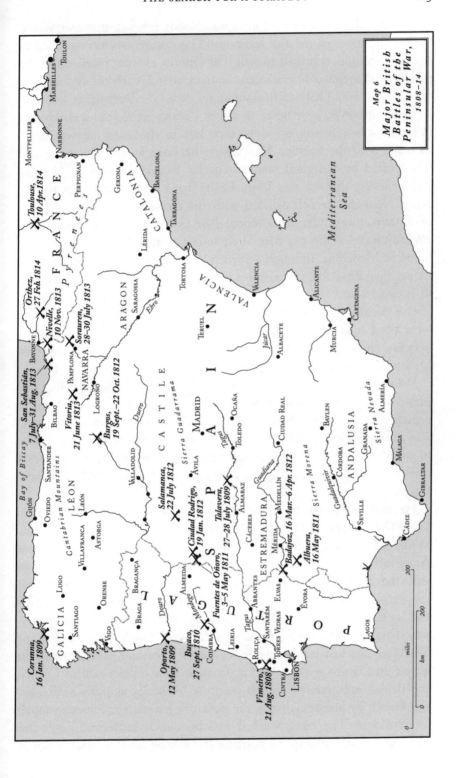

Map 6
Major British Battles of the Peninsular War, 1808–14

Corunna, 16 Jan. 1809

Oporto, 12 May 1809

Buçaco, 27 Sept. 1810

Vimeiro, 21 Aug. 1808

Fuentes de Oñoro, 3–5 May 1811

Ciudad Rodrigo, 19 Jan. 1812

Salamanca, 22 July 1812

Talavera, 27–28 July 1809

Badajoz, 16 Mar.–6 Apr. 1812

Albuera, 16 May 1811

Burgos, 19 Sept.–22 Oct. 1812

Vitoria, 21 June 1813

San Sebastián, 7 July–31 Aug. 1813

Sorauren, 28–30 July 1813

Nivelle, 10 Nov. 1813

Orthez, 27 Feb. 1814

Toulouse, 10 Apr. 1814

Bay of Biscay

Mediterranean Sea

FRANCE
SPAIN
PORTUGAL
GALICIA
LEÓN
CASTILE
ARAGON
CATALONIA
NAVARRA
VALENCIA
ESTREMADURA
ANDALUSIA

Cantabrian Mountains
Pyrenees
Sierra Guadarrama
Sierra Morena
Sierra Nevada

Duero
Ebro
Tagus
Guadiana
Guadalquivir
Júcar
Mondego

MARSEILLES
TOULON
MONTPELLIER
NARBONNE
PERPIGNAN
GERONA
BARCELONA
LÉRIDA
TARRAGONA
TORTOSA
VALENCIA
ALICANTE
CARTAGENA
MURCIA
ALBACETE
TERUEL
SARAGOSSA
PAMPLONA
LOGROÑO
BAYONNE
BILBAO
SANTANDER
GIJÓN
OVIEDO
LEÓN
ASTORGA
VILLAFRANCA
LUGO
SANTIAGO
ORENSE
VIGO
BRAGA
BRAGANÇA
ALMEIDA
COIMBRA
LEIRIA
SANTARÉM
ABRANTES
TORRES VEDRAS
CINTRA
ROLIÇA
LISBON
ÉVORA
ELVAS
LAGOS
CÁCERES
MÉRIDA
MEDELLÍN
ALMARAZ
ÁVILA
MADRID
TOLEDO
OCAÑA
CIUDAD REAL
CÓRDOBA
SEVILLE
CÁDIZ
GIBRALTAR
MÁLAGA
GRANADA
ALMERÍA
BAYLEN
VALLADOLID

miles
km
0   200
0   200

on all sides, the French were forced into bloody reprisals that only served to generate more hatred and resistance. The Portuguese, having failed to stop his invasion, managed to stall it at Oporto, as what remained of the regular and irregular forces of the state cut the French off and isolated them. Soult would have to sit tight and wait for reinforcements.

These, however, were never to arrive. Victor's route into and through Portugal was a matter of contention, but in the event he was never to make it to the frontier. Increasingly harassed by irregular forces, he was bluffed by the gentleman adventurer Samuel Wilson at Almeida into believing that the tiny Loyal Lusitanian Legion was a large regular army. Then the French collided with the reconstituted Spanish Army of Estremadura under the command of General Antonio Cuesta. On 29 March, the same day that Soult took Oporto, Victor fought a stiff battle at Medellín. Although a French victory, the fight had been much harder than expected, and with his rear threatened by increasing numbers of irregulars and militia, and with no chance of support from Madrid, Victor decided to halt until he received news from Soult. So numerous were the bands of guerrilla and other irregulars that communications between Spain and Portugal were effectively severed. Soult's force in Oporto was ripe for the picking.

When Wellesley arrived in Lisbon on 22 April 1809, then, he faced two immediate threats to the security of his army and of the Portuguese capital: the first from Soult in Oporto; the second from Victor, who was apparently entrenching his position at Medellín. It would take time to establish the necessary logistical base at Lisbon, so Wellesley elected to attack Soult first, although he believed Victor represented the greater threat.[9]

He marched north to attack Oporto at the beginning of May with 17,000 British and 11,000 Portuguese troops. Further to the east, Marshal William Beresford, who had been appointed to command the Portuguese Army in February 1809, marched with a flanking column of 6,000 troops with the objective of cutting off Soult's retreat east from Oporto. This, though, was not the army Wellesley had commanded at Vimeiro. That still lay in tatters in England after the Corunna campaign. Of the twenty-five battalions marching north, only five had fought at Vimeiro, and Wellesley had just five complete regiments of cavalry. Nevertheless, the attack on Oporto went exceptionally well. Fifty miles south of Oporto, the British encountered French outposts. Wellesley skilfully outflanked the French by manoeuvring to the west, using naval amphibious support as he did so. The tactic worked well because it convinced Soult that Wellesley would attempt to outflank the French on the western side of

Oporto. When Soult reached the city, he withdrew across the Douro, blew up the pontoon bridge, and brought all the boats to the northern bank. He then concentrated his defensive efforts in the west of the city.

Wellesley took up a position at the Monastery de Serra do Pilar on the south bank of the river. From here he could see a bishop's seminary on the northern bank on the eastern edge of the city, out of sight of the 11,000 French troops in the west, and apparently undefended. He quickly learned that there was a sunken ferry two miles upstream at Avintas. Wellesley promptly sent two battalions of the King's German Legion to refloat the ferry, cross the river and approach the city from its eastern outskirts. Soon after, news also arrived of four hidden wine barges, which were seized and used to ferry across thirty men apiece, an extremely daring manoeuvre in broad daylight. A platoon of the 3rd Foot was the first to cross; finding the seminary unguarded, they occupied it and began reinforcing it in expectation of a French counterattack. It took an hour for the French to recognise the danger. By then, the seminary had been secured by 600 troops. Sat atop a steep incline, the seminary was easily defended; the first two French counterattacks quickly faltered, and Soult, who had only just been woken, decided to make a third attack with the brigade of troops most readily to hand: those guarding the harbour. As soon as those troops evacuated the harbour, the inhabitants of Oporto poured into the streets, sailed a small flotilla of barges and skiffs to the southern bank and began ferrying across the main element of Wellesley's force. Soult's position quickly became untenable, and he joined his troops in a headlong retreat from the city. Finding their way cut off by Beresford's flanking column, the French had to utilise tiny goat tracks in their flight north to Galicia. In the process, Soult lost his baggage, all his guns and 4,000 men, many of whom fell victim to Portuguese irregulars who tortured those they captured, 'nail[ed] them up alive on barn doors [and] stripped many of them, emasculated them, and then placed their amputated members in their mouths ...'[10] Nevertheless, Soult escaped to Galicia, where he received support from the forces of Marshal Ney, who was facing his own difficulties against the emerging *guerrilla*. After five days, Wellesley cancelled the pursuit.

With Soult out of Portugal and his flank protected, Wellesley could now turn his attention to Victor. Before doing so, however, he faced an increasingly serious problem. From the inception of its operations in Portugal, the British Army had been accruing debts to local merchants and suppliers. Wellesley had received barely a quarter of the amount of money he required to settle these debts and pay the soldiers: the latter were by June two months in arrears. Failing to pay the troops meant they had no money with which to purchase food to supplement the meagre diet provided by army rations. The problem quickly evolved into plunder and, despite harsh penalties, it was impossible to stop. 'I have long been of the opinion that a British Army could bear neither success nor failure,' wrote Wellesley to John Villiers, the British minister in Lisbon, 'and I have proof of this opinion in the recent conduct of the soldiers of this army ... They have plundered the country most terribly ...'[11] Wellesley was concerned that the British might alienate the population as the French had done.

Wellesley penned furious letters to the government, directed at both Castlereagh and Huskisson, to no avail. In consequence of the massive cost of establishing and maintaining an army in Portugal, Wellesley recalculated the annual cost at £2.5 million, much higher than his original estimate of £1 million, but still less than Huskisson had predicted. Despite promises that 'he would attempt to keep the army's expenses as low as possible', Wellesley still received no response and, more importantly, no money, from Huskisson.[12] Faced with a wall of silence, Wellesley complained to Villiers that he suspected 'the ministers in England are very indifferent to our operations in this country',[13] and then effectively bullied the wine merchants of Oporto into lending him £10,000 so that he might pay his men, even though this covered only about 10 per cent of the total owed in arrears. The wine merchants complained, and the row escalated to the Portuguese Regency. 'I believe I did shame them into lending us a sum of money,' Wellesley explained, but 'the sum was not more than £10,000, and this is what [they] call "severe"?' Now that the Oporto wine merchants were free of the French, Wellesley argued, the sum they could expect to make from renewed trading possibilities was 'a hundred times the amount' of the loan.[14]

The lack of money in the army's coffers was therefore having a three-fold effect. It was compromising Wellesley's logistics system by denuding him of the cash he needed to pay merchants and, most importantly, his men. Lacking funds to supplement their rations, his men plundered the local countryside and alienated the population. In an effort to stop this, Wellesley had created a diplomatic row which had reverberated to the highest levels of the Portuguese government. Sadly, it was a problem that would not going away. Wellesley wrote increasingly inflammatory letters home. 'The operations of the [British Army] would be cramped for want of money,' he moaned, this time to Castlereagh.[15] The Secretary for War came to Wellesley's rescue in the nick of time. After Wellesley refused to continue operating against the French (for very practical reasons, if nothing else – his soldiers had no shoes, and no money to buy new ones),[16] Castlereagh wrote in early July to inform him that £230,000 was on the way to relieve Wellesley's immediate debts, but that thereafter the coffers were dry. More bullion was coming from South America, but when this was due to arrive was uncertain.[17]

Crisis had been averted, but temporarily. The episode demonstrated the short-termist view that held sway within the government. Huskisson was not alone in wanting to avoid a protracted conflict. The pressure on Wellesley to deliver decisive victories against the French would be intense. Yet the pressure on Wellesley to ensure the safety of the British Army was also intense. These political requirements were currently incompatible, and Huskisson's reluctance to provide financial support reflected tensions that were to manifest themselves throughout the war. Wellesley would have his work cut out devising a strategy that successfully addressed these tensions.

Nevertheless, the coffers were replenished for the time being, and Wellesley could now confidently take the initiative against Victor, for which he received permission on 12 June. Taking advantage of the delay imposed by monetary shortage, Wellesley had reorganised the army into a divisional structure. The brigade structure served a small force well enough, but, as the army expanded, Wellesley recognised the need to organise these into permanent higher formations. Wellesley initially created four divisions, each containing two or three brigades. The strength of the new divisions was between three and four thousand troops, except the First Division which had a complement of 6,000. A company of riflemen was attached to each infantry brigade, to enhance skirmishing capabilities. Once Portuguese troops were integrated into the divisional structure in February 1810, the complement of each division was nearly 6,000 men.[18] As the army expanded up to March 1811, Wellesley created an additional four divisions, as well as two separate cavalry divisions. The divisional structure increased the manoeuvrability of the Anglo-Portuguese Army and was the marked organisational feature of Wellington's successful battles against the French. Lacking the corps formation preferred by Napoleon, which adopted a combined arms approach and also increased manoeuvrability, but was unsuitable for the Peninsula, the British divisional structure nevertheless enhanced communications between the separate elements of the army, with all divisions having an identical headquarters and staff structure.

Each division rapidly developed its own identity, complementing the regimental structure of the British Army. The First and Third Divisions, for example, became known as the Fighting Divisions after the heroism of the former at Talavera and the latter at Salamanca. The Second, commanded by Wellington's most trusted subordinate, Sir Rowland Hill, became known as the Observing Division, not for want of its commitment to battle, but because Wellington trusted Hill more than anyone to protect his flank in battle and on operations. Frequently Wellington detached the Second Division some distance from the main army to watch the enemy. The most famous division was probably the Light Division. Whilst most of the divisions were composed of regular line infantry, the Light Division was a crack unit of highly trained light infantry that could be deployed by Wellington quickly and effectively to secure a flank or plug a hole in defences during a battle. Over the course of the war, it became the most highly trained and reliable of Wellington's divisions. The tenacity and fighting spirit of the men of the Light Division came to define many histories of the British Army in the Peninsula. Often overlooked in the history of the Peninsular War, Wellington's seemingly inconsequential reorganisation of his army was one of the most enduring aspects of its success.

*   *   *

Wellesley's preferred course of action against Victor was in concert with Cuesta's reconstituted Army of Estremadura – now back to a strength of approximately 36,000 troops – and the Army of the Centre, under Javier Venegas, numbering 23,000. In mid-June, the plan of operations which Wellesley had been developing with Cuesta was abandoned when Victor retired from Medellín, having found his position over-exposed and his want of supplies too great to manage. A revised plan of operations was therefore developed. Venegas and the Army of the Centre would act to prevent General Horace Sebastiani and Joseph, in Madrid, from coming to Victor's aid, while Wellesley and Cuesta would join forces in the Tagus valley and attack and defeat Victor. If Venegas failed to stop Sebastiani and Joseph from marching to Victor's aid, Madrid would still be exposed, whilst together Wellesley and Cuesta still outnumbered the French. At the very least, then, Madrid should be liberated, dealing a stinging, though not fatal, blow to French power in Spain.

From the outset, the plan appeared to work well. On 23 July, Wellesley and Cuesta agreed to attack Victor after pursuing him to the east of the town of Talavera de la Reina. There, Victor had taken a strong defensive position behind the River Alberche. At the last moment, Cuesta refused to move, and Wellesley, furious, was forced to halt his own advance. 'I find General Cuesta more and more impracticable every day,' exclaimed Wellesley. 'It is impossible to do business with him, and very uncertain that any operation will succeed in which he has any concern.'[19] In the event, this proved fortuitous, for it was unlikely that the allied attack on a

French force in such a strong position would have succeeded, as Wellesley himself admitted,[20] but what annoyed Wellesley more was Cuesta's failure to inform the British of his new intentions. Facing ever increasing logistical difficulties – 'it is certain that at the present moment the people of this part of Spain are either unable or unwilling to supply [our wants]; and in either case, and till I am supplied, I do not think it proper, and indeed I cannot, continue my operations in Spain'[21] – Wellesley refused to advance beyond the Alberche. Cuesta nevertheless did so, and on 25 July found himself badly over-exposed facing not just Victor, but Sebastiani and Joseph as well – a total French force of 46,000 troops to the Spanish 30,000. Venegas had failed to prevent reinforcements marching to Victor's aid, and had instead launched a futile attack against Toledo.

Unsurprisingly, Cuesta turned tail and fled back to the Alberche, his retreat being covered by the First and Third Divisions of Sherbrooke and Mackenzie. Once the Spanish were across the river, the two commanders agreed to offer battle on terrain selected by Wellesley immediately north of the town of Talavera. Wellesley's 23,000 Anglo-Portuguese troops occupied strong defensive slopes on the northern half of the battlefield, the allied left, whilst Cuesta and some 30,000 Spaniards held wooded ground running into the town of Talavera itself and on to the bank of the Tagus, on the allied right. Victor decided to attack before the whole of his force was in position, and a confused night action developed in the evening of 27 July, during which the British managed to hold the line against an attack on their left. This was renewed in the morning, but the British again held their ground, bayonet charges featuring heavily in the defence. Thereafter, a lull occurred in the fighting as Victor, Sebastiani and Joseph argued over the best course of action. Fearful that the British might escape, Joseph was browbeaten by Victor into agreeing to another assault. Thus began a horrific artillery assault, in which heavy losses were sustained – the allied forces could only bring to bear 55 guns to Victor's 80.

> Just as my company got into line, the captain told me to close the files on the right, and ... at that moment a round shot passed through the bodies of the front and rear rank men, killing them both. I was struck with one of their muskets on the breast and stunned for a few minutes ... A sergeant who assisted me up instantly reeled and fell, and was carried about six yards to the rear.[22]

Soon after, the French began a coordinated assault on the British line. To the north, two infantry divisions were to attempt to outflank the British left. Anticipating this move, Wellesley had dispatched a cavalry brigade, which despite overstretching itself and sustaining heavy losses, managed to hold the French back. Meanwhile, Victor threw three divisions against the British centre. Advancing in three columns, the French initially received heavy fire from Spanish cannon on the far right. The southernmost French division, commanded by General Leval, soon advanced against the British right, held by the Fourth Division under Campbell. The British, supported by some Spanish battalions, defended well with successive volleys of musket fire, which brought Leval to a halt. The French were then put to flight by a bayonet charge. Generals Rey and Lapisse, who commanded the other two attacking divisions, were confronted with Sherbrooke's First Division. Here, the legendary thin red line of disciplined British troops was more than apparent. The French advanced to within fifty yards of the British line, whereupon a single, devastating volley was let loose, and 'the Brigade moved forward to the Charge, & completely routed the enemy'.[23] Sherbrooke's troops overstretched themselves, though, and came into contact with Rey and Lapisse's supporting troops, suffering heavy casualties as a result. Reinvigorated, the French renewed the assault, but the reserves of Mackenzie's Third Division, and a battalion sent down by Wellesley, had plugged the gap. A prolonged firefight ensued until, unable to break the British infantry and harassed by cavalry, the French eventually fell back. The final attack of the battle was made by Leval once more on the British right, but Cuesta sent out a brigade of Spanish troops, who successfully attacked Leval's left flank and forced him to retire. The Battle of Talavera was over. British casualties numbered in the region of 5,000 killed, wounded or missing – fully a quarter of the total British strength – whilst the French had sustained 7,000.

If the allies achieved a tactical victory at Talavera, they failed to convert this into operational and strategic success. On 30 July 1809, Wellesley received intelligence that an enemy force under Soult numbering 20,000 troops was 'threatening the pass of the Puerto de Baños, which leads to Plasencia, in which object, if they should succeed, they would cut off ... communication with Portugal, and may otherwise do ... infinite mischief'.[24]

On 3 August, Wellesley elected to retreat to a secure position south of the Tagus to ensure his lines of communication were not cut.[25] A day later, intelligence was received that the French were, in fact, much stronger than had been previously supposed, consisting of 30,000 men. Anxious that he would be cut off from the British, Cuesta also retreated from Talavera, leaving Wellesley's wounded behind.[26]

The retreat, although hurried, was disciplined, and largely free of harassment from the French. Although the advances made in the Talavera

Campaign had been lost, Wellesley had been able to carry off his army in good order. Moreover, in terms of a defensive strategy, the threat Victor had posed to Lisbon had now been neutralised. Wellesley dressed the result as 'the best, if not . . . the most brilliant' to be hoped for.[27] The same could not be said of Anglo-Spanish relations. Wellesley and Cuesta had not seen eye to eye from the outset of the campaign, with Wellesley concluding that 'the obstinacy of this old gentleman is throwing out of our hands the finest game that any armies ever had'.[28]

Strategic differences aside, the principal point of contention was that of supplies. The British and Spanish armies had united on 22 July, and immediately Wellesley had difficulties procuring transport for his supplies. The problem escalated and, after his troops went unsupplied for two days, Wellesley threatened to return to Portugal.[29] The situation did not improve after the battle. By the middle of August, Wellesley had had enough. In the last month, 'the troops have not received ten days' bread', he complained. As a consequence, 'the sickness of the army . . . has increased considerably'.[30] Moreover, general concern was emerging about the quality of the Spanish troops. Although they had acquitted themselves reasonably well in the battle, there were instances when the raw recruits of the Spanish Army had deserted even before the enemy had commenced firing. Inevitably, it was this image that stuck in Wellesley's mind, and he concluded that 'they are troops by no means to be depended on'.[31]

Wellesley decided to abandon his position on the southern bank of the Tagus, and retreated to the Portuguese border, where supplies were more plentiful. Although Wellesley believed that the dispersed nature of the French forces in central Spain represented no threat to Cuesta's army, he wrote, 'if I had been certain that the enemy could and would attack the Spaniards on the day after my departure, I could not, with justice to the army have remained any longer . . .'[32]

The British retreat to the Portuguese border had, for now, the support of the ministers in London. 'If the result should be that there is no mode in which the British Army can act in Spain creditably and advantageously,' wrote Canning despondently when he heard of the fallout after Talavera, 'the next object is to get creditably out of the difficulty.'[33] Wellesley, meanwhile, was rewarded with a peerage, and, on the suggestion of his brother William duly became Viscount Wellington of Talavera. This, though, was all the thanks Wellington would get. Public opinion was swinging violently against the war in the Peninsula. Although the early public and political reaction had been favourable, news of Wellington's retreat to the Portuguese frontier engendered a change of mood. 'Lord Wellington, without knowing the force of his enemy, without being furnished with that which constitutes an army, advanced to Talavera. The idea of entering Madrid turned his brain. If not quite mad,' raged an article in the *Examiner*, 'that brain must certainly be disordered which could even think of such a plan.' Wellington was also criticised in Parliament by Sir Edward Milton. Wellington, Milton argued, 'had imprudently brought his army into a critical situation, was forced to give battle, and was attacked by the enemy'. Talavera was nothing more than 'a decisive victory followed by a precipitous retreat'. In such circumstances, 'what "thanks" would Parliament bestow on an admiral, who first ran his fleet on the rocks and shoals and then evidenced great skill and ability in getting them off again?'[34]

Wellington was experiencing the fickleness of British public and political opinion. In the wake of the liberation of Oporto, Wellesley had received the exact opposite criticism for failing to take the initiative against Soult's retreating force, whilst a disgruntled officer – one of the 'croakers', as Wellington called them – reportedly described British operations as 'snail paced', arguing that he 'could do more damage to the French army with one brigade'.[35] In the wake of the disastrous Walcheren expedition, there was little the government could say or do to defend Wellington, being, as it was, on the brink of collapse. It was soon also consumed by internal fracture, when Castlereagh challenged Canning to a duel in late 1809. Canning had unreasonably blamed Castlereagh for the Walcheren disaster. The two met at dawn on 21 September 1809, on Putney Heath. Canning – no marksman – missed his target, and Castlereagh shot Canning in the leg. Both resigned, and departed for the political wilderness for several years, depriving the government of two of its ablest politicians at a time when their skills were most needed. The Portland ministry thus fell, and George III asked Spencer Perceval to form a new coalition government. Canning refused to join, as did Huskisson, so at the end of 1809, Richard Wellesley was appointed Foreign Secretary, and Lord Liverpool became Secretary of State for War. Despite this change of emphasis in London, there was little appetite for shoring up Wellington's position. In the first instance, the government had to prepare itself for a savage onslaught from Parliament over Walcheren, whilst the increasingly vitriolic letters Wellington had dispatched regarding the supply of money to his army had alienated some cabinet members, and many were beginning to question the wisdom of the campaign in Spain and Portugal.

Canning's instructions, shortly before his departure from office, that the British could only campaign in Spain under certain conditions – namely, with a regular system of supplies and with Wellington as overall Commander-in-Chief – were partly designed to contain the increasingly

1 General Sir David Baird commanded the force that stormed Seringapatam on 4 May 1799. His wife had this painting commissioned following his death. Baird was actually nowhere near Tipu Sultan when his body was found. Nor was Wellesley, who can be seen in Baird's shadow, peeking over his shoulder. No doubt a comment of Baird's opinion of Wellesley.

2 Wellesley can be seen rallying his troops in the face of stiff resistance from the Marathas. Wellesley considered this the bloodiest and greatest of his victories (along with the Nivelle). The battle had a major influence on Wellesley's approach to warfare and imbued in him a respect for South Asian warriors, rare among British soldiers of the period.

3 Mornington was responsible for Wellesley's early political experience, and for keeping him on the straight and narrow. Unfortunately, despite his best efforts, Wellesley was unable to return the favour and, in 1805, Mornington was sacked. After a few years in the political wilderness, Mornington became the Foreign Secretary between 1809 and 1812, when he, Wellington and Henry formed a triumvirate of Wellesley's who effectively governed British strategy.

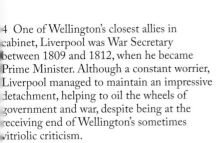

4 One of Wellington's closest allies in cabinet, Liverpool was War Secretary between 1809 and 1812, when he became Prime Minister. Although a constant worrier, Liverpool managed to maintain an impressive detachment, helping to oil the wheels of government and war, despite being at the receiving end of Wellington's sometimes vitriolic criticism.

5 A lifelong friend, Castlereagh was instrumental in ensuring Wellesley was appointed to command in the Peninsula after the Convention of Cintra debacle. Soon after, Castlereagh resigned from office for three years following a duel with the then Foreign Secretary, George Canning. Castlereagh returned to public office in 1812 as the new Foreign Secretary. During this period, he became Britain's most famous diplomat, and ensured that British interests were secured at the Congress of Vienna in 1814-15.

6 Four of Wellington's greatest generals. Sir Thomas Graham and Sir Rowland Hill became Wellington's most trusted corps commanders in the Peninsular War, often being sent on independent missions. Sir Thomas Picton was infamous for being foul-mouthed and ill-tempered, but he frequently achieved startling results on the battlefield before his death at Waterloo. Henry Paget was second-in-command at Waterloo, and was in overall command of the cavalry.

Wellington can be seen receiving intelligence from the peasant Zuarte during the opening stages of the Battle of Vitoria. The battle was the culmination of a strategic masterstroke that had seen the Anglo-Portuguese Army march nearly 400 miles in three weeks across the width of Spain. In so doing, Wellington was invoking his experience of warfare from India.

Spanish peasants bring Wellington information as he rushes to the village of Sorauren in the Pyrenees, aware that the right wing of his army is under attack by Marshal Soult. The battle was an allied victory largely because Soult was unable to manoeuvre in the mountainous terrain. The fate of the French army at Sorauren taught Wellington a great deal about fighting in the Pyrenees and informed his planning for the invasion of France.

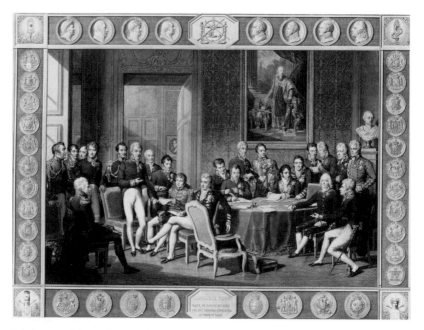

9 The assemblage of monarchs and diplomats at the Congress of Vienna determined the course of European history for the next century. The Congress itself nearly resulted in a new European war as the Prussians and Russians faced off against the British, Austrians and French over the fate of Poland and Saxony. The failure to reach conclusive decisions at the Congress was one of the reasons for allied tensions during the Waterloo Campaign. Wellington can be seen on the far left of the painting.

10 The French cavalry charge on the afternoon of 18 June was one of the pivotal moments of the Battle of Waterloo. It is unclear why Marshal Ney ordered the cavalry charge, but the impact was devastating for the French. The British, having formed square, received repeated French cavalry attacks for several hours. Had Ney or Napoleon ordered a simultaneous infantry attack, the redcoats would have stood no chance. The lack of combined arms warfare at Waterloo was one of the primary reasons Wellington's thin red line survived.

1 It was at Blucher's insistence that the Prussian Army marched to support Wellington at
Waterloo, having itself received a bloody nose two days before at Ligny. Without the timely arrival
of the Prussians, Wellington's centre would almost certainly have broken. Blucher met Wellington
after the battle at La Belle Alliance, and actually suggested that this should be the name of the
battle. Wellington would have none of it. La Belle Alliance was not to last long.

2 Blucher can be seen receiving Napoleon's captured hat and sword. Standing in the foreground,
left of the picture with his back to us, is Blucher's chief of staff, August von Gneisenau, who
had repeatedly expressed suspicion of Wellington's motives, whilst seated second to the right of
Blucher, facing us is (possibly) Karl von Zieten, whose timely arrival on the battlefield at Waterloo
enabled Wellington to redistribute his forces in time to meet Napoleon's final attack.

13 'Paint a telescope if you must, but no pocket watch.' This portrait of Wellington originally depicted him holding a pocket watch, to denote him waiting for the Prussians at Waterloo. Wellington was reportedly very angry at the suggestion, not least because it ruined the carefully cultivated version of events whereby the Prussian arrival was relatively unimportant to the allied victory. The truth, of course, was that without the Prussians, Wellington would have lost the Battle of Waterloo.

unpleasant political fallout from the war. If Wellington remained in Portugal, there seemed to be little that could go wrong. After all, Wellington himself had argued that Lisbon was easily defended against a force numbering less than 100,000. Containing the war in Portugal ensured the safety of the British Army, reduced the cost of a protracted engagement there, and undermined the nay-sayers in Whitehall. Wellington, though, had other plans.

* * *

Wellington had learned much from the Talavera Campaign. First and most obviously, the British could not rely on the Spanish for supplies of victuals and ammunition, or for transportation. Considerable time and effort would therefore have to be expended on building a logistics system and a supply train capable of supporting the British Army on long-term and distant operations. For this to work, a magazine system was essential. Fortunately, Wellington had the requisite experience from India to prepare such a system.

Secondly, friendly relations would have to be built and maintained with the Portuguese and Spanish. The nadir of Anglo-Spanish relations in 1809 had, on the surface, been reached primarily because of the logistical difficulties that the British encountered. In reality, however, the lack of supplies had only accentuated underlying political and cultural differences. At the root of this issue was the difference in perception of the nature of the war. For the British it was a means of containing and draining French strength. For the Spanish, it was literally a war of national survival, but, in the event, the Spanish were incapable of strategic prioritisation. A sense of paralysis therefore permeated the Spanish provisional government, exacerbated by Wellington's hostility and a latent but inherent xenophobia throughout the country. Fortunately for Wellington, his chances of overcoming these difficulties improved dramatically at the beginning of 1810, when his younger brother, Henry, arrived in Cadiz as the British Ambassador to Spain. In Lisbon, meanwhile, the experienced diplomat Sir Charles Stuart had succeeded John Villiers as British minister-plenipotentiary in Lisbon.

Thirdly, it was now obvious that Wellington could expect very fickle support from Whitehall. The one bright aspect in this regard was the news that his eldest brother was to become Foreign Secretary, whilst another Wellesley ally, Liverpool now sat in the War Department. Nevertheless, the fact still remained that the strategic direction of the war in the Peninsula was very poor, and that this war, for the foreseeable future, was going to be fought on a shoestring.

Fourthly, Wellington had realised that his intelligence department was ineffective. The surprise discovery of Soult's corps descending on the British lines of communication in the immediate aftermath of the Battle of Talavera had shocked Wellington. Although the allied capacity for acquiring information on the enemy disposition was above average for the period – the guerrillas constantly intercepted and delivered French dispatches to the Spanish and British – Wellington's intelligence collection evidently left something to be desired. Efforts were therefore being made to establish one of the most sophisticated intelligence systems yet seen in Europe. Charles Stuart, who had already acquired vast experience in intelligence gathering during an earlier mission to Madrid, and Henry Wellesley would be at the centre of this organisation.[36]

Within months of his arrival in Lisbon, Stuart managed to organise a system of agents running from Lisbon to the French border. There, they watched as French troops crossed into and out of Spain. Their reports in early 1810 were very disturbing. Some 138,000 troops were on their march to Spain.[37] Earl Grey, a leading member of the opposition and significant opponent of the war, had predicted this as early as May 1809. 'As soon as Bonaparte was finished ... in Austria, he would find no difficulty in settling affairs in the Peninsula.'[38] Wellington was no idiot, and had reached the same conclusion. The intelligence only confirmed what he knew was inevitable.

On 7 October 1809, Napoleon announced his intention to gather a massive invasion force on the Franco-Spanish border. 'I propose to assemble 80,000 infantry and 15,000 or 16,000 cavalry by the beginning of December,' he wrote, 'and to enter Spain with these reinforcements.'[39] It was not immediately decided what this force was to be used for – whether to complete the subjugation of Spain or begin the invasion of Portugal. In the event, Napoleon went first for the subjugation of Spain, arguing logically that only when Spain was settled could the British be beaten. Soult therefore invaded Andalusia in the autumn of 1809, and it was not until the end of May 1810 that a plan for the invasion of Portugal was finalised. Although it was rumoured that Napoleon himself would lead the invasion, the French emperor eventually elected to stay in Paris, and appointed, instead, Marshal André Massena to the command of at least 50,000 troops for the invasion of Portugal, but emphasised that operations should not commence until 'September, when the heats are over, and above all, after the harvest ...'[40]

Yet this was ordered before Spain was completely subjugated. Reflecting Napoleon's inaccurate perception of events in the Peninsula, this mistimed decision would ultimately contribute significantly to French problems in the Peninsula. It also reflected the chaotic system of command and control in the French camp, with Napoleon constantly undermining Joseph's authority. Wellington was aware of this. 'There is something discordant in all the French arrangements for Spain,' he wrote to Henry in June 1810. 'I should suspect that the impatience of Napoleon's temper will not bear the delay of the completion of the conquest of Spain; and that he is desirous of making one great effort to remove us by the means of Massena.'[41] Arguably, Spain could be subjugated, or Wellington defeated, but not both together. Impatience got the better of Napoleon, and he was to pay for it.

Wellington, then, knew an invasion was coming, but he also knew that it would take some months for Napoleon to assemble the troops he needed. Thus, on 20 October 1809, Wellington outlined his plans for the defence of Lisbon. He expected a two-pronged invasion of Portugal, from the north and from the south. The northern column would fix the defenders, while the southern column outflanked them. If the Anglo-Portuguese Army could avoid this trap, and fall back on Lisbon, they would stand a good chance of defending the Portuguese capital. The Anglo-Portuguese Army was to 'oblige the enemy as much as possible to make his attack with concentrated corps', to prevent the soldiers from foraging and attacking the population. This would allow the population to evacuate the provinces north of the Tagus – where Wellington expected the main thrust of any attack – and engage in a scorched earth policy as they did so, 'carrying with them or destroying all articles of provisions and carriages, not necessary for the allied army'.[42]

The centrepiece of the defence would be three lines of fortifications, redoubts and earthworks running between the Tagus and the Atlantic Ocean. The hilly terrain just to the north of Lisbon provided numerous defensive opportunities, and, utilised properly, this natural feature could be supplemented by fortifications to make the route to Lisbon impassable. The first and second lines were 29 and 22 miles long respectively; the third covered the port of São Julião and would protect the British embarkation if the French managed to break through. Essentially, though, the Portuguese capital would become a fortified peninsula, impenetrable from the north, and bounded by river and ocean on the east, south and west. In time, these works would become known as the Lines of Torres Vedras, and, without question, they were a masterclass in strategic defence. Wellington's eye for terrain, astute at Vimeiro and Talavera, would once again prove decisive.

Wellington's earliest thinking reveals that he never intended to fight a battle between the Portuguese border and Torres Vedras with the explicit aim of defeating the invasion attempt. If any action was fought, it would be with the aim of delaying the advance of the enemy. To the untrained observer, though, Wellington's strategy would look very much like a devastating retreat. Unsurprisingly, given the fickle comments published in the British press and uttered in Parliament, Wellington anticipated a negative reaction:

> During the continuance of this contest, which must necessarily be defensive on our part, in which there may be no brilliant event, and in which, after all, I may fail, I shall be most confoundedly abused, and in the end I may lose the little character I have gained; but I should not act fairly by the Government if I did not tell them my real opinion, which is, that they will betray the honour and interests of the country if they do not continue their efforts in the Peninsula, which, in my opinion, are by no means hopeless . . . [43]

Wellington – in warning that there would be 'no brilliant event' – was asking for the government's confidence to allow him to execute the campaign free of interference from London. This, however, was easier said than done. Wellington had no intention of telling Liverpool, or other members of the government, how he planned to defend Portugal. The reason was the continuing media indiscretion in printing the operational plans and objectives of the British Army. 'The newspapers have recently published an account of the defensive positions occupied by the different English and Portuguese corps,' Wellington wrote in frustration to Liverpool towards the end of November 1809. 'This intelligence,' he continued, 'must have reached the enemy at the same time it did me, at a moment at which it was most important that he should not receive it.' [44] With the success of the defence of Lisbon dependent on the enemy not knowing what awaited them when they reached Torres Vedras, Wellington could not risk another leak to the media. Despite Liverpool's denials that the media's information did not come from the War Department, Wellington refused to give him any details of his campaign plan.

Aware only of the vaguest facts about Wellington's plans, Liverpool came under intense pressure in Parliament. The new government was facing serious criticism over the handling of the Walcheren fiasco, whilst questions continued to be asked about the escalating cost of the war in the Peninsula and its likelihood of success. 'To carry on the war under the present scale of expense . . . is impossible,' wrote one political observer, [45] and others were more effusive. In the debate about the continued subsidy to Portugal, one Member of Parliament complained that 'it would probably have been better, if not a single English regiment had ever been sent to the Peninsula. It reinforced to the Spanish and the Portuguese people, to look toward the English people and not to themselves.'[46] News then arrived of further Spanish defeats, notably at Almonacid de Toledo in August, and then at Ocaña in November. 'When will the Spanish be cured of fighting battles under circumstances when nothing but disaster can be expected?' wrote Liverpool in horror after news of Ocaña.[47]

Then, of course, came intelligence of the French reinforcements. 'The intelligence which has lately been received of the defeat of the Spanish Armies ... may when combined with the advance of the considerable reinforcements from France,' wrote Liverpool despondently, 'produce a material effect on the probable success of the contest in the Peninsula, and may render all the efforts of the British and Portuguese armies for the defence of Portugal, ultimately unavailing.'[48] In short, with Spain on the brink of collapse, and ever greater numbers of French troops pouring across the Pyrenees, Liverpool was seriously thinking of throwing in the towel. 'I should apprise you that a considerable amount of alarm exists within this country respecting the safety of the British Army in Portugal,' Liverpool wrote to Wellington in February 1810. 'I have no difficulty in stating that under all circumstances you would rather be excused for removing the army a little soon than by remaining in Portugal a little too long.'[49] Others, such as the king's military secretary, questioned the wisdom of defending Lisbon. 'The superior importance of Cadiz must be acknowledged ... [Cadiz] actually contains the concentrated naval means of Spain. [Lisbon] offers no comparative advantage.'[50]

This prompted Liverpool to question Wellington's judgement directly. 'Is it not true that Cadiz and some part of southern Spain might be defended if Portugal were lost, but Portugal could not be defended if Andalusia were in French possession?'[51] Wellington was losing patience, but, unwilling to provide details of his plan, he could only try to defend his position with rhetoric:

As long as we shall remain in a state of activity in Portugal, the contest must continue in Spain; ... the French are most desirous that we should withdraw from the country, but know that they must employ a very large force indeed in the operations which will render it necessary for us to go away; and I doubt whether they can bring that force to bear upon Portugal without abandoning other objects, and exposing their whole fabric in Spain to great risk.[52]

Nevertheless, with the twin pressures of an inquiry over Walcheren, and a vote looming on whether or not to continue the subsidy, tensions were running high. There were those in the cabinet who were willing to hang Wellington out to dry. 'I understand your instructions direct you to not risk the army,' Wellington's second brother William wrote nervously in early April. 'I hope . . . you will strictly obey them – for be afraid . . . If you fight a bloody battle and afterwards evacuate Portugal – you will not be safe.' Meanwhile, the cabinet was 'completely paralysed', and it seemed Parliament was moving for peace.[53] Wellington felt he had no alternative but to take full responsibility for his plans. 'I am willing to be responsible for the evacuation of Portugal,' he wrote to Liverpool. 'I am perfectly aware of the risks that I incur personally . . . All I beg is, that if I am to be responsible, I may be left to the exercise of my own judgement; and I ask for the fair confidence of Government upon the measures which I am to adopt.'[54]

Wellington thus threw down the gauntlet. Either the government would accept his military judgement and leave him be, or they should send detailed instructions that he would execute to the letter. In the event, the crisis blew itself out. The government survived the inquiry over Walcheren, and a vote on the subsidy to Portugal was passed by 213 votes to 106. In fact the government agreed to send Wellington nearly £1 million, so he could pay off the army's debts to Portuguese merchants, pay the army its arrears, and pay British officers in the Portuguese Army.[55] Thus, Liverpool gained renewed confidence. Suddenly, 'the greatest satisfaction and the fullest sense of confidence is placed in your discretion in the important and delicate service in which you are engaged'.[56]

Wellington had persuaded the government to support a defensive strategy about which it knew little. This was the product of the cabinet's collective relief at surviving the Walcheren crisis, and the influence of Wellington's reputation among key figures, not least Liverpool and Wellesley. 'I have looked to the great result of our maintaining our position on the Peninsula,' Wellington argued, 'and have not allowed myself to be diverted from it by the wishes of the allies, and probably of some of our own army.'[57] That 'great result' was the long-term defeat of France. Wellington realised that lightning strikes against French forces would, for the moment, be futile. They might achieve short-term tactical success, such as at Talavera, but French strength in the Peninsula as a whole was so great that the tiny Anglo-Portuguese force would be incapable of translating tactical victories into strategic success. The only option, then, was a defensive war of attrition, with the British and the Portuguese safely supplied from the sea, and the French over-extended and isolated in the barren and scorched countryside north of the Tagus. 'If they should be able to invade [Portugal], and should not succeed in obliging us to evacuate, they will be in a very dangerous situation; and the longer we can oppose them, and delay their success, the more likely are they to suffer materially in Spain.'[58] Such a strategy would invite criticism, as no battle victories – which the press and Parliament so yearned for – would be forthcoming. But with French strength weakened, the Anglo-Portuguese force might be able to take to the field once more and challenge the French in such a way as to achieve strategic as well as tactical success. Wellington had convinced his supporters in government of the sense of this strategy. Yet, there were many in Parliament who remained deeply sceptical. Whatever the perception in London, the great test of Wellington's defensive strategy was about to begin. In July 1810, Marshal Massena began the third French invasion of Portugal.

*   *   *

First on Massena's list of targets was the Spanish border fortress of Ciudad Rodrigo. Initially, progress for the French was slow. But by the middle of June, Hill, who was keeping an eye on developments on the border, noticed that the French were making preparations to lay siege to Ciudad Rodrigo. 'The Plot,' wrote Hill, 'begins to thicken around us.' 'The Enemy appears to be bringing everything from Old Castile, Leon, and the North towards Ciudad Rodrigo, near which place are the Corps of Ney and Junot composing a force of upwards of 50,000 men.'[59] By 24 June, Massena's batteries were ready to open fire. The town held out for seventeen days, but after a breach was created in the town's walls, the garrison surrendered on 10 July. Anglo-Spanish relations suffered another setback, after the governor of Ciudad Rodrigo, Don Andrés Pérez de Herrasti, wrongly anticipated aid from Wellington. When none arrived Herrasti angrily accused the British of betrayal and cowardice. The immediate effect of this was an intelligence shortfall. 'We have not received a letter from Spain,' wrote Wellington to Henry, 'or any intelligence, for the last ten days, and the officers who are out on the flanks of the army tell me, that not only can they get no intelligence, but [they] can scarcely procure any body to carry their letters. This is not encouraging.'[60] But Wellington nevertheless defended his decision. 'I must leave the mountains and cross the plains to relieve Ciudad Rodrigo, as well as two rivers, to raise the siege,' he explained. 'Is it right, under these circumstances, to risk a general action to relieve or to raise the siege of Ciudad Rodrigo? I should think not. To this add that there is nothing to relieve the place excepting the stores belonging to this army.'[61]

After the fall of Ciudad Rodrigo, Massena's army finally entered Portugal on 21 July. To the south, Hill was watching a corps commanded by Reynier and guarding the allied flank. Massena, meanwhile, marched on Almeida. Eager for action, the commander of the Light Division, Robert 'Black Bob' Craufurd, defied orders to fall back as the French advanced, and ended up nearly trapped on the wrong side of the River Coa. Intense fighting ensued as the Light Division covered its own withdrawal across the single bridge 'of very few feet in width'.[62] The skirmish had been unnecessary and had resulted in 400 casualties. Wellington was privately furious at Craufurd for ignoring his explicit instructions to retire in the face of overwhelming force. Craufurd had at least atoned for his blunder by ensuring his force withdrew in order, but French morale was raised. Then, on 26 August, just thirteen hours after firing on the fortress walls of Almeida had commenced, a freak shot ignited the fortress store of gunpowder. The resulting explosion all but destroyed the fortress, killing 500 of the Portuguese garrison. The remainder of the garrison could only hold out for two more days. The loss of Almeida in such a short space of time was a blow to Wellington's plan. The siege had been meant to last weeks, eroding French resources and galvanising the allied defence. News of the skirmish at the River Coa and the destruction of Almeida undermined Portuguese confidence in Wellington's plans, whilst Wellington's critics in the army – the so-called 'croakers' – were vocal once more. 'These unpleasant affairs have produced much conversation in the Army, and also serious animadversions, from the Commander of the Forces,' wrote Lieutenant-Colonel John Elley, the assistant Adjutant-General. 'Although the French have collected a very formidable force, to act on one point I am persuaded the conquest of Portugal is not immediately at hand. The country we have to retire through, if obliged, is strong and without supplies.'[63]

Despite the quick success at Almeida, it was another three weeks before Massena could resume his march. Wellington's scorched earth policy was already having an impact, and the French were experiencing both subsistence and transportation shortages. To Wellington's consternation, Massena appeared to be moving the majority of his force north of the River Mondego, taking a more northerly and difficult road, described by the British general as 'decidedly the worst in the whole kingdom'.[64] The usual explanation for Massena's decision to take this route is that poor maps and the incompetence of his own guides misled him. In all likelihood, however, Massena had actually been informed of the defensive preparations Wellington had carried out on the most accessible routes to Lisbon, and chose to take his force by a less well defended road.[65] Undefended it might be, but it was also close to impassable. Massena's army therefore endured a harrowing and extended march through barren countryside and along roads that were barely capable of accommodating the troops and equipment. Hill, meanwhile, now joined by the new commander of the cavalry, Sir Stapleton Cotton, was keeping a close eye on Reynier's corps, which had been a constant threat to Wellington's southern flank. Despite fears that Reynier would march along the Tagus valley, it soon became clear that he was moving north to join Massena.

Facing a single enemy force, Wellington chose to delay their advance by offering battle on an eight-mile-long ridgeway known as the Serro de Buçaco, across which Massena would need to pass to capture the strategic town of Coimbra and continue his advance on Lisbon. 'We have an excellent position here,' he wrote to Cotton on the evening of 21 September, 'in which I am strongly tempted to give battle. Unfortunately Hill is one day later than I expected and there is a road upon our left by which we may be turned and cut off from Coimbra. But I don't yet give up hopes of discovering a remedy for this last misfortune.'[66] This remedy was the Portuguese brigade commanded by Nicholas Trant, who were ordered to guard the road to Coimbra. Offering battle at Buçaco presented a number of benefits for the allies. It gave Wellington the chance to test his new Portuguese battalions in the heat of battle; provided him with political ammunition to defend his actions when the inevitable criticism began in London; promised to delay the French advance sufficiently to allow more of the population to get to Lisbon; and also gave him the opportunity to halt the French invasion in its tracks.

In the event, the French were so badly delayed by the poor state of the roads to the north of the River Mondego that Wellington had five days in which to concentrate his forces on the ridge. The Army of Portugal did not get to Buçaco until 27 September. Massena's plan was flawed from the outset, based, as it was, on poor intelligence. Mistaking Wellington's centre for his extreme southern flank, Massena chose to attack here with Reynier's II Corps. This, he imagined, would turn Wellington's right flank and allow Reynier to roll up the British line from the south while Ney launched the main attack towards the convent at Buçaco, on Wellington's centre-left. Instead of encountering a flanking force, Reynier attacked the strongly posted Third Division under General Sir Thomas Picton. Reynier made three attacks on this division between five and six in the morning, each stalled by the steady, disciplined fire of the Third Division, and repulsed by the shock action of a bayonet charge. During this defence, Leith sent two regiments, the 9th and 38th, from the Fifth Division, to support Picton. These arrived in time to help repulse Reynier's second attack. Sergeant James Hale of the 9th Regiment recalled that his regiment continued marching in column 'until we got within 100 yards of them, where we were ordered to wheel into line and give them a volley which we immediately did and saluted them with 3 cheers and a charge'. The French stood their ground until the British 'got within 20 yards of them, but seeing it was our intention to use the bayonet, they took to their heels'.[67]

Meanwhile, Ney's attack on the convent to the north began a couple of hours after Reynier's initial attack. Ney ordered General Louis Loison to advance to the north of the Buçaco convent with his division. Throwing forward his skirmishers, Loison's men advanced up the steep and rocky incline, easily forcing the British riflemen out of their positions. Their objective was a small unit of German infantry and a battery of guns. As they neared the crest, the guns were pulled back and nearly 2,000 British infantry of the Light Division were revealed. Craufurd had used the dead ground offered by the ridge well, completely hiding his main force from French view. The shock of seeing the British infantry was not in itself enough to halt the French advance, but the three volleys delivered at close range, followed by a bayonet charge, sent the French into headlong retreat. In the words of Jonathan Leach of the Rifles:

> The instant the attacking columns were turned back, they were exposed to the fire of our whole division; whilst our battalion and some caçadores [Portuguese Light Infantry] were ordered to pursue, and to give them a flanking fire, and the horse artillery continued to pour on them a murderous fire of grape, as they were struggling through the narrow streets ... and trampling each other to death in their great haste to escape. Men, muskets, knapsacks, and bayonets, rolled down the side of the mountain in such a confused mass, as it is impossible to convey a just idea of.[68]

The battle was not yet over, although it must have been blatantly apparent that Massena could not break the British on such a strong defensive position. Ney sent forward the division of Marchand, this time at the Portuguese brigade posted to the right of Craufurd's Light Division. These troops, commanded by Colonel Dennis Pack, performed well, as most Portuguese troops did throughout the battle. Holding fire until the French were within range, they then managed to turn the final attack of the day into a rout. In the course of the battle, Massena suffered 4,500 casualties, the British just 1,250.

By midday, Massena gave up attempting to force Wellington from the ridge. In the evening his scouts discovered the road around the northern edge of the ridge; it was unguarded. Trant had not received his orders and was not in position, and by morning Wellington had learned that the French were outflanking his left. There was no option but retreat, and the morale of the army, temporarily boosted by the triumph at Buçaco, once more plummeted. Nevertheless, Buçaco had been an important victory. Massena had received an unexpectedly bloody nose, and the Portuguese troops had proven their worth on the battlefield. Moreover, the Anglo-Portuguese Army had proven itself a cohesive fighting force. The victory also demonstrated, once more, Wellington's ability to identify strong defensive terrain and deploy his force effectively. This was the foundation of British military success in the first half of the Peninsular War.

The use of a ridge allowed the deployment of troops on the reverse slope of the battlefield, which then helped to protect them from French artillery fire, and increased the shock impact they made on the French infantry, when the latter discovered the true nature of the force they were attacking. In selecting a battlefield, though, Wellington was only doing half the job. The British infantry – and by September 1810, the Portuguese as well – were trained to a high standard. It must be remembered that this was not all Wellington's doing. The reforms instituted by the Duke of York, Sir David Dundas and Sir John Moore had developed an extraordinarily successful infantry tactical drill.[69] The success of the Battle of Buçaco resided in the disciplined fire and bayonet charges of the British infantry. Wellington was not responsible for this innovation, although he selected terrain that enhanced its success.

As always, Wellington was not one to unduly apportion credit. 'The army was and indeed still is, the worst British Army ever sent from England,' he wrote to his brother William in September. 'The General Officers are generally very bad and indeed some of them a disgrace to the service.'[70] Whilst there were a few bad apples, such criticism, although unspecific, seems inappropriate, especially considering the performance of men like Craufurd, Hill, Picton and Leith. It was their tactical dispositions that had taken advantage of the ground Wellington had selected at Buçaco. William warned Wellington that he was being too harsh, or failing to recognise the success and gallantry of others. 'You are not saying enough in praise of your officers,' he had written after the Battle of Talavera.[71] It seems Wellington did not take this advice, and continued to criticise his men and officers after Buçaco.

The Anglo-Portuguese Army joined the rest of the population in a lengthy, although well-ordered, march to the Lines. Conditions were, needless to say, unpleasant. 'To attempt a description of our misery would be a task too hard for my old pen,'[72] wrote one soldier. The Portuguese population, meanwhile, were worse off. Schaumann, a commissary in the army, recalled seeing women who were 'wading in torn silk shoes ... through the mud',[73] and their prospects did not improve once behind the lines, where there was 'an immense population hemmed up in a small space of country, hundreds of them without a house to cover them or food to eat'.[74] News of the retreat from the Portuguese frontier had begun to trickle into London. 'Not one officer ... expressed ... any confidence as to probable success,' noted Liverpool, whilst most believed 'in the necessity of a speedy evacuation of the country'.[75]

By 10 October, the Anglo-Portuguese Army had fallen behind the Lines. The retreat had ended successfully, and Massena's army, now depleted to no more than 40,000 by desertion, disease, battlefield casualties and the need to garrison Almeida, could go no further. Nor were the French leaving. The Portuguese had ignored Wellington's instructions: there was still food and forage to be had for those willing to look, and the French were expert foragers. Thus began a six-month-long stand-off. Wellington could have attacked the French, but, to his mind, such a move was unnecessary, as the enemy would eventually be forced to retreat. His priority remained the security and strength of the British Army, and he refused to risk the lives of his men on such an attack.

News of the retreat, following the success at Buçaco, was not received well in London. The cost of the war had escalated dramatically from £2.7 million in 1809 to £9.2 million in 1810. The additional costs were attributed to the need to maintain transports in the Tagus for the possible evacuation of the army, but the government was feeling the pinch. With Wellington unable or unwilling to drive the French out of Portugal by force, the government began to question whether the campaign was worth pursuing. Ministers faced a choice 'between a steady and continued exertion upon a moderate scale, and a great and extraordinary effort for a limited time'. Liverpool wondered whether, 'if ... the latter would bring the contest to a speedy and successful conclusion', it would be the wisest course. However, 'the experience of the last fifteen years [was] not encouraging in this respect'. It seems the British government still considered it possible to inflict a single decisive blow on French power.

The problem was very real. To Parliament, it looked as if the government had spent millions of pounds funding a campaign that consisted of, in the words of one Whig, 'having lost almost all of Portugal'.[76] Wellesley began to 'doubt whether [the] government have the power or the inclination, or the nerves to do all that ought to be done to carry the contest on'.[77] Wellington had so far navigated a difficult and obstacle-strewn path in convincing the government that they should support a long-term strategy against the French. He had staked his military career on its success. He had also recognised the political imperative of ensuring the safety of the British Army at all costs. The new alliances with Portugal and Spain, and even defeating the French in battle, were subordinate to this necessity. Yet he had not done so cheaply. His estimate that defending Portugal would cost no more than £1 million had proven wildly optimistic; by 1810, the cost of the war was ten times as much, and such expenditure for little return was political dynamite to the peace-supporting opposition in London. It is a constant problem in political–military relations that the military feels under-resourced and the politicians fear they are being taken advantage of. For Wellington, it was no different. Perhaps the stresses of the campaign were beginning to tell, because his political intuition promptly deserted him.

Despite the economic problems and political opposition the government faced, Wellington demanded still more cash and now also started demanding reinforcements. His complaints met with short shrift. Liverpool was having none of it. If Wellington could promise to defeat the French decisively in the near future, then the government would provide him with more money and reinforcements. But if he wanted to continue with his long-term strategy of wearing down French strength, he would have to make do with what he had, or 'we must otherwise look, at no very distant period, wither to a reduction of the scale of our exertion or to the necessity of withdrawing our army altogether'.[78] Wellington had badly misjudged the political climate at home. The winter of 1810–11 was, therefore, very uncomfortable for him. Faced with limited resources, and playing a waiting game that alienated his allies, it was far from obvious that this defensive strategy would work.

CHAPTER 6

England's Oldest Ally

THE LIBERATION OF PORTUGAL, 1811

Depend upon it that Portugal should be the foundation of all your operations in the Peninsula. If they are to be offensive, and Spain is to be the theatre of them, your commanders must be in a situation to be entirely independent of all Spanish authorities.

Wellington
Villa Formosa, Portugal, 7 May 1811[1]

ARGUABLY, Wellington's greatest challenge – besides the French – was overcoming the constant difficulties posed by his Portuguese and Spanish allies. In late 1810, the Spaniards were aggrieved at the British withdrawal to Lisbon, but the more pressing problem was the deteriorating Anglo-Portuguese relations. Portugal was England's oldest ally; the original treaty between the two nations dating back to 1373. Probably one of the moments of greatest tension between the two powers came in the winter of 1810–11. As soon as the Anglo-Portuguese Army was secure behind the Lines of Torres Vedras, Wellington faced political pressure from London and the Portuguese Regency over the escalating cost of the war, deplorable conditions in Lisbon and its outskirts, and apparent military inactivity despite an increasingly weak French force some 30 miles away in Santarem. Massena had retreated there in November 1810 after a month in front of the Lines. This minor breakthrough had given Wellington a small respite from some of the political pressure – it at least proved that the British Army was not in immediate danger. But a political storm was brewing in Lisbon. Since the withdrawal of the army from the Portuguese frontier, Anglo-Portuguese relations had all but disintegrated and were at their worst since the war began.

The collapse in relations was the product of two separate circumstances: long-running divisions within the Portuguese Regency; and the British command of the Portuguese Army and plans for the defence of Lisbon. The Regency consisted of a council, which theoretically wielded sole decision-making authority. Outside of the council were several key secretaries, who undertook the regular administration of the government. In practice, these secretaries were the real decision-makers. A key British ally was Dom Miguel Pereira Forjaz, who, as Minister for War, State and the Marine, was one of the secretaries to the Regency, and had overseen the reorganisation and reconstitution of the Portuguese Army and the appointment of Beresford as its commander. A quiet and hard-working administrator, Forjaz preferred a 'behind the scenes' role that allowed him to get on with his job with minimal political interference.[2] Beresford and Forjaz were, to some degree, cut from the same cloth, and worked well together. The two worked miracles in the year or so that they had had to rebuild the army.

In the wake of Talavera, Wellington was deeply sceptical about the prospects of success in reforming the Portuguese Army. To his mind, the average Portuguese was neither capable nor willing to serve in the military. Such troops as had been conscripted 'have lately deserted to an alarming degree; and, in fact, none of the regiments are complete', he wrote to Castlereagh in August 1809.

In order to improve retention, then, the morale of the Portuguese Army would need to be raised significantly. A series of basic reforms was instituted; a new system of training was introduced; the punishment of crimes and misdemeanours was centralised and regularised; and the bloated officer corps was purged of the chaff: no fewer than 215 officers were cashiered and a further 107 pressed to retire. They were replaced by volunteers from the British officer corps – a decision that Wellington did not agree with, but did not overrule – who were given a promotion on entry into the Portuguese service. To maximise integration and ensure the smooth running of battalions, British officers were posted with Portuguese seconds.

The reorganisation of the officer corps began to reap immediate rewards. 'Their discipline is most wonderfully improved, perhaps fully as good as necessary for active service, and only wants confirming,'[3] observed Sergeant William Warre. That confirmation was delivered at Buçaco on 27 September 1810. Beresford had waited anxiously for the battle, concerned that the troops he had trained and disciplined for the last year would still be unequal to the task. But his concerns were to prove groundless. Wellington, who was with Beresford at the battle, tapped the latter on the shoulder and shouted, 'Well, Beresford, look at them now!'[4] The battle gave Wellington the opportunity to test the Portuguese troops, and give them 'a taste for an amusement to which they were not before accustomed'.[5]

The successful reorganisation and reconstitution, under predominantly British command, of the Portuguese Army did not sit well with all members of the Regency in Lisbon, however. Worried that the growth of British influence within the army was for ulterior motives beyond the immediate defence of the country, members of the Regency began to agitate against Wellington and Beresford, and their main supporter, Forjaz.[6] When the Regency was reorganised in August 1810, Dom Rodrigo de Sousa Coutinho became a key member of the Regency Council. The reorganisation had been designed, in part, to increase Britain's influence on the council: Charles Stuart was also given a seat. The Sousa family was seen to be pro-British. Dom Domingo de Sousa, one of Rodrigo's brothers, was the Portuguese minister in London (another, the Conde de Linhares, was the Portuguese Prince Regent's Minister of State in Rio de Janeiro). The Sousas, however, had a different agenda. With a misplaced sense of patriotism, they wanted to undermine the influence of the British in Lisbon, whom they viewed as increasingly powerful – and reduce the authority of the secretaries to the Regency, notably Forjaz.

When Wellington outlined his plan for the defence of Lisbon, however, and advocated a scorched earth policy that would inevitably ruin the already poor economies of Beira and Estramadura, Sousa took exception. The British refusal to fight the French on Portugal's frontier was a step too far. Sousa began manoeuvring to oust Forjaz and take control of the military defence of Portugal. In this scenario, Wellington would need to defer to Sousa in all decisions.[7] Despite Wellington's complaints, Sousa argued that if the British were going to evacuate Lisbon – which seemed a distinct possibility in September 1810 – then control of the Portuguese Army would fall anyway into the hands of the Regency. Sousa was therefore duty bound to act now to prevent a calamity being visited upon Portugal from which it might never recover. The only thing preventing Sousa from taking control was his inability to obtain a majority on the Regency Council. Stuart, anticipating trouble, had managed to persuade the other members to support Forjaz and Wellington.

The criticisms continued, however, and, indeed, intensified, as the army neared Lisbon. Increasingly the population believed the British were fleeing. To the casual observer, the abandonment of territory without resistance looked very much like defeat. To some degree, the victory at Buçaco changed this perception, among the population at least. But the criticism from Sousa continued. Buçaco had come too late: the only hope of a successful defence, according to Sousa, had been on the frontier. Soon the ink was flowing from Wellington's pen in a flood of hyperbole. 'I will not suffer them, or any body else,' wrote Wellington melodramatically to Stuart, 'to interfere with' the operations of the army. 'I know best where to station my troops, and where to make a stand against the enemy. . . I am responsible for what I do, and they are not.'[8]

Sousa's primary motivation was the power struggle within the Regency: Sousa wanted to discredit Forjaz, and Wellington played straight into Sousa's hands by writing directly to the Portuguese Prince Regent on 30 November. It was Sousa's fault, Wellington argued, that 'the enemy have found, in Portuguese Estremadura, everything which could tend to their comfort and subsistence, and to enable them to maintain their position in Portugal'. He went on to accuse Sousa of attempting to 'thwart and delay' his plan of operations. He concluded by reluctantly asking that Sousa be dismissed from the government.[9]

The request backfired dramatically. Sousa's other brother, the Conde de Linhares, as Minister of State in Rio de Janeiro, had informed the Prince Regent that Forjaz and Stuart had been deliberately feeding Wellington inaccurate information. In this version of events, Sousa had not been interfering or criticising Wellington; merely requesting clarification. In an attempt to usurp the authority of the government, Forjaz and Stuart had deliberately maligned it.[10] In his reply to Wellington in February 1811, then, the Prince Regent dropped a bombshell. Sousa would only be dismissed if Stuart also left the Regency, whilst Forjaz was ordered immediately to sail for Brazil to explain his actions.[11]

It became clear that Stuart's position on the Regency Council was untenable, and he stepped down in the spring of 1811. But both Stuart and Wellington agreed that Forjaz's loss would be 'irreparable' when it came to the success of allied operations in the Peninsula.[12] Wellington saw that he had been played; the political intrigue in Portugal was as bad as, if not worse than, that he had experienced in India. The problem was exacerbated by the conflicting views expressed at various times by London, Lisbon and Rio de Janeiro; by the fact that Portugal effectively had two governments, the junior of which – in Lisbon – was forced to take more critical decisions without recourse to the senior – in Rio de Janeiro; and by the four-month delay in gaining approval from the Prince Regent in Brazil. In some ways the communications delay played into British hands as Sousa was forced to wait for the Prince Regent's response and, while he waited, the status quo continued. Unable to act, Sousa could only grumble as the British went on waiting for the French either to surrender or evacuate. And on 5 March 1811 Wellington was vindicated, as Massena began to withdraw his starving and diseased army.

Throughout spring 1811, the intrigues and accusations against Forjaz continued, and Wellington's frustration at the paralysis within the government reached boiling point. Forjaz was 'accused of being a partisan of the French, ... then accused of disobeying the Prince's orders ... and of founding his opposition on the support ... from [the British]'.[13] Concerned that Forjaz might be forced out of the Portuguese government, Wellington, having exhibited a shortfall in political insight throughout the controversy, now recovered some political acumen and delivered something of a blow to Sousa's intrigues.

On 7 May 1811 he wrote to the Prince Regent, defending Forjaz to the hilt, arguing that it was because of him that the machinery of government had continued to function so as to provide adequate support for allied operations. Then, rather than rashly threatening to resign, as was Wellington's preferred tactic on such occasions, he politely apologised for having incurred the wrath of the Prince Regent over his interference in the government of Portugal, and suggested he be relieved; this, of course, despite his successful liberation and defence of Portugal three times in as many years.[14] At the same time, Wellington reminded the government in London that Portugal was absolutely fundamental to continued British operations in the Peninsula.[15] Success depended on adequate and efficient support from the Portuguese government, and this was best provided by Miguel Forjaz.

The strategy worked effectively. Dual pressure was brought to bear, in Rio de Janeiro by Wellington and by Richard Wellesley at the Foreign Office. The Prince Regent, faced with the possible withdrawal of Wellington and at the same time appearing to be ungrateful for British assistance, backed down. Forjaz and Stuart were both exonerated, and Sousa would be asked to resign from the Regency if the British wanted him to go.[16] The delays in getting responses from Rio meant it was another year before the controversy was formally ended, although by this point the storm had blown itself out. With the matter taking months to resolve it was clear Sousa and Forjaz needed to find some sort of accommodation, and an uneasy truce descended, no doubt aided by the movement of the scene of military operations to the Portuguese frontier in the summer of 1811.[17]

Meanwhile, with the Regency paralysed by internal power struggles, the inefficient Portuguese supply system had completely collapsed. Beresford's difficulties were 'increasing so fast, that matters are ... coming to a crisis', meaning that mass desertion or, worse, mutiny, could be expected at any moment.[18] Beresford's chief of staff, Benjamin d'Urban, was equally worried. 'The whole civil branch of the army is in such a state of confusion that I hold it utterly impracticable to carry on operations with it ...'[19]

Wellington suggested doubling the subsidy to cover 'the real amount of the expense of 30,000 men, which we have engaged to maintain'.[20] Such an increase could be offset by reducing the size of the loans Britain made directly to the Portuguese government. Since he controlled how the subsidy was spent, he could then bring influence to bear on the Regency to reform the commissariat and transportation services. This was a cunning political ploy, designed to undercut the power struggle currently under way within the Regency.

Unsurprisingly, such a suggestion met with strong opposition in Whitehall. A furious debate about the propriety of the war in the Peninsula once more commenced in Parliament. The excessive cost of the 1810 campaign had rendered the cabinet fearful that an increased tempo in operations in 1811 might further increase the annual cost of the war. The government now apparently preferred a totally defensive strategy, which would draw in French troops and drain the enemy army of resources, but pose a minimum risk to the security of the British Army.[21]

For Wellington, this was not good enough. If the government was unwilling to pay for constant operations, 'it may also be asked why we should spend our money, and why these troops should not go on as the French troops do, without pay, provisions, magazines, or anything? The French Army is certainly a wonderful machine,' he wrote, responding to his own question, 'but if we are to form such a one, we must form such a Government as exists in France, which can with impunity lose one half of the troops employed in the field every year, only by the privations and hardships imposed upon them.'[22]

Wellington was overstating the case here, but his point is important, as it went to the heart of British strategic concerns in the Napoleonic Wars. The French were successful, but at high cost. Napoleon's strategic priorities did not include the safety of his army – he could find more troops when he needed to – but this was the first concern for the British. Any deficiency in the supply of the British Army – and now also the Portuguese Army, since the two were so closely integrated and reliant on one another – was as much a threat as the French Army itself was. In short, the British could fight in one of two ways: either by adopting a 'total war' mentality, and in so doing embracing the very concepts with which the country was at odds, or by directly paying the full cost of fighting a war on the continent.

As usual, however, such a powerful political argument fell on deaf ears when not backed up by credible military success. News of Massena's retreat reached London on 26 March 1811, and soon critics and supporters alike were falling over themselves to compliment Wellington. One observer noted that 'those who were before abusing his delay are now applauding his foresight and wisdom'.[23] The government, meanwhile, now approved the increase in subsidy. 'You know our means both military and financial are limited, but such as they are, we are determined not to be diverted from the Peninsula to other objects,' Liverpool wrote to Wellington soon after news of Massena's retreat arrived. 'If we can strike a blow, we will strike it there ...'[24]

The winter of 1810 had been militarily quiet but politically tumultuous for Wellington. He had engaged in political bargaining, not unlike that he had engaged in when in India – the parallels here with the negotiations between the British, the Peshwa and Sindhia are obvious. Ultimately, he was successful. Forjaz retained his position and continued to support the development of the Portuguese Army throughout the remainder of the Peninsular War. Despite some hiccups, Wellington continued to exhibit political intuition rare among his peers. His strategy might not always have been in tune with that of either of the governments, in Lisbon or in London, but it was entirely focused on achieving victory, albeit in the long term.

*   *   *

On 5 March 1811, when Massena evacuated Santarem and began a precipitate retreat through the Portuguese countryside, the allies were taken by surprise. Wellington belatedly ordered an advance and came up with Massena's rearguard at Pombal on 11 March, and again at Redinha on the 12th. After fighting small rearguard actions on the 14th and 15th, Wellington was forced to pause his advance as he had outstripped his supplies. In the French camp, as he neared the frontier, the ignominy of his position must have caught up with Massena, and in an attempt to salvage something of the invasion, he turned south towards the River Tagus in a misguided attempt to outflank Wellington's advance. The military wisdom of this decision was questionable. The already starving French army was being asked to march into an even more barren area of Portugal.

Wellington seized the opportunity to engage Reynier's advanced column in battle at Sabugal, about 35 miles south-west of Ciudad Rodrigo, on 3 April. Fought in thick fog, the battle degenerated into a confused action, with the Third Division marching to the relief of the over-extended and beleaguered Light Division, a situation generated largely by the incompetent decisions of the temporary commander of the division, General William Erskine. Although a tactical mess, the combat at Sabugal prevented Massena's further advance south, and forced him to fall back to Ciudad Rodrigo. The third French invasion of Portugal thus ended on 11 April 1811. Massena's losses were devastating – some 25,000 men were missing from the ranks of the Army of Portugal, 8,000 of whom had been taken prisoner.

With the French now out of Portugal, Wellington turned his attention to offensive operations in Spain, but he had to wait for government acquiescence before invading. In the meantime, he could turn his sights on the border fortresses of Almeida, Ciudad Rodrigo and Badajoz. Any Anglo-Portuguese invasion of Spain would be predicated on the successful capture of these fortresses. The main challenge in 1811 would be besieging and capturing them rapidly, before the French armies in the country could concentrate in sufficient strength to force the allies to retreat. This was a constant problem throughout the year. Intelligence indicated that the strength of the Army of Portugal (swiftly reconstituted after its evacuation of Portugal) and the Army of the South was so great as to pose a constant threat to Wellington. The story, then, of 1811, is one of stalemate.

Beginning with Almeida, Wellington opted to isolate the fortress and starve its garrison into submission. In order to prevent Massena relieving Almeida, the allies fought a lengthy battle around the village of Fuentes d'Oñoro, just inside Spain, between 3 and 5 May. The majority of the fighting on the first day took place within the village itself, against which Massena threw a whole corps, commanded by Loison. Seeing that Fuentes was close to being overwhelmed by the French, Wellington, who was watching the battle from a small ridge behind the village, ordered in 2,000 additional reinforcements from Spencer's First Division. The 71st Regiment, which was under the command of Lieutenant-Colonel Cadogan, charged a French stronghold in the left of the village.[25] The fighting was intense, with British troops engaged in hand-to-hand combat with their French counterparts.[26] Several French assaults were made on the village, and although they managed to gain small footholds inside Fuentes, all were ultimately beaten back. In the evening, Massena gave up the attack, his men retreating, leaving 650 dead and wounded on the streets.

The fight was not over, however. During 4 May, Massena reconnoitred his position and moved a corps south in front of Fuentes d'Oñoro. Wellington perceived that Massena was attempting to outflank the British to the south by attacking the small village of Poço Velho, and cut the British communications with Portugal.[27] Demonstrating his impressive ability to out-think his enemy, Wellington moved the Seventh Division consisting of 4,500 infantry and 1,500 cavalry, under Major-General Houston, to occupy the village of Poço Velho, south of Fuentes.

Although he had predicted his enemy's intent, Wellington did not quite appreciate the magnitude of the French assault on Poço Velho. Massena sent in the whole of Loison's corps again, whilst leaving General Jean-Baptiste Drouet, Comte d'Erlon, with a corps to threaten Fuentes from the east. It was swiftly apparent that the Seventh Division, which had only been raised in March and consisted of troops who were new to the Peninsula, was severely outnumbered. A fraught battle developed, as Wellington struggled to get reinforcements to Houston's beleaguered troops. The French advanced rapidly and 'took about 200 [prisoners] before they could clear [Poço]', recalled John Insley of the 1st Dragoons. 'Our regiment fell back and the French Cavalry charged our Guns and then 2 Squadrons of our Regiment charged their Cavalry and killed and took about 200 and saved our Guns.'[28]

Wellington ordered the Light Division, which had been sent north on the 4th to protect the road to Almeida, to retrace their steps and cover the retreat of the Seventh. The Light Division's 95th Rifles found their new comrades in a dire situation. 'Opposed, with their conspicuous red dresses, to the old trained French tirailleurs, it is no wonder that the gallant 85th should have suffered so severely,' recalled Rifleman Edward Costello. Arriving in the nick of time, the more practised and accurate fire of the rifles of the Light Division managed to halt the French advance, giving time for the Seventh Division to fall back.[29] It was now patently obvious to Wellington that he had over-extended his position. He decided to consolidate his forces by abandoning Poço Velho and withdrawing to a gentle ridge running west to east, with the east flank anchored on Fuentes.[30]

In falling back on this new line, though, the Light Division was nearly overwhelmed. 'The French were playing a deep game,' wrote Costello. 'They had succeeded in moving a regiment of infantry, with some cavalry, through the wood in our rear. The alarm, however, was immediately given, and our company . . . had to run for their lives into a square formed by the Fifty-Second.'[31] There now ensued an arduous retreat under heavy fire and constant threat of a cavalry charge. 'This was done by alternate squares under a heavy cannonade, the balls sometimes hopping in and out of the square,' remembered Lieutenant Dobbs of the 52nd. 'The distance was about three miles, and marching in square a most difficult operation, as, if the correct line is not kept by the front or rear faces, or the sides in file marching not locked up or well covered, the square must be broken.'[32] Nevertheless, the crack training and discipline of the Light Division ensured the successful completion of this complex manoeuvre. 'The execution of our movements presented a magnificent military spectacle as the plain between us and the right of the army was by this time in possession of the French cavalry, and, while we were retiring through it with the order of a common field day, they kept dancing around us and every instant threatening a charge, without daring to execute it.'[33] The new allied position was very strong, and the French declined to attack, preferring to open an artillery bombardment. This effectively marked the end of the battle to the west of Fuentes.

Wellington's quick reaction to events, and the phenomenal training of the Light Division in particular, had saved the day. However, seeing that Loison's outflanking manoeuvre to the south appeared to be gaining ground, D'Erlon had pushed on the attack on the village itself, which was held by the left of Picton's Third Division. The battle here ebbed and flowed through the streets of the village, with the French nearly gaining control of all the buildings on two occasions. Each attack was successfully countered, however. William Grattan, of the Connaught Rangers (88th Regiment) led the final counterattack:

> On reaching the head of the village, the Eighty-Eighth was vigorously opposed by the Ninth Regiment, aided by some hundred of the Imperial Guard, but it soon closed in with them, and . . . drove the enemy through the different streets at the point of the bayonet, and at length forced them into the river that separated the two armies. Several of our men fell on the French side of the water.[34]

The successful defence of the village of Fuentes d'Oñoro effectively ended the battle. The fighting had been intense, possibly the worst of the whole war, particularly in the village itself, where hand-to-hand combat was common. Walking through the streets later, Schaumann observed 'an English and a French soldier with their bayonets still in each other's bodies'.[35] In many ways, the battle was a turning point in the struggle against France. Allied failure here would have opened up Portugal to a new invasion, but victory had reinforced its successful liberation. It had been an unquestionably close fight. Wellington himself perceived it to be the closest of the war. The successful outcome for the allies was the result of a combination of Wellington's skilled generalship, his eye for terrain, and the exemplary command and training of the Light Division. If Craufurd's men had been overrun on the plain between Poço and Fuentes, then it is possible to envisage the whole of the allied line collapsing. As it was, Fuentes d'Oñoro had secured Wellington's liberation of Portugal, even if the victory was tarnished by the successful escape of the French garrison from Almeida.

Wellington was furious. He had given explicit instructions that the garrison not be allowed to get away, ordering Erskine, who was now in command of the blockade, to close all routes from Almeida. Lackadaisical implementation of these orders gave the garrison commander, General Brennier, and his men, the opportunity to break out on 6 May, although not without significant loss. 'They had about 13,000 men to watch 1,400,' Wellington raged. 'There they were all sleeping in their spurs even: but the French got off.'[36] Wellington was increasingly of the opinion that he alone was competent to command the army, and he began to view his subordinates with mounting distrust. 'I am obliged to be everywhere, and if absent from any operation, something goes wrong,' he wrote to Liverpool.[37] That this statement is often repeated is sometimes offered as proof of its accuracy, but the Battle of Fuentes d'Oñoro had demonstrated the skill and ability of Wellington's divisional commanders. That Wellington's quick thinking saved the day is clear, but this on its own would have counted for nothing without the tactical skill of Craufurd, Picton and Houston.

Wellington's belief that he alone was capable of successfully commanding the army in battle was only reinforced by events in the south. There, Beresford's detachment of 35,000 British, Portuguese and Spanish troops (the latter under the command of General Blake) was tasked with besieging Badajoz. Appallingly supplied with siege guns (some were 200 years old), the siege progressed so slowly as to allow Soult to muster a force of 20,000 men to march from Andalusia to try and relieve the French garrison. In anticipation of Soult's approach, Beresford deployed his force on a commanding defensive ridge behind the village of La Albuera about 10 miles to the south-west of Badajoz. Here, one of the bloodiest battles of the war was fought on 16 May.

Beresford expected Soult to make a frontal assault through the village, so deployed his army facing east, with the Portuguese holding the northern flanks, the British Second Division, under Stewart (Hill was in London, recuperating from an illness), in the centre, and the Spanish divisions, of Zayas, Ballesteros and Lardizabal, protecting the southern flank. Cole and the Fourth Division were still marching to the front when the action commenced, and thus acted as a secondary reserve.

The battle opened with an apparently heavy attack on the village, as expected, but it quickly emerged that this was a feint, and the real attack was in the south against the Spaniards. Beresford was slow to react. Convinced that the attack on his southern flank was a feint, designed to get him to weaken his centre, he instead reinforced the village. It was only when the attack in the centre started to fade that Beresford recognised his mistake. He immediately sent General William Stewart's Second Division to support the now heavily outnumbered Spaniards. Charles Leslie recorded the march of the Second Division from the allied centre to the right. 'We were suddenly thrown into open column, and moved rapidly along the heights to our right flank for nearly a mile under a tremendous cannonade . . . [The French] were at the same time attacking the Spaniards with great vigour, having put them into some confusion . . .'[38]

Soult's decision to attack the Spaniards was sensible enough given their historic inability to stand and fight, but the divisions of Zayas, Lardizabel and Ballesteros were hardened veterans, and would not flee at the sound of their own musket fire. Zayas's division was the first to be engaged by General Jean-Baptiste Girard's column, and a prolonged musketry duel developed. Support from the Second Division arrived in the nick of time, though, as the addition of General Horace Gazan's division to the fight meant the French now significantly outnumbered the Spanish. Stewart threw Colborne's brigade in too hastily, however, and 800 Polish Lancers caught the troops in open terrain. Leslie watched in horror as Colborne's brigade was all but wiped out. Three 'regiments were in line . . . when a body of [Polish] lancers, taking advantage of the thick weather and heavy showers of rain . . . broke them and swept off the greater part as prisoners into the French lines.'[39] During this attack, the staff was overrun and Beresford himself had to fight off a Lancer, grappling with his assailant's weapon and throwing him to the ground.

Beresford, presumably suffering some sort of shock, now became paralysed with indecision, and it appears that Stewart assumed nominal command. He advanced his remaining two brigades, under the command of Hoghton and Abercrombie, but at the same time the Spanish line finally collapsed, the exhausted troops streaming towards the advancing British. 'Many of the Spaniards threw themselves on the ground, others attempted to get through our line,' recalled Leslie. 'We being in line on the slope of a bare green hill, and such a rush of friends and foes coming down upon us, any opening made to let the former pass would have admitted the enemy also. We had no alternative left but to stand firm and in self-defence to fire on both.'[40] The Lancers fell back and the Spanish were thus allowed to pass through the British line, which then continued to advance to contact with the French. A terrible firefight broke out, as the French, exhausted from their duel with the Spanish, were unable to fall back because of the sheer weight of numbers in their rear. 'The murderous contest of musketry lasted long,' recalled Sherer, who was in Abercrombie's brigade. 'The slaughter was . . . dreadful: every shot told.'[41]

With the sides evenly matched, a bloody battle of attrition now developed which was to last for four hours. The decisive moment was the timely arrival of Cole's Fourth Division, which bore down on the French line from the north-west. Although the French were reinforced with Werlé's division, they now found themselves caught in terrible crossfire, as Cole's division entered the fight on their left. 'Under the tremendous fire of the enemy our thin line staggers, men are knocked about like skittles, but not a step backward is taken,' recalled John Cooper of the 7th Foot. 'We close the enemy's columns; they break and rush down the hill in the greatest mob-like confusion ... We followed down the slope firing and huzza'ing till recalled by the bugle.'[42] The battle was over. The allies lost 5,380 dead or wounded, whilst the toll for the French was much higher, between six and eight thousand. The French, out-fought, fell back in some disarray, but the British were in no fit state to pursue them, and Soult was allowed to return to Seville, although the retreat he embarked on was itself gruelling. Some believed that had the British pursued Soult, his entire army could have been destroyed.[43] The blame for this effectively lay with Beresford, whose poor understanding of the terrain had ultimately caused the bloodiness of the battle and rendered pursuit impossible.

Beresford's command in the battle had also been questionable. His misreading of the French disposition at the beginning of the fighting had led to command-paralysis, and it was only on the initiative of his aides-de-camp that the orders to redeploy the Second and Fourth Divisions were sent. When he arrived at Badajoz on 27 May, Wellington was extremely concerned about Beresford. 'The battle of Albuera was a strange concern,' he wrote to his brother William later in the year. 'They were never determined to fight it; they did not occupy the ground as they ought; they were ready to run away at every moment from the time it commenced till the French retired . . .'[44]

After the battle, Beresford was devastated, and his depression was reflected in the dispatch he authored for Liverpool. 'I consented to oppose Soult,' he wrote despondently, 'we have by beating him escaped our total destruction which must have been the consequence but I am very far from feeling happy after our triumph.'[45] Wellington could not allow such a downcast account of what had been a hard-fought allied victory to get to London. Years later, Wellington recalled that on reading the dispatch, he told Beresford that 'this won't do, write me down a victory'.[46] Nevertheless, the high casualty figures spoke for themselves. Many in London questioned Wellington's appointment of Beresford to such an important field command, and, more generally, whether an offensive against French forces in Spain was sustainable. 'Beresford's action is considered here as proof of the astonishing bravery of the British troops, which appears to have saved him and his army,' wrote William to Wellington, but, he warned, 'there are so many letters from the army detailing particulars that everybody knows the whole story, even to the General's loss of head ...' The sooner Hill recovered to resume the command, the better, with Beresford best left to 'arrange the Portuguese'.[47]

Still, Albuera and Fuentes d'Oñoro had proved that the British were capable of holding their own against the French at the very least. Moreover, Albuera had demonstrated that the British and Spanish could work together, although Wellington subsequently downplayed the Spaniards' role, even going so far as to blame them for some of the problems Beresford experienced, arguing that their very immovability had been a disadvantage, forcing Beresford 'to apply the British everywhere'.[48] The Spaniards, meanwhile, came close to viewing Albuera as another Bailen, sharing none of the credit with the British. 'The news of the victory in Extremadura has filled the minds of the people ... with the most determined belief of the superiority of the Spanish Army,' complained Sir Thomas Graham, one of Wellington's most trusted divisional generals, from Cadiz, 'which now in the public opinion neither admits of nor requires improvement, being already perfect.'[49]

The successful liberation of Portugal, and the fighting prowess demon-strated at Fuentes d'Oñoro and Albuera, convinced the government that Wellington could engage in offensive operations in Spain,[50] but it was becoming apparent that a stalemate was developing. It was impossible for Wellington to besiege and storm Badajoz and Ciudad Rodrigo before significant French forces could concentrate against him.

This became obvious over the next fortnight, as, in late May, Wellington took command of Beresford's corps, and once more laid siege to Badajoz in late May. Massena had been sacked from the command of the Army of Portugal and replaced by Marshal Auguste Marmont, who, having received an appeal for reinforcements from Soult in the wake of Albuera, promptly marched south. Although Wellington had estimated that two weeks would be sufficient to take Badajoz,[51] the decrepit state of his elderly siege artillery, which he had still been unable to persuade the Master-General of the Ordnance to replace, rendered this objective wildly unrealistic. Marmont and Soult rendezvoused in Mérida by 18 June, bringing to bear no fewer than 60,000 troops. It was a threat Wellington could not ignore. By 10 June, he knew he would soon be outnumbered. Later he commented that it was good intelligence which had allowed him to make a 'guess of the enemy's probable movement, as described in the letter from our friends'.[52] On the evening of 11 June, after two unsuccessful attempts to storm the fortress, Wellington pulled the siege guns back to Elvas.

Thwarted at Badajoz, Wellington moved north and besieged Ciudad Rodrigo, having been misinformed that the garrison was low on supplies, when in fact it had several months' worth.[53] After relieving Badajoz, Soult and Marmont once more went their separate ways, and Wellington felt that the threat of Marmont's force alone was insufficient to force him to raise the siege of Ciudad Rodrigo. Intelligence had indicated that Marmont had received 20,000 reinforcements, but even this 'can in no measure enable them to attempt further than establish their conquests already within Spain'.[54] In fact, Marmont had received closer to 40,000 troops, but Wellington remained unaware of these until they appeared in his front.[55] He hastily abandoned the blockade (no attempt had been made to begin a bombardment) and fell back to protect his communications. The French were so strong that they felt confident enough to threaten a brigade of the Third Division at El Bodon on 25 September. There, 1,000 infantry had to make a fighting withdrawal in square under constant pressure from 2,500 cavalry.

Wellington and Marmont faced off against one another, but Marmont declined battle, despite overwhelmingly outnumbering Wellington, and the British were allowed to escape on 27 September. Marmont also retreated, and Wellington was allowed to use the Light Division once more to isolate Ciudad Rodrigo, but the constant threat of the Army of Portugal rendered any siege works futile. Aside from an action at Arroyomolinos on 28 October, when Hill surprised the division of General Girard, capturing 1,300 prisoners, all their artillery and baggage and inflicted several hundred wounded, this marked the end of combat operations in 1811.

After a wildly successful start, the campaign had proven rather disappointing. The French were just too strong to enable offensive operations. Wellington had been holed up on the Portuguese frontier, and the morale of his army was suffering. Unsurprisingly, with his reputation and strategy at stake, he put as positive a spin as possible on the outcome of the campaign. 'Although our success has not been what it might and ought,' he wrote home at the end of the year, 'we have at least lost no ground, and with a handful of British troops fit for service, we have kept the enemy in check in all quarters since the month of March. Till now they have gained nothing, and have made no progress on any side.'[56] The stagnation of the campaign only confirmed the fears of the opposition in London. Grenville wrote of the 'desperate and hopeless character of waging war on the continent', whilst Grey perceived that the French were 'on the point of making a great effort ... which Lord Wellington will find himself unable to resist'.[57] The implication was that Wellington was too weak and unskilled, and the government too cash-strapped to continue the campaign.

Events were to prove Grey wrong. A series of factors outside Wellington's control combined to give the latter the opportunity to strike at the heart of French power in Spain. The first was a spectacular collapse in Franco-Russian relations. The reasons for Napoleon's invasion of Russia in 1812 are many and varied. On the one hand, it was a very realistic, and initially limited attempt to secure more satellites and therefore manpower, in the east. But on the other hand, it seems that Napoleon, frustrated at the lack of progress in a long and draining war in the Peninsula, decided to flex some military muscle in an attempt to reaffirm his military, and therefore political, credibility. Whatever the cause, Napoleon's invasion of Russia was a gift to Wellington. In preparation, at the end of 1811, the French emperor began assembling a colossal invasion force, withdrawing select forces from across the Peninsula. The first to be recalled were the Imperial Guard, then significant elements of the Armies of the North, South and Catalonia – some 6,000 troops each.[58] Wellington, constantly supplied with intelligence from agents throughout Spain, as well as via intercepted dispatches, was aware of the withdrawals. In March and April alone, intelligence showed, some 34,749 French troops had been withdrawn.[59] At the same time, Napoleon ordered General Louis-Gabriel Suchet, Commander of the Army of Catalonia, now critically short of troops, to conquer Valencia. For Wellington, the prospect of the loss of Valencia carried significant strategic implications. Valencia had become one of the last outposts of financial revenue for patriot Spain. Denuded of income, many patriots might now be forced to accept French rule. Worse, if the irregular resistance in south-east Spain could be overcome, and the population subdued, Suchet would 'then be disposable on the left of Soult or to support those more immediately opposed to us'.[60]

To facilitate the capture of Valencia, Napoleon authorised the dispatch of 15,000 reinforcements to south-eastern Spain from elsewhere in the Peninsula. Joseph in Madrid could muster 2,000, so it fell to Marmont to supply the remaining 13,000. This finally tipped the balance decisively in favour of Wellington, who became aware of the French movements as early as October 1811.[61] Previously, Marmont had possessed too large a force to enable the allies to attack him with any hope of success. This reduction, combined with a general thinning of the numbers of French troops, and with the personal vendettas of the various marshals – notably Soult, who could not be uprooted from Andalusia – meant that, unlike in 1811, the French would be unable to concentrate in sufficient force on the Portuguese border to threaten Wellington. The Anglo-Portuguese Army, meanwhile, had been substantially reinforced, and was now in possession of a powerful siege train.

Ironically, Marmont need not have sent the reinforcement to Suchet. Napoleon had delivered the order when he received news of an apparent reversal of Suchet's force at Sagunto. Suchet, in fact, had been able to defeat a force of 27,000 Spaniards under Blake – including the divisions of Lardizabel and Zayas, that had performed so well at Albuera – with only 13,000 troops. Slow to capitalise on his success, however, it was not until late December that Suchet fought a decisive battle outside Valencia, which capitulated on 8 January.

Wellington was deeply concerned about the fall of Valencia, but his expectation that Spanish resistance would immediately collapse proved overly pessimistic. With the Army of Portugal now badly undermanned, and strung out across Old Castile, southern Galicia and Estremadura, Wellington was able to take the opportunity to launch a lightning assault on Ciudad Rodrigo. In freezing conditions, and after a six-day bombardment, two breaches were made in the fortress walls. Wellington decided to storm Ciudad Rodrigo on the evening of 19 January. The attack was ultimately successful, although casualties were high, including 'Black Bob' Craufurd, who fell mortally wounded at the head of his division near one of the breaches. There now followed a night of pillaging, which won the British soldiery few friends among the population of western Spain. Only the 'voice of Sir Thomas Picton, with the power of twenty trumpets', who 'began to proclaim damnation to everybody', was able to bring the worst excesses under control.[62]

Ciudad Rodrigo had been taken in eleven days, completely surprising Marmont, who remained unaware of the siege until 14 January, by which time it was too late to act. Wellington took the garrison prisoner, but, in so doing, had set an alarming precedent. Tradition had it that a garrison that was summoned and refused to surrender was put to the sword if the fortress was captured. Barbarous as this act might sound, it had an important deterrent effect, for garrisons of subsequent fortresses to be besieged by the same army would be less willing to hold out when terms were offered. In the fact that he acted humanely, the impact of Wellington's experiences in India can clearly be seen. Having witnessed barbarous slaughter there, he had no wish to see this repeated unnecessarily in Spain. But in so acting, he quite possibly made his job more difficult, as next on his list was Badajoz, and that garrison now felt free to resist in perpetuity, safe in the knowledge that it did not mean certain death. It was to cost Wellington's men dearly.

Time, though, was of the essence. The siege of Ciudad Rodrigo had given the game away. Marmont's assumption, based on the British performance in 1810 and 1811, that Wellington would not act aggressively had been comprehensively shattered. Wellington decided to make his main assault from the southern approach to the fortress.

On the evening of 19 March, a sortie by the garrison – which numbered in total 4,500 – attacked the siege works, injuring Colonel Richard Fletcher, Wellington's chief engineer, causing 120 casualties, and making off with the tools the British had left in the trenches in their haste to escape. Conditions were atrocious, and the trenches quickly filled with water and mud. The rain did help prevent some of the French shells from exploding, but the gunfire from Badajoz remained devastating. Only three hours after one battery began firing on 31 March, for instance, its magazine exploded when it received intensive counter-fire from the fortress. The battery was in ruins. An engineer 'met two artillerymen carrying in a blanket a wounded gunner from this battery, the left side of whose head had been struck by a cannon ball . . . His brains in the unbroken membrane (like a bag) hung on his shoulder.' Unsurprisingly, the unfortunate soldier died soon after.[63]

By 6 April, although two breaches had been established in the fortress walls, they were barely practicable, but Wellington nevertheless decided that, given that Soult was bearing down on his position, the best thing to do was to storm the fortress without hesitation. The Fourth and Light Divisions were assigned the task of attacking the breaches, whilst the Third would conduct a feint against the high eastern walls of the fortress, and the Fifth would conduct a second feint from the west, attacking the north-west corner. Those defending the main breach had booby-trapped the debris, and were armed with hand grenades, incendiary bombs and extra muskets. The attackers had to cross a ditch along which a cheval-de-frise – effectively, large barbed wire – had been laid, climb over an unfinished counterscarp, and then ascend the steep rubble-strewn sides of the breaches. Inside, the defenders had also constructed a second ditch some seven feet deep, over which the attackers would have to cross, before they were even in sight of the town itself. The casualties sustained by the main attacking force were horrendous. William Lawrence was injured in the initial attack, but was unable to go to the rear, 'for on arriving at the ladders, I found them filled with the dead and wounded, hanging . . . just as they had fallen. . .'[64]

Simmons, fighting in the 'Forlorn Hope' of the Light Division encountered a 'most dreadful fire . . . that mowed down our men like grass'. Ladders were positioned on the counterscarp, and once past this, the troops 'rushed forward to the breaches, where a most frightful scene of carnage was going on'. The breaches were repeatedly stormed, 'without effect, the French cannon sweeping the breaches with a most destructive fire ... I had seen some fighting,' Simmons recalled, 'but nothing like this.'[65] The fighting continued for two hours, whereupon Wellington decided to call off the attack, resigned to failure on this occasion. However, the attacks meant as feints on the western and eastern sides had been unexpectedly successful, although the Third Division, which had proceeded to attack the castle of Badajoz, had suffered heavy casualties as well. Under heavy fire, the attackers managed to get ladders on to the 30-foot-high walls, but several broke under the weight of the men ascending them. 'The poor fellows who had nearly reached the top were precipitated a height of thirty to forty feet and impaled on the bayonets of their comrades below,' recalled one participant named Donaldson. 'Other ladders were pushed aside by the enemy on the walls, and fell with a crash on those in the ditch, while those who got to the top without accident were shot on reaching the parapet, and, tumbling headlong, brought down those beneath them. This continued for some time, until at length, a few having made a landing ... enabled others to follow.'[66] Having taken the castle, the Third Division then rounded on those defending the main breaches, where they were joined by the Fifth Division troops who had successfully stormed from the north-west, which had been relatively under-protected. Attacked from the rear, the defenders were thus forced to surrender.

So horrific had the fighting been that the troops now embarked on an orgy of pillage and rapine. 'Men, women and children were shot ... for no other ... reason than pastime; every species of outrage was publicly committed,' wrote Blakeney after witnessing the tumult. 'The infuriated soldiery resembled ... a pack of hell-hounds vomited up from the infernal regions for the extirpation of mankind ...'[67] As many as 250 Spaniards were killed by the rampaging British troops, whose mayhem continued unabated for three days. Wellington ordered the plundering to cease after a day, and had a gallows erected, but on the whole he appeared ambivalent. In turn, he was horrified by the losses his army had suffered in the attack.

The day after the attack, Wellington, weeping openly, encountered Picton, notoriously hard-hearted, while surveying the carnage amidst the main breach. 'I bit my lips and did everything I could to stop myself for I was ashamed he should see it, but I could not, and he so little entered into my feelings that he said "Good God, what is the matter?"'[68] Wellington's feelings and humanity, so rarely displayed in public, were now memorably on show. The loss of so many troops was truly devastating. Given the events that followed, it is unsustainable to argue that he became overly cautious as a result, although it made Wellington extremely nervous when conducting sieges. Quite possibly, though, Badajoz inspired in Wellington the phenomenal level of planning which marked the autumn campaign of 1812, and the Vitoria and Pyrenees Campaigns of 1813. Combined with the failure at Burgos the following November, the high casualty rates sustained in siege warfare might also have persuaded Wellington to avoid such battles in the future. Taken together, then, Badajoz was a turning point. A subtle shift in Wellington's approach to warfare began after this bloody siege.

CHAPTER 7

England's Essential Ally

The Invasion of Spain, 1812

If this game had been well played, it would have answered my purpose. Had I any reason to expect that it would be well played? Certainly not. I have never yet known the Spanish army to do anything, much less do anything well.

Wellington
Ciudad Rodrigo, Spain, 25 November 1812[1]

IN 1812, Wellington was finally able to strike at the heart of French power in Spain, but the political problems with his Spanish allies were as time consuming as his military problems with the French. With the keys to Spain – Ciudad Rodrigo and Badajoz – in Wellington's hands, he now had to decide which part of Spain to attack. His main concern was preventing the Army of Portugal under Marmont and the Army of the South under Soult from uniting. Marmont's force, according to intelligence from intercepted dispatches, numbered 22,295 men at Salamanca, plus a further 20,000 dispersed around Castile and Estremadura.[2] Soult, although he had 56,000 men in Andalusia, had to maintain the siege of Cadiz, retain garrisons at Seville, Granada and Malaga, and would also need to keep an eye on Ballesteros, who maintained a force on the peripheries of Andalusia. 'Marmont's then being, what may be called of the two, the operating army', if Wellington marched against Soult, then Marmont could go to his aid, and the enemy would be able 'to bring the largest body of men to act together on one point'. This 'would be a false movement, and must by all means be avoided'.[3] Rather than Soult, Marmont and the Army of Portugal would be Wellington's main target.

His strategy decided, Wellington wanted to keep Marmont in the dark as to his true intentions for as long as possible. The *guerrilla*, who proved repeatedly successful at intercepting French dispatches and capturing French scouts and guides, constantly hampered French intelligence efforts. Wellington capitalised on this by keeping his army spread out across the Portuguese frontier between Ciudad Rodrigo and Badajoz. This was a risky move. It relied on a delicate balance of French knowledge and ignorance. Wellington needed Marmont to know enough about British dispositions to keep him guessing as to the true target of Wellington's army, but at the same time he needed Marmont to be ignorant of the true strength of the British force. So effective were the *guerrilla* that Wellington was confident 'that the French will not find out how weak we are at all points'.[4] At the last moment, Wellington would concentrate his forces and strike at Marmont's army at Salamanca. Not everyone was as confident. Graham wrote privately to Wellington of his concerns 'that Marmont will have the means of getting sound intelligence of the movements of the divisions of [the] army, & will regulate his accordingly ...'[5] It was a risk Wellington was willing to take.

In addition, Wellington coordinated several diversionary operations around the Peninsula. Sir Home Popham, commanding the naval squadron off the northern coast of Spain, was ordered to work with the Spanish Seventh Army to neutralise the Army of the North. This he did very effectively, launching a number of amphibious raids along the Cantabrian coastline, which comprehensively tied down General Maximilian Caffarelli commanding the Army of the North. The Sixth Army, meanwhile, was to besiege Astorga, and the Fourth and Fifth Armies were to cooperate with Hill to pin down Soult in Andalusia. Finally, a British force sent from Sicily was to cooperate with the Second and Third Armies to prevent Suchet from sending reinforcements to Marmont. Crucial to success was the requirement that the forces remained an unremitting threat to the French so as to provide constant diversion. This was more important than attempting to achieve tactical success. If any diversions were decisively defeated, then the French force would be free to support Marmont. To the commander of the Second Army Wellington wrote, 'I only request that you may not be defeated again, and to accomplish this object you must not attack the French if success is not quite certain. Threaten as much as you can, but do not engage in serious affairs.'[6]

Fearful that Soult might dispatch reinforcements to Marmont, in mid-May Wellington sent Hill on an expedition to destroy a pontoon bridge across the Tagus at Almaraz. Although successful, the operation gave away Wellington's intentions to Marmont, who began to concentrate his widely dispersed forces. In Madrid, meanwhile, Joseph began concentrating some 13,000 troops to reinforce Marmont, a force that, remarked Wellington, 'may make some difference in the situation of us all'.[7] In early June, Wellington learned that Marmont's force was much larger than previously thought – nearly 60,000 troops.[8] 'I did not calculate that the enemy's army of Portugal was so strong when I determined upon this expedition,' he wrote to Liverpool, but 'I shall not give up the plan ... unless I should see that success is not to be looked for.'[9] Nevertheless, the knowledge that Marmont was much stronger weighed heavily on Wellington's mind over the next six weeks. Worse still, when the Anglo-Portuguese Army reached Salamanca, Wellington found two improvised forts to be far stronger than he had previously expected. As he had marched without sufficient artillery for a siege, there now ensued a long delay in reducing the defences, a delay which gave Marmont extra breathing space to concentrate his force.

The garrison of the forts only surrendered on 27 June when the roofs of the convents were set alight with red-hot shot. In the meantime, Marmont approached Salamanca, and the two armies prepared for battle on the heights of San Cristóbal, to the north-east of the city. Wellington, in an extremely strong position, refused to attack Marmont, who also declined battle, and the French slunk away in the night of 21 June. Wellington was criticised by some of his subordinates for not attacking the French, but he retorted that although 'the superiority of numbers in the field was on our side, the superiority was not so great as to render an action decisive of the result of the campaign, in which we would sustain great loss'. In other words, 'Marmont will not risk an action unless he should have an advantage; and I shall certainly not risk one unless I should have an advantage; and matters therefore do not appear likely to be brought to that criterion very soon.'[10]

Wellington chased Marmont north to the River Duero, where the French encamped for a fortnight on the northern bank. The British occupied positions between Tordesillas and Pollos. During this lull in operations, the armies mingled amiably in the cool waters of the Duero, but the stalemate ended on 17 July, when Marmont outflanked Wellington in a surprise crossing on the allied right.

The Anglo-Portuguese Army now fell back to the south-west, towards Salamanca. There followed a series of confused skirmishes at Castrejón and Castrillo on the banks of the Guareña, before the armies fell into a parallel line of march. 'It was a fine sight to see the two armies in motion at the same time,' recalled one participant. 'They moved parallel to each other, and at no time were more than two miles distant ... Their object is to get between us and Portugal, thereby obliging us to move as they do and eventually it must end in us being obliged to quit Spain or fight.'[11] These movements taught Wellington a valuable lesson. Marmont's army, unencumbered by a lengthy supply train, had been lighter and more manoeuvrable than the Anglo-Portuguese Army. Discounting any unforeseen French mistakes, Wellington's army would itself have to become lighter and nimbler if it were to stand a chance of outmanoeuvring its enemy.

Fortunately, the French were to make a catastrophic mistake that would give Wellington the opportunity he needed to attack. On the morning of 22 July, Marmont tried to outflank Wellington a few miles south of Salamanca. As he wheeled his army to the right, his line became overextended, and a gap appeared between the leading French divisions and the rest of the Army of Portugal.

Thomières, an ambitious young general in command of the leading French division, had marched on too fast, and was now advancing rapidly to the west, towards a small range of hills, the Monte de Azan, which overlooked any route Wellington would retreat along. Marmont was about to send counter-orders to Thomières when a chance artillery shot from the British battery blew his left arm off. In the British camp, Wellington was eating his lunch in a farmyard that had a view across the plain between the British and French armies. At about half past two, he was 'walking about … munching, with his field-glass in his hand, and constantly looking through it. On a sudden he exclaimed, "By G——, they are extending their line; order my horses." ' Wellington realised that Thomières was marching his division straight into line with the Third Division, under the temporary command of Edward Pakenham, which that morning had been sent to the far west flank to provide cover for any possible retreat. 'He galloped straight to Pakenham's division and desired him immediately to begin the attack.'[12]

At this point, with the joining of battle still a couple of hours away, Thomières's mistake can only have been apparent to the practised eye. By now Maucune, who commanded the second French division, had deployed his force between Thomières's extended division and the dominant feature of the battlefield, the Greater Arapile – a 90-foot-high isolated hill with excellent views of the whole area, and from which Marmont had commanded the army until his injury. The British, meanwhile, occupied the second dominant feature of the battlefield, the Lesser Arapile, a few hundred yards to the north. Had Marmont not been injured, Thomières's advance would have been stopped, and it is difficult to predict how the attack of the Third Division would have unfolded. Wellington's decision was no simple matter, and carried with it enormous risk.[13]

Having delivered instructions to Pakenham to advance and attack Thomières's divison when he found it, Wellington now galloped back to his main line and told Leith and the Fifth Division to prepare to advance in line towards Maucune's division, in what was to become the French centre. Leith was to begin his attack as soon as battle was joined by the Third Division on the far right. Next, Cole was ordered to advance with the Fourth Division to attack the French around the Greater Arapile, while Pack's Portuguese brigade was given the task of attacking the Greater Arapile itself. The Light and First Divisions were ordered to protect the British left flank, which was threatened by two French divisions commanded by Foy and Ferey.

The Third Division advanced along the road toward Thomières's division, which was hidden from view by the undulating terrain. Arriving at the base of the Pico de Miranda, a steep hill, the Third Division formed into three lines, each a brigade in strength, and began to advance up the hill. When the leading brigade, commanded by Colonel John Wallace, made contact with the French, the right and left flanks were able to curve inwards, creating a crescent shape which completely surrounded the French. William Grattan bore vivid witness to the initial attack:

> The soldiers ... speedily got footing upon the brow of the hill, but before they had time to take breath, [Thomières's] entire division, with drums beating and uttering loud shouts, ran forward to meet them, and belching forth a torrent of bullets from five thousand muskets, brought down almost the entire of [the front] rank ... The brigade staggered back from the force of the shock, but before the smoke had altogether cleared away, Wallace, looking full in the faces of his soldiers pointed to the French column, and leading the shattered brigade up the hill, without a moment's hesitation, brought them face to face [with] the French ... Astounded by the unshaken determination of Wallace's soldiers, [Thomières's] division wavered; nevertheless they opened a heavy discharge of musketry, but it was unlike the former ... At length their fire ceased altogether, and the three regiments, for the first time, *cheered*! The effect was electric; [Thomières's] troops were seized with a panic ...[14]

Meanwhile, the British cavalry regiments of Arentschildt and D'Urban swept around the British right to neutralise the threat posed by Curto's light cavalry. Having suffered a devastating blow, and now outflanked by British cavalry, Thomières's division collapsed, and began a headlong retreat back along the Monte de Azan, where it collided with Maucune's division, which was by now facing its own threat.

Maucune, meanwhile, had brought his artillery to bear on the exposed British troops of the Fifth Division, behind the village of Los Arapiles.

Leith, having received his orders, told his men to lie down, 'though he sat on horseback, exposed to the fire as calm as possible'. He then delivered an inspirational speech, which reveals once more the importance of the bayonet to British infantry morale. 'The day shall be a glorious day for Old England,' he said: 'if these bragadocian [sic] rascals dare but stand their ground, we will display the point of the British bayonet, and where it is properly displayed no power is able to withstand it.'[15] Hearing the clash of arms to his right on the Pico de Miranda, Leith now ordered the advance of the Fifth Division. It must have been a spectacular sight, the quintessential thin red line of British soldiers stretching over 1,500 yards. But this was not Maucune's first consideration. Behind the British infantry, which now advanced out of sight of the French troops into the undulations in the terrain, Maucune could see Le Marchant's cavalry brigade preparing a charge. Anticipating a cavalry assault before Leith's infantry, Maucune ordered his division into square. Leith's troops now reappeared closer than Maucune had anticipated. 'General Leith ordered the line to fire, and charge: the roll of musketry was succeeded by that proud cheer that has become habitual to British soldiers on similar occasions.' As soon as the British troops saw the French in square, 'we gave a shout opened a tremendous fire and ran into them directly so that that line was in a few minutes killed and taken prisoners'. The same story, of a single musket volley followed by a charge 'according [to] the English custom ... show[ing] them the point of the bayonet', is told all along the line.[16]

From the west Le Marchant's cavalry now thundered in, sweeping up the remnants of Thomières's division and Maucune's left flank before attacking the leading regiment of a third French division, commanded by General Taupin. This had been sent up in support by the new French commander, General Clausel. The French left, under attack from the advancing infantry of Pakenham's Third and Leith's Fifth Divisions, as well as the cavalry of Le Marchant, now disintegrated. Things were not proceeding quite so successfully in the centre, however. Clausel counterattacked with two divisions, to the west of the Greater Arapile, against the troops of Cole's Fourth Division who were advancing from the Lesser Arapile. The fighting here became intense. The French front rank failed to make any headway, and fell back on the much stronger rear echelon, numbering some 3,000 troops. 'The French ... came up the hill with a brisk and regular step ... our men fired wildly and at random among them,' recalled John Burgoyne, who was on the right of the Fourth Division's advance. 'The French never returned a shot, but continued their steady advance. The English fired again, ... but men in such confusion had no chance against the perfect order of the enemy, and when the French were close upon them, they wavered and gave way.'[17]

Outflanked on the right by Clausel and with his centre also threatened by the failure of Dennis Pack's brigade to take the Arapile itself, Cole's position became untenable. Even before Cole's attack faltered, Wellington sent in the Sixth Division in support. Allowing the fleeing troops of the Fourth to pass through its ranks, the Sixth now advanced afresh on the two divisions making Clausel's counter-attack. 'The brigade . . . advanced in line and entered the plain in front of the enemy's position, and within range of their batteries, which commenced a fire upon us,' recalled one officer.[18] The fighting became intense, but, suffering from damage inflicted by the British artillery on the Lesser Arapile, Clausel's counterattack collapsed and his men retreated headlong behind the Greater Arapile.

The action now moved to the undulating wooded ground to the south of the Greater Arapile. There, General Ferrey formed two divisions in a rearguard defensive line, allowing the five shattered French divisions to retreat. Wellington ordered the Sixth Division to attack this strong defensive line, supported by the Third and Fifth, whilst the remains of the Fourth, now restored to order, would attack Ferrey's northern flank. There was great unhappiness with the decision to attack directly. Pakenham preferred to attack Ferrey's left, and reportedly said that 'to do otherwise, is taking the bull by the horns'.[19] Another participant, Colonel de Lancey, the acting Quartermaster-General, also expressed disquiet. 'The enemy retired from the Field of Action towards Alba de Tormes and to cover his retreat occupied a strong height on the road,' he wrote to Sir George Murray. 'The height however was attacked and carried by the 6th Division but at the expense of 1,000 men.'[20] The fighting, indeed, was intense. The Sixth Division 'had approached within two hundred yards . . . before the fire of musketry began . . . and was accompanied by constant discharges of grape', recalled Captain Harry Ross-Lewin of the 32nd Foot. 'An uninterrupted blaze was then maintained, so that the crest of the hill seemed to be one long streak of flame.'[21] The Sixth persisted in its attack, however, and, with the remains of the Fourth Division outflanking his right, Ferrey gave way. The Battle of Salamanca was over. It had been extremely bloody. The allies sustained 5,000 casualties, including 700 dead. French losses were 12,500, including nearly 7,000 prisoners.

By now darkness was falling, and the Anglo-Portuguese Army was too exhausted to pursue the retreating French. In any event, Wellington expected their route to be cut off by the brigade of Carlos d'España, who had been given orders to hold the bridge at Alba de Tormes. However, the latter had not done so, giving the French the opportunity to escape.

Wellington was, of course, furious, but there was little that could be done. To be fair to d'España, the overwhelming impression he had got from Wellington's movements on 20–21 July was that the Anglo-Portuguese Army was about to retreat, leaving his brigade cut off. He prudently, although mistakenly, opted to retreat himself. His gravest error was not informing Wellington.

In fighting the Battle of Salamanca, Wellington had transformed the military situation in Spain. Soult's position in Andalusia was rendered untenable by the advance of the allies, and the French Marshal was inevitably forced to give up the siege of Cadiz and evacuate south-western Spain. Wellington thus achieved two objectives in attacking Marmont. Salamanca also marked a sea change in his approach to warfare. Gone – but not forgotten – was the caution witnessed at Talavera and Buçaco, to be replaced by the confident opportunism which had driven Wellington's tactical decisions in India. Wellington still faced three French armies in Spain: the North, the South and Catalonia, to say nothing of the remnants of the Army of Portugal, now in the capable hands of Clausel. If the Anglo-Portuguese Army was to stand a chance of attacking and defeating them, it would need to become a far more manoeuvrable and flexible force. Unfortunately, the autumn campaign of 1812 was to demonstrate the importance of this lesson – and Wellington's failure adequately to implement it.

* * *

The Battle of Salamanca concluded a troublesome eighteen months for Wellington. Although it was ultimately successful, the toll on his army had been heavy, and he still faced his political opponents in London. Following the fall of Badajoz, Grey remarked cynically that the 'news from Portugal . . . is just enough to show that all this immense expense of blood and treasure is fruitless'.[22] The continued military success of the Anglo-Portuguese Army did keep the political opposition in check, but, as usual, it was crises within government that caused Wellington more angst. In May 1812, an insane Norfolk farmer assassinated the Prime Minister, Spencer Perceval, in the lobby of the House of Commons. The government consequently suffered a major upheaval, with Lord Liverpool becoming Prime Minister, the War Department going to Lord Bathurst, and Castlereagh returning to the government as Foreign Secretary.

The last appointment was probably the most disconcerting for Wellington, for it occurred not because of the assassination of Perceval, but because his brother, Richard, resigned from office in March in an elaborate, and ultimately unsuccessful attempt to oust Perceval and Liverpool, acquire the keys to Downing Street for himself, and restore his old friend

Canning to office. If only he had waited. Wellington was forced to assign his loyalty to either the government or his brother, a difficult decision given the intense family loyalty that existed between the Wellesley brothers. On the surface, Richard could hope for Wellington's support. The brothers agreed that neither Perceval nor Liverpool was wholly committed to the war in the Peninsula. Wellington believed that Perceval had been complicit in the attempts by the Treasury to starve him of money, an exaggerated view, but unsurprising, given the close ties between Perceval and the Treasury. Liverpool's crime was failing to support Wellington in every single bad-tempered request the General had made. 'Mr Perceval was a very honest man,' he wrote to William, 'whose views were rather limited by professional habits and those acquired by long practice . . . I think he did not take a sufficiently enlarged view of our situation here; nor does Lord Liverpool.'[23] Wellington might not have been totally wrong about Perceval, but his attitude to Liverpool was wholly unfair. Under the most difficult of circumstances, Liverpool had constantly defended Wellington's actions, with little or no support from his cabinet colleagues. Pressured by the financial crisis of 1811, it was no surprise that he had been unable to meet every one of Wellington's innumerable demands.

Wellington, though, saw which way the wind was blowing. He backed Liverpool as Prime Minister in the wake of Perceval's death. His decision was politically motivated and completely dispassionate. Realising that Richard lacked the support in Parliament to form an administration, he needed to maintain his relationships with those in charge: Liverpool's administration remained committed to the war. It must have been a terrible decision to make, and marked the end of a political alliance that had endured ups and downs since 1798. Wellington was the only brother not to offer Richard his support. William lost his place in government because he supported his brother, and Henry considered resigning. It is fortunate that he did not, as Wellington would need Henry's support in Spain in the months ahead. Unsurprisingly, Wellington's decision precipitated a break with Richard that would never be fully repaired.[24]

Shattering though this must have been, it was not the only political obstacle Wellington faced in the first six months of 1812. The other problem, was a continued shortage of funds. 'I can scarcely believe that the Treasury is aware of the distresses of this army,' Wellington ranted to the ever-patient Liverpool in April 1812. 'We owe not less than 5 million dollars; the troops are two months in arrears and I have been able to allot only 100,000 dollars to the payment of the Portuguese subsidy . . .' On top of this, the commissariat had run out of money to pay for supplies, and there was no money with which to pay the mule drivers who brought supplies up from the coast. 'It is not improbable,' concluded Wellington, 'that we may not be able to take advantage of the enemy's comparative weakness in this campaign for want of money.'[25] Wellington could complain all he liked, but there was nothing Liverpool could do. The coffers were dry. To make matters worse, a new war with the United States had severely limited British trading opportunities, and the government also had to fork out vast amounts to subsidise the Russian war effort against Napoleon. Attempts by the Treasury to circumvent the lack of specie by issuing promissory notes and Treasury certificates were not working because local supply merchants placed little value on the former – they were fearful the British would evacuate the Peninsula without making good on these debts – and the latter were driving up the exchange rate between the dollar and pound. There seemed no solution.

A reprieve came, morbidly, with the assassination of Perceval. Liverpool's replacement at the War Department, Henry, Earl Bathurst, was a less strait-laced politician. Perceiving the desperate state of affairs in Spain, he used a little-known legal loophole to compel the Bank of England to release its gold reserves for payment of troops abroad. By the autumn of 1812, Bathurst was able to send £100,000 a month to Wellington. Although not everything Wellington asked for, it went some way to alle- viating the British General's immediate monetary worries.[26] Bathurst's actions carried considerable political risk. 'For this I shall have my head off, if we should not succeed,' Bathurst remarked to his friend Charles Harrowby.[27] In the summer of 1812, with Wellington triumphant and the French in retreat, the possibility of failure must have seemed remote.

With the shattered Army of Portugal now fleeing north, Wellington was free to advance on Madrid, entering the city on 12 August, having faced no resistance from Joseph. All who entered Madrid recorded scenes of adulation and joy amongst the population. Many a soldier's cheek was kissed by a pretty lady, but Private Wheeler recalled an altogether different experience:

Amidst all this pleasure and happiness we were obliged to submit to a custom, so unenglish that I cannot but feel disgust now I am writing. It was to be kissed by the men. What made it still worse, their breath was so highly seasoned with garlic, then their huge moustaches well stiff- ened with sweat, dust and snuff, it was like having a hair broom pushed into one's face that had been daubed in a dirty gutter.[28]

Jubilant though the celebrations were, Wellington was well aware he was riding from a military battle into a political storm that had been brewing for three years. Ever since Wellington had begun fighting in the Peninsula, there had been talk of making him Commander-in-Chief of all allied military forces, including the Spanish Army. Until now, the provisional Spanish government had resisted appointing a foreigner as commander of its armies, but Wellington's victory at Salamanca and the liberation of Madrid now set the conditions for his appointment.

Reluctant to accept it, Wellington nevertheless knew that he needed to be made Commander-in-Chief of all allied forces in the Peninsula, to have any chance of assembling a force large enough to defeat all of the French armies in Spain. The main problem was one of coordination. With no overall commander, the British, Portuguese and Spanish Armies could not be coordinated in a combined operation against the French. Instead, the same story would repeat itself:

> The enemy will collect ... a larger body of troops than the allied British and Portuguese army can bring into the field, and will oblige us to take the defensive, and they will experience no danger or even inconvenience from their weakness in all other parts of the Peninsula in consequence of their collecting their whole force to oppose us because the Spanish Armies are neither disciplined nor provided nor equipped in such a manner as that they can perform any operation even of the most trifling ...[29]

Indeed, this had been the story since Wellington arrived in the Peninsula, and continued to be the case throughout 1812. Although the allies repeatedly achieved extraordinary tactical success, the French were repeatedly allowed to escape and concentrate in greater force, preventing the allies from turning tactical victory into strategic success. One of the primary reasons for these failures was the fact that the Spanish were unable or unwilling to operate in partnership with Wellington.

Wellington's opinion of his allies had been heavily influenced by the numerous military failures that had engulfed the Spanish armies between 1809 and 1811, many of which Wellington considered to have been avoidable. In 1809, as Napoleon had crammed Spain full of French troops, and Wellington had recognised the need for the British to retire into Portugal, he suggested that the Spanish government adopt a defensive strategy. Instead, for a wide variety of reasons, chiefly its own political security, the government ordered a general offensive. The defeats that followed were as inevitable and futile as they were calamitous. 'I declare that if they had preserved their armies, or even one of them, the cause was safe,' Wellington had written in late 1809. 'But no! Nothing will answer excepting to fight great battles in plains in which their defeat is as certain as the commencement of the battle.'[30] Rather than planning for the long term, the Spanish government, army, press and population looked only for the next short-term success and were incapable of organising or mounting a sustained defence of their own nation. 'The Spanish nation will not sit down soberly and work to produce an effect at a future period,' Wellington wrote in frustration to Henry. 'Their courage and even their activity is of a passive nature, and must be forced upon them by the necessity of their circumstances, and is never a matter of choice or foresight.'[31]

Wellington's problem was that he could only view events in Spain through a military lens, and could therefore only conceive of a military solution. But Spain was also in the throes of political revolution. After Soult's invasion of Andalusia in late 1809 and the capture of Seville in early 1810, the Central Junta was deposed in favour of the Council of Regency, headed for the next two years by military personnel – first Castaños, and then the Anglophobe, Blake – based in Cadiz. The key difference between this council and the Central Junta was the establishment of a Cortes – a Spanish Parliament. The new Spanish government marked a shift to liberal politics, which was not wholeheartedly supported throughout Spain. The Spanish armies, meanwhile, remained bloated, top-heavy, corrupt organisations. Refusing to appoint a Commander-in-Chief, as they were fearful of the power such an office would hold, and because they did not want to relinquish strategic decision-making themselves, the Regency Council had, in December 1810, reorganised the Spanish military into six regional armies, each with its own headquarters. Far from improving coordination, this merely produced increasingly isolated enclaves, which became dependent on their locale for supplies. The system effectively paralysed Spanish military capability, and left the troops themselves chronically short of equipment and supplies. 'All the Spanish troops I see are of a most despicable description, neither clothed, paid, disciplined or even organised, and but precariously fed,' observed one commentator.[32] Continued Spanish military failings, notably at the Battle of Barrosa in March 1811, and the unnecessary capitulation of Badajoz in the same month, further darkened Wellington's opinion of his allies. 'This defeat goes to the vitals of the cause,' he wrote to Henry, 'and it would certainly have been avoided if the Spaniards had been anything but Spaniards.'[33]

The combination of poor military performance, political revolution and incompetent and decentralised command also meant there was no obvious Spanish candidate for the role of Commander-in-Chief. 'There is not a general officer in the service of Spain whose character has not in some

way or other suffered in the opinion of his countrymen by the events of
the revolution,' Henry reported in March 1811. 'All these generals have
their partisans and followers in the different armies so that if one of them
happens to be appointed to a command he is certain of finding two thirds
of his army prepared to counteract his views.'[34] On the one hand, then,
Wellington knew that a single unified Commander-in-Chief was needed
to bring order to the chaos that was the Spanish military. On the other
hand, he was reluctant to volunteer for such a role, bearing in mind the
obstinacy and incompetence that he perceived were the hallmarks of his
counterparts in the Spanish Army.

To both Richard and Henry Wellesley, though, it was apparent that
Wellington was the best candidate, and, probably as early as 1809, the two
began manoeuvring to have Wellington appointed Commander-in-Chief.
The parallels with the political campaigns that preceded Wellington's
military operations in India are clear. As in India, military success in Spain
would only be achieved once a sense of political direction and clarity was
established between the allies. Throughout the Peninsular War, the
Wellesley brothers spent a great deal of time and energy attempting to have
Wellington appointed Commander-in-Chief. As in India, one of the most
serious obstacles was convincing the Spaniards that the British had no
ulterior motive, but Britain's conduct in the war so far had reinforced the
opinion in Spain that all issues were subordinate to Britain's key interests.
The key issue was the opening of the South American market to British
trade. From Britain's perspective, this would guarantee a ready supply of
bullion that would, in turn, sustain the war effort in Spain. For Spain, this
manoeuvring, combined with ambiguous British support when rebellions
broke out in South America, suggested that Britain wanted to take control
of all of Spain's colonies. This was not an unreasonable conclusion, based
on the evidence of Britain's failed military escapades in Buenos Aires in
1806. Closer to home, Wellington's actions in 1809, and the abandonment
of Spain to defend Portugal in 1810, only accentuated the belief in Cadiz
that Britain's commitment to the war in Spain was questionable.

It was something of shock, then, when the Spanish Cortes appeared to
give consideration to offering Wellington the position of Commander-in-
Chief in early 1811, even before Massena had retreated from Portugal and
the gamble of the Torres Vedras campaign was justified. 'There seems to be
a strong disposition in the Cortes to appoint you Generalissimo of the
Spanish Armies, and to employ English officers in the army,' wrote Henry
to Wellington in January. 'I think it very probable that these questions may
soon be brought forward in the Cortes, who seem to be perfectly aware that
their own officers are good for nothing.'[35] Wellington smelled a rat. In any

event, he decided, he could not accept the command of the Spanish Armies without the authority to conduct root and branch reforms to the pay, supply and equipment infrastructure of the military. Without such reforms, his appointment would 'certainly not answer any purpose whatever excepting to throw upon me additional trouble, and the blame and odium of certain ultimate failure'.[36] This changed the nature of the Anglo-Spanish relationship. Wellington was proposing a fundamental reorganisation of the central government departments. At the very least, Henry was aware that Spain could not currently afford this. 'I see no prospect of any improvement in the Spanish armies, and without a complete change in their military system it is in vain to hope for success against the French,' he wrote despondently to Richard. In the event, the offer was never made. Futile as the episode had been, it had at least clarified in Wellington's mind the terms on which he would accept the command of the Spanish Armies.

The opportunity for Wellington to press his reforms on the Spanish government came in 1812. Alongside the ongoing military success of the Anglo-Portuguese Army, the Spanish military continued to suffer a string of defeats, culminating with the loss of Valencia. As a result, the Blake Regency was deposed in January 1812, and was replaced with a new government, headed by the more liberal-leaning Duque del Infantado, who immediately began drafting a new constitution that transformed Spain into a limited constitutional monarchy, under the representative leadership of the Cortes. Simultaneously, Wellington's popularity increased in the wake of the capture of Ciudad Rodrigo and Badajoz. In April, for example, he was forced to wave to the admiring crowds in Ciudad Rodrigo for an hour and a half, a circumstance which he must have loved and hated in equal measure. The Order of the Golden Fleece was then conferred on him for the victory at Salamanca. Wellington was also building political bridges. Despite serious reservations, as he advanced through Spain he proclaimed the new Constitution of 1812.[37] The Regency also ordered its generals to support Wellington, and most did their best to support British operations in Salamanca. By mid-September, observers reported that 'from the respect and confidence which all the Spanish officers place in his military talents ... he now exercises almost as much authority as he could do under a regular commission from the government'.[38] Nevertheless, Wellington was aware that this authority was fleeting, if not illusory. This was never more clearly demonstrated than in d'España's failure to hold the bridge at Alba de Tormes after the Battle of Salamanca. Only official appointment as Commander-in-Chief would allow him to exercise real authority and decision-making power.

With little other options available to it, then, the Spanish government, in secret session, voted on 22 September to make Wellington Commander-in-Chief of the Spanish armies. But the appointment was misleading. Although Wellington was appointed Commander-in-Chief, the position carried with it none of the criteria that he believed would be necessary for him to accept the post. For instance, he had no control of civilian authorities, meaning he was unable to reform the supply, payment and equipment systems of the army: regional civilian governments controlled these. Indeed, the offer of the command was so carefully worded that Wellington would effectively be subordinated to the Spanish government, which still retained control of the strategic direction of the war.[39] Although Wellington never realised the full implications, he clearly had suspicions, which inflamed his concerns about accepting such a role. 'The consequence of entering into such a convention,' he had written as early as March 1812 to Liverpool, 'would be that I should bind myself ... to perform a certain operation even after my own judgement should have convinced me that ... I ought to discontinue it.'[40] Worse still, that the offer was made at all enraged some of the other potential candidates for the position, most notably General Ballesteros. When he heard of the offer to Wellington, Ballesteros attempted to usurp the government, but he failed to carry the support of his whole army, which had been watching Soult in Andalusia. Placed under arrest, Ballesteros was eventually sent to the Balearic Islands in disgrace.

Needless to say, when the offer was made, Wellington was deeply sceptical, but the prospect of being able to coordinate the combined forces of Britain, Spain and Portugal, now that he was so far advanced into Spain, was too good to refuse outright. Still, Wellington was unconvinced by the offer. He referred the decision on whether to accept to London, promising to 'guard against the pretensions which the Spanish Government might form to direct the operations of the war in consequence of this appointment of me to command the Spanish armies'.[41] It was inevitable that Whitehall would agree that Wellington should accept the command, but, in the event, Wellington did not receive confirmation until late November. Had he accepted it at once, he could have used the political credibility established by his military success to extract concessions from the Spanish government. As it was, Wellington accepted the command as the Anglo-Portuguese Army retreated headlong back to the Portuguese frontier, his plans for the consolidation of the allied control of Madrid, and his military reputation alike, in tatters.

*   *   *

Wellington's decision to liberate Madrid had always been politically, rather than militarily motivated. Although possession of the Spanish capital offered several military advantages, most obviously the opportunity to concentrate a central defence, there were also severe shortcomings to the position, notably the over-extended lines of supply and communication which rendered the allied flank vulnerable to assault. For the French, meanwhile, Wellington's liberation of Madrid provided the opportunity to regroup and concentrate in force against the allies. Had Wellington kept up his momentum, and directly attacked one of the other armies in Spain, possibly Soult in Andalusia, or Cafferelli and the Army of the North, he could have prevented such a union. On the other hand, his army was not in good condition. True, morale was high, but in the course of operations in the first six months of 1812, it had accumulated over 10,000 casualties of its own. Constant operations would further wear down its strength. Weighing the pros and cons of his decision, then, it seems there was little option but to move on Madrid, allow his army to rest and recuperate, and reap the political benefits that came with such a move.

As expected, the forces of the remaining French armies in the Peninsula soon began to concentrate in Valencia against the allies, and it became clear that the French aimed to pursue one of two options. Wellington had become concerned with the surprise threat of a revived Army of Portugal under the command of General Bertrand Clausel, which had reoccupied Valladolid[42] and now threatened to either encircle the allies, or combine with Joseph, Soult and Suchet on the line of the River Ebro. The belief that the French were following the latter stratagem was still prevalent as late as 18 October when Edward Pakenham wrote of Soult's 'liberty either to come up in a direct line to the Tagus, or by Turning [his force] put the Ebro in his rear, over which he could best retire in the event of accident; I rather imagine they suppose the latter to be his plan from the inclination of our Light Corps in that direction'.[43]

Wellington had three options. He could advance with his entire force against one of the French armies, probably the Army of Portugal, and hope the momentum of the advance forced the Armies of the South and Centre to retreat as well. There was significant risk attached to such a strategy, however. Continuing the advance risked over-extending the lines of supply and communication and opening them up to attack from the south, if Soult and Joseph decided to attack Madrid rather than retreat behind the Ebro. Alternatively, Wellington could advance, with a portion of his force, against the Army of Portugal while it was in Valladolid. With enough strength, he might be able to destroy Clausel's army in detail, and return to Madrid in time to face Soult and Joseph as they advanced from Valencia. This operation required precision timing and buckets of luck. Thirdly, Wellington could consolidate his position.

Wellington chose to advance against Clausel in Valladolid, with 22,000 men, supported, in theory, by the Spanish Sixth Army, which had recently captured Astorga. Defending Madrid was a political imperative, so Wellington once again divided his force, leaving Hill to defend the Spanish capital. Having apparently learned the lesson of the Salamanca Campaign, Wellington sought to ensure his forces were light and manoeuvrable by taking only three guns with him. However, the advance of his detachment was anything but speedy, and, when the Sixth Army, delayed by supply problems around Astorga, failed to reinforce Wellington, causing the advance against Valladolid to stall, the British general decided to adopt the third option, of consolidating his position, and advanced to Burgos. There, he sought to establish a strong defensive position running from south of the River Ebro, in the north-east of Spain, to the north of the River Tagus, south of Madrid. Capturing Burgos was critical to the plan's success, 'as it commands the great road to Madrid by Aranda; as well as that to Valladolid; and gives us with the River Arlanzon an excellent winter position for the defence of the Northern provinces'.[44] This would have given the allies a means of holding their position for the winter and forcing the French north in the New Year.

Aware that the heavy rains of the autumn would swell the Tagus, Wellington was proposing to use the natural barriers of the Peninsula to prevent the French attacking Madrid. This was made all the more urgent by the fact that if the enemy intended to move on Madrid, although the combined force of Joseph and Suchet was not large enough to do so, with Soult, the French had a total of 73,000 troops.[45] If Wellington wanted to defend Madrid successfully and make the Tagus his southern defensive line, then he had to prevent Joseph, Suchet and Soult from combining early enough to cross the Tagus before it flooded. In August, he therefore ordered Hill to 'move with activity upon Drouet [Comte d'Erlon, who commanded part of Soult's force] ... and to threaten to enter Andalusia'.[46] In late October, he also ordered the destruction of all the bridges across the river, from Toledo to Alcántara.[47] At what point Wellington concluded on this course of action is unclear. Certainly, it was after he had left Madrid, which would explain why only three guns accompanied the allies on their advance to Burgos. Alternatively, false intelligence from Popham in Santander that the French had evacuated Burgos[48] might have induced the British general to advance with just a light siege train to facilitate rapid movement.

On 19 August, Soult was preparing to leave Granada and evacuate Andalusia. He planned to move north and east in combination with D'Erlon, pressing Hill to retreat.[49] By 21 September, Hill had indeed retreated to Toledo and Aranjuez, leaving Alten's Light Division and

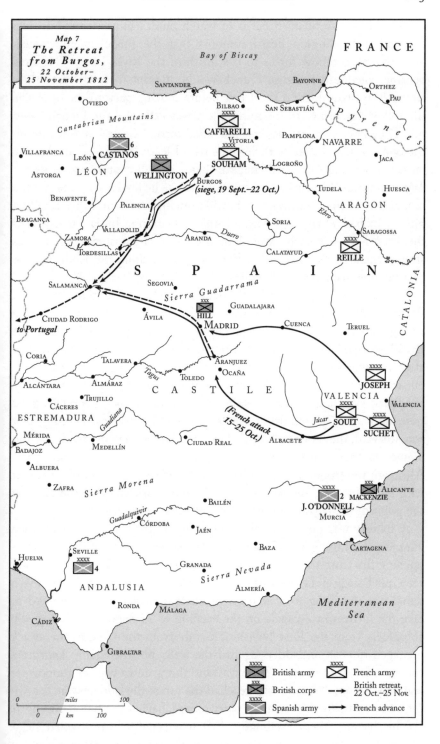

Map 7
The Retreat from Burgos,
22 October–
25 November 1812

Carlos d'España's Spanish corps to watch Soult's movements.[50] In late September, Wellington heard rumours that the French were, indeed, preparing to combine forces to the north of the River Ebro.[51] He thus became convinced that the French would attempt to consolidate their strength in Spain behind the Ebro, before moving back to the offensive the following spring. To his mind, there was little else the French could do. 'They have to guard against the allied force collected at Alicante on the one hand, and against Ballesteros who I learn is to be about Alcáraz on the other, and can hardly believe that they will continue towards the Tagus in force.'[52] In coming to this conclusion, he obviously preferred the judgement of his intuition to what his intelligence sources were telling him, as he had when faced with a similar situation in India. He expected the French to act as he would in the same circumstances. This was strengthened by the fact that a French retreat behind the Ebro was the best possible scenario for the allies.

Having failed to force a battle with Clausel's reconstituted Army of Portugal, Wellington fell, instead, upon Burgos in an attempt to form a strong defensive line. The siege began successfully enough when the British stormed a hornwork to the north of the main fortress immediately after arriving before Burgos on 19 September. 'The night was very dark, but we were soon perceived by the enemy,' recalled a corporal in the 42nd, the Black Watch, 'and in an instant all the works opened upon us a most tremendous fire of roundshot, shells, grape and musketry.' Forcing their way forward, the 'Forlorn Hope' placed the ladders against the walls and 'found, to their great grief, that they were about two feet too short'. Although the frontal assault failed, a diversionary assault on the rear met with less resistance, and was to enter the hornwork, carrying the place 'at the point of the bayonet in the course of fifteen minutes'.[53]

A battery was quickly established with the three guns – nicknamed Thunder, Lightning and Nelson, after the latter lost one of its trunions – opening fire from the north-east on to the outer walls. Wellington, eager for a quick siege and conscious that he needed to act to secure his southern flank, was unwilling to wait for a practicable breach, and attempted to take the fortress by escalade on the evening of 22 September. Using 400 volunteers from the First Division, mainly from the Guards, the attack managed to position ladders against the walls, but the enemy 'kept up a constant fire from the top of the wall and threw down bags of gunpowder and large stones'.[54] Those who reached the top of the ladders were thrown off, and eventually the storming party retired, having lost half its strength.

This having failed, Wellington had to engage in a protracted siege. Owing to his lack of guns, he resorted to the time-consuming process of mining, but had still not been provided with a corps of sappers or miners, despite a request for one after Badajoz. A second parallel was dug to the north-east against the relatively weak outer wall. A mine was exploded on 29 September, but was found to have been positioned too far from the wall and did little damage. A second, successful, attempt was made to storm the outer wall on 4 October, using two breaches created by new batteries. Now the British faced an imposing inner defensive wall, whilst being effectively 'kettled' within the perimeter of the outer wall. They were thus exposed to constant harassment from the garrison, including repeated sorties. One particularly bloody attack, costing no fewer than 120 casualties, took place on 7 October, when 'aided by the most tremendous fire which I ever saw of cannon, they succeeded in driving us out ... but a small party of about thirty of our men maintained themselves behind a breastwork ... from their spirited conduct the work was regained.'[55]

Finding the wall on the north corner impenetrable, Wellington decided on a last-ditch assault on 19 October. A feint would be made against the north corner, while two simultaneous attacks would be launched: from the south-west, starting from the base of the hill on which the fortress was built, and from the north-east, from the direction of the hornwork, where a small breach had been established. Facilitating the assault from the south-west, a mine had been dug under a chapel which had been improvised as a bastion at the base of the outer defences of the fortress. Each storming party was composed of 300 volunteers from the Guards and the King's German Legion. Attacking from the bottom of the hill, one participant recalled that 'a most tremendous fire opened upon us from every part which took us in front and rear. They poured down fresh men, and ours kept falling down into the ditch, dragging and knocking down others ... The fire was tremendous: shot, shell, grape, musketry, large stones, hand grenades and every missile weapon were used against us.'[56]

The resistance was too fierce, and the small storming parties were eventually overcome. The siege failed partly because the attempts to lay mines hadn't had the desired effect, partly because Wellington did not have his best troops with him, partly because the three walled defences of the citadel were too strong, and partly because the three guns Wellington had brought with him were completely unsuitable for the task at hand. But the siege mainly failed because of Wellington's caution and reluctance to engage in sieges properly. Wellington has been blamed for the tactical mismanagement of the siege, not unfairly. Devastated by the losses he encountered at Badajoz, where entire divisions had been used to overcome the French defenders, Wellington attempted to keep casualties to a minimum, but in doing so he doomed them to failure. This did not go unnoticed within the army, with one commentator noting that confidence 'in all desperate cases is to be acquired by numerical superiority'.[57] Wellington was therefore accruing a seriously poor record in siege warfare.

On 19 October he wrote to Hill:

> I hope that the rain which annoys us so much reaches you likewise and I should state that you will have the Tagus in such a state as I feel no apprehension in regard to the enemy's operations be their numbers what they may. It is quite clear to me however, that the King, Soult and Suchet are joined on the frontier of Murcia and Valencia from the accounts from Madrid, of the 9th that I received today, and from letters from Alicante of the 29th.[58]

Unfortunately, the plan had come unstuck. In the south, Soult's force had proven too strong for Hill, partly because diversionary support, promised by Ballesteros, failed to materialise when the latter chose instead to try and usurp the government. There was little Hill could do, then, to prevent a conjunction of the three French commanders in late September. Despite Hill destroying bridges in Toledo, Almáraz and Alcántara,[59] the three French commanders were able to manoeuvre towards Madrid. The rains that drenched Wellington at Burgos came late in Madrid and the Tagus valley and the river did not flood as early as it had in previous years, allowing the French the opportunity to ford the river, thereby threatening Hill's communications with Wellington.[60]

On top of this, Wellington was unaware that Cafferelli, commanding the Army of the North, had temporarily vanquished the *guerrilla* in Cantabria, and was now bearing down on Burgos, in support of Souham, who had succeeded Clausel in command of the Army of Portugal. Wellington later admitted that he 'had no notion that the enemy could have been so much reinforced, particularly in cavalry, or that the army of the North could come so far down . . .'[61] With the siege progressing badly, he settled upon a retreat. The gamble, then, had not paid off. On the night between the 21 and 22 October 1812, with news that Soult and Joseph were advancing in overwhelming force in the direction of Madrid, Wellington raised the disastrously unsuccessful siege of Burgos. The ensuing retreat to the Agueda in October and November 1812 was highly demoralising and arduous for the allied army. Between 15 and 19 November alone, about 3,000 men were lost.

It is difficult to know what else Wellington could have done. With superior French forces bearing down on him from all sides, he certainly could not sit and do nothing. In allowing his intuition rather than intelligence to guide him, Wellington may have been persuaded to adopt a course of action that would result either in outright success or outright failure; if he had paid more attention to the intelligence at his disposal, which plainly suggested the French were preparing to advance decisively on Madrid, he might have adopted a different course. By getting bogged down in the siege of Burgos, Wellington effectively ended any possibility of posing an adequate obstacle to Soult and Joseph's advance on Madrid. A swifter, more decisive march towards Valladolid might have suppressed the threat of the Army of Portugal from the north, even if Wellington was unable to bring Clausel to battle. He could then have returned to Madrid with plenty of time to spare to confront Soult and Joseph on the Tagus. Instead, Wellington chose to believe that Soult and Joseph intended to withdraw behind the Ebro. Only with this belief could Wellington have reached the conclusion that he was safe to continue a protracted siege operation at Burgos.

The autumn campaign was a tactical and operational failure, and reversed many of the successes won at Salamanca. There had been benefits: Soult had evacuated Andalusia, and as such improved the strategic situation for 1813. But 1812 had ended in failure, and, unsurprisingly, Wellington blamed everyone but himself. Particularly at fault, of course, were the Spaniards. Although not totally to blame, the Spanish armies had indeed performed remarkably badly. Ballesteros had refused to occupy Alcáraz, then indulged in a power-grab in Granada that had resulted in his acrimonious dismissal. The Spanish *guerilla* leader, Gabriel Mendizabel, had not been cooperative with Sir Home Popham in the amphibious operations conducted on the northern coast, and was therefore partly responsible for allowing Caffarelli to go to Souham's support. Finally, the Sixth Army under Castaños had failed to coordinate its movements with the Anglo-Portuguese Army, and only brought forward one third of its 30,000 troops. Wellington thus concluded that the Spaniards were the worst allies he had ever had. 'If the Spanish officers had knowledge and vanity like the French, or ignorance without vanity as our allies in India, something might be done with them,' wrote the diplomat, Thomas Sydenham after a conversation with Wellington. 'But they unite the greatest ignorance with the most insolent and intractable vanity. They can therefore be neither instructed nor persuaded nor forced to do their duty.'[62] If any success was to be had in the Peninsula, reform was plainly necessary.

His army once more in winter cantonments in and around Ciudad Rodrigo, Wellington went to Cadiz over Christmas to negotiate with the Cortes on the precise terms of his command of the Spanish Armies. He travelled with a range of objectives in mind. As before, he was convinced that the Spanish military was incapable of sustained military success without root and branch reform of the ways in which the men were paid, supplied and equipped. But his experiences in Spain thus far had shown that 'the evil ... requires a stronger remedy than the mere removal of the ... want of pay, clothing and necessaries'.[63] He proposed organisational changes, including a reform of the seven military districts established in December 1810, the streamlining of the general staff, and a purging of the officer corps, including the power to appoint and dismiss officers according to his own judgement. These demands were mild in comparison to his main objective. Above all, Wellington wanted 'to establish some authority in the provinces which should exercise the powers of government, ... superintend the realisation of the resources of the country, and ... be responsible for their application to the service of the army'.[64]

Wellington was calling for the establishment of military-led regional governments throughout Spain. 'It cannot be expected that any province of Spain should be in a state fit to be governed according to the best principles,' Wellington argued, in a memorandum to the Spanish government. 'Even in countries where these systems and principles are perfectly understood ... and of which the tranquillity has not lately been disturbed by a foreign enemy, it has frequently been necessary [to impose military rule] therefore, must it be in the provinces just recovered from the enemy in which the authority of the government is imperfectly established ...'[65] Wellington was conscious of the controversy such a request would generate. 'I am aware that it is wrong in principle to invest military men with civil powers,' he reasoned, 'but when the country is in danger that must be adopted which will tend most directly to save it.'[66] In reaching this conclusion, he cannot but have been influenced by his tenure as governor of Seringapatam, during which he had overseen a dramatic improvement in the infrastructure of Mysore.

Predictably, the liberal press in Cadiz was aghast at such proposals, which flatly contradicted the principles of the Constitution of 1812. 'Is it credible that Lord Wellington, who was born and brought up in a free country, where such a union of authorities is entirely unknown because it is contrary to the liberty of the citizens, could have made such a proposal?' raged one vituperative journalist. 'How could a general destined to have the glory of bringing liberty to a nation which esteems it so much ... have made so absurd a mistake?'[67] On 4 December, the Regency issued a decree which went some way to meeting Wellington's demands, including the reform of the military districts, the streamlining of headquarters and the introduction of systems for the pay and supply of its soldiers. If the Regency thought it could get Wellington to back down on the issue of regional military governance, then it was sadly mistaken. 'It is impossible to perform these duties as they ought to be performed unless I shall possess sufficient powers,' he wrote on Christmas Day. 'If [the government] . . . have not confidence in me to trust me with the powers which I think necessary, I beg leave to relinquish the command of the Spanish armies.'[68] Wellington insisted that political and military authority be concentrated in the hands of the Captains-General of a province, and that an Intendant-General should also be assigned, who would be responsible for the administration of the pay and supply systems within an entire province. The measure was put to a vote in the Cortes on 6 January, and, faced with losing the only general shown to be capable of sustained military victory in Spain, the Cortes let Wellington have his way. 'There was little difference of opinion between the government and me after they understood I was in earnest,' wrote Wellington once he had returned to Ciudad Rodrigo to prepare his next offensive. 'If the system is not fairly acted upon by the government, or for any reason whatever should fail, it will always be time enough to resign the command, and affairs cannot be in a worse state than that in which I found them . . .'[69]

Wellington had achieved his objective of sole command of the Spanish Armies, combined with enormous political influence in Spain. This enabled him to plan a much more dynamic campaign in 1813. But although he had no nefarious motives, the decision caused considerable resentment in Cadiz, and throughout Spain generally. According to Henry, the Cortes had been jealous 'of conferring unlimited authority upon the principal officers of the army who are generally supposed to be adverse to the Cortes, and to be dissatisfied at the restraints imposed upon them by the regulations of the Constitution'.[70] For many in Spain, this was a worrying precedent and a step towards military dictatorship. In degrading their principles in order to achieve freedom from Napoleon, they were jeopardising their future ability to enact them. 'Such a step on the part of this warrior would tarnish all his glorious actions for ever,' bemoaned the liberal press, 'and discredit him in the eyes of his own nation, which has not given us its aid so that we can be enslaved.'[71] Small wonder that, despite the powers granted him in Cadiz, Wellington would continue to encounter problems in controlling the Spanish armies in the remaining year of the campaign.

The challenges confronting the British, then, were still great. Facing armies of greater combined strength, Wellington realised that his force would need to adapt to meet the challenge they posed. Already there were signs of this adaptation, although Wellington's attempts to improve the speed and flexibility of his force had ultimately resulted in failure. The main impediment to success in 1812 had been the need constantly to lay siege to the fortresses that guarded the main supply routes throughout Spain. The delay that such a siege entailed meant Wellington's forces lost momentum, and gave the enemy the chance to regroup, concentrate and move against him. If he was to succeed in throwing the French out of Spain, Wellington would need to find a way around this problem. The year 1813 would see an unusual military development. Tactics and operations designed for and developed in India would be exported to Europe. Wellington was about to unleash 'Light and Quick' operations against the French, and, in so doing, he would bring Bonapartist Spain to its knees.

CHAPTER 8

'I Will Beat Them Out, and with Great Ease'

The Liberation of Spain and the Invasion of France, 1813–1814

'These fellows think themselves invulnerable, but I will beat them out, and with great ease.' 'That we shall beat them,' says Colborne, 'when your lordship attacks, I have no doubt, but for the ease—' 'Ah, Colborne, with your local knowledge only, you are perfectly right; it appears difficult, but the enemy have not men to man the works and lines they occupy. They dare not concentrate a sufficient body to resist the attacks I shall make upon them. I can pour a greater force on certain points than they can concentrate to resist me.' 'Now I see it, my lord,' says Colborne.

Captain Harry Smith, 52nd Regiment, Light Division
La Rhune, the Pyrenees, Franco–Spanish border, 8 November 1813[1]

THIS remarkable exchange, recorded some decades later by the inimitable Harry Smith, provides one of the most personal accounts of Wellington's thought processes, planning and decision-making. Wellington, Colonel Colborne, the commander of the 52nd Regiment, and Major Harry Smith were reconnoitring the battlefield of the Nivelle, while Wellington was planning a huge offensive that would see allied forces invade France for the first time since 1794. Shortly after, Smith continued, Wellington 'was lying down, and began a very earnest conversation. General Alten, Kempt, Colborne, I, and other staff-officers were preparing to leave the Duke, when he says, "Oh, lie still." After he had conversed for some time with Sir George Murray, Murray took out of his sabretache his writing-materials, and began to write the plan of attack for the whole army.' Murray then read out the memorandum, and as he did so, 'the Duke's eye was directed with his telescope to the spot in question. He never asked

Sir G. Murray one question, but the muscles of his face evinced lines of the deepest thought. When Sir G. Murray had finished, the Duke smiled and said, "Ah, Murray, this will put us in possession of the fellows' lines. Shall we be ready to-morrow?" "I fear not, my lord, but next day." [2]

Smith portrays Wellington as the all-seeing, all-knowing military genius that has made him an enduring 'great man' of British military history, in contrast with the less well-informed subordinates, notably Colborne, who possessed 'local knowledge only'. The only officer portrayed by Smith as of a similar calibre is Murray, the Quartermaster-General, and unquestionably the man chiefly responsible for translating Wellington's tactical vision into reality. But men like Colborne, with their 'local knowledge', were just as important to Wellington's military successes. We have already seen the tactical genius of men such as Craufurd and Picton, but by 1813 the crop of high-quality officers was much larger. They led an army that was now the best the British Army was ever likely to be. But the final full year of campaigning was not to be without its problems, some of which would need to be surmounted, others merely tolerated and ameliorated. Before Wellington could lie at the summit of La Rhune in the foothills of the Pyrenees and plan his invasion of France, he would have to march his army the length of Spain, in the face of the continued presence of a still superior French force. To do this, Wellington would resuscitate an approach to operations that he had long thought irrelevant.

By resurrecting 'Light and Quick' operations, Wellington was using tactics and operational planning designed in the East for irregular opponents, but was using them to fight other Western forces. I am not suggesting that Wellington deliberately sought to develop an approach to military operations that depended on Eastern cultural influences: he was not trying to outfox the French by using an alien approach to warfare. If he did so, then he left no evidence that this was his intention, and it would anyway have been totally out of character. Rather, he was using – as he always had used and always would – the best methods for the situation that were available to him from his vast array of military experience. Napoleon was right. Wellington was a 'sepoy-general'. The 1813 campaign was the unique product of such a mind.

*   *   *

Wellington began making his plans for 1813 almost as soon as he completed his retreat from Burgos. His successful negotiations concerning the command of the Spanish armies around Christmas finally gave him a numerical advantage over the French forces in Spain. In the event, Wellington quickly became aware that he would not need all the Spanish forces that were ostensibly at his disposal. First of all, Napoleon's invasion of Russia had not gone well. The detritus of the once Grande Armée had begun its ignominious retreat from Moscow. Of the 600,000 men who had marched into Russia, barely 10 per cent made it out. Even having suffered such a calamity, Napoleon was still not finished, and he swiftly drew on more reinforcements from across his empire, including Spain. In a repeat of the events at the beginning of 1812, in 1813, Wellington's intelligence network once more kept tabs on where French forces were in Spain, and by early spring it was becoming obvious that significant quantities of troops were being withdrawn. By mid-February, reports confirmed the withdrawal of 15,000 troops and officers including Marshal Soult himself.[3] This left a total of 150,000 French troops in Spain, most of whom occupied the vast region from Salamanca to Catalonia, and north to Cantabria.[4]

Much more serious for the French were the successes of the guerrillas, notably those under the command of Espoz y Mina and Francisco Longa, two of the most active *guerrilleros* of the war, who operated predominantly in northern Spain. After Caffarelli sent reinforcements to support Souham against Wellington at Burgos in the autumn of 1812, the guerrilla forces in Navarre, Cantabria and the Basque Provinces rallied and achieved their greatest successes of the whole war. In late January, Wellington noted the 'great mischief' that these guerrilla forces had done to Caffarelli.[5] In response, Gazan, who had taken over from Souham and was now watching Wellington from Salamanca, was forced to send significant reinforcements to help Caffarelli re-establish control. Of the six infantry divisions directly opposed to Wellington, five and a half were ordered to support the Army of the North. This opened an enormous hole in the French defences in front of Wellington, and now decisively shifted the balance of power in his favour. As Pakenham noted, 'the enemy have fallen back from the Tormes, ... the numbers stated were 4000 Dragoons and 30,000 Infantry; should this prove the case, the enemy will voluntarily or of necessity evacuate the Peninsula next Spring'.[6]

The withdrawal of French forces alleviated one of Wellington's greatest concerns. He was now able to plan an operation free from the worry that the Spaniards would once more prove unreliable. Previously, he had thought he needed the Spaniards to bring a balanced force against the French. With the virtual withdrawal of the Army of Portugal, he was no longer under such a constraint. The Anglo-Portuguese Army was strong enough to take on the French forces without significant Spanish support. This was fortunate timing. The agreement he had negotiated in Cadiz had quickly shown signs of discord. In practical terms, the reforms agreed to the supply system would plainly take too long to enact, and what

Spanish forces were available remained poorly supplied and equipped throughout 1813. This was nothing, though, compared to the exaggerated concerns the liberals had that Wellington was conspiring to establish a military dictatorship. As a result, the Cortes was not abiding by the simplest terms of its agreement with Wellington. It still, for example, continued to communicate directly with the Spanish armies, ignoring Wellington's explicit insistence that it do so only through his headquarters. Command and control remained a constant difficulty. At the extreme end, there remained those who wanted Wellington replaced by a Spanish general, perhaps Ballesteros. Undoubtedly, Wellington would have preferred to utilise the Spanish forces, and in June he made a last ditch effort to persuade the Spanish government to establish 'in the provinces some authority to which the people will pay obedience, and which will ensure their resources for the purposes of the war; otherwise,' he argued somewhat disingenuously, 'the cause of the country will be lost'.[7]

Such pleas having failed, the problem of the Spanish command became chronic but nevertheless manageable, rather than a terminal issue. Despite the clear weakness of the French Army, to the ill-informed observer the preparations for the allied offensive were painfully slow. Bearing in mind the French withdrawals were made in January and February, the fact that Wellington seemingly unaccountably delayed his advance until late May drew additional criticism from the Spanish press. The Spanish newspaper, *El Conciso*, for example, accused Wellington of deliberately delaying the advance to prolong the war and weaken Spain.[8] The true reason for the delay, though, was the complexity of the planning involved in the operation, combined with the fact that Wellington refused to give details of the whole of the operation to any of his subordinates. The previous year had seen repeated breaches of operational security, leading to the publication of Wellington's plans in the British press.[9] As would become obvious, the success of the 1813 offensive depended on duping the French. Wellington kept his plans totally secret. We must piece these plans together from a series of apparently unrelated General Orders and dispatches over the course of the six months to the end of May.

Wellington's plan, although nobody but he knew it, was to march his army, in three columns, from the Portuguese border to north-eastern Spain. Rather than taking the main road, as he had done in 1812, Wellington would march through the rather less navigable terrain north of the River Duero. Hilly and inaccessible, the terrain through which the army would march was badly mapped. The only passable roads were too narrow for large artillery or supply trains. Captain Henry Booth of the 43rd recalled the 'winding . . . valleys' through which the army marched.

At one point, 'we found we had been marching parallel to a French division commanded by General Maucune; but this circumstance had been concealed from us by the high hill which divided our line of march between them'.[10] Also blocking the army's path was a series of rivers that ran vaguely north to south, most of them tributaries of the Duero.

Why did Wellington set his army such a difficult task? In the first instance, it was the last thing the French expected him to do. They had used these obstacles to protect their northern flank while they concentrated their main force on defending the large road that ran from Ciudad Rodrigo through Salamanca, Valladolid, Burgos and Vitoria, and on to France. This was the only route by which the large supply and siege trains upon which the British were dependent could manoeuvre. Yet, if he were to use this road Wellington would be delayed, as he had been in 1812, by the need to lay siege to and capture the various fortresses that commanded the road. Instead, in 1813, he proposed to outflank those positions, knowing that as he did so, any French defence based on these fortresses would be rendered untenable.

Yet, he took a massive risk with his army. For them to use the roads north of the Duero, his force would have to advance with limited supplies. If he were to succeed, he would need his troops to be as lightly laden as possible; he would need regular and precise intelligence on the position of the enemy and on the nature of the roads his force would march along; and he would need to be sure that when his army reached north-eastern Spain it could be resupplied. If one of these three critical factors were to fail, then not only would the success of the entire operation be jeopardised, but, along with it, the safety of the Anglo-Portuguese Army.

The similarities between this operation and the campaign against Dhoondiah Vagh in 1800 are obvious. Both required swift movement to keep momentum up against the enemy and to reach new supplies. Both were undertaken in unmapped terrain, dependent on intelligence on possible routes and on the positions of the enemy. But preparing a force of 4,000 to march for a few weeks on minimal supplies, as Wellington had in 1800, was quite different from preparing 80,000 to do the same. In March, Wellington ordered that tents be supplied to the army, one for every six men, thereby removing the need for heavy greatcoats under which the men had previously slept.[11] Similarly, iron camp kettles were replaced with lighter and bigger tin kettles that would be transported by mules. This amounted to a significant reduction in the weight soldiers had to carry. In its place, the men could now carry more food.

Despite Wellington's best efforts, however, the logistics for the 1813 campaign – at least until the army made contact with the navy at

Santander – was never as efficient as he would have wished. Simply too
little food was available to sustain the men. 'My heart aches for the unfortunate infantry,' wrote one lieutenant in the 18th Hussars: 'I saw ... such
numbers laying on the roadside unable to stir a step further'.[12] This was
not a new or unfamiliar problem. Despite a system which historians of
Wellington's generalship have lauded as highly successful, Wellington's
logistics and supply systems frequently failed to deliver enough food to his
men.[13] The old argument that Wellington kept his men on the march and
at fighting strength by keeping their stomachs full is patently false.
Instead, as Ed Coss argues, the small group dynamics that existed at the
very lowest levels in the army – the relationship between a group of six
men who ate, slept, marched and fought together – more comprehensively
accounts for the tactical and fighting prowess of the British redcoat. It was
fear of ostracism by this group that kept the men in line in battle, and
limited indiscipline in the ranks outside of battle. Pillaging was permitted
– how else would the men get the sustenance they really needed? – but
any spoils had to be shared. This suggests that Wellington's relationship
with the men of the army was much more complicated than the standard
command history would suggest. Fear of the lash and drill training were
only part of the reason men stayed in the field. This also helps explain
how Wellington was able to march his entire army several hundred
miles through inhospitable terrain in the sweltering heat of June 1813. As
with the reliability and support of the Spaniards, the supply problems
of the army were never comprehensively addressed, just ameliorated
and endured.

On top of this, Wellington was aware that he needed to cross at least
three rivers to accomplish this plan. He was unlikely to be able to utilise
existing bridges as these would form the lynchpin of any French defensive
lines. Outflanking those lines would require a pontoon train to enable the
army to cross the rivers where the French least expected. A pontoon train,
though, was conventionally drawn by bullocks, but the roads along which
the train would need to travel were unsuitable for large pack animals.
Wellington instead decided to use the horses from the artillery, but this
left a backlog of artillery guns and ammunition in the rear. He therefore
developed a staggered system as more horses were brought up from
Lisbon.[14] The big guns would be brought along the larger road. By then,
the French defences and fortresses would have been outflanked, so the
road would be open. With the route of advance still kept secret, Wellington
gave no indication as to why a pontoon train should be given precedence
over the artillery of the army. Yet his entire concept of operations depended
on the pontoon train, as he could not be delayed by time-consuming

searches for fords and bridges that might give away his intentions to the enemy.

Success depended on the ability of army intelligence personnel to keep an eye on the French, and on the Quartermaster-General, Sir George Murray, finding suitable routes along which the army could march. By 1813, the army had a cache of skilled draughtsmen who more often than not volunteered their services to Murray to move ahead of the army and make topographical sketches of the terrain. In addition, the Corps of Guides, originally raised by Lieutenant-Colonel Scovell, was formally established by a General Order, with a complement of 105 officers and men under the command of Lieutenant-Colonel Sturgeon.[15] By 1813, these were highly skilled topographical intelligence collectors who could report daily on suitable roads along which the three columns of the army could march. By early evening, Murray would be in a position to devise the next day's route of march. He would then send a copy of the memorandum to every division in the army. Wellington sought to improve communications and therefore suggested that all divisional headquarters be arranged in an identical fashion. 'There is to be an officer of the General Staff at all times present in the camp or cantonment of each division of the army, who is to receive all orders sent to the division, and who is to be responsible that the orders are immediately communicated to the senior officer present,' Wellington instructed. 'In camp, the tent, or hut of the above mentioned Staff officer is to be placed always in the same situation in the division, and it is to be known to the quarter guard of each regiment, so that any person arriving in the camp of the division with orders may be immediately conducted to it.'[16]

The final piece of the jigsaw puzzle was the supplies the army would need when it reached north-eastern Spain. For this, a new supply base would be needed in Santander, which required close cooperation with the Royal Navy. This was by no means guaranteed. Generally speaking, Wellington had enjoyed a reasonably good, if occasionally fractious, relationship with his naval counterparts in the Peninsula. The strongest relationship had been between Wellington and Berkeley, commander of the Lisbon station in 1809–10. He had been replaced by Keith, whom Wellington had initially disliked, but for whom he had developed a grudging respect during Keith's two-year long command. By 1813, Lisbon was under the command of Admiral Martin, and Wellington enjoyed a well-balanced relationship with him. Unfortunately, the Lisbon station did not extend to northern Spain, which was the remit of the Channel Fleet, now under Keith. With a much wider area of sea to control, Keith could not help being overstretched when a war with America broke out in

1812. The result was a chronic, if unavoidable, under-resourcing of the Bay of Biscay. By 1813, Captain George Collier commanded just one large warship, the *Surveillante*, and five smaller vessels on the northern coast of Spain

For Wellington, who was deeply concerned that American privateers might intercept and capture his supply vessels, the obvious solution was to extend the command of the Lisbon station to include northern Spain. 'I think it is not impossible that we may hereafter have to communicate with the shipping in one of the ports in the North of Spain,' he wrote to Martin in late April. 'Under these circumstances, the communication along the coast becomes of the utmost importance, and I acknowledge that I feel a little anxious upon the subject, adverting to the weakness of the squadron under your command . . .'[17] Focused entirely, as he was, on the Peninsula, and unable to comprehend the competing demands placed upon the Admiralty, Wellington became increasingly irate. 'For the first time I believe that it has happened to any British Army,' he wrote, 'its communication by sea is insecure.'[18] He also attempted to influence Bathurst on the subject. 'The loss of one vessel only,' he wrote with some exaggeration, 'may create a delay and inconvenience which may be of the utmost consequence.'[19] If this were truly the case, then, as Christopher Hall has pointed out, Wellington had much more to fear from shipwreck than Yankee privateers.[20] In truth, Wellington's fears were overblown. As Melville said to Wellington, 'ten times the amount of Admiral Martin's force could not give that entire protection against an active and enterprising enemy'.[21] As long as the convoy system was used, for which there were ample resources, then Wellington's supplies would not be in danger. Wellington, still unsatisfied, had to accept this conclusion, although inter-service relations would again fracture later in the year.

By May, with preparations complete, if not complete to Wellington's impossibly high standards, it was time to unveil his plan of operations. He proposed to turn the enemy right, by approaching from the north bank of the Duero. An attack would be made by Hill from the south upon Salamanca, ostensibly to cover the left of the army, but this would also serve to divert French attention from the main attack. Although Wellington's plans beyond the capture of Zamora and Toro remained unclear, it seems he intended to outflank the French repeatedly, pushing them back until he found a ground upon which he felt he had a reasonable prospect of victory if he attacked.[22]

The plan had been kept so secret that it surprised some senior officers. 'From the 10th to the 16th of May the Divisions of the Army in the rear, closed up to the Coa, and every preparation having been made for the advance on Salamanca,' wrote one officer. 'On the three following days six Divisions unexpectedly turned to the left, crossed the Duero, and advanced in three columns on the Esla . . .'[23]

The operational movements of May and June 1813 can be divided into three phases. Phase one involved the concentration of the entire allied army north of the Duero, turning the left of the enemy army position along the northern bank of that river. Phase two was the allied advance, now also comprising flank support from the 23,000 troops of the Spanish Fourth Army under the command of General Giron, past the River Pisuerga turning the enemy defensive line just outside Burgos. Phase three culminated in the Battle of Vitoria and involved the crossing of the Ebro, outflanking the third enemy defensive line along that river. As with previous 'Light and Quick' operations, as well as being dependent on intelligence, the operational plan of 1813 was reliant on speed and precision, outwitting the enemy, and on the timely reaction of the allies to French actions. With confrontations with the retreating enemy a daily possibility, Wellington was keen to keep his line as tight as possible, and 'the cavalry and infantry should be kept together, in order to support each other'.[24]

With the left of the Anglo-Portuguese Army preparing to advance to the north of the Duero inside Portuguese territory, Wellington accompanied Hill in his advance to Salamanca, giving the impression of a genuine assault from that direction. These troops arrived in Salamanca on 27 May, before advancing on and crossing the Duero on the 30th.[25] The initial advance upon Salamanca successfully convinced the French that Wellington was invading along the Great Road. The French had constructed defensive works and redoubts to hamper the allied movement and aid in any battle or skirmish that took place. In the event, Wellington sidestepped these works completely, turning the French right as he crossed the Esla. Alten's feint at Fresno on 31 May accelerated the French withdrawal from Zamora and Toro, and Hill crossed the Duero there on 3 June.[26]

On their right, meanwhile, the French had carelessly left their flank unguarded, when the British began fording the Esla at two in the morning of 27 May. 'The enemy did not expect us so early [and] was taken by surprise and out of about sixty men, that formed the squadron . . . not more than 10 escaped,' recalled Lieutenant Woodberry of the 18th Hussars. The British pushed on relentlessly. 'This was certainly the most fatiguing march I have experienced since I have been in the army,' thought Woodberry. The enemy retreated to a plain in front of the village of Morales de Toro, some 37 miles east of the Esla. Here, a short but bloody cavalry rearguard action took place. 'It was impossible to distinguish the enemy from our own Hussars such was the confusion.' With that, Wellington had successfully outflanked the first French defensive position on the Duero. His men exhausted, a halt was called while Wellington 'employ[ed] himself reconnoitring & arranging everything on the march'. Woodberry thought the General seemed 'very confident that we shall drive the enemy out of the country'.[27]

By 10 June, Wellington had advanced as far as the Pisuerga, and the second phase of the operation began. The British successfully turned the enemy right by crossing at Melgar. The French then fell back upon Burgos, leaving a rearguard under General Reille, the right of which extended to the village of Hormaza, whilst the left commanded the heights of Estépar. In total, the enemy rearguard amounted to 11,000 infantry and 300 cavalry.[28] Wellington decided to attack this position head-on with part of Hill's southern column while the rest of the column, comprised of two cavalry brigades and the Light Division, outflanked the French.[29] After some cavalry skirmishing, when the enemy infantry, which was drawn up in lines, saw the British infantry begin their advance, the French, 'instantly commenced [their] retreat, in squares of Battalions our cavalry pressing them & the Horse Artillery firing on them occasionally'.[30]

Defeated, then, with little effort, the French withdrew behind the Ebro and the third phase of the operation began. Wellington and Murray ordered Sir Thomas Graham to detach some of his 'cavalry down the left bank of the Ebro [on 14 June] to the place opposite to Puentearenas' for reconnaissance purposes. Wellington intended to waste no time in establishing where to cross the Ebro, thus maintaining an element of surprise over the French,[31] who interpreted this as a move to secure Bilbao. When Graham unexpectedly crossed the Ebro, he caught three divisions under Reille at San Millan and Osma on 18 June, 25 miles south of Bilbao. Reille fell back 12 miles to the River Bayas where he was ordered to delay Wellington, whilst the armies of the centre and south fell back towards Vitoria. Reille successfully held Wellington off for the afternoon of the 19th. Wellington had once more ordered a frontal assault, this time by the Fourth Division, and planned to turn the French southern flank with the Light Division. He personally directed the attack, but upon discovering the much stronger retreating French divisions on the Great Road, called a halt.[32]

The next day, Wellington reconnoitred the terrain around Vitoria. He realised the French were going to make a stand, and saw he could completely cut off their retreat. The French were drawn up in three defensive lines inside the large bowl in which the town of Vitoria sits, surrounded on all sides by high ridges.

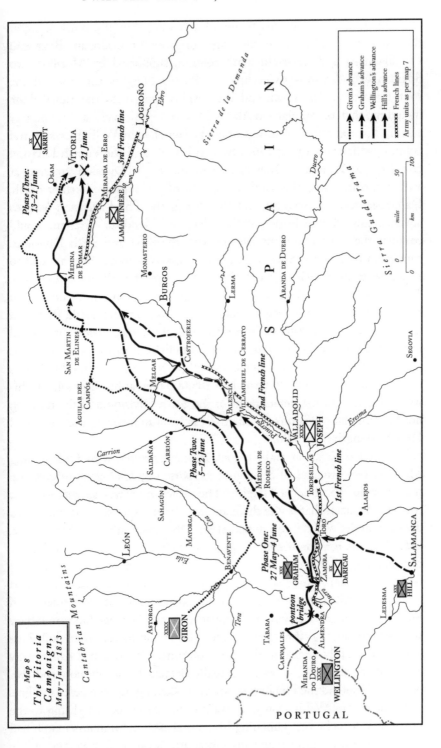

Map 8
The Vitoria
Campaign,
May–June 1813

Wellington continued his theme of attacking frontally, outflanking at the same time. Hill (with the three brigades of Cadogan, Bing and O'Callaghan) and the right-hand column, supported by Morillo's two Spanish brigades, was to occupy the Puebla Heights that formed the southern rim of the bowl, and the various spurs into the valley floor, including that of Subijana d'Alava. This was principally a diversionary assault. The main frontal assault would be launched by Wellington's central column, which was divided into two, with Cole and the Fourth Division crossing the Zadora at Nanclares, and the Light Division crossing at Villodas, comprising the southern section of the column. Further north, Dalhousie and the Seventh, and Picton and the Third Division were to advance towards the bridge at the village of Mendoza. Graham would conduct the outflanking manoeuvre with the First and Fifth Divisions, supported by Longa's Spaniards. He was tasked with cutting the road to Bayonne, to do which he would have to occupy the villages of Gemarra Mayor and Durana, along with their bridges. In response to rumours that the British were descending the mountain road from the north, Reille, on the afternoon of the 20th, withdrew from his third line outside Vitoria and reinforced the northern sector of the battlefield, throwing two divisions north of the Zadora. Total allied strength at the outset of the battle was approaching 80,000 (Wellington had 105,000 men at his disposal, but this was reduced with the detachment of the Sixth Division and the decision not to utilise all of Giron's Spaniards), easily outnumbering the combined French strength of 57,000.

The attack began at eight o'clock in the morning, with Hill sending Morillo's two brigades of Spaniards, supported by Cadogan's brigade, up the slopes of the Puebla Heights. The attack here was so successful, it persuaded Gazan that it was the main assault. In response, he dispatched a division, under Villate, to try and stymie the allied advance. Meanwhile, O'Callaghan's brigade became engaged in Subijana village. Joseph Sherer, commanding a light company of the 34th was ordered 'to carry [the village] with the bayonet'. 'Not a soul was in the village,' he remarked, 'but a wood a few hundred yards to its left and the ravines above it were filled with French light infantry. I, with my company, was soon engaged in some sharp skirmishing among the ravines, and lost about eleven men killed or wounded.'[33] Hill's attack on the right continued all day, but it had already achieved its objective. Gazan eventually detached one division and two brigades to defend the Heights, seriously weakening his own defensive line.

In the centre, Wellington was awaiting the outbreak of fighting to the north of Vitoria before launching his frontal assault. Graham's march had been long and circuitous, and his initial attack on Reille's defensive line was cautious and lacklustre, as he had anticipated a far stronger force. The First Division and Longa's Spaniards encountered stiff resistance, but Longa's Spaniards in particular distinguished themselves, and managed to bring fire down on the main road, effectively cutting it. The Fifth Division, however, encountered much heavier fighting at Gemarra Mayor. Major-General Andrew Hay deployed his brigade in support of the initial attack, commanded by Frederick Robinson. Hay recalled that he 'was leading the centre . . . in to the village when I never in my life met with a more tremendous fire of musketry and cannon'.[34] Hay's son and ADC, Captain George Hay, was mortally wounded in the fighting, the result primarily of the French cannon fire from the opposite bank. The intense and bloody confrontation continued for upwards of two hours, and effectively prevented Graham from attacking further south.

At 11.30, with Graham's attack well under way, but with no sign of Picton or Dalhousie to the north of Mendoza, Wellington decided to press on the attack in the centre. As he gave the order to attack, a Spanish peasant named Zuarte came forward with the news that the bridge at Tres Puentes was unguarded, and that troops could be marched there through a ravine created by a hairpin bend of the river, unobserved by the French. Wellington ordered Kempt to march with his brigade to Tres Puentes, thereby outflanking on the left the first French defensive line. Kempt's brigade seized the bridge, but found it overlooked by a French column, which fired its artillery at the advancing British. Only two shots were fired before Kempt was able to deploy his troops under cover of the steep hillside that formed the southern bank of the hairpin bend. The second shot decapitated the unfortunate Zuarte. Kempt's new position now threatened the north-western French flank, but an expected counterattack never materialised.

The belated advance of the Third Division on the bridge at Mendoza had distracted the French. An artillery breakdown had delayed the march of the Seventh and Third Divisions. Picton had arrived at Mendoza before Dalhousie, and seeing that the French were vulnerable to an attack from the northern bank of the Zadora, was becoming impatient. 'Damn it! Lord Wellington must have forgotten us,' he raged. Finally, an aide-de-camp arrived, but had orders for Dalhousie. Picton angrily demanded to know what they were, and the aide-de-camp responded that the Seventh Division was to advance and take the bridge at Mendoza, and that the Fourth and Light Divisions were to support. Picton, now clearly boiling with rage, told the aide-de-camp, 'you may tell Lord Wellington from me, Sir, that the Third Division, under my command, shall in less than ten minutes attack that bridge and carry it, and the Fourth and Light may support if they choose.'[35] Picton's advance was so rapid that one eyewitness described it as 'shooting like a meteor' towards the bridge.[36]

Picton carried with ease both the bridge and a ford, some 300 yards upstream. From the latter, Colville's brigade joined up with Kempt's as it advanced from Tres Puentes. The French now found themselves attacked on all sides: from the south by Hill, from the front by Wellington, from the north by Picton, and from the rear by Graham. Seeing his first line completely outflanked, Jourdan ordered a general withdrawal. From the Puebla Heights, Brigadier Charles Ashworth observed 'the attack on the centre ... their army was completely routed ... flying in all directions'.[37] This is perhaps an exaggeration. Jourdan and Joseph, abandoning their position on Arinez Hill, redeployed Gazan's battered divisions to the south of the main road to Vitoria, and positioned D'Erlon's divisions to the north of this road to meet the advance of the Third and Seventh Divisions. 'The enemy allowed us to gain the high ground without opposition but opened a tremendous fire from behind the village ... which brought us to a momentary check,' recalled Duffy of the 43rd. The several villages on the plain in front of Vitoria now became the scene of bloody firefights, in which the British won out, eventually occupying a position roughly where the second French defensive line had originally stood.

A brief lull in the combat now ensued, during which Wellington prepared his forces for a general advance, while Jourdan struggled to plug the holes in his line. Desperately short of troops, Jourdan now sent for his reserve, Villate's division, which had been deployed earlier in the day to arrest the advance of the Second Division along the Puebla Heights. Recalling Villate was problematic because of the distance involved, and the terrain across which the troops had to march. In the event, when Wellington ordered the general advance, Villate had been unable to plug the hole in Jourdan's line. From north to south, Wellington's army prepared for the final advance. The Seventh, Third and Light Divisions were advancing on the north of the Great Road, while Cole's Fourth Division had made contact with Hill and the Second Division and both were advancing south of the road. At the same time, the artillery reserve was brought up and positioned in the centre of the allied line. A massive artillery duel thus commenced, the largest of the war, with 75 allied guns versus 76 French. Most diarists recalled the ferocity of the bombardment. For Leach, 'except ... at Waterloo, I do not remember to have experienced a more furious cannonade'.[38]

Under this heavy bombardment, the British line advanced, with seven brigades in the front line, supported by another five. On the far left, George Wood, of the 82nd, 'advanced through the tumultuous scene with a battery in our front, dealing out dire destruction'. 'Men and officers fell in every direction,' he continued. 'Our front was exposed to the full range of this, and had to contend with a French regiment on the right of the battery, but, after politely receiving us with a few sharp volleys, which we as politely returned, they ... retreated into a thicket. Towards this we advanced firing, and drove them furiously before us till they were completely routed.'[39] Casualties were heavy – the 76 French guns exacted their toll on the leading British brigades. 'I really thought that, if it lasted much longer,' recalled John Green in the 68th Foot, on the far left, 'there would not have been a man left to relate the circumstance.' So severe was the fire that Green took refuge in a ditch. Ordered forward to skirmish in front of a general advance by the Light Division brigades of Kempt and Vandeleur, Green and his comrades 'immediately sprang over the ditch, gave three cheers and charged the enemy, the Light Division breaking their ranks in haste to join us'. News that the road to Bayonne had been cut now reached the French defenders and their morale collapsed. First to break was Gazan, outflanked on the left by Morillo and Campbell at the vanguard of Hill's column advancing from the Heights. This left D'Erlon in a perilous position. In the face of a seemingly fearless British advance, the French line disintegrated. 'The enemy could not withstand the shock, but were panic-struck, and fled in confusion,' recalled Green. 'We followed them shouting and huzza'ing, and gave them no time to form, but drove them before us like cattle to destruction.'[40]

The main road might have been cut, but Graham's attack from the north had stalled. Meeting serious resistance at Gemarra Mayor, he declined to press home an attack with the First Division. Had he done so, he would have encircled Vitoria and completely cut off all avenues of retreat for the French. In the event, a smaller road, leading due east, provided an avenue of escape for the disintegrating armies. Upon hearing of the British attack in his rear, Reille swiftly abandoned his position on the south bank of the Zadora opposite Graham, and joined the French retreat. There was very little pursuit of the defeated armies. Wellington has been criticised for exercising too much caution, but he was, in reality, now facing a significant logistics problem. Duffy, of the 43rd, noted that 'the [Light] Division reduced by constant marching and privation to nearly one half of their original numbers' since the beginning of the campaign, only received a supply of bread for the first time after the battle, on 27 June.[41]

A more creditable pursuit might have been possible had the army not fallen upon the baggage of the French Army, which clogged the roads out of Vitoria. Particularly at fault here was the cavalry, which had not seen much action during the day and so might have completed the destruction of the enemy army. The baggage contained the loot the French had accumulated during their six-year occupation. Officers and men alike stopped to break open carriages and ransack the contents. One officer, finding a heavy box, sequestered four men to help him break it open. When they did so, gold doubloons spilled out on to the ground. Suddenly realising he was the only officer present, after taking a small share, the unnamed individual felt 'in a rather awkward position'. 'I said they might have the rest of my share. There was first a look of surprise, and then a burst of laughter, and I trotted away.'[42] Especially noteworthy were the 14th Light Dragoons, who fell upon Joseph's baggage and to this day still sup from the King's silver chamber pot in celebration of Vitoria.

Wellington was understandably furious. 'We started with the army in the highest order and up to the day of the battle nothing could get on better,' he wrote in frustration to Bathurst, 'but that event has, as usual, totally annihilated all order and discipline.'[43] Moreover, a concerted pursuit was next to impossible owing to the chaos outside Vitoria itself. 'Cannon, overturned coaches, broken-down wagons, forsaken tumbrels, wounded soldiers, French and Spanish civilians, women and children, dead horses and mules, absolutely covered the face of the country.'[44] This problem got worse when bad weather set in, turning the clogged roads into muddy quagmires. Poor Ashworth was knocked unconscious by a lightning strike that killed a lieutenant in the 34th Regiment riding next to him.[45] In this situation the army remained for close to three weeks. By 9 July, Wellington still had 12,500 soldiers unaccounted for. 'They are not in hospitals, nor are they killed, nor have they fallen into the hands of the enemy,' he exclaimed.[46] The failure of the army – and the fault here lies with the junior officers who participated in the looting, and then failed to restore order – to engage in an effective pursuit of the retreating French gave the enemy the chance to regroup. Marshal Soult was dispatched to restore order to the battered army, and in late July he was in a position to launch a counterattack. 'We have the scum of the earth as common soldiers,' wrote Wellington, 'and as of late, we have been doing everything in our power to relax the discipline by which alone such men can be kept in order.'[47]

*   *   *

Vitoria had been a decisive victory for the allies. It effectively ended the Bonapartist kingdom of Spain, and was a fitting climax to Wellington's 'Light and Quick' operation. Although the French armies escaped to fight another day, Wellington could be satisfied with the success of his operational plan first put into action at the end of May. His casualties had been large – 5,100 – but those of the French were larger – no fewer than 8,000 – whilst all but two of Joseph's 153 guns were taken, along, of course, with the treasure and plunder. Wellington had successfully marched his army, which, with the Spaniards, numbered 105,000, in the region of between 350 and 400 miles, taking into account outflanking manoeuvres. This was truly a 'Light and Quick' operation. It had been reliant on intelligence throughout, but it had been logistically challenging. Although Wellington had made contact with the northern coast, he was yet to receive supplies, and with the discipline of the army itself in tatters, it was small wonder that a lull in combat operations now commenced.

As usual, military success brought with it almost unqualified political support. Wellington had faced questions over where the British Army could be deployed most effectively once Spain was liberated. Contenders included northern Europe – where Britain might conclusively demonstrate her continental commitment – and southern Italy.[48] Wellington dismissed both suggestions for reasons of cost; the time needed to withdraw and redeploy; the fact that the war in Spain had shown that military intervention carried with it significant political difficulties; and that the British Army was a drop in the ocean compared with the forces arrayed against Napoleon.[49] As long as it was deployed in the Peninsula, the British Army would continue to have an effect disproportionate to its size. As if to demonstrate this point, the victory at Vitoria sent shock waves through Europe. Austria, still undecided on whether to join the alliance against Napoleon, was reportedly persuaded to do so because of Wellington's success. Unsurprisingly, then, the government decided to 'entertain no objection to your pursuing the great object of the war by whatever course your Lordship shall deem most effectual'.[50] The Prince Regent, having received Jourdan's captured marshal's baton, promoted Wellington to the rank of Field Marshal. 'You have sent me, among the trophies of your unrivalled fame, the staff of a French Marshal,' wrote the Prince, 'and I send you in return that of England.'[51]

Wellington now advanced to the French border, and after some combat at the passes of Maya and Roncesvalles, succeeded in forcing the devastated French armies across the Pyrenees by 8 July. First in Wellington's sights were the fortresses of San Sebastian and Pamplona. The latter he decided to starve into submission, but the former, as it controlled the coastal road, would have to be besieged and taken by storm. Wellington required significant naval support for the siege: he requested that Collier blockade the port and transport siege artillery and magazines of ammunition and supplies.

Unfortunately, Collier had acted lackadaisically since receiving the request for support from Wellington in May. 'Ammunition required for the army has lately been delayed at Lisbon for want of a convoy, and it has not yet arrived at Santander,' Wellington wrote in fury to Bathurst. 'I am obliged to use the French ammunition, of a smaller calibre than ours.' Facing the prospect of having achieved a decisive victory but with no means to exploit it, Wellington was insistent that the Admiralty act quickly to establish the new supply base at Santander. 'The army cannot remain in this part of the country without magazines,' he wrote. 'These magazines must be brought by sea.'[52] Two months later, and after an unsuccessful attempt to take the fortress by storm, Wellington again complained of the lack of naval support. 'I have never been in the habit of troubling the Government with requisitions for force, but have always carried on the service to the best of my ability with that which has been placed at my disposal,' he wrote disingenuously. 'If the Navy of Great Britain can not afford more than one frigate ... to cooperate with this army in the siege of a maritime place ... I must be satisfied and do the best I can.'[53] Make no mistake, though, unless the Admiralty adopted 'measures to give us secure and easy communication along the coast, and the means of using its harbours with convenience ... they will be responsible for any failure that may occur'.[54]

The deterioration of inter-service relations escalated when Wellington learned that the French were able to bring in supplies, reinforcements and evacuate casualties in *trincandores*, small craft piloted by two or three seamen. The truth was that Collier was unable to maintain a constant blockade because of the shallow waters around San Sebastian, and the inclement weather conditions that frequently blew frigates and sloops off stations. Wellington typically failed to understand the problems. 'The blockade of the coast is merely nominal,' he wrote. 'The enemy has re-inforced *by sea* the only two posts they have on the north coast of Spain.'[55] The First Lord of the Admiralty, Lord Melville, was unforgiving. 'Our military officers on the frontiers of Spain do their duty most admirably,' he wrote privately to Lord Keith, 'but they seem to consider a large ship within a few hundred yards off the shore of San Sebastian as safe in its position and as immovable by the winds and waves as one of the Pyrenean Mountains.'[56]

Melville informed Wellington that the problem was not necessarily the number of ships the navy had available, but the lack of sailors. Undoubtedly, more ships and men would be made available if a small-armed expedition could be sent to destroy the French naval ports that required constant blockade, but this, Melville smugly pointed out, would draw troops away from the Peninsula.[57] None of this sated Wellington's anger, which was further inflamed when Melville publicly suggested that the blockade of San Sebastian had never been broken, and if it was, then the boats that made it to harbour were so small that they carried 'nothing more than letters or eggs and fowls'.[58] Any attempt by Melville to cut short 'this paper warfare' was undermined when he wrote to Wellington insincerely, 'I will take your opinion in preference to any other person's as to the most effectual mode of beating a French army, but I have no confidence in your seamanship or nautical skill.'[59]

This unseemly spat continued into the winter, and undermined Wellington's relations with the navy, whose support now was crucial. The problem was that Collier exhibited no aptitude for joint operations. 'This is no joint service,' Wellington exclaimed angrily. 'All that is required from His Majesty's navy is to convoy the supplies for the army coming from England and elsewhere, and to convoy back the empty transports.'[60] The problem remained intractable, and eventually the Admiralty alighted on one of its fundamental causes. In January 1814, it replaced the ineffective Collier with Rear Admiral Sir Charles Penrose, enabling Wellington to start afresh with a new squadron commander. What efficiencies were made, were done so swiftly, but in the main Penrose faced the same shipping shortages as Collier had, and so the supply difficulties caused by the failure of inter-service relations continued until the end of the war.

In July 1813, though, Wellington's deteriorating relations with the navy and the consequent shortfall in supplies and ammunition was just one of his problems. With no reinforcements forthcoming from the Admiralty, Wellington had to make do. However, with a shortage of ammunition, Wellington was forced to make a hasty assault on San Sebastian on 25 July, which failed. At the same time, Soult launched a counterattack through the Pyrenees. In the space of three weeks, Soult had successfully reconstituted the French Army, now known as the Army of Spain. The army was divided into three 'lieutenancies', effectively corps by another name. These were under command of Reille (Right), D'Erlon (Centre) and Clausel (Left). Instead of attacking along the northern coast, as Wellington expected, in an effort to relieve San Sebastian, Soult instead marched his troops through the Pyrenees, and attacked Wellington's weak right wing via the mountain passes of Maya and Roncesvalles, which were guarded by Cole and Picton with the Fourth and Third Divisions. Although they held out for a while, both perceived their positions to be untenable and withdrew to a strong defensive position at the village of Sorauren.

Wellington, unusually, was wrong-footed by the precipitate withdrawal of his forces, and raced to Sorauren in an attempt to stem the flow. He arrived in the nick of time, just as Soult was commencing his attack on 28 July. There now ensued some difficult close-quarter fighting, with positions changing hands at the point of the bayonet, whilst the mountainous terrain added to the exhaustion and fatigue of battle. Wellington's presence was crucial, as he directed brigades to plug holes in the allied line. The battle developed into one of attrition, with the allies managing to hold out until darkness fell. The following day, Soult sought to rally his depleted forces, and decided to change tack and attempt to cut Wellington off from San Sebastian. His plan was foiled by the rough terrain, which, saturated by heavy rainfall, caused a long delay in the redeployment of his forces. As 30 July dawned, Wellington observed three French divisions moving across his front in column, unprepared for battle. The opportunity was too good to miss. During the course of the day, these French divisions were all but annihilated, resulting in absolute catastrophe for Soult, who ordered a general retreat north. Unfortunately, Wellington had only one division available for pursuit, and the remnants of Soult's Army of Spain were afforded the opportunity to escape. By 3 August, slowed by the hard terrain and continually harried by the British vanguard, Soult was back in France, his grand counter-offensive at an end.

For many, Wellington's speedy reactions and personal direction of the battle had rescued the precarious situation in which Cole and Picton found themselves. This is probably an unfair criticism of two of Wellington's most trusted divisional commanders, but it is impossible to predict how either would have performed without Wellington had he not arrived in time to assume command at Sorauren. 'Never did I see such hard fighting as we have had. The 28th was hell. I escaped as usual unhurt; and I began to believe that the finger of God is upon me,' he wrote to William. But then, 'if I had been two minutes later, the entire position would have been lost'.[61]

In the event, though, a severe toll had been exacted on the French – some 13,000 casualties, to the allies' 7,000. The defensive line had been restored, and Pamplona and San Sebastian remained blockaded. Moreover, it had become clear, from the fractured nature of the operations of both the allies and the French in the Pyrenees, that swift, initiative-based operations were impossible. The broken and rough terrain precluded easy communications of intent, whilst opportunities could not be easily exploited. How to achieve success in the Pyrenees would require careful consideration, and plans would have to be sufficiently detailed to ensure that units were coordinated even if communication between them was impossible. Meanwhile, political pressure was exerted subtly from Whitehall, which was looking for a quick victory or peace. Wellington was more than aware of both political and military pressures. 'The British government or nation ... forget that we have but one army,' he wrote in August, 'and that the same men who fought at Vimeiro and Talavera fought the other day at Sorauren; and that, if I am to preserve that army, I must proceed with caution.'[62] If Wellington was to invade France, it was going to be a slow and deliberate process.

San Sebastian town finally fell to an allied assault on 31 August; the garrison, which had retreated to the castle, was bombarded into submission a few days later. On the same day, Soult, having recovered from the losses suffered at Sorauren, launched one final attack to try to relieve San Sebastian, assaulting a strong defensive position, the heights of San Marcial, on the southern bank of the Bidassoa. This position was resolutely defended by the troops of General Manuel Freire, who had succeeded Giron as commander of the Spanish Fourth Army. The Spaniards defended against two spirited French attacks led by Reille, before themselves launching a decisive bayonet charge. To the right, however, Clausel launched a flanking attack across the river near the village of Bera. A sudden thunderstorm flooded the river, cutting off the French retreat, with one of the few means of escape being a tiny bridge across the Bidassoa, held by the second battalion of the 95th Rifles. Observing from the heights behind Bera, General Skerret, commanding a brigade of the Light Division, was advised by his aide-de-camp, Harry Smith, to send in the 52nd to reinforce the bridge. 'Oh, is that your opinion?' responded Skerret, to which Smith replied, impertinently, 'and it will be yours in five minutes'. When the French stormed the bridge and took the houses on the far bank, Skerret admitted his error, and ordered the 52nd to retake the bridge and houses. This completed, Skerret, much to Smith's fury, unaccountably ordered the bridge to be held by a picket of fifty men. Commanded by Captain Daniel Cadoux, the men fought tirelessly throughout the night holding the bridge against repeated French attacks. The death of Cadoux, shot in the head on horseback, destroyed his men's morale, and the French once more captured the bridge, making good their escape. Had the bridge been held, most of Clausel's corps might have been cut off. Wellington was understandably furious that another opportunity to capture a significant portion of the French army had been lost, and Skerret went home on sick leave shortly after.[63] Despite this setback, with San Sebastian in allied hands, the way was now open for the invasion of France.

* * *

On the exact line of the Franco–Spanish border lie the impressive battlefields of the Bidassoa, Nivelle and Nive, three rivers that run east to west from the Pyrenees into the Bay of Biscay. In the moments when thick cloud does not envelop the 900-metre summit of La Rhune, the highest point on the combined battlefield, one can see the Bay of Biscay, about eight miles to the west, whilst to the east, the steep slopes of the foothills of the Pyrenees disappear into the distance. In this direction, one can see about 12 miles before the imposing slopes of the Pyrenean mountains proper provide a striking horizon. Everything that can be seen by the human eye from this point forms part of the battlefields that Wellington used to stage his invasion of France. In all, the entire battle front extends some 17 miles.

The three battles that comprise the invasion of France represent another transformation in Wellington's approach to warfare: Wellington did not achieve, nor did he seek, a decisive battle. Before each battle, he planned to capture certain objectives that would make the next advance possible. As a whole, these battles were designed to force the French to a more traditional battlefield where Wellington stood a good chance of defeating his enemy in a conventional battle.

Following the Battle of San Marcial, Wellington was unsure of the strategic situation in northern Europe. It remained unclear whether the Great Powers would conclude a formal alliance aimed at the total defeat of Napoleon. Wellington did not want to invade France from the south only to find that Napoleon had concluded separate peace treaties with his enemies on his eastern front, thereby allowing him to redirect his force against Wellington. He also wished to avoid a similar catastrophe to that which had befallen Soult in July, so he decided to take what can best be described as an operational pause. Wellington has been criticised for losing the momentum gained at San Marcial, but he chose instead a measured and concerted approach. It is important to note that an allied invasion of France was not necessarily the natural outcome of the liberation of Spain. What is more, Spain was not yet liberated: Pamplona and Santoña still held out against an allied blockade, whilst Suchet remained a menacing threat to Wellington's right flank in Catalonia. Wellington, then, gave some consideration to turning back and clearing Catalonia before contemplating an invasion of France. Politically and publicly, though, he found himself under pressure to invade France. 'I see, as usual, the newspapers on all sides are raising the public expectation, and that the Allies are very anxious that we should enter France,' Wellington wrote to Bathurst in mid-September.[64] Privately, Wellington expressed frustration, which manifested itself, typically, through sarcasm. 'Such extravagant expectations are excited by the excessively wise and useful class of people, the editors of newspapers,' he remarked to Lord William Bentinck the governor of Sicily, and commander of the British expedition of South eastern Spain. 'If I had been at any time capable of doing what these gentlemen expected, I should have been on the moon ... or at least at Bordeaux ...'[65] Nevertheless, Wellington accepted the political expediency of an invasion of France, and recognised that such a move was not without its military benefits. Moreover, Suchet was well contained by the Spanish armies in Catalonia and unlikely to pose much threat to Wellington's flank, whilst a successful invasion of France could only render Suchet's position increasingly tenuous, as the Army of Catalonia became cut off from communication and reinforcement from France. It was with these factors in mind, then, that Wellington wrote to Bathurst that he thought he 'ought and will bend a little to the views of the Allies, if it can be done with safety to the army, notwithstanding that I acknowledge I should prefer to turn my attention to Catalonia'.[66]

For the invasion of France, he needed to collect topographical and tactical intelligence on his enemy's dispositions, and to devise a plan to cross the River Bidassoa into France. A decisive victory against the French was unlikely, a fact reinforced by Soult's problems in July, and Wellington could not afford the luxury of risking his army in an ill-planned crossing. The operational pause was undoubtedly the correct decision. When it came, the crossing of the Bidassoa, the first stage of what became a three-stage invasion of France, was a complete success.

With the western approaches into France secured by the estuary of the Bidassoa, Soult anticipated Wellington's main assault some time in late September or early October to come in the 12-mile stretch of terrain to the east of La Rhune, and it was here that he positioned the majority of his forces, six of his nine available divisions. A total of 14,000 troops manned two lines of defensive redoubts and earthworks north of Urdax. Further east, Clausel occupied the terrain between La Rhune and the River Nivelle. Fortifications were constructed on the various spurs from La Rhune itself, including Bayonnette Ridge, which ran steeply into the village of Bera. In total, 15,000 men, including Soult's reserve, which was further to the rear, defended this sector. The weakest defences were opposite the Bidassoa estuary, in the eastern sector of the battlefield, and comprised just 10,000 men. Soult clearly thought the wide estuary to be an insurmountable obstacle.

On the morning of 7 October, three brigades of the Fifth Division surprised Soult's right with a daring estuary crossing at Hendaye. They crossed at 7.15 in the morning, at which point the water at three fords across the estuary, previously identified by helpful local shrimpers, was just three feet deep. So surprised were the French that the Fifth Division was able to traverse the estuary without receiving fire. One and a half miles upstream, upon observing the Fifth make their attack, the First Division would cross at Behobie, the site of a ruined bridge. Again advancing under very light resistance, the First Division had achieved its main objectives by eleven o'clock.[67]

At La Rhune, meanwhile, Giron's Spanish division assaulted all enemy positions south of the mountain, and then attacked La Rhune itself. The Seventh Division supported Giron in reserve, while the Light Division ascended the strong feature of the Bayonnette Ridge to the south-west of La Rhune, taking the fieldworks that the French had thrown up in defence, including the Star and Bayonnette redoubts. The ascent would also outflank La Rhune. Fighting here was more severe than at the estuary, and Colborne and the 52nd suffered heavy casualties when they were forced to storm the Star redoubt twice before the division could continue its ascent. The Bayonnette redoubt fell with less resistance, as skirmishers swarmed around it, and the 52nd stormed it frontally. 'The 52nd Regiment . . . with their bayonets sharp and glistening in the sun . . . were advanced under a most heavy fire, but . . . it was not near so destructive as we expected,' recalled Harry Smith, now Colborne's aide-de-camp. 'Still more to our astonishment, the enemy did not defend their well-constructed work as determinedly as we anticipated.'[68]

La Rhune itself held out against fierce attacks from the Spaniards, but, outflanked, the position was abandoned the following day. Occupying new positions that needed a thorough reconnaissance, and still uncertain of the credibility of the alliance against Napoleon on the northern front, Wellington once more took an operational pause, taking the time to collect intelligence on his enemy.

Over the next month, a three-pronged assault, based on intelligence and surprise, took shape in Wellington's mind. Immediately after the operation to cross the Bidassoa succeeded, Wellington and his Quartermaster-General, George Murray, began collecting intelligence in preparation for the next assault. The Light Division, in particular, was asked to monitor the 'position and force of the enemy's troops seen from any of the most commanding situations from which you have had observations made'.[69] It soon became clear, however, that Soult was planning a terrain-based defence. The hills that stretched from the coast to the steep foothills of the Pyrenees, combined with the anchorage of the River Nivelle on the French left, provided an apparently strong defensive line that Soult chose to occupy in strength. Soult occupied every hilltop and fortress which existed on the French border with Spain west of the Pyrenean mountain range: a defensive line which stretched 17 miles in total.

Wellington again planned an advance in three columns against the French positions. The centre column, consisting of five divisions, would punch through and turn the French line, by outflanking or capturing the many redoubts and fortresses between La Rhune and the French town of Ascain. The high ground before Ascain was Wellington's ultimate objective for the day. The right, commanded by Hill and consisting of two divisions, would provide a supporting manoeuvre, outflanking the French left. On the coast, where, after being outflanked here in October, Soult had hastily reinforced the defences, the British left, commanded by the newly arrived Sir John Hope, would act as a deception, advancing in three mini-columns, the first along the coast between the heights of Urrugne, the second between the towns of Urrugne, Ciboure and St-Jean-de-Luz, and the third would advance as necessary to maintain communication with the centre. It was not 'intended that the operations in this quarter should be pushed forward as a real attack; it is meant only to fix the attention of the enemy, and prevent his detaching troops to the support of other points of his line'.[70]

In the centre, Soult's position was defined by three interconnected defensive lines of small fortresses and redoubts, which were mutually supporting, covering each other's flanks. Wellington's command post on La Rhune was opposite the smaller rocky ridge of La Petit Rhune, with three stone redoubts and a star fort – known as Mouiz – behind it. The lynchpin of the second line was the heavily fortified Signals redoubt. This was supported by the double forts of the Col de St Ignace and the Louis XIV redoubt. The third French position in the town of Ascain itself was anchored to the north-west by the River Nivelle, and to the north-east by a third defensive line of forts. The fundamental weakness of the French defences was their interdependence. Wellington realised that the capture of a few positions would precipitate the disintegration of the entire French line. The first objectives of the day were the three redoubts on La Petit Rhune and the Mouiz Star Fort. This, the Light Division was charged with.[71]

The attack was dependent on the surrender of Pamplona, and when that fortress capitulated on 31 October, preparations began for the advance. Snow and rain prevented the right flank from coming up, and the attack was delayed first until the 9th and then 10 November. The Light Division's 'attack was made on the enemy's position in seven columns, nor did we ever meet a check, but carried the enemy's works, the tents all standing, by one fell swoop of irresistible victory', recalled Smith. 'Such was the attack and such the resistance, that a few prisoners whom we took declared that they and their officers were perfectly thunderstruck, for they had no conception any force was near them.'[72]

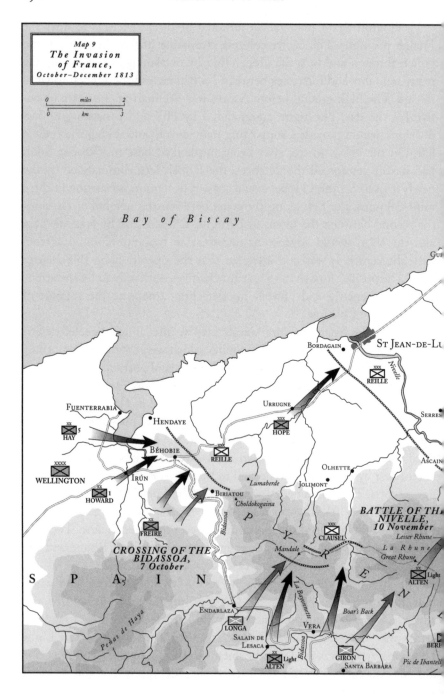

Map 9
The Invasion of France,
October–December 1813

0   miles   2
0   km   3

Bay of Biscay

GUI

St Jean-de-Lu

BORDAGAIN

REILLE

FUENTERRABIA

HENDAYE

URRUGNE

SERRES

HAY 5

BÉHOBIE

HOPE

WELLINGTON

REILLE

OLHETTE

ASCAIN

IRÚN

BIRIATOU

Lumaberde

JOLIMONT

HOWARD 1

Choldokogaina

BATTLE OF TH
NIVELLE,
10 November

FREIRE

CLAUSEL

Lesser Rhune

CROSSING OF THE
BIDASSOA,
7 October

Mandale

*La Rhune
Great Rhune*

S   P   A   I   N

ALTEN Light

Peñas de Haya

ENDARLAZA

Boar's Back

LONGA

VERA

BERE

SALAIN DE
LESACA

GIRON

Pic de Ibantell

ALTEN Light

SANTA BARBARA

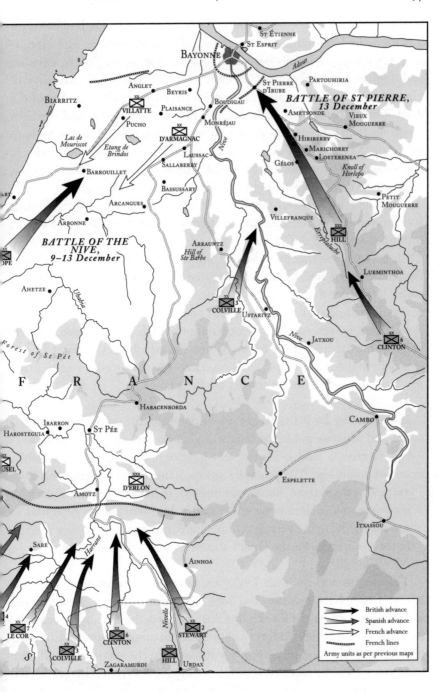

St Étienne
St Esprit
BAYONNE
Adour
Partouhiria
Anglet
Beyris
St Pierre
d'Trube
Boudigau
BIARRITZ
VILLATTE
Plaisance
Monréjau
BATTLE OF St PIERRE,
13 *December*
Pucho
Ametsonde
Vieux
Mouguerre
D'ARMAGNAC
*Lac de
Mouriscot*
*Etang de
Brindos*
Laussac
Hiriberry
Marichorry
Losterenea
BARROUILLET
Sallaberry
Gélos
*Knoll of
Horlopo*
Bassussary
Arcangues
Arbonne
Villefranque
Petit
Mouguerre
BATTLE OF THE
NIVE,
9–13 *December*
Arrauntz
*Hill of
Ste Barbe*
HILL
Ahetze
Ubabia
Lurminthoa
COLVILLE
Ustaritz
Nive
Jatxou
CLINTON
Forest of St Pée
Habacenborda
Cambo
Ibarron
Harosteguia
St Pée
Espelette
D'ERLON
Amotz
Itxassou
Sare
Harrant
Ainhoa
LE COR
Niveille
STEWART
CLINTON
COLVILLE
HILL
Urdax
Zagaramurdi

British advance
Spanish advance
French advance
French lines
Army units as per previous maps

The capture of La Petite Rhune was the key to the battle. It allowed for a flanking and frontal assault on the second defensive line. The capture, however, was possible only because Anson's brigade of the Fourth Division and Inglis's brigade of the Seventh captured the small redoubts of Grenade and Santa Barbara, which provided covering fire on some of the dead ground before La Petit Rhune. The Third, Fourth and Seventh Divisions then mounted an assault on Sare, which opened up the route to the Louis XIV redoubt. The first line of defence had broken, but with it, the advantage of surprise had been lost. The assaults to take the St Ignace, Signals and Louis XIV redoubts would be much more laboured.

The Light Division temporarily lost communication with the Fourth and Seventh Divisions, having outstripped them by some distance, combined with the difficulties of the terrain between the two columns. Their advance was therefore delayed, but to the commander of the second French defensive line, Clausel, it appeared that he was receiving an attack on his left rather than in his front. This was not an incredible assumption to make: Wellington had specialised in surprise turning manoeuvres in the past. It was, however, an incorrect assumption. Clausel reinforced his left flank, at the expense of his centre. When the assault on Col de St Ignace was delivered by the Light Division, although they took casualties, the resistance was therefore somewhat weakened.

> In descending La Petite Rhune, we were much exposed to the enemy's fire, and when we got to the foot of the hill we were about to attack, we had to cross a road enfiladed very judiciously by the enemy, which caused some loss. We promptly stormed the enemy's works and as promptly carried them. I never saw our men fight with such lively pluck; they were irresistible; and we saw the other Divisions equally successful, the enemy flying in every direction. Our Riflemen were pressing them in their own style, for the French themselves are terrific in pursuit.[73]

The Fourth and Seventh Divisions, however, suffered heavily on the left at Louis XIV redoubt, but took the position when they received artillery support. As the French line disintegrated, the Signals redoubt, the only completed defensive fort, was the one remaining obstacle. Colborne realised it would soon be completely turned, and the garrison would have to surrender, but he received an oddly worded order from Alten, delivered by the Assistant Quartermaster-General of the Light Division, Charlie Beckwith: 'Move on'. Colborne was shocked: 'What, Charlie, to attack that redoubt? Why, if we leave it to our right or left, it must fall, as a matter of course; our whole army will be beyond it in twenty minutes.' But

Beckwith pressed the point, and there was no shortage of enthusiasm amongst the troops. Colborne sent Smith to get clarification from Alten, while he led the assault on the redoubt. The 52nd tried attacking the redoubt twice, but both assaults failed because the defences were so well constructed. Most of the regiment's 240 casualties died unnecessarily in a ditch surrounding the redoubt.

Realising the futility of the attack, Alten ordered Smith to call off the assault. While he was riding to Colborne, Smith's horse was shot from under him, 'her blood, like a fountain, pouring into my face ...' Smith lay trapped under the horse and witnessed 'one of the enemy jump on the parapet of the works in an undaunted manner and in defiance of our attack, when suddenly he started straight up into the air, really a considerable height, and fell headlong into the ditch. A ball had struck him in the fore-head.' By now, the rest of the army was outflanking the redoubt. 'Colborne, in the most gallant manner, jumped on his horse, rode up to the ditch under the fire of the enemy, which, however, slackened as he loudly summoned the garrison to surrender. The French officer, equally plucky, said, "Retire, sir, or I will shoot you!" Colborne deliberately addressed the men. "If a shot is fired, now that you are surrounded by our army, we will put every man to the sword."'[74] Colborne implied that he would leave the French troops in the hands of Giron's Spaniards. This was enough to persuade the French officer to surrender.[75] Smith, meanwhile, remained trapped under his horse, until rescued by some of the men, who believed him dead. 'Well, d—— my eyes if our old Brigade-Major is not killed, after all,' exclaimed one soldier. 'I am not even wounded, only squeezed,' replied Smith. Having missed the attack, Smith 'had to limit his triumph to carrying off his good and precious English saddle, which he performed with his accustomed coolness to the amusement of observing friends and enemies'.[76]

Following the collapse of the French centre after Wellington's attack on the Nivelle, Soult withdrew his forces north of the River Nive. The Nive flowed south-east to north-west into the Adour (itself flowing east to west) at Bayonne, which was a heavily defended fortress town. Here, in occupying a strong defensive line running south-east, with his right anchored on the fortress at Bayonne, Soult hoped to stymie Wellington's advance by containing him in a triangle of land with Bayonne at its apex. However, on receiving intelligence that Wellington was planning to outflank this position, Soult decided to withdraw most of his forces to Bayonne, where they could easily be deployed in response to whatever action Wellington took.

In the event, Wellington halted his advance, once again pausing to plan his next move, allow his forces to come up and, most important of all, wait for news that the allies in Northern Europe were going to proceed with the invasion of France and not come to terms with Napoleon after the decisive allied victory at Leipzig between 16–19 October. On 17 November, Wellington established his headquarters at St-Jean-de-Luz. After gaining the trust of the initially suspicious French population, the British were able to arrange for supplies to be brought in by sea from Pasajes in Spain, and up the Nivelle to Ascain, which became the main allied depot. By early December, however, Wellington had concluded that he did not want to spend the winter holed up behind the Nive, and thought it best to extend his position to the Adour. By taking control of that river, the allies could effectively curtail French attempts to resupply Bayonne, forcing Soult to withdraw further into France. There now ensued several actions over three consecutive days between 9 and 12 December to the south of Bayonne, as the French tried to halt this final advance of the allied invasion of France.

At dawn on 9 December, Hill's right-hand column began the advance by crossing the Nive at the fords at Cambo. His instructions were to outflank the enemy left and roll up their defensive positions by advancing north-west towards Bayonne. In his path stood Foy, but on seeing his position outflanked, the French general gave up his terrain with little resistance. Beresford, in command of the centre column, was ordered to cross the Nive at Ustaritz. The resistance here was also light, and Clinton's Sixth Division was able to advance up the riverbank, slowed only by the deep mud. Upon connecting with Hill, the British began their advance on Villefranque. Seeing that only two battalions defended the village, Hill decided to attack and take possession of the town before dusk. D'Erlon counterattacked, but Hill retook the town later in the afternoon. That night, the French lit fires to hide their withdrawal, allowing Hill to advance close to Bayonne the following day.

On the left, Hope was again instructed to make a demonstration movement towards Bayonne. His divisions, the First and Fifth, with flanking support from the Light and Fourth, advanced unhindered until they encountered skirmishers at Anglet. These were eventually outflanked by the King's German Legion and forced to retire. Having achieved his objectives, Hope then inexplicably sent the First and Fifth Divisions some eight miles to the rear. Soult had withdrawn D'Erlon's corps from in front of Hill's column in order to launch a counterattack to the south-west of Bayonne, against Hope's now considerably weakened flank.

As a result, at dawn on 10 December, the Light Division's advanced pickets were surprised around the village of Bassussary. Quickly falling back on a prepared defensive position at the chateau and church at

Arcangues, the Light Division withstood a heavy artillery bombardment for the rest of the day, although Clausel never pressed home an infantry assault after receiving news that Wellington had withdrawn the Third and Sixth Divisions to reinforce the Light Division at Arcangues. Meanwhile, on the far left of the British line, Reille had been ordered to make a diversionary assault. Finding the defences much weaker here, the attack succeeded in pushing the weak British pickets back a mile before Campbell's brigade was able to halt the French advance temporarily. Seeing Clausel's attack at Arcangues peter out, Soult instead reinforced Reille with two additional divisions. Heavy fighting now ensued, in which the British found themselves in a precarious position, until the First Division, with Hope himself at its head, came up after a four-hour forced march. Arriving in the nick of time, the First Division stabilised the situation by nightfall, thus preventing the whole British line from being outflanked. That evening, 1,400 Germans from Villate's division deserted and were transported back to Germany. This prompted Soult to disband a number of foreign regiments under his command. During the Battle of Leipzig, Saxony had switched sides, and allied with the Great Powers against Napoleon. Soult now could not trust his foreign troops, particularly the Germans. Desultory fighting continued for another day or two, but the Fifth Division, brought up to hold the line, managed to hold the French back, but at some cost. Soult now withdrew all his divisions bar two across the Nive in preparation for an attack on Hill's greatly weakened flanking force at St Pierre d'Irube.

On 13 December, Soult attacked Hill at St Pierre d'Irube, about a mile south-west of Bayonne. Abbé's division pressed Hill's centre hard for most of the day, and at one point it looked as though the allied centre would collapse. Hill committed his reserve, which eventually stabilised the centre, while Foy pressed Hill's right and Darricau attacked on the left. Both were forced back with heavy losses on both sides. Wellington, meanwhile, had been prevented from sending reinforcements by the collapse of the pontoon bridge across the Nive because heavy rain had flooded the river. Only near the end of the battle did the Sixth Division arrive on the field ultimately to decide the contest. The French fell back to a position north of the Adour, whilst the allies settled into their winter cantonments.

The Battle of the Nive, designed to secure strong defensive positions for the winter and enable the continued allied advance in France, had been rather less successful than Wellington would have liked. True, the objectives had been achieved. The allies were now established on the Adour, and could threaten the French at any number of points. True, also, Bayonne had been invested, and marginalised as a strategically important defensive fortress. That said, the crossing of the Nive had cost the allied army dearly, compared with its predecessors on the Bidassoa and the Nivelle. When asked by a major, who was making out the returns of killed and wounded, whether he would like to establish a grand total, Wellington replied that 'he would not have every drummer boy and every officer ... killed or wounded in the last five days, all added up in one grand total'. No, he far preferred that the 'croakers should have the trouble themselves of adding up all the different losses'.[77] Wellington was clearly upset at the costly final battle, but was also anticipating the inevitable criticism in the liberal press at home. That said, the three battles of Wellington's invasion of France arguably mark his greatest victories. Wellington himself thought the Nivelle his greatest triumph, alongside Assaye – not because of what was achieved on the day (although this was not inconsiderable), but because it represented his talents on a grand scale: namely clarity of planning, communicated with simplicity, despite the complexity of the scenario in an operation based on surprise and deception, which maintained the political primacy of Britain's campaign in Spain. They were also Wellington's greatest victories because the battles had limited aims, fitting into a larger, multi-faceted operation.

Anticipated criticism notwithstanding, Wellington now faced far more acute problems with his Portuguese and Spanish troops. As the allied army had advanced further into Spain, so the Portuguese government had grown restive at the use of its soldiers so far from its borders. The Portuguese were becoming increasingly concerned about their deteriorating relations with Spain. It was clear by 1813 that a resolution to a dispute over the border area of Olivenza was not in sight, whilst each government alleged the other owed vast sums of money in war debts. Hard-line factions within the Portuguese government expected post-war difficulties with Spain, and began pressuring the Regency to recall its troops home. This problem emerged as others continued to hamper Anglo-Portuguese relations. The subsidy agreement had recently been revised, effectively reducing the sum Britain gave Portugal each year, whilst Wellington had been forced to arrange for the supply of the independent Portuguese units in his army. In addition, in late 1813, the Portuguese Regency complained to the British government that its troops were not afforded the same rights as Spanish troops. They began demanding that Portuguese troops be commanded independently, as the Spaniards were.

In early 1814, these problems combined to prevent the Regency dispatching the requisite number of reinforcements to Wellington's army. Wellington initially reacted with indignation. 'The Portuguese Government should recollect, that their engagement to keep 30,000 men in the field is

not with the Spanish Government, but with His Majesty,' he wrote obsti-
nately to Stuart.[78] In Wellington's opinion, the Portuguese troops would
not perform well independent of British command. On their own, he
argued, 'they could not field a respectable' force.[79] Consequently, he came
down hard on the Regency for hampering his operations, and changed the
terms of the subsidy agreement to reflect the number of troops the
Regency provided to the allied army. Running an already unmanageable
budget deficit, the Regency had no option but to comply, sending the
required reinforcements to Wellington by March 1814.

As usual, however, any problems with the Portuguese were vastly overshadowed by those Wellington encountered with his Spanish allies. In the
wake of the crossing of the Nivelle, the Spanish troops under Longa's
command sacked the village of Ascain, whilst those under Morillo plundered Espelette. Wellington was deeply concerned that Spanish aggression towards the French populace might result in the sort of reprisals that
had generated the *guerrilla* in Spain. With limited troops at his disposal,
he could not afford to leave large forces in his rear protecting his lines of
communication. At all costs, the population in southern France must be
appeased. Part of the motivation of the Spanish troops had been their lack
of supplies: they were forced to plunder out of necessity. 'Without pay and
food they must plunder,' remarked Wellington after the Battle of the
Nivelle. 'If they plunder they will ruin us all.'[80] These fears were in part
borne out in January, when troops from Mina's irregular division ransacked
the villages of Bidarray and Baigorry. This, as expected, alienated the
population to such a degree that they began harassing the British cantonments, doing 'more mischief than the French Army'.[81]

Wellington had no option but to withdraw the majority of the
Spaniards from his army. He sent the whole Fourth Army into cantonments over the border, the troops being escorted out of France under arms.
Longa, as its commander, was sent to Spain in disgrace. Freire and Longa
complained at Wellington's treatment of them, but the British general
was having none of it. 'I have not caused the death and wounding of
thousands of officers and soldiers so that the survivors can pillage the
French,' he wrote in irritation.[82] Morillo's Spaniards remained in France
as a flanking force on the far right, where it was deemed they could do no
mischief. For extra security, the troops were placed under arms in daylight
hours only. Whilst the Spanish troops were by no means paragons of
virtue, neither were they alone in their plundering activities. The British
and Portuguese soldiers also pillaged and robbed the French inhabitants
on arrival in the country, but received no such stiff punishment. Wellington's
treatment of the Spaniards under his command, who had by now proven

their loyalty to him as Commander-in-Chief, only served to alienate his allies.

The fact remained, though, that abuses by Spanish troops had a disproportionate effect on the population. Both French civilians and soldiers repeatedly expressed their fear at being left to the mercies of the Spanish soldiery. And who could blame them, with promises from prominent Spanish commanders that the troops would soon be able to avenge 'the atrocities committed by the enemies of humanity' the French?[83] Politically, Wellington had no option but to ensure the French population was protected from the brutality they feared at the hands of the Spaniards.

If Wellington's handling of the Spaniards appeared harsh, it was because this latest transgression came at the end of a long list of mistakes, failures and deliberate insubordination. Anglo-Spanish relations really soured after the storming of San Sebastian had given way to a torrent of pillaging, which resulted in an inferno that destroyed most of the town. The local junta accused the British of deliberately destroying the town in order to prevent it threatening British trading supremacy. Moreover, the continued indiscipline of the British troops was alienating the locals, whose initial delight at liberation swiftly soured when their liberators robbed and pillaged their property. Such was the weight of ill feeling among local Spaniards that the British began to see their supply lines hampered by passive resistance from Spanish authorities. Imports were embargoed in order to be searched for contraband goods, and Bilbao outlawed the transportation of supplies through its streets because of the damage the wagons caused to the road surfaces. Perhaps the final straw came when the whole of Santander, Wellington's main supply depot, was quarantined with a mystery illness. Demonstrating acutely Wellington's earlier concerns about the incoherent nature of the civilian control of supplies to the military, these activities exacerbated supply problems for the Spanish troops. This produced outbursts of violence between British and Spanish soldiers as the winter set in. Wellington was forced to offer supplies to the Spaniards, lest he lose their support for the invasion of France. As the allied army invaded France, what was supposed to be the moment of decisive victory should have been the subject of celebration within the Anglo-Spanish alliance, but instead Wellington's relations with his allies were at breaking point.

He could take no more. Charles Esdaile has suggested that the accumulated irritation at what Wellington perceived to be repeated attempts by the Spanish government, authorities and now, through the poor behaviour of the Spanish troops, the military, to hamper his operations, had become 'so severe as to deprive him of all sense of proportion'.[84] This is not an unreasonable conclusion. What came next was totally at odds with the political campaign Wellington had engaged in since arriving in the Peninsula. On the brink of complete and decisive victory over France, Wellington wrote in late November to Whitehall, calling for the withdrawal of the British Army unless certain conditions were met. First, Wellington wanted to weaken the liberal regime by reducing Britain's diplomatic representation at Madrid, and force the Spanish government to admit British troops to San Sebastian, thus establishing direct control over the lines of supply and communication of the army. This was all for the good of Spain, Wellington argued. 'You may rely upon this, that if you take a firm, decided line, and show your determination to go through with it,' he wrote, 'you will have the Spanish nation with you, you will bring the government to their senses . . .' What was more, unless Britain acted now to extinguish the anti-British rhetoric emanating from Madrid and Cadiz, 'if we do not show that we are sensible of the injury done to our characters, and of the injustice and unfriendly nature of such proceedings, we must expect that the people at large will soon behave towards us in the same manner, and that we shall have no friends'.[85] In other words, Britain's wider diplomatic credibility would be harmed, perhaps irrevocably.

This suggestion came at the least convenient moment for the British government. With Napoleon defeated in Germany, and the allied powers of Austria, Russia and Prussia preparing to invade France and sign a treaty that promised to continue the fight until Napoleon was deposed, the diplomats were now more concerned with the fate of post-Napoleonic Europe. Britain's credibility in such negotiations hinged on her ability to argue that she had contributed materially to the war effort, not just in a financial sense, but in the same way that the Great Powers had: by the commitment of land forces to the defeat of Napoleon. Wellington and his army was the only defence Lord Castlereagh, leading the British contingent in the negotiations at allied headquarters in northern Europe, had against charges of 'Perfidious Albion'. Withdrawal now might jeopardise British chances of influencing any post-war negotiations. Thus, when Bathurst sent his reply to Wellington's request, it was a firm negative. The reasons given were entirely military: 'I doubt very much whether the Spanish army would be equal to defend their own frontiers,' he wrote severely, 'and the jealousy and pride of Spain will not trust a Portuguese army' to aid in its defence.[86] The motives, though, were wholly political. The need for power and influence with the Great Powers trumped the need for power and influence in Spain. Wellington's request was denied, and his conditions for staying in France were firmly ignored. Wellington would continue his invasion of France, and Anglo-Spanish relations would remain tense until the end of the war.

It is hard not to sympathise with Wellington's criticism and anger at his allies. The Spaniards were proving mercurial partners. Now that Spain was liberated, her attention understandably turned inwards. The internal motivations that had given rise to the rebellion against the French and the proclamation of a liberal constitution were now denied a common enemy, and began to fracture. Britain, and Wellington in particular, was used as a scapegoat for many of the ills Spain had suffered over the past seven years. This was the inevitable product of a national war of survival, but Wellington appeared to take the criticisms personally, rather than dividing the specific problems that his army was suffering from the general hostility to the British. More seriously, Wellington was clearly treating his Spanish allies with contempt, perceiving their requirements as subordinate to those of the British Army. It is hard not to draw comparisons with Wellington's similar treatment of his Indian allies, a decade earlier. His over-reaction and attempt to have the British Army withdrawn at the point at which it could achieve decisive victory demonstrated the limitations of Wellington's political acumen. He had lost sight of the fact that Spain's very survival had been at stake, and never properly understood the wider pressures and tensions that had afflicted his allies throughout the campaign. It was a spiteful move, designed to teach the Spaniards that they could not get by without British support, but one, fortunately, that the level-headed Bathurst saw through. Wellington was once more reminded of the subordination of military operations to political objectives. Wellington's continued presence in the south of France guaranteed Britain's voice at the negotiating table. This was a point, after all, that Wellington had made after Vitoria, when the government had briefly considered withdrawing the British Army from Spain.

*   *   *

Wellington was forced into winter cantonments because the army had outpaced its supplies. 'My posts are already so far distant, that the transport of the army is daily destroyed in supplying the troops.'[87] Undoubtedly, though, Wellington was himself exhausted. 'I am quite certain the Government are tired of me and my operations; and I wish both to the devil,' he wrote to his brother. By February 1814, supplies had been re-established with mule trains traversing the narrow coastal roads to Bayonne, and the British were now able to purchase supplies from the local population. The allied army was ready to take to the field once more, and the advance Wellington planned on Orthez and Toulouse – designed to bring the French Army to a conventional battle and destroy it once and for all – would, of course, be the last of the Peninsular War.

Before advancing, however, Wellington had to consider the political scenario into which he was marching. The allies had not yet decided on the shape of the French government in the wake of Napoleon's defeat. The Austrians, and some elements of the British political scene, wanted to come to terms with Napoleon himself, but the Tories, and the Russians and Prussians, wanted to depose him. Wellington was concerned that Britain was not devising what might be termed an effective post-war strategy. In February, he received Louis Antoine de Bourbon, Duc d'Angoulême, the nephew of Louis XVIII, at his headquarters.[88] Such was the pro-Royalist feeling in the south that Wellington became convinced that France was ready for the restoration of the Bourbon monarchy. 'I find the sentiment in the country still more strong against the Bonaparte dynasty and in favour of the Bourbons,' he wrote to Liverpool. 'Any declaration from us would raise such a flame in the country as would soon spread from one end of it to the other, and would infallibly overturn' Bonaparte. In this estimation, Wellington was deluded by the enthusiasm of the Royalists in the south and assumed it translated into a general feeling across France.

In this febrile atmosphere, Wellington once more took to the field against Soult, who had lost a further 20,000 troops, sent north to reinforce Napoleon. Wellington now distinctly outnumbered Soult. Dividing his forces, he left 30,000 troops under Hope blockading Bayonne, while he marched with the rest of the army, striking east towards Orthez.

Hill and Beresford's march east was initially a diversion. Soult responded by stringing out his forces defending the northern bank of the Adour. He did not anticipate that Hope's forces would stage a bridging operation to the west of Bayonne. Although delayed by inclement weather, this was completed by 14 February, allowing Wellington to move with purpose to attack Soult now that the blockade of Bayonne was complete, and his rear thus protected. Wellington decided to attempt to outmanoeuvre Soult by sending Hill east, and then having him turn north outflanking Soult's position from the south, whilst Beresford would move to the north and form a blocking line to prevent Soult's retreat. Realising he had been outmanoeuvred from the south, Soult concentrated his force on a strong defensive position, north of Orthez. Wellington did not expect Soult to stand at Orthez, but when the French Marshal showed no signs of budging, Wellington had to halt to wait for Beresford to catch up. Soult, perceiving the allied troops to his south to be another diversion, readjusted his line, adopting an even stronger defensive position facing west, but leaving his southern flank open to attack.

On 27 February, when Beresford's column joined the rest of the allied army, Wellington attacked Soult's position in three columns. On the left, Beresford, with the Fourth and Seventh Divisions, was to roll up the enemy right, while the Third and Sixth Divisions were to attack Soult's centre. Hill would attempt to outflank Soult from the south and rear. The initial attack by Cole and the Fourth Division was successful in forcing the French from the outlying village of St Boes, but the British were counterattacked, and the entire attempt to roll up the French right stalled. Wellington now threw more effort behind Picton's Third and Clinton's Sixth Division attacks in the centre. Fighting here was extremely serious, but eventually Foy's defensive line on the French left disintegrated after its commander was wounded. This precipitated a general collapse of the French line, as each defensive position was rendered untenable by the collapse of its support. With Hill attacking from the south, Soult realised the game was up, and ordered an immediate retreat. Hampered by the hilly terrain, the allied pursuit was less effective than it might have been, with only the 7th Hussars achieving any success. During the battle, Wellington again escaped serious injury by a hair's breadth, when a musket ball hit his sword hilt. The impact temporarily incapacitated him, causing painful bruising from which it took him some days to recover.

At this point, Wellington received word from the mayor of Bordeaux that the city was willing to surrender to allied troops if they appeared before its gates. Soult, having elected to attempt to draw Wellington away from Bayonne and Bordeaux by falling back on Toulouse, was surprised once more by the allies' failure to pursue him with vigour. Wellington sent Beresford with the Fourth and Seventh Divisions to accept the surrender of Bordeaux, and then continued his offensive against Soult in mid-March, arriving at Toulouse at the end of the month. It was not until 7 April that the allied army had secure communications across the River Garonne, which flows through the heart of the city. Hill remained on the western bank outside St Cyprien, whilst, clockwise from north of the town, Picton's Third Division and the Light Division under Alten were to attack the outlying French pickets of Darriceau. The Spanish division of Morillo would launch the main attack on the north-western defences of the city, manned by Conroux and D'Armagnac, simultaneously with an attack launched by Cole and the Fourth and Clinton's Sixth Division, under Beresford's overall command, the latter having been recalled from Bordeaux with the Fourth Division. This column was positioned further to the north, but would march south to outflank Soult's defences to the south-west of the city.

The attack began at dawn on 10 April, and proceeded well until Picton over-extended himself and was beaten back twice with heavy losses. The

Spaniards, however, advanced too soon, misinterpreting action on their left as indicating that Beresford was launching his attack. Consequently, facing the focused fire of D'Armagnac, despite a gallant advance, the Spaniards were beaten back with heavy losses. Eventually, the Fourth and Sixth Divisions manoeuvred into position and attacked from the south-west. Soult withdrew from his first line of defence, establishing a second line facing south and running west from the western suburb of St Etienne. At about half past two in the afternoon, Beresford launched an assault on this line, coordinated with a second attack from the north by the Spaniards, which was again held up by heavy French fire. In the south, though, the Sixth Division led the attack, taking some heights over-looking St Etienne, while the Fourth Division and its cavalry support offered flank protection and prevented any successful French counter-attack. The redoubts outside the city then became the subject of continued contest, which saw them change hands repeatedly. Only when Lambert's brigade from the Sixth Division was committed was the battle decided. The French retired into the town at about five in the evening, finally evacuating the city on the evening of 11 April. Wellington entered Toulouse early the next day, to acclaim from the Royalist population. That evening, Colonel Ponsonby arrived from Bordeaux with some astonishing news. Napoleon had abdicated on 6 April. The battle at Toulouse had been fought unnecessarily. The war was over.

Following the Battle of Leipzig in October 1813, Napoleon's power was all but smashed, but the allied armies of Russia, Austria and Prussia also suffered greatly – some 50,000 casualties out of a total of over 300,000. The pause in allied operations also reflected the tensions within the allied camp over precisely what terms they wished to impose on France. Austria wanted to maintain Napoleon on the throne to provide a counter to increasing Russian strength. Russia still preferred Napoleon, but in order to counter British strength. Prussia, on the whole, wanted to be rid of Napoleon, although this policy was far from concrete. The Frankfurt Memorandum, issued on 1 December, proposed peace with Napoleon in return for the withdrawal of French power behind her 'natural frontiers'; in other words, the Rhine in the east, the Alps in the south, and the Pyrenees in the west. Britain found the proposals unacceptable, as they left the Low Countries in French hands. Lord Aberdeen, the British diplomat present at allied Headquarters, was young and inexperienced, and outclassed by the devious Metternich, Austria's Chancellor. It also seems that the dreadful sights Aberdeen witnessed at Leipzig may well have affected his judgement. In any event, Napoleon, reflecting his increasing disengagement from reality, refused the terms, and thus blew the last chance he had of reasonable peace terms. Britain, relieved to have dodged this particular bullet, dispatched Castlereagh to ensure her position was adequately represented. The allies invaded France at the beginning of January 1814.

Napoleon's defence of France was possibly one of his greatest military campaigns. Here was the dynamic general that had dominated Europe from 1796 to 1805. But it came too late. Dodging the strong French defensive fortresses in the north, the allies invaded from Switzerland. The invasion campaign once more reflected the tensions between the allies. The Prussian and Russian Army of Silesia, commanded by General Gebhard Leberecht von Blücher, the seventy-two-year-old hero of Prussia's wars against Napoleon, attacked along a northerly axis towards Paris, while the Austrian and Russian armies, under the allied Commander-in-Chief, the slow and methodical Austrian Field Marshal, Karl Philipp, Prince of Schwarzenberg, invaded along a southerly route from Basle. Blücher, a charismatic and slightly mad risk-taker, pressed on rapidly, whilst Schwarzenberg, reflecting his personal preferences and the Austrian desire for a compromise peace with Napoleon, marched his army at a snail's pace.

In mid-February, Napoleon inflicted damaging defeats on Blücher in the north before darting south and forcing Schwarzenberg to retreat. Blücher, suffering from mental and physical exhaustion, descended into a world of paranoid delusion, including alarming hallucinations of being pregnant with an elephant. The Prussian advance ground completely to a halt. Forced back, it seemed as though the allied campaign would fall at the final hurdle. Instead, the Great Powers rallied, convinced now that Napoleon's power had to be decisively defeated, and on 1 March 1814 Great Britain, Austria, Prussia and Russia signed the Treaty of Chaumont. By the terms of this accord, each of the powers promised not to reach a separate peace with Napoleon; agreed that they would continue to fight until terms satisfactory to all of the allies were achieved – namely the imposition on France of her 1792 borders (somewhat less generous than the 'natural' borders offered in Frankfurt the previous December); and promised to maintain an armed force ready to prevent any resurgence of illegitimate French power for the next twenty years. With a renewed sense of purpose, the allies began their final onslaught on the French capital. Napoleon, convinced that an attack on the allied rear and communications would force Schwarzenberg to retreat, gambled, and lost. Instead, the allies pressed on to Paris, which fell on 31 March. Once there, Napoleon's devious foreign minister, Talleyrand, switched sides, and sought to negotiate the removal of Napoleon and the restoration of Louis XVIII. The allies agreed, and refused to negotiate with Napoleon or his family. Six days later, with the remains of his army abandoning him, Napoleon abdicated.[89]

In the south, Soult refused to accept this news, and asked for an armistice to ascertain its truth. Nor did General Thouvenot, the governor of Bayonne believe the news and on 14 April he staged a daring sortie, which took Hope by surprise. In the fighting, both sides sustained heavy casualties and Hope himself was wounded and captured. Having received confirmation of the news from Paris, Soult and Wellington signed the Convention of Toulouse on 18 April. Thus ended the Peninsular War. Toulouse had been a bloody battle, fought unnecessarily, a darkly appropriate conclusion to a brutal and remorseless conflict, which had cost as many as a quarter of a million lives, among them those of 40,000 British soldiers.

On the face of it there was not much about the allied invasion of France that can be described as 'Light and Quick'. Having used a variation of 'Light and Quick' operations to bring his army to Vitoria, thereafter Wellington seemed to abandon the approach to operations that had won him much success. That said, it is clear that Wellington always chose the best and most expedient option available to him, and many of the principles that had defined the original concept were present after June 1813: frequent operational pauses to allow logistical arrangements to catch up with the well-advanced army; major advances designed to overawe the enemy and force him to retreat; the seizure of objectives designed to shape the actions of the enemy and force a battle on allied terms; and a constant eye kept on political considerations. There just was not much that was quick about the invasion of France. Perhaps a better name would have been 'Light and Decisive'.

Wellington had moulded an army from a rabble composed of the 'scum of the earth', had trained it in the course of six years of high-intensity warfare, had developed his tactical prowess from defensive to offensive, and had worn down, divided, and all but annihilated an opponent whose ubiquitous military skill had conquered much of Europe. Thus, the battles that comprise the invasion of France were outstanding victories in their own right, but as a key event in Wellington's career they deserve much more recognition, and were it not for what happened on a small ridge south of Brussels in Belgium a year later, they might well have been remembered as Wellington's greatest victories.

The campaign, of course, had not been without its problems. Interservice relations between the army and the navy had caused some unnecessary difficulties, but Wellington here was as much to blame for failing to understand the competing pressures on the Admiralty. There were also the constant problems with the allies. Anglo-Spanish relations had never been anything short of fractious, and Wellington fell into the trap of treating his Spanish comrades in the same way as he did his Indian allies, that is to say, not as equals. In India, the alliances Wellington had forged had been with powers that placed a disproportionate emphasis on military force. In Spain, the government with which Wellington had such a difficult relationship was fighting for the survival and liberation of its nation. To some degree, Wellington failed to respect this, and treated his allies and their objectives as subservient rather than equal to the wider necessity of defeating Napoleon. Spain's contribution to its own liberation is often overlooked. British campaigns aside, the Spanish Army had continued to fight Napoleon's armies for the duration of the conflict, whilst the irregular forces had also posed a constant problem for the French. Combined, this provided a drain on French resources so strong that it gave Wellington many of the opportunities he capitalised on in 1812 and 1813. Despite its problems, then, the alliance survived and ultimately produced victory.

In the wake of Toulouse, there was, of course, much to celebrate. Napoleon had finally been defeated, and Britain had played an important, if peripheral role in the collapse of his empire. This gave Castlereagh, who was preparing for the consuming negotiations that were about to redraw the map of Europe, a very good hand to play in the discussions with his counterparts from Austria, Prussia and Russia. The government could not fail to recognise Wellington's contribution to this political success, and bestowed upon him a dukedom, whilst peerages were given to no fewer than five of his most senior officers. Nevertheless, in the wake of military victory, politicians have a habit of forgetting the doubts they had expressed about the feasibility of a war. Bathurst, it seems, was no exception.

'What had distinguished the English Nation in the late war with France?' he asked a rapturous Parliament. 'It was not merely the greatness of her exertions, nor was it the skill of her generals.' No, in fact 'it was the firmness and perseverance with which the country had maintained the contest and the pertinacity with which it upheld the independence of the Peninsula', he claimed. Britain, he said, held 'up a pillar of fire amidst the surrounding darkness, which marked out to other nations the path to the Promised Land – to the haven of safety and independence'.[90] Clearly, this speech was aimed at the opponents of the war in Parliament, and to Britain's allies who needed reminding that, far from being perfidious, Albion alone had maintained the fight against Napoleon, even when all seemed lost. True, Wellington can be criticised for losing sight of how the Peninsular War fitted into Britain's wider strategy, but it was he who originally conceived a grand strategy in a seemingly insignificant backwater, fending off criticism and indifference from every angle. With a raised eyebrow, then, might Wellington reflect on the irony of Bathurst's statement, as he remembered his own dark days of conflict in the Peninsula. Days such as those when he had to fight to maintain his command; when he had to engage in constant debate with the Treasury to maintain a supply of money to pay his soldiers; when he had to keep up a barrage of angry letters to Whitehall to sustain awareness of his needs, and press home the severity of his situation; when he had to deal with acrimony in Britain's alliances with Spain and Portugal that threatened the very future of the war; or when he had to handle incompetent subordinates, argue an obvious case with the Admiralty, and punish soldiers who pillaged because they had not enough food. But, most of all, when he wept at the burials of his fallen men.

CHAPTER 9

Wellington's Waterloo

THE BATTLE FOR THE BALANCE OF
POWER IN EUROPE, 1814–1815

I should not do justice to my own feelings, or to Marshal Blücher and the Prussian Army, if I did not attribute the successful result of this arduous day to the cordial and timely assistance I received from them.

Field Marshal the Duke of Wellington,
Commander-in-Chief Allied Forces
Brussels, Belgium, 19 June 1815[1]

T HE Battle of Waterloo was as much a great Prussian military victory as it was a great British military victory. The timely arrival of Blücher's Prussian army on the left of Wellington's Anglo-Dutch line undoubtedly sealed Napoleon's fate. True, Wellington only fought at Waterloo because he had received a guarantee from Blücher that the Prussians would support him (although the chances of a successful retreat either on the evening of 17 June, or on the morning of the 18th, looked extremely slim). True, also, that Wellington's army held out for a considerable period of time under a sustained and brutal attack, and it is doubtful that any other commander would have deployed his forces in such a way as to withstand such an onslaught. But, ultimately, it was the arrival of the Prussians that decided the day, and to them went the spoils of victory.

Or not, as the case may be. Because, however great the Prussian contribution to the military victory at Waterloo, it was unquestionably solely a British political victory. This was the result of politicking and manoeuvring in the weeks preceding and succeeding Waterloo. To explain this, we must understand what the Battle of Waterloo was really fought for. Napoleon had to be defeated, true, but his defeat would have been guaranteed by a timely withdrawal of allied forces from Belgium, allowing the sizeable Austrian and Russian forces to come forward. Why, then, did Wellington fight in Belgium? The battle fought at Waterloo was not solely about defeating Napoleon and laying to rest the threat of a resurgent Imperial France; it was also about securing the peace that had been won in 1814.[2] For Britain, this meant establishing political dominance over her allies, notably Prussia. Waterloo was as much about alliance politics as it was about defeating Napoleon.

*   *   *

The five months following the end of the Peninsular War were frenetic for Wellington. He had arrived in Paris in May to a rapturous welcome as Britain's new ambassador, and on visiting the opera, for example, the audience rose and cheered 'Vive Wellington'.[3] Soon, though, unwelcome news had arrived from Spain of impending civil war, and Wellington was sent to Madrid in an effort to restore order. After his restoration, Ferdinand VII had swept away the liberal reforms introduced by the Regency and Cortes during the years of French occupation. Unsurprisingly, those who had been dispossessed by the new liberal regime greeted this turn of events with jubilation, whilst the proponents of the Constitution of 1812 sought support to fight for its principles. For a time, civil war seemed certain, not least because the liberal proponent General Manuel Freire commanded the Fourth Army, which had recently returned from France, and seemed poised to fight for the Constitution. In the event, the situation was less perilous. Wellington, when he arrived on 24 May, found intervention unnecessary. He attempted to persuade his former subordinates that they needed to 'prevent factious persons ... influencing the conduct of the officers and troops in order to produce a civil war'.[4] Taken by the Spanish authorities, and Ferdinand in particular, as Wellington's grudging acceptance of the restoration of absolutism, it was, in fact, an attempt to enforce a separation of political and military power. Throughout his tenure as Commander-in-Chief, Wellington had sought constantly to prevent military intervention in domestic politics, and when he advocated it, it was only as a last resort. Sadly, this principle was lost when he resigned the Spanish command on 13 June, soon after his departure for the last time from Madrid.[5]

From Spain, Wellington travelled to Bordeaux, where he also relinquished the command of the Peninsular Army, which was being disbanded. Some units would travel to North America; others were destined for the West and East Indies and Ireland. Unsurprising though the decision was, the disbandment of Wellington's army was one the British government and Wellington would come to rue a year later. Wellington then returned to England, via the French capital, where the Treaty of Paris had just been concluded. Sailing in to a rapturous welcome at Dover, Wellington was returning home for the first time in five years. He was not to stay for long. By August he was in Brussels, discussing the defence of the Low Countries against future French aggression. Before travelling back to Paris to resume his embassy at the court of the restored King Louis XVIII, Wellington took the opportunity to survey the defensive terrain south of Brussels.

'The face of the country is generally open, and affords no feature upon which reliance can be placed to establish any defensive system,' Wellington wrote. The terrain was 'intersected by roads, canals and rivers, running in all directions'. Manoeuvrability and communication would be slow and unreliable. An invading force capitalising on the broken terrain could easily outflank any defending army. Any British force defending the Netherlands would be placed at a disadvantage because its communications with the Channel offered an invading force an easy target. On the bright side, there were plenty of suitable strong defensive positions 'between Tournay and Mons; ... about Nivelle; ... and' the ridgeway of Mont St Jean.[6] Despite the strength of these positions, Wellington would continue to worry that any army could be easily outflanked.

Back in Paris by late August, Wellington was immediately the centre of a social whirl and was the guest of honour at numerous soirées and balls, whilst also partaking in hunting trips with the royal party. He reputedly conducted affairs with at least two of Napoleon's former mistresses. Although taking mistresses was *de rigueur* in restoration France, the indiscretion with which he conducted these affairs – in full view of his wife when she finally arrived from England – began a swift process of disillusionment. Wellington did not help matters by appearing aloof and rude in public. 'The negligence of the Duke of Wellington's manner and the familiarity of his nods are quoted in every company as proofs of his insolence,' recorded one English visitor. 'He has neither courtesy nor display enough to be popular at Paris.'[7] As French society realised that the restoration of Louis XVIII brought with it economic hardship, opinion turned decisively against the Bourbons, as well as the British. Wellington was a particular target for discontent by disenfranchised Bonapartists, and he narrowly escaped assassination at the end of October. By late November, 'the feeling [was] now so strong and so general against' the British, noted the same visitor, 'as to make the residence of Paris really unpleasant'.[8]

It soon became apparent to Liverpool that Wellington had become a focus of French discontent and that his presence in Paris was contributing to the difficulties of the restored Bourbon regime. Wellington would have to go elsewhere. William Wellesley-Pole suggested offering Wellington the North American command, but the Duke refused. The war with America broke out in 1812 largely because of disputes over Britain's implementation of the 'Orders in Council', which were devised in reaction to Napoleon's Continental System. The 'Orders' restricted neutral trade and enforced blockades against French ports. This inevitably hindered American trade with Europe. The United States objected to this flagrant abuse of power, and war was declared in 1812. Wellington perceived the war to be a fool's errand, and did not want a command in America, which he felt would lead nowhere. By December, a new possibility presented itself. Castlereagh, having spent the whole autumn in Vienna negotiating the settlement of post-war Europe, was required to account for his action in Parliament. Wellington was the ideal choice as his replacement. On 1 February 1815, Wellington's carriage trundled into the Austrian capital, depositing the Duke in the centre of a diplomatic whirlwind that had nearly resulted in a new European war, and would define the coming final contest with Napoleon.

* * *

The Congress of Vienna had been convened to resolve the outstanding issues arising from the French defeat. Napoleon's conquest of Europe had fundamentally redefined its identity and a mere return to the status quo ante bellum was swiftly ruled out as impossible to enforce. The Treaty of Paris, signed on 30 May 1814, had settled European concerns about French strength, but the issue of what to do with the rest of Europe remained undecided. The principal issues that needed addressing were the composition and governance of the Italian states; whether Poland should be partitioned, given independence or fall under Russian influence; how Prussia was to be reconstituted; what was to be done with the other German states – notably Bavaria, Saxony, Brunswick, Württemberg and Hanover; and how the differences between Denmark and Sweden were to be reconciled. All the Great Powers had interests in all of the issues, and reaching decisions on the format of the Congress, let alone on the final resolution of these problems, had taken months.

Britain was in a reasonably good position: the Treaty of Paris had satisfied all of her war aims. Under this treaty, France had been forced to accept her pre-war frontiers, whilst Antwerp and the Scheldt estuary had been incorporated into an independent Holland, which now also included the whole of Belgium. Elsewhere, the acquisition of colonies such as Malta, the Cape of Good Hope, Tobago and Mauritius had ensured Britain's strategic mastery of the seas, and with it communications in the Mediterranean and with the West and East Indies. The Great Powers might grumble – Metternich himself had called 'England's dominion on [the seas] ... no less monstrous than Napoleon's on the continent'[9] – but there was little they could do about it. Castlereagh had gone to Vienna, then, perceiving himself to be a mediator rather than a player. He would be swiftly disabused of this notion. The terms of the Treaty of Paris had been really quite generous to France – 'No murders, no torture, no conflagration, how will the pretty women of London bear it?', quipped one English satirist[10] – and the other Great Powers, particularly Prussia, were aiming for a renegotiation of the treaty's articles. To Castlereagh and, later, Wellington, it was obvious that nothing less than the balance of power in Europe was at stake.

Following the abdication of Napoleon in April 1814, Castlereagh, along with all the other European powers, perceived the major threat to continental stability to be France. She certainly remained the biggest threat to the independence of the Low Countries, that all-important strategic trigger for British intervention on the continent. It was for this reason that Wellington had been assessing the defences of southern Belgium in August 1814. In order to counter French hostility to the Low Countries, Castlereagh undertook to reinforce German strength in that region of Europe to act as a deterrence:

> There can be no doubt that the support of so highly military a Power as Bavaria on the left flank, with Prussia in second line to Holland ... presents a much more imposing front to France than Holland spread out to the Moselle ... with Prussia behind the Rhine ... The great question ... is to weigh what is the best security for peace, and for keeping the Low Countries out of the hands of France.[11]

France, however, was concerned about the increasing German, and particularly Prussian, strength so close to her borders, perceiving a threat to the balance of power in Europe. It was a position the British would soon come to understand, but for the moment Castlereagh found such a notion ridiculous, arguing that 'France need never dread a German league; it is in its nature inoffensive, and there is no reason to fear that the union between Austria and Prussia will be such as to endanger the liberties of other states.'[12]

Swiftly, though, other bogeymen were identified among the Great Powers, with France the least worrying, as Liverpool observed in late December 1814:

> The more I hear and see from the different Courts of Europe, the more convinced I am that the King of France is (amongst the Great Powers)

the only Sovereign in whom we can have any real confidence. The Emperor of Russia is profligate from vanity and self-sufficiency, if not from principle. The King of Prussia may be a well-meaning man, but he is the dupe of the Emperor of Russia. The Emperor of Austria I believe to be an honest man, but he has a minister in whom no one can trust; who considers all policy as consisting in finesse and trick, and who has got his government and himself into more difficulties by his devices than could have occurred from a plain course of dealing.[13]

Wellington agreed. 'The situation of affairs in the world will naturally constitute England and France as arbitrators at the Congress, if those Powers understand each other.'[14] While in Paris, Wellington's key diplomatic goal had been securing the support of Louis XVIII for Britain's objectives in balancing power in Europe.

The intricacies and vicissitudes of the negotiations that occurred in Vienna between September 1814 and March 1815 are complicated, but the main bones of contention that were to have lasting repercussions were Russia's claim on Poland and Prussia's claim on Saxony. The two problems were interconnected and appeared insoluble. 'With respect to the Polish question,' wrote Castlereagh instructively, 'you must always combine it, to a certain degree, with that of Saxony, as Austria can ill afford to be foiled on both these points.'[15] Tsar Alexander of Russia, perceiving himself to be the liberator of Europe, had pledged a united Poland, with the caveat that he became its king. Specifically unacceptable to Austria, which would be seriously threatened and weakened by a Russian presence that far west, Alexander's proposals were also deeply unattractive to Castlereagh and Talleyrand, who both sought to balance Russian power in Europe. Alexander's only ally in his pursuit of Polish territory was King Frederick William of Prussia, and his chancellor, Hardenberg. Prussia, having been all but wiped from the map by Napoleon in 1806, and having played a key role in his eventual defeat, had been promised Saxony, whose king and army had remained allied to Napoleon until the Battle of Leipzig. In return, Prussia had promised to turn over South Prussia and New East Prussia to Russia. But, territory alone was not enough. Also being negotiated were populations, to provide much needed income through taxation, and conscripts for future military campaigns. It quickly became apparent that two alternatives for the peace of Europe were presenting themselves: 'a union of the two Great German Powers, supported by Great Britain, and thus combining the minor states of Germany, together with Holland, in an intermediary system between Russia and France – or a union of Austria, France and the Southern States against the Northern Powers, with Russia and Prussia in close alliance'.[16]

For the moment, Prussia's demands in Saxony were the lesser of two evils. 'I am confident I speak the universal sentiment, when I declare my perfect conviction,' wrote Castlereagh pessimistically, 'that unless the Emperor of Russia can be brought to a more moderate and sound course of public conduct, the peace, which we have so dearly purchased, will be but of short duration.'[17] He therefore decided to try and break the Russo-Prussian alliance by persuading Metternich to accept Prussian demands in Saxony, in return for Prussian support against Russia over Poland. This was the best possible outcome for Castlereagh, who wanted a strong Prussia to counter the threat of a remilitarised France.[18] Unfortunately, although he won both Metternich and Talleyrand over to the idea, and even managed to persuade Hardenberg to convince Frederick William to break with Alexander, British public opinion cared little for Poland, and was incensed at the treatment of Saxony. 'I ought to apprise you that there is a strong feeling in this country respecting Saxony,' reported Liverpool. The British public, it seems, took exception to the erasure of a country and nation from the map of Europe. 'The case against the King [of Saxony] appears to me, I confess, to be complete, if it is expedient to act upon it; but the objection is to the annihilation of the whole of Saxony as an independent Power . . .'[19]

Castlereagh was ordered to reverse course and renege on his promise to Hardenberg. Prussia would not be allowed to annex the whole of Saxony, and would be compensated elsewhere. Unsurprisingly, this drove Hardenberg and Frederick William back into the arms of Alexander. War now became a genuine possibility, and Castlereagh began speculating as to how Britain might become involved, albeit against her will:

Take the case of Russia and Prussia: if they are determined to make common cause on their respective objects, and cannot succeed in prevailing upon the other powers to acquiesce in their demands, it will not suit the exhausted finances of Prussia to remain long armed and inactive; nor can Russia expose herself indefinitely to the encumbrance of large armies remaining unemployed beyond or on the verge of her own frontier. I think the probability therefore is, that one or both of these Powers, if they do not relax in their pretensions, will provoke rather than procrastinate the war. If war should, under these circumstances, arise, I think it has every prospect of becoming general in Germany. That France must now and will enter into it, I have no doubt, and with Holland, the Low Countries, and Hanover exposed, in addition to the interest we must take in the fate of the Continent, it will be difficult for Great Britain long, if at all, to abstract herself from the contest.[20]

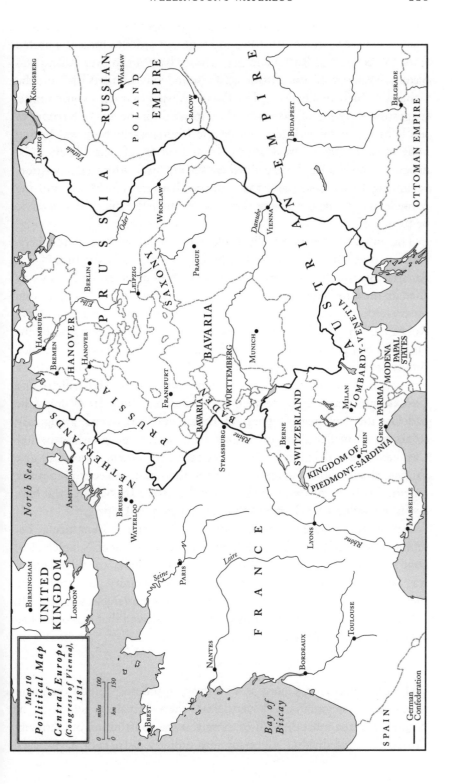

Map 10
Political Map
of
Central Europe
(Congress of Vienna),
1814

miles 100 150
km
0

North Sea

UNITED KINGDOM
•BIRMINGHAM
LONDON•

RUSSIAN EMPIRE
•KÖNIGSBERG
•WARSAW
POLAND
•CRACOW
•DANZIG
Vistula

PRUSSIA
•BERLIN
Elbe
WROCŁAW•
Oder
SAXONY
•LEIPZIG
•PRAGUE

AUSTRIAN EMPIRE
•VIENNA
Danube
•BUDAPEST
•BELGRADE
OTTOMAN EMPIRE

HAMBURG•
BREMEN•
HANOVER
•HANOVER

NETHERLANDS
AMSTERDAM•
BRUSSELS•
•WATERLOO

PRUSSIA

BAVARIA
FRANKFURT•
•MUNICH
WÜRTTEMBERG
BADEN
•STRASSBURG
Rhine

SWITZERLAND
BERNE•

LOMBARDY-VENETIA
MILAN•
KINGDOM OF PIEDMONT-SARDINIA
TURIN•
GENOA
MODENA
PARMA
PAPAL STATES
•MARSEILLE

FRANCE
Seine
•PARIS
Loire
•NANTES
•BREST
•LYONS
Rhône
•BORDEAUX
•TOULOUSE

Bay of Biscay

SPAIN

German Confederation

Tensions became so extreme that Castlereagh suggested a secret defensive alliance between Britain, Austria and France, in order to present a united front to Prussia and Russia and get them to back down over Poland and Saxony. Wellington was instructed to sound out Louis XVIII on the viability of such an alliance.[21] The Prussians tried to reach a compromise, suggesting the King of Saxony be recompensed for the loss of territory in southern Germany with territory on the Rhine. Castlereagh was having none of it. 'To place a weak Prince, from a variety of causes likely to be dependent on France,' he explained caustically, 'in so advanced a position, occupying Luxembourg and the countries between the Meuse and the Moselle, was to expose all our defences on the left bank of that river to be turned.'[22]

The impasse was eventually broken by, of all people, Hardenberg. Frustrated at what he perceived to be the betrayal of Great Britain and Austria, he sought to curry favour with Alexander and permanently alienate the latter from Metternich and Castlereagh by presenting to him his correspondence with them about their attempts to split Prussia from Russia over the Polish question. Alexander was, of course, outraged by the machinations going on behind his back, but in his defence Metternich simply presented his correspondence with Hardenberg on the issue, which revealed that the Prussians were in fact complicit in Metternich's and Castlereagh's actions. Hardenberg had blundered badly. In so doing, he had lost the diplomatic support of Russia and was forced, grudgingly, to accept a smaller share of Saxony than he had previously expected. Castlereagh was delighted. 'The arrangement in contemplation will give Prussia about eight hundred and fifty thousand subjects in Saxony, together with the fortresses on the Elbe. The King [of Saxony] will have about one million two hundred thousand, including Leipzig.'[23]

Prussia was rather less satisfied with this arrangement. In particular, her senior generals felt that their exertions in the final defeat of Napoleon had gone unrewarded. Suffice it to say that the issue, to their minds, was far from settled, and, the moment an opportunity presented itself, they would reopen the question and seek a more tolerable solution. On 7 March, just such an opportunity arose. News arrived that Napoleon had escaped his exile on Elba.

* * *

Wellington arrived in Vienna as an uneasy calm descended on the major issues under negotiation. Nevertheless, there remained issues to be decided, and the most difficult of those was the constitution of Germany. Prussia favoured dividing Germany into military districts or *Kreise*, each to be headed by one of the larger German states – Austria, Prussia, Hanover, Bavaria and Württemberg – which, among other things, would administer and command the armed forces that fell within that district.[24] Austria, in contrast, wanted a centralised authority with limited powers. Effectively, this became a battle for the manpower available in Germany, and Wellington's role was initially limited to defending the rights of Hanover. This role expanded when Napoleon landed in France and once more posed a military threat to the rest of Europe.

A council of war was convened to decide on the allied response. Wellington represented Britain, Barclay de Tolly stood for Russia, Schwarzenberg for Austria, and Kleist for Prussia. In the wake of the surprising turn of events in Paris, and bearing in mind the extraordinary nature of the threat Napoleon posed, Prussia sought to take command of all available troops in the northern German states. This was the first of a series of attempts by Prussia to exert military authority over Germany as a whole. Austria, unsurprisingly, objected, and in the end Schwarzenberg prevailed. An Austrian force was sent south to deal with Murat, who had remained King of Naples, and now marched in favour of Napoleon. An army would be deployed to the Low Countries, consisting of Kleist's Prussian corps, the garrison of Mainz and the troops supplied by the smaller German states, including Brunswick, Saxony, Hesse-Kassel Hesse-Darmstadt and Nassau, along with the British, Hanoverians and the Dutch and Belgians. This was to be commanded by Wellington. A third army would occupy the Upper Rhine, under Schwarzenberg's command, but would take some time to assemble. The strategy was clear. The allies, having reaffirmed the Treaty of Chaumont on 25 March, sought to encircle Napoleon as they had done so successfully in 1814. The Russians would form a reserve in Württemberg.[25]

However, the situation became more urgent when news arrived that the Bourbon regime was not going to be able to resist Napoleon's advance. The Royal Fifth Regiment, sent to stop Napoleon at all costs, refused to fire, and promptly switched sides. Soon after, Marshal Ney followed suit, despite having promised Louis XVIII that he would bring Napoleon back to Paris in a steel cage. The next one hundred days would see the allies, and Wellington in particular, consistently underestimate the speed with which Napoleon could regain control and reconstitute the forces of Imperial France. A second council of war was convened. Schwarzenberg was aware that the speed of Napoleon's resurgence had strengthened the Prussian hand, and now sought to protect Austrian interests, specifically by preventing Kleist getting his hands on the contingent from Hesse-Darmstadt. All other concerns were secondary. The Prussians now successfully lobbied for command of all the troops north of the Main, as well as Oldenburg and Brunswick. Schwarzenberg left it to Wellington to fight it out with the Prussians over the precise allocation of resources. Wellington was aghast at what was widely perceived as a Prussian move 'to procure for herself a military supremacy over Northern Germany'.[26]

Wellington could delay his own departure to the headquarters of his new command – in Brussels – no longer, leaving Earl Cathcart, Castlereagh's, original deputy (and the son of Wellington's former commander on the Copenhagen expedition), to fight Britain's corner against the Prussians. Clearly Hanover would fall under Wellington's command, but what of the other German states? Kleist yielded on Brunswick, the Hanseatic Cities and Oldenburg, but points of contention remained over Nassau, the Hessians and, of course, Saxony. The latter three fell under Prussia's projected *Kreise*, and the Prussians were unprepared to lose the opportunity of enforcing their idea of the future German constitution. But precisely because they could see their sovereignty being eroded, the leaders of Nassau, Hesse-Kassel and Saxony preferred that their troops served under Wellington. The Nassau contingent, based on a past relationship with Wellington in the Peninsula, was placed under his command, but for the same reason the Hessians were allocated to Blücher, who was appointed to the Prussian command in the Low Countries. As for the Saxons, it was decided that those troops who came from the territory newly annexed by Prussia would fall under Blücher's command, whilst those who remained in Royal Saxony would be given to Wellington. Small wonder then that, as a consequence of being divided, the Saxon contingent mutinied on 2 May. The corps – an ordinarily extremely disciplined and reliable force – never saw action, not least because Blücher's firing squads saw off what remained of its fighting quality.[27]

Politics had clearly not been left on the negotiating table in Vienna. The Prussians, justifiably or unjustifiably, were utilising Napoleon's return as a means of increasing their own authority and power within Germany. Although Prussia was the weakest of the Great Powers, benign as she might be in 1815, she nevertheless represented a distinct threat to the balance of power in Europe. Wellington, now implicitly involved in the political negotiations before and after Napoleon's return, would have been more than aware of what was at stake. The only way to ensure that Britain's interests were adequately represented after Napoleon was defeated was to ensure that Britain played a perceptibly crucial role in that defeat. If Prussia could claim to have defeated Napoleon alone, or with minor support from Britain, then her political authority in the subsequent peace negotiations would be almost insurmountable. Worse still, if none of the allies – Britain, Austria or Prussia – could defeat Napoleon outright, the Russians might sally forth and inflict a crushing defeat on Napoleon's by then mangled army. The consequences were worrying. Russia would be able to exert a level of control in Europe that might seriously destabilise the continent in Britain's eyes. For this reason, Castlereagh had subsidised German rather than Russian troops in the run-up to war.[28] The politics of Waterloo, then, was in balancing Prussian and Russian expansion, whilst ensuring Britain was a key participant. Only then would Britain's interests be adequately defended. The political pressure on Wellington to exact a quick and decisive victory over Napoleon was clear. In this atmosphere, the Iron Duke arrived in Brussels. If he did not take the offensive, then he had to defend terrain which earlier reconnaissance had shown favoured a well-organised attacker. In Wellington's opinion, any position he defended, no matter how tactically strong, could be easily outflanked, particularly by Napoleon, the master of envelopment and the famous *manoeuvre sur les derrières*. It was this issue that was to play on Wellington's mind for the whole campaign, and that was to lead to a series of mistakes by the British general that nearly cost him the campaign, and his reputation.

*   *   *

Between March and May, Wellington organised his forces in Belgium. His disparate band of troops was, by June, 93,000 strong, composed of Britons, Netherlanders and Germans, approximately a third each. Wellington considered this ragtag horde to be 'an infamous army, very weak and ill equipped, and a very inexperienced Staff'. He worked to remedy his chronic shortage of competent staff officers, but, in his opinion, the politicians were 'doing nothing in England. They have not raised a man; ... [and] are unable to send me anything ...'[29] Wellington, as usual, was underestimating the competing pressures facing Horse Guards, the administrative headquarters of the British Army in Whitehall, but his complaints reflect widespread concerns over a creaking military machine in desperate need of reform. As war approached, and Wellington surveyed his poorly trained army, he wished he 'could bring everything together as I had it when I took leave of the army at Bordeaux, and I would engage that we should not be the last in the race; but, as it is, I must manage matters as well as I can.'[30] It was quite apparent that this army would be incapable of the complex tactical manoeuvres that had won decisive victories at Salamanca, Vitoria and the Nivelle.

Despite these reservations, Wellington and his allies could not conceive how quickly Napoleon would be able to reconstitute his forces, and so the weight of military planning up to June 1815 was for an invasion of France. The glaring political differences between the British and the Prussians were apparent from the outset. Gneisenau, the Prussian chief of staff, expected a concerted drive on Paris. For the Prussians, capturing Paris was the key to defeating Napoleon, whilst the French capital would also prove a valuable bargaining chip in any subsequent peace negotiations.[31] Gneisenau's plan was blatantly politically motivated. Wellington, on the other hand, perceived that the key to Napoleon's defeat was the army itself. It had swung behind the emperor when he returned from Elba, and it was unquestionably his centre of gravity. Defeat the army, and Napoleon would be no more.[32] As neither ally realistically expected Napoleon to take the offensive, both envisaged that the decisive battle would be in the vicinity of Paris. The difference was that the Prussians perceived the city itself to be the prize, whilst the British considered the freedom of Paris as central to their post-war plan.

Neither Wellington nor Gneisenau were stupid enough to discount the possibility of Napoleon taking his army on the offensive, particularly after the Austrians and Russians refused to sanction the invasion of France until June or July, when their forces would be able to play a decisive role. Wellington therefore had to consider how to defend terrain he believed largely indefensible. His solution was to string his forces along a 62-mile front, guarding four of the five paved roads through Belgium, and with them the routes to Brussels, Antwerp and Ghent. He did so in a fashion that would allow him to concentrate his forces anywhere along that line in response to an attack. 'All the dispositions are so made,' wrote Wellington to Uxbridge, his second-in-command, at the end of April, 'that the whole army can be collected in one short movement, with the Prussians on our left.' He nevertheless recognised the inherent weakness of his position.

> In the situation in which we are placed at present neither at war nor at peace, unable on that account to patrol up to the enemy and ascertain his position by view, or to act offensively upon any part of his line, it is difficult, if not impossible, to combine an operation, because there are no data on which to found any combination. ... All we can do is to put our troops in such a situation, as, in case of a sudden attack by the enemy, to render it easy to assemble, and to provide against the chance of being cut off from the rest.[33]

It was a dangerous situation. Wellington would only concentrate his force when he was sure of the location of the main attack and certain that he was not being duped by one of Napoleon's legendary feints. The conflicting aims and priorities of the allies became wholly apparent. Wellington positioned his troops to defend his lines of communication with the sea, and with the strategic centre of Brussels, and the main route to Antwerp, the key Channel port about the sovereignty of which the British were desperately concerned. The Prussians were understandably more concerned with defending Germany itself.

Both Gneisenau and Wellington thought it likely that, as the smaller of the two defending forces, the Anglo-Dutch Army would be the first to be attacked by Napoleon in the event of a French offensive. Gneisenau therefore pledged to cooperate with his allies, indicating as early as April 'that he sincerely wishes to operate in concert with the Duke of Wellington and to move the troops under his orders to the places required without awaiting a general plan'.[34] For his part, Wellington clearly expected to be outflanked on his right. The Anglo-Dutch outposts extended west of Tournai, running east, parallel with the French border, through Mons, meeting the Prussian outposts at Charleroi. Wellington then positioned his two corps in deep defensive postures. I Corps, under the command of Prince William of Orange, occupied the terrain south of Brussels, in front of the forest of Soignes. II Corps, under the command of Sir Rowland Hill, occupied the ground to the west of Brussels from Tournai in the south to Ghent in the north. Wellington himself commanded the Reserve in the vicinity of Brussels. Wellington's instructions, issued at the end of April, expected Napoleon to attack on the Anglo-Dutch right, striking at the British communications and the Scheldt river.[35]

Blücher was similarly widely spread, occupying territory between Charleroi and Liège. Charleroi, where the two armies met, was the weakest point in the allied line. If the Prussians were attacked first, then they were to fight a delaying action long enough to allow the rest of their forces to concentrate at Sombreffe, while the Anglo-Dutch Army gathered at Quatre Bras.[36] This was the plan of action agreed upon by Wellington and Blücher when they met at Braine-le-Comte on 27 May. Wellington was 'inclined to believe that Blücher and I are so well united, and so strong, that the enemy cannot do us much mischief', were the French to attack.[37] Blücher had been eager to take the offensive, but Wellington could not until the Austrians and Russians were ready. 'Marshal Blücher is ready and impatient to begin,' wrote Wellington to Schwarzenberg on 2 June. 'But I told him today it appears to me that we will not be able to do anything until we are certain of the day you will commence and have a general idea of your plans.'[38]

Everyone recognised that if Napoleon went on the offensive, no one would be able to defeat him alone. Wellington and Blücher were reliant

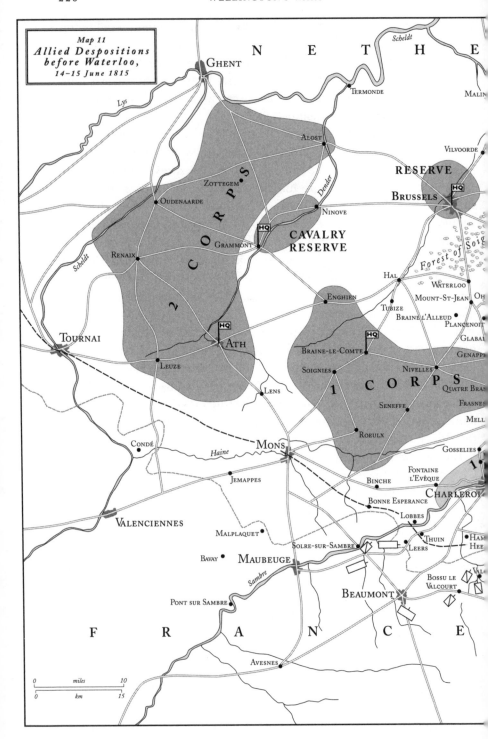

Map 11
*Allied Despositions
before Waterloo,*
14–15 June 1815

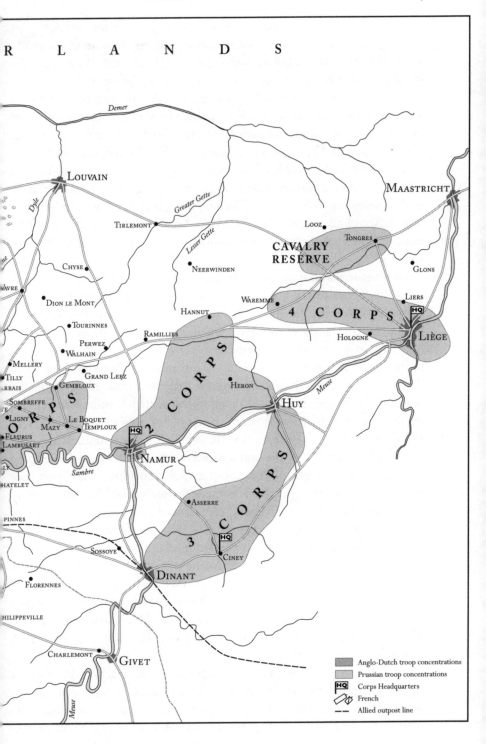

R L A N D S

Demer

LOUVAIN

MAASTRICHT

Dyle

TIRLEMONT

Greater Gette

Lesser Gette

LOOZ

TONGRES

CAVALRY
RESERVE

GLONS

CHYSE

NEERWINDEN

LIERS

AVRE

DION LE MONT

WAREMME

4   C O R P S

HQ

HANNUT

HOLOGNE

LIÈGE

TOURINNES

RAMILLIES

PERWEZ

WALHAIN

Meuse

MELLERY

GRAND LEEZ

HERON

TILLY

GEMBLOUX

RBAIS

SOMBREFFE

O R P S

C
O
R
P
S

HUY

LIGNY

LE BOQUET

MAZY

TEMPLOUX

HQ

2

FLEURUS

LAMBUSART

NAMUR

Sambre

3

C
O
R
P
S

HATELET

ASSERRE

PINNES

HQ

SOSSOYE

CINEY

DINANT

FLORENNES

HILIPPEVILLE

CHARLEMONT

GIVET

Meuse

	Anglo-Dutch troop concentrations
	Prussian troop concentrations
HQ	Corps Headquarters
	French
- - -	Allied outpost line

on one another. The only impediment was coalition politics, and Wellington, having just left Vienna, was undoubtedly aware of the political problems that existed between the British and the Prussians. It is possible he did not care, but such an attitude would fly in the face of a military career underpinned by political acumen. Blücher, though, probably took a personal decision to leave politics in Vienna. He was a military man to the core, and had witnessed the two-faced tendencies of his allies in the past. When invading France in 1814, he had sustained heavy losses whilst Schwarzenberg advanced at a snail's pace. Then, he had refused to allow coalition politics to interfere with the ultimate military goal of defeating Napoleon, and he was not going to allow it to interfere now.[39] Above all else, Blücher hated the French and wanted to see their military power crushed, and permanently removed as a threat to Prussian security.

Wellington was not incapable of understanding Blücher's perspective. 'I can easily conceive the objection which [Blücher] has to the French,' he wrote to Hardinge, the British liaison officer at Prussian Headquarters. 'Long and constantly as we have been at war with [the French], we have not had such an intimate acquaintance with the treachery of their proceedings as other nations, and we are more inclined to trust them than others.'[40] Nevertheless, he realised that the forthcoming campaign was 'a political question',[41] and therefore instructed Hardinge to 'remove these prejudices (whether founded or not is not now the question) from [Blücher's] mind'.[42] Realistically, though, Wellington understood that his greatest problem in the wake of a French defeat would be keeping the Prussians in check. 'I imagine that our difficulties will commence on the day that we shall have completely succeeded,' he remarked to Metternich on 20 May.[43] Having experienced and been at the heart of coalition politics throughout his career – from the Marathas in India, to the Spanish and Portuguese in the Peninsula – and having engineered military solutions to political problems, he was not about to stop doing so now. If Blücher was military to his core, Wellington was political to his. By the beginning of June, the uneasy allies were waiting to see who would strike first. Coalition procrastination had handed Napoleon the initiative. Wellington relied now on intelligence to keep him informed of French intentions. It would fail him.

As usual, Wellington had at his disposal a wide-reaching intelligence network. During his embassy in Paris he had actively cultivated informants in Paris and northern France, and they continued to supply him with information right up to the eve of war. According to Müffling, the Prussian liaison officer in Wellington's headquarters, the Duke considered

'Blücher's espionage was very badly organised', but 'was himself certain of his, and would hear immediately of everything in Paris'.[44]

Privately, Wellington was less sure of his own espionage network. 'There is a good deal of charlatanism in what is called procuring intelligence,' he wrote in frustration to Bathurst on 22 May.[45] Despite having a number of agents and informants, Wellington was unsure of Napoleon's intentions. By late May, it was clear the French were going to attack before the allies were strong enough to take the offensive themselves. Wellington therefore wanted to know the likely point at which Napoleon would strike. He dreaded being outflanked most of all, so it was to that scenario that he paid closest attention. Wellington seems to have virtually discounted the other possibility, that Napoleon would attack the allies at their weakest point, the hinge where the Anglo-Dutch and Prussian armies joined. If Napoleon could punch through in the centre, the armies would be forced to separate and then be vulnerable to defeat in detail. Throughout May and June, the main role of Wellington's intelligence collectors was to identify which of these options seemed more likely, but judging by Wellington's actions on 15–16 June, he had already decided which course Napoleon would pursue.

Under the overall command of Colonel Colquhoun Grant, intelligence officers were deployed across the allied outposts by early May, providing observations on the enemy troop numbers as they gathered near the French border.[46] Meanwhile, Colonel George Scovell, who had commanded the Corps of Guides in the Peninsula, managed communications. 'It is quite impossible for me,' wrote Wellington, 'to superintend the detail of the duties of these departments myself, having already more to arrange than I am equal to.'[47] This was a rare admission by Wellington, although he clearly devolved staff duties both during the Peninsular War and at Waterloo. Grant supervised a network of informers, whilst Scovell ensured rapid communications between the outposts, the corps headquarters and the Headquarters of the allied armies in Brussels and Namur. With these two in command of intelligence and communication, Wellington should have been provided with timely and reliable intelligence. Unfortunately, the picture that emerged was so confused and contradictory that Wellington's initial belief that Napoleon would outflank him only seemed more plausible.

By the beginning of May, Wellington had received news that Napoleon had successfully mustered 130,000 troops.[48] Although the allies, with 170,000 effective troops between them, outnumbered the French, the fact remained that the British and the Prussians were defending a perimeter of more than a hundred miles. To be able to concentrate rapidly enough,

Wellington needed to know where Napoleon was likely to strike. At this point the picture began to grow complicated. Preliminary indications were that the French were taking a defensive position. Napoleon was holding ground to the south of the River Sambre, just beyond the French border, and were 'breaking up roads and bridges'.[49] By piecing together a series of reports from the outposts, and from informants across the French border, Wellington believed that the majority of Napoleon's forces were gathering between Valenciennes, Maubeuge and Avesnes, south-west of Mons.[50] This indicated that the likely line of Napoleon's advance would be through Mons or Tournai, which seemed to be confirmed by rumours that the French were pulling up the roads south of Charleroi. More and more evidence was suggesting that Napoleon would attempt to outflank Wellington's position rather than attack the allied centre.

Dörnberg, who was in charge of intelligence collection in Mons, continued in early June to report that the French were concentrating at Valenciennes.[51] At the same time, a report arrived from the Prussians, apparently obtained from Paris, which seemed to confirm Wellington's worst fears. It alleged that Napoleon was travelling to the Belgian border on 6 June and would launch a feint against Charleroi, before launching the main assault on Mons and Tournai.[52] Whether the report was fabricated or not is immaterial, but it was the complete opposite of Napoleon's actual intention. This was compounded by inaccurate information from Dörnberg on 9 June. 'A peasant arriving from Mauberge assures [me] that Bonaparte came there yesterday at two o'clock, and left it this morning at seven o'clock for Valenciennes,' he reported. Meanwhile, 'the Dutch outposts on the Mauberge road near Havay, have been reconnoitred'.[53] All this pointed to a French attack on the British right. All of it was wrong. Wellington, though, was duped. 'I have received intelligence that Bonaparte arrived at Mauberge yesterday,' he noted to Hardinge on 10 June. 'I believe he has gone along the frontier towards Lille.'[54] Wellington appeared increasingly convinced that Napoleon was planning to outflank him. In fact, Napoleon only left Paris on the evening of 12 June.

Further intelligence received up to 13 June confirmed that Napoleon was concentrating his army in and around Mauberge. This information offered no concrete suggestions as to where Napoleon would attack – from Mauberge, he could easily attack Tournai, Mons or Charleroi. Then, on 13 and 14 June, new information appeared to suggest Napoleon was shifting his focus to the Prussians. Hardinge summarised this in a report to Wellington on the evening of the 14th, which would have arrived in Brussels on the morning of 15 June. 'The troops collected at Mauberge are in movement from thence on the road to Beaumont,' wrote Hardinge.

Meanwhile, 'the fires of a body of troops ... were seen last night in the direction of Thirimont, near Beaumont, and also in the vicinity of Mirbes ... The prevalent opinion here,' he concluded, 'seems to be that Bonaparte intends to commence offensive operations.'[55] Wellington reassured Blücher that he would be able to concentrate his forces at Nivelles or Quatre Bras a mere twenty-two hours after the first gunshot.[56]

But still, Wellington doubted Napoleon's intentions. Among others, Hofschröer has asked whether this was a case of Napoleon convincing Wellington by disinformation, or a refusal by the Duke to believe the information in front of him.[57] In truth, it was a combination of the two. Wellington's fears that an apparent Prussian victory over Napoleon would give them political leverage in any subsequent peace negotiation caused him to seek a leading British part in any campaign. Now, although the news that Napoleon planned to outflank the Anglo-Dutch Army on its right was a nightmare scenario, it would ensure that the British would take a leading role in the forthcoming campaign. Napoleon's disinformation campaign accidentally reinforced this, and news that he appeared to be planning to attack the Prussians merely conformed to the earlier suggestion that the French were planning a diversionary campaign before outflanking the British. Thus, Wellington did not act, as he remained convinced that Napoleon would attack Mons or Tournai. If he concentrated his forces at Nivelles or Quatre Bras, he would leave his right flank wide open. Not for the first time, Wellington trusted his intuition above the intelligence in front of him. Not for the first time was he wrong.

When, on 15 June, Napoleon in fact attacked from the south towards Charleroi, striking at the weak link between the Anglo-Dutch and Prussian forces, Wellington was clearly surprised. His actions after learning of Napoleon's advance are difficult to account for. Wellington himself claimed that he did not learn of the French attack until 3p.m., whereupon he gave orders immediately to concentrate his forces on the Nivelles–Quatre Bras road. Subsequent evidence has emerged which suggests that Wellington learned of the French attack several hours earlier still, on the morning of 15 June.[58] Wellington can therefore be accused of failing to react sufficiently quickly to concentrate his force, procrastinating for three or four vital hours. This would leave the Prussians to face Napoleon's main attack on 16 June, the implied reasoning for such inaction being a deliberate plan to weaken the Prussian force, and thereby secure more glory for himself and the British.

On the one hand, this argument fits well with Wellington's wider political objective in the campaign: that is, to undermine Prussian diplomatic leverage in post-war negotiations. On the other hand, the scenario ignores the fact that literally in the space of a few hours, the situation had changed dramatically. Wellington was more than aware that he needed the Prussians to defeat Napoleon and he would not have jeopardised the whole allied army in such circumstances. The political objective of undermining Prussian diplomatic strength could be obtained only if the main military objective – the defeat of Napoleon – was achieved first. Therefore, Wellington's failure to react rapidly enough was a genuine mistake, and can only have been made because he still could not believe that Napoleon was making his main assault on Charleroi, rather than on Mons or Tournai. Indeed, it was not until late in the evening, when Wellington and his men were enjoying an evening's entertainment at the Duchess of Richmond's Ball in Brussels, that the notion of an outflanking manoeuvre was proven to be mere fiction. As he observed irately in an anteroom to the ball, 'Napoleon has humbugged me, by God; he has gained twenty-four hours' march on me'. The situation was plainly serious. 'I have ordered the army to concentrate at Quatre Bras,' said the Duke, 'but we shall not stop him there.' Looking at a map, he pointed at the ridge of Mont St Jean. 'If so I must fight him there,' he said.[59]

Wellington remained at the ball, receiving further communications throughout the evening, and only left Brussels early the following morning, riding south to Frasnes. At 10.30 he wrote to Blücher explaining that 'the Army Corps of the Prince of Orange has one division here and Quatre Bras, the remainder at Nivelles ... The Reserve is on the march from Waterloo on Genappe where it will arrive at midday.' Meanwhile, 'Lord Hill's Corps is at Braine-le-Comte.'[60] The last sentence was wrong. Perhaps Wellington genuinely believed this. According to Wellington's acting Quartermaster-General, Colonel William de Lancey Evans, most of the army was dispersed between Braine-le-Comte and Ath, with the Third and Fifth Divisions on the road from Brussels to Quatre Bras. Optimistic assessments put the whole of the army at Quatre Bras by early afternoon.[61] The reality was much more serious. The majority of the army was in fact further west, and would only reach Quatre Bras in dribs and drabs throughout the afternoon.[62] Hofschröer claims that Wellington deliberately lied to Blücher in order to persuade the Prussians to fight at Ligny, where they would certainly receive a pasting, not least because of the ill-advised manner in which Blücher had deployed his forces.[63]

Whatever the truth, and we will never know for certain, the sequence of events reflects badly on both Wellington and the Prussians. If Wellington provided inaccurate information but genuinely believed it, then his understanding of his own forces' deployments was seriously questionable. If he deliberately misled the Prussians then the implication is that he did not trust them to fight Napoleon at Ligny unless they could be certain of Anglo-Dutch support at Quatre Bras. If the Prussians retreated from Ligny too early, Wellington's concentrating forces would have been outflanked and picked off one by one. In any event, the Prussian action at Ligny conformed entirely to the plan of action agreed by Wellington and Blücher on 27 May; that is, to fight a delaying action until the Anglo-Dutch forces could concentrate. Upon meeting with Blücher at Brye at about one in the afternoon, Wellington reportedly promised that he would 'see what is standing against me' at Quatre Bras and support the Prussians if he was able to.[64] In the event, he was caught short at Quatre Bras, and fought a decidedly hot action against Marshal Ney, displaying brilliant generalship as he plugged holes in his line with reinforcements as and when they arrived.

The fact that Wellington went undefeated at Quatre Bras is as much the result of Ney's incompetence as of Wellington's brilliance. Ordered by Napoleon to capture the key strategic crossroads at Quatre Bras, Ney dithered, unsure if he was advancing into a Wellingtonian trap, the sort that had repeatedly caught him out in the Peninsula. So convinced was Napoleon that Ney would have no difficulty in taking that crossroads, that he actually ordered Ney to detach a large portion of his force to help fight at Ligny. Not only did Ney not follow this order, but he countermanded a second order to D'Erlon, who was advancing from Charleroi with another corps, and whom Napoleon had intended should also join the fight at Ligny. Owing to the confusion, D'Erlon's corps never saw action on 16 June. Had it done so, wherever it fought it would probably have had a decisive effect. The Prussians were soundly beaten at Ligny, but were able to withdraw. Rather than retreating east into Germany, the Prussian Army instead retreated north towards Wavre. Doing so kept communications open with the Anglo-Dutch force, and enabled combined operations later in the campaign. Wellington fought Ney to a stalemate at Quatre Bras, so was also able to disengage in relatively good order throughout 17 June. The Battles of Ligny and Quatre Bras were no mere skirmishes, but had cost the allies dear: 16,000 Prussians were killed or wounded, and 9,000 British and Dutch troops were put out of action.

'Old Blücher has had a damned good licking and gone back to Wavre, eighteen miles,' Wellington commented on the morning of 17 June. 'As he has gone back, we must go too.' Typically, Wellington had an eye on the political ramifications. 'I suppose in England they'll say we have been licked. Well, I can't help it.' But the political situation was now the least of his problems. The Anglo-Dutch Army thus followed the Prussians and fell back, assembling on the slopes of Mont St Jean. The cavalry fought a series of important, and largely overlooked, rearguards throughout the 17th, in torrential rain, fending off a somewhat half-hearted French advance. Napoleon meanwhile dispatched a corps under Marshal Emmanuel de Grouchy to pursue the Prussians. Unsure of the route the Prussians had taken, Grouchy marched first on Gembloux, before turning towards Wavre, leaving Blücher sufficient scope to send a force south to support the Anglo-Dutch Army. Wellington told Müffling that he would only fight at Waterloo if the Prussians committed support.[65] Thus, on the stormy night of 17 June, Wellington received word from Blücher that the Prussians would march at first light with three corps in the direction of Waterloo. This was much more than the single corps Wellington had been expecting, and helped reinforce the Duke's confidence on the morning of 18 June. It also explains Wellington's tactical dispositions on the slopes of Mont St Jean. The right and centre of Wellington's line were heavily reinforced, whilst the left was comparatively weak. It was here that the Prussians would advance when they finally reached the battlefield.

Napoleon's 'humbugging' of Wellington and his attack on the central position on 16 June put paid to any political manoeuvring to reduce the importance of the Prussian contribution. Napoleon's central attack, attempting to divide the Anglo-Dutch and Prussian forces, reduced the campaign to a very basic level: the primary objective was the defeat of Napoleon, and Wellington and Blücher recognised this. At heart, despite Wellington's political experiences, they were both now military men, and both sought the decisive battle. This explains Wellington's agreement to fight at Waterloo, and Blücher's trust that he would, and his subsequent decision to march to support. Wellington knew he could only win at Waterloo if his Prussian allies arrived in time. It is, however, difficult to see what Wellington could have done besides fight. Having successfully retreated from Quatre Bras on 17 June, it is unlikely Napoleon would have let Wellington escape again. Waterloo, then, was a panicked battle. With no other option, Wellington had to stand and fight. His political calculations had misfired, his planning come to naught. At least Mont St Jean offered a strongly defensible position, and one of Wellington's choosing.

There was a torrential thunderstorm on the night of 17 June. So much rain had fallen that the fields were sodden and muddy. Napoleon was obliged to delay the attack to allow the ground to dry sufficiently to enable his gunners to bring the artillery battery into position. Only at around eleven o'clock, then, did he finally commence the Battle of Waterloo. With the majority of his force ensconced behind the reverse slope of the ridge of Mont St Jean, Wellington's troops were sheltered from the worst effects of the bombardment. At about the same time, Napoleon ordered Reille to attack the chateau of Hougoumont on Wellington's right. If Napoleon was to have any chance of breaking through Wellington's line, he needed to take Hougoumont. Its position effectively controlled the battlefield, and, along with La Haye Sainte, in the centre, it forced the French to attack Wellington at his strongest point – where he had positioned the most reliable British troops. Napoleon intended that the attack on Hougoumont should draw in Anglo-Dutch reinforcements and be a drain on Wellington's manpower. Instead, it evolved into the opposite. Hougoumont was held by 2,600 men, but occupied the attentions throughout the day of a total of 12,700 French soldiers. The fighting here was intense and devastating, and the position was nearly lost several times, but the British held on, preventing Napoleon outflanking Wellington's right.

At half past one, Napoleon ordered D'Erlon's corps – some 16,000 men – to attack Wellington's centre-right, between Hougoumont and La Haye Sainte. The corps achieved some success, taking the garden and orchard at La Haye Sainte, breaking through a tall hedge at the summit of the ridge of Mont St Jean, and managing to advance as far as the sunken road that traversed the ridge. There, it was greeted by a brigade of Dutch and Belgian troops, which, badly mauled as they had been at Quatre Bras, and having sustained heavy casualties under artillery bombardment for the last hour and a half, promptly broke and fled. D'Erlon's men therefore successfully established a foothold in the middle of the Anglo-Dutch line, and there was considerable potential for them to exploit this position, as more forces arrived. Behind the Dutch and Belgian troops, however, were Picton and the Fifth Division, standing firmly against the enemy, 'who approached so close that there could not have been above two yards between their front rank' and Picton's division, recalled Colonel Andrew Barnard of the 95th Rifles. 'A fire ensued, which was very heavy, but of short duration', followed by a legendary bayonet charge, during which Picton was killed, shot through the head as he ordered the advance.[66]

Shaken by the resolve of their enemy, D'Erlon's troops wavered. At this point, Uxbridge – Wellington's second-in-command, and commanding the cavalry – ordered the Union and Household Cavalry brigades to charge. 'The Enemy stood very well till we came within 20 yards,' recalled Captain William Elton of 1st Dragoon Guards. 'Those who could escape lost no time, the others were blocked up in a corner ... These men were all killed by our people.'[67] Witnesses in Picton's infantry were awestruck by the cavalry's attack. 'It was fearful to see the carnage that took place,' recalled one observer. 'The dragoons were lopping off heads at every stroke, while the French were calling for quarter.'[68] This precisely timed attack devastated D'Erlon's corps, which broke and fled. Drunk with success, however, the Union Brigade continued on into the French lines, inflicting some losses on the gunners in Napoleon's Grand Battery. Over-extended and blown, the British cavalry were taken in the flank by French lancers and cuirassiers. Of the 2,500 cavalry that charged, over a thousand did not return. Wellington, with reason, chastised his cavalry commanders – those who survived – but was also disappointed with Napoleon's performance so far. None of the dynamic flair that had become Napoleonic legend was in evidence. 'He just moved forward in the old style, in columns, and was driven off in the old style.'[69] Heavy though the fighting had been, Wellington had successfully held off a strong French attack. Napoleon, meanwhile, had left the battlefield briefly, leaving Ney in command. It was a decision he was to regret.

There now ensued a brief lull in operations, as Napoleon sought to reconstitute D'Erlon's mangled force. Ney then attacked, but failed to take, La Haye Sainte. The cause of what happened next is unclear. Some have suggested that it was the result of Ney's misinterpretation of Wellington's realignment in his centre, which he took to be the beginning of a general retreat; others that he was over-eager to reassert his reputation in the wake of the fiasco at Quatre Bras; or perhaps that it was simply over-excitement among the cavalry in anticipation of a charge. Whatever the reason, a massive cavalry charge now began – some 43 squadrons totalling 5,000 sabres. Wellington saw the charge begin and ordered his forces to form square. When Ney's cavalry crested the ridge of Mont St Jean, they encountered 13,000 infantry formed in a chessboard arrangement of squares. Ensign Macready of the 30th Regiment of Foot was in a prime position to observe the French cavalry attack unfold:

> Their first charge was magnificent. As soon as they quickened their trot into a gallop the Cuirassiers bent their heads so that the peak of their helmets looked like visors and they seemed cased in armour from the plume to the saddle – not a shot was fired till they were within thirty yards when the word was given – and our men fired away at them. The effect was magical – thro' the smoke we could see helmets falling – cavaliers starting from their seats with convulsive springs as they received our balls; horses plunging and rearing in the agonies of fright and pain and crowds of the soldiery dismounted – part of the squadrons in retreat but the more daring remainder backing their horses to force them on our bayonets. Our fire soon disposed of these gentlemen. The main body reformed in our front were reinforced and rapidly and gallantly repeated their attacks. In fact from this time (about four

o'clock) till near six we had a constant repetition of these brave and unavailing charges. There was no difficulty in repulsing them but our ammunition decreased alarmingly – at length our artillery waggon galloped up, emptied two or three casks of cartridges into the square and we were all comfortable. The best cavalry is contemptible to a steady and well supplied infantry regiment – even our men saw this and began to pity the useless perseverance of their assailants and as they advanced would growl out 'here come these damned fools again'...[70]

Repeated charges failed to break the allied squares, whilst the French compounded their mistake by failing to carry with them the tools necessary for spiking the guns that had been temporarily abandoned by the artillerymen as they sought shelter inside the squares. The musketry of the defenders took out numerous French horses, which now became further obstacles to the cavalry charge. Ney made repeated attempts to break the allied squares – perhaps fourteen in all – but although not all performed well, none was broken. The fighting, however, was heavy, and Wellington was observed to appear 'perfectly composed; but looked very thoughtful and pale' as he took shelter in one square.[71]

Returning to the battlefield, Napoleon recognised Ney's error, but failed to correct it. Arguably, if the Imperial Guard had been committed now, or the artillery sent in at close range, the French would have broken the vulnerable infantry squares. Instead, he sent in another thirty-seven squadrons of cavalry. For two hours, between four and six in the evening, the French cavalry repeatedly charged, ultimately to no avail. By six o'clock, the majority of French cavalry were exhausted, blown, or lay wounded or dead on the battlefield. Failure here had been twofold. Ney had tried to deploy an enormous number of cavalry through a relatively narrow stretch of ground between Hougoumont and La Haye Sainte. This forced it to charge on a narrow front, which drastically reduced its effectiveness and shock value. Worse, though, was the failure to deploy a combined arms attack. Had infantry or artillery been brought up in support, the allied line would have broken. That neither Ney, nor Napoleon, thought it wise to commit the other arms in support of the cavalry charge is inexplicable.

By half past one, Napoleon had become aware that he was facing a Prussian contingent on his flank, but he had no idea of its strength. By four, he became all too aware. Bülow's corps (numbering some 30,000 troops) attacked the French right which was defended by 7,000 troops under Lobau in and around the chateau of Frischermont and behind it the village of Plancenoit. After some heavy fighting, during which the

Prussians skilfully manoeuvred their entire force into action, Lobau was forced to give way. Recognising the threat to his right, and that his potential line of retreat had been cut off, Napoleon ordered in a detachment of the Old Guard to retake Plancenoit, which they successfully did by 6.45p.m. Meanwhile, Zieten's corps was coming into action on Wellington's left. After Müffling informed Wellington of this, the latter realigned his forces, moving two brigades from his left, to reinforce his mauled centre.[72] This was a timely realignment. La Haye Sainte had fallen to Ney, and it was clear that another massive French infantry assault was about to commence. The fall of the farmhouse in Wellington's centre – its defenders, elements of the King's German Legion, had run out of ammunition – allowed the French to bring up guns with which to assault directly the Anglo-Dutch centre. This was perhaps the most desperate point of the battle. Wellington himself led the Brunswickers to plug a hole in his line. 'Of such gravity did Wellington consider this great gap in the very centre of his line of battle, that he not only ordered the Brunswick troops there, but put himself at their head,' noted one observer. 'At no other point of the day were his great qualities as a commander so strongly brought out, for it was the moment of his greatest peril as to the result of the action.'[73]

With the Prussians beaten back on his right, and Wellington's centre buckling, Napoleon now sought to commit his trusted 'Invincibles' – the Imperial Guard. They advanced in three echelons. A deserting cavalry officer had advised Wellington of the point at which the Guard would attack, and the Duke had repositioned his forces accordingly. Nevertheless, from the descriptions of British observers, it is easy to see why the Guard had acquired the nickname of the 'Invincibles'. The reputation and experience of this elite and highly trained band of soldiers were clear for all to see in the confidence with which they marched towards the allied line. The advancing troops instilled confidence in the wavering French infantry, and fear into the exhausted ranks of the British, Dutch and Belgian defenders. 'A black mass of the Grenadiers of the Imperial Guard with music playing and the great Napoleon at their head, came rolling onward from the farm of la Belle Alliance,' noted one astonished eyewitness.[74] The first echelon crested the steep slope between Hougoumont and La Haye Sainte at about half past seven in the evening. By now the battlefield was shrouded in smoke.

The Grenadiers emerged out of the smoke into the sights of no fewer than thirty guns that Wellington had hastily thrown together, each firing canister, blowing huge holes in the French line. Nevertheless, the Guard pressed on. Part of it was engaged and repulsed by tenacious Dutch and Belgian troops who successfully charged the French Grenadiers, whilst the

33rd and 69th Regiments briefly wobbled, but nevertheless held firm against the French onslaught. The second and third echelons now crested the ridge. Wellington, though, had moved the 1st Foot Guards and hidden them in the tall corn just behind the ridge. 'Whether it was from the sudden and unexpected appearance of a Corps so near them,' recalled one participant, 'or the tremendously heavy fire we threw into them, *La Garde* ... suddenly stopped.'[75] At the same time, the British artillery fired constantly into the French ranks. Then came the killer blow. Wellington ordered the Guards to fix bayonets and charge the frozen French troops. The second attack of the Imperial Guard stalled, wavered and collapsed. The final French line came up against the sturdy troops of Colborne's 52nd Regiment. Under sustained fire from the front, and then the rear, as the defenders of Hougoumont turned upon them, the Imperial Guard finally disintegrated. Sensing victory, Wellington rode to the crest of the ridge and waved his hat as a signal for a general advance. Soon the entire French Army was fleeing the battlefield as the Prussians closed in from the left and redcoats streamed down the slopes of Mont St Jean. The Prussian cavalry cut down many a fleeing Frenchman, as any semblance of order gave way to irrevocable panic, effectively destroying the Grande Armée once and for all.

The luck of the day was with Wellington. The French had blundered at almost every turn. The fight at Hougoumont had been allowed to consume an unwarranted number of French troops, whilst the failure of either Ney or Napoleon to use combined arms during the infantry or cavalry attacks certainly constituted a missed opportunity. Had any of these moments been exploited properly, then Wellington's line would have cracked.[76] Unquestionably, only an army under Wellington's command could have withstood for so long the assaults Napoleon dealt out at Waterloo. The Anglo-Dutch troops proved more than a match for the task set for them, although it is unlikely Wellington could have used them in any sophisticated offensive campaign. It is perhaps the ultimate irony that Waterloo, a battle fought on the defensive with poorly trained troops, should overshadow Wellington's more impressive victories at Salamanca, Vitoria and the Nivelle, battles fought on the offensive by an army at the peak of its training and capability. Blücher, in contrast, had proven at Ligny that he was unable to withstand a concerted Napoleonic bombardment, simply by his choice of dispositions, although the Prussians performed more effectively on the offensive at Waterloo. Wellington's presence on the battlefield at Waterloo had genuinely contributed to victory. He had been there to restore confidence and reorganise his forces as and when necessary. He needed to be. Many of his trusted divisional generals were either absent or lay dead around him.

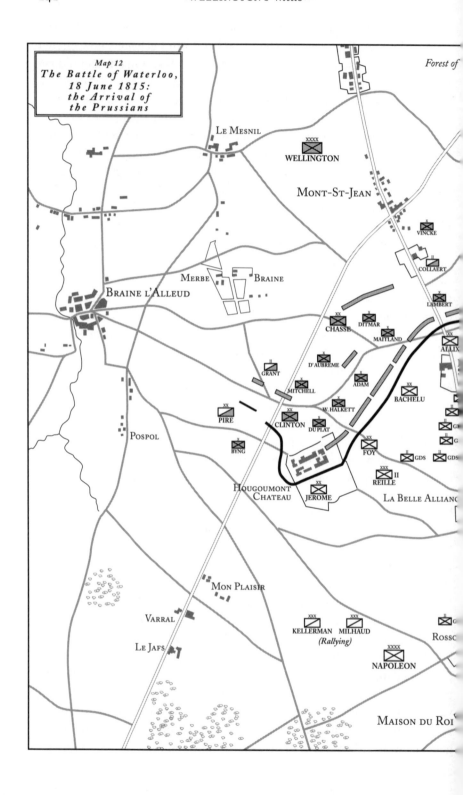

Map 12
The Battle of Waterloo,
18 June 1815:
the Arrival of
the Prussians

Forest of

LE MESNIL

WELLINGTON

MONT-ST-JEAN

VINCKE

COLLAERT

MERBE   BRAINE

BRAINE L'ALLEUD

LAMBERT

CHASSE   DITMAR

MAITLAND

ALLIX

D'AUBREME

GRANT

MITCHELL   ADAM

BACHELU

PIRE

W. HALKETT

POSPOL

CLINTON   DU PLAT

BYNG

FOY

GDS   GDS

HOUGOUMONT
CHATEAU   JEROME

II
REILLE

LA BELLE ALLIANCE

MON PLAISIR

VARRAL

KELLERMAN   MILHAUD
(Rallying)

ROSSC

LE JAFS

NAPOLEON

MAISON DU ROI

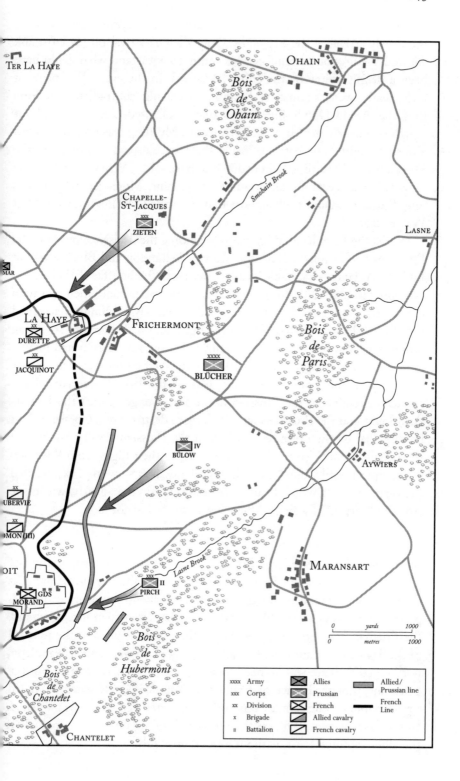

TER LA HAYE

OHAIN

Bois
de
Ohain

Smohain Brook

CHAPELLE-
ST-JACQUES
××× 1
ZIETEN

LASNE

MAR

LA HAYE
××
DURETTE

FRICHERMONT

Bois
de
Paris

××
JACQUINOT

××××
BLÜCHER

××× IV
BÜLOW

AYWIERS

××
UBERVIE

××
MON (III)

Lasne Brook

MARANSART

OIT

GDS
MORAND

×× II
PIRCH

Bois
de
Hubermont

	yards	1000
0	metres	1000

Bois
de
Chantelet

CHANTELET

××××	Army	Allies
×××	Corps	Prussian
××	Division	French
×	Brigade	Allied cavalry
II	Battalion	French cavalry

Allied/
Prussian line

French
Line

Yet he would not have been able to make these readjustments but for the timely arrival of the Prussians. Only Zieten's arrival on his left flank allowed Wellington to reinforce his centre to withstand what could have been a decisive blow by the Imperial Guard. In the event, this piece of luck nearly went against Wellington. Receiving contradictory reports that the Anglo-Dutch line had actually collapsed, Zieten halted his march and nearly turned back. Fortunately, Müffling was on hand to put Zieten straight. 'The battle is lost if the First Corps does not go to the Duke's rescue,' Müffling later claimed to have said.[77] Whether this is true or not, it was certainly an accurate assessment. More generally, it was only Blücher's guaranteed support that persuaded Wellington to fight at Waterloo at all.

Whilst the British could lay claim to landing the decisive blow, only the Prussians had enabled it. At nine o'clock, Wellington and Blücher met at La Belle Alliance – a suitable location, perhaps. 'Quelle affaire!' Wellington is reputed to have said. But no sooner had the two military men met than the politicking began. In his dispatch the next day, Wellington accepted that Bülow had distracted Napoleon's right, and had therefore struck an important blow, but he did not acknowledge the role Zieten had played. An oversight perhaps, but it is likely that Wellington was deliberately downplaying the Prussian role, not least if the British were to have a chance of reining in the Prussian desire for revenge against the French. Any doubt that the Prussians were looking to destroy French power might be dispelled by the excessive retribution the Prussian cavalry exacted on the fleeing French Army. 'That the French in their flight from Waterloo were unnecessarily butchered during many hours by the exasperated Prussians, is a fact, which I can more easily explain than justify,' wrote one British observer.[78] La Belle Alliance was not to last for long.

*   *   *

As the British suspected, the Prussians were seeking the renegotiation of the Treaties of Paris and Vienna. They sought further territorial gains at the expense of France, with the aim of permanently weakening French power. This was unacceptable. For the French, in particular for Talleyrand, the Prussian position was a betrayal of the earlier treaty and the renewal of the Treaty of Chaumont. The allies had gone to war against Napoleon, not France, so there was no need to renegotiate the peace treaties. For the Prussians, though, France had rallied to Napoleon's side when he called for her support. The country was not to be trusted and had to be punished. In the first instance, this was the problem Wellington encountered when the allies captured Paris, without a fight, on 7 July.

On the 8th, Castlereagh, who had also travelled to Paris, informed Liverpool of the vengeful attitude the Prussians adopted once the French capital was captured:

> The immediate difficulty is how to keep Blücher and the Prussians within any bounds towards this town. They have notified [Wellington] today that they have laid on the city of Paris a contribution of 110,000,000 and equipments for 110,000 men; and they are at this moment mining the bridge of Jena, with a view of blowing it up. The Duke has written to urge them at least to suspend all measures of this nature 'til the arrival of the Sovereigns; and we propose tomorrow morning to pay the Marshal a visit at St Cloud, together, to stop, if possible, these measures of arbitrary and unconcerted severity.[79]

Wellington, meanwhile, was concerned about the impact Prussian actions were having on the French population, a concern which harked back to his command in India. 'It is my decided opinion,' wrote the Duke on 14 July, 'that we shall immediately set the whole country against us, and shall excite a national war, if the useless ... oppression practised upon the French people, is not put a stop to; if the troops of the several armies are not prevented from plundering the country.'[80]

Soon, however, allied attention turned to how to punish France for its latest transgression. Prussia, predictably, favoured a major reduction of French territory, for ever, theoretically, removing the threat of French aggression. Wellington, though, saw the folly of this view. As Ambassador to Paris after Napoleon's abdication, he had witnessed French nationalism at first hand. 'The general topic of conversation,' he argued, 'was the recovery of the Left bank of the Rhine, and the unpopularity of the Government was attributed to its supposed disinclination to go to war to recover these possessions.' Better to occupy France temporarily, to give the inhabitants an understanding that, one day, France would be restored to her pre-Revolutionary status. To fail to do this would encourage further nationalist revolution in France. 'Revolutionary France,' Wellington argued, 'is more likely to distress the world than France, however strong in her frontier, under a regular Government; and that is the situation in which we ought to endeavour to place her.'[81] Underlying this argument was the inherent recognition that French strength would need to be maintained at a moderate level to ensure an equal balance of power in Europe, and to counter growing Prussian strength, not to mention the already quasi-superpower status Russia enjoyed.

In the event, the British, with the support of a surprisingly moderate Tsar Alexander of Russia, won the day, largely because of the influence Wellington had gained from being seen as the man who had ultimately defeated Napoleon. Historian Paul Schroeder believes that this was decisive. 'Wellington,' he argues, 'in quickly ending the war, performed the inestimable service of keeping these dangers within bounds.'[82] Of course, Wellington had not defeated Napoleon alone, but his cunning management of information in the wake of the battle, starting with the infamous dispatch that downplayed Blücher's role, kept Prussian post-war influence to a minimum. What many have assumed was a hubristic attempt to hoard glory for himself was in fact a calculated move to ensure that British interests were served.

The terms of the Second Treaty of Paris reduced French territory but not to the degree that the Prussians desired. Instead, an army of 150,000 troops, composed of all nations, was to occupy eastern France for five years. Wellington was to be its commander. In the course of a few months, France had turned from being the major obstacle to peace in Europe to being its guarantee. Britain, and Wellington in particular, recognised that whilst being restrained, French power also needed to be retrenched sufficiently to resist exploitation from the east, and to counter any remaining revolutionary spirit still left within France itself. The question is, did these issues influence Wellington's decision-making in the lead up to the Battle of Waterloo?

His troop deployments in the Low Countries before Napoleon invaded suggest that Wellington was gravely worried that his position was to be turned, but, viewed with the allied political situation in mind, these deployments suggest also that Wellington hoped to engineer a situation that achieved both political and military objectives. Arguably, this resulted in a failure to understand Napoleon's true intentions. Wellington, as he had done in the past, both in India and the Peninsula, had superimposed his interpretation on events and assumed that Napoleon would act in the way he expected him to, or, more accurately, wanted him to. Critically, Wellington's deployments reveal the major sticking point that the British always encountered. They, with a ragtag assortment of poorly trained and newly recruited troops, from a myriad nations across Europe, could not defeat Napoleon alone. As always, Britain, and specifically Wellington, was reliant on an alliance for success. But, as in India and the Peninsula, fighting as part of that alliance did not necessarily support political objectives. In this case, if Prussia could claim victory over Napoleon, then the chances of stopping an enormous assault on French territorial strength would be significantly reduced.

Entirely reliant on the Prussians for support at Waterloo, Wellington was nevertheless aware that he needed to mitigate their influence in any post-war negotiation. Political issues influenced Wellington throughout his career. On many occasions, he was presented with political requirements that contradicted both themselves and the military aims he needed to achieve. The relationship Wellington had with his allies was always critical. In India, alliances were made which Arthur Wellesley knew he would eventually betray. In the Peninsula, despite being deployed to support the Spanish alliance, he could not do so effectively or convincingly for five years, because of the greater political requirement to safeguard his own force. And at Waterloo, despite fighting for the common purpose of defeating Napoleon once and for all, the political necessity of ensuring the continued balance of power in Europe was one of Wellington's key concerns. Fêted in history as a military genius, more importantly Wellington was a political general of the highest calibre.

Conclusion

From Sepoy General to Military Statesman

COMETH the hour, cometh the man. In 1808, Britain found itself in
dire straits. Facing military defeat, or the prospect of a devastatingly
long war against Imperial France, this was Britain's darkest hour. Worse,
she had no hero on whom to rely. Nelson, a man eminently suitable for
the role (embodying, as he did, a level of pomposity and vanity that only
a British naval officer could attain), had fallen at the moment of his
greatest victory.[1] Britain needed a hero, someone whom the mainstream
political class and public could set atop a pedestal, if only for the liberal-
leaning press and politicians to throw stones at. In 1808, there was little
sign that Nelson was going to be replaced. A year later, a relatively junior
lieutenant-general wrote a strategic memorandum which offered a possible
new way forward in this seemingly unwinnable war. And so began Arthur
Wellesley's rise to glory. Six years later, he had liberated Spain, defeated
Napoleon and secured Britain's position as the dominant military power
of the age, while the Great Powers of Europe were balanced precariously
against one another, preventing each other from dominating the continent, and therefore from threatening Britain's global hegemony. Waterloo
cast a long shadow across the nineteenth century. It perpetuated the belief
that wars could be settled in single decisive battles.[2] More specifically, the
British establishment stared into the face of a continental army and
decided it did not like it. British attention therefore became firmly focused
on imperial matters for almost a century. Despite the growth of Prussian
power and the eventual unification of Germany Britain only fought one
war in Europe between 1815 and 1914.[3] The Crimean War against Russia
was, for Britain at least, the result of imperial rather than continental
causes. It is nearly impossible to separate the legend of the Battle of

Waterloo from the reality of Wellington's career as a whole. The fact is that, without Waterloo, Wellington's greatest victories would have been the infinitely more militarily important Salamanca, Vitoria and Nivelle. The irony of this is that, without Waterloo, these victories might not have been remembered at all.

If Wellington was a military genius, then three important and linked pillars supported this genius. The first was his ability to develop and adapt fundamentally different approaches to operations based on the tactical and strategic circumstances he faced. In an era when the operational level of war, that which connected tactical action to strategic objectives, was ill defined, Wellington was able to develop, synthesise, evolve and perfect new ways of operating his army that allowed him to capitalise on his intuitive ability to out-think the enemy. His export of 'Light and Quick' operations from India to the Peninsula is the most obvious example of this phenomenon. Secondly, he developed and utilised an intelligence system that was far more sophisticated than any of its predecessors in Europe and that would not be surpassed for over a century. It was Wellington's ability to integrate this intelligence into his own intuitive understanding of the battlefield and his operating environment that marked him out as a possible military genius. Finally, and most importantly, his political understanding allowed him to link the strategic objectives of his government, balance the concerns and demands of his allies with the inherent contradictions that existed within British governmental priorities, and develop a clear and precise understanding of how to achieve his military objectives by establishing the parameters of political success early in a campaign. All three of these pillars had their foundations laid in India, and it is there that Wellington learned his trade.

But this is to view Wellington's generalship, his decisiveness, planning and genius, through rose-tinted spectacles. He had his shortcomings, and these were very nearly disastrous. First among them was the balance between caution and risk-taking. Wellington's historical reputation, founded on the defence of Lisbon at the Lines of Torres Vedras and, of course, Waterloo, is one of caution. This is both unfair and inaccurate. After the victory at Salamanca in 1812, Wellington fought only two more defensive battles, at Sorauren and Waterloo. With 'Light and Quick' operations reinvented for the Peninsula, Wellington demonstrated himself to be a calculated risk-taker, willing to go on the offensive if he considered the situation to be suitable and his army to be sufficiently trained and capable.

This was based on experiences wrought not from success, but from failure in India. There, he in part based his approach to warfare on inaccurate racial assumptions, appearing to subscribe to the view that a

European force must never retire in the face of a native enemy; that to do so would be to fatally undermine the moral ascendancy of European military power on the subcontinent. Far from cautious, in India Arthur Wellesley was overtly aggressive, bordering on reckless. But this aggression was not just the product of Wellesley's inaccurate racial assumptions, it was a fundamental aspect of his personality, and this continued to be the case in the Peninsula. Even at the outset of the war, battles such as Vimeiro and Talavera, although themselves defensive, were the climax of offensive campaigns. Marshalled well, Wellesley's risk-taking led to unbridled success; but when applied in the heat of the moment when the pressure was on, serious shortcomings were exposed.

One of these shortcomings was an occasional but devastating propensity to recklessness. On the whole, of course, Wellington was far from reckless. The majority of his decisions were founded on reliable and accurate intelligence, and a strong appreciation of his own capabilities and vulnerabilities. The decision to advance north from Madrid towards Burgos in 1812, with less than half his force and only three antiquated guns, is less easy to explain. Wellington here appears either to have been over-confident or to have underestimated his enemy. To be fair, he based some of his decisions on intelligence, but this was one of the few occasions in the Peninsula when intelligence had been uncertain. His plan of attack in 1812 was therefore a gamble, and it failed. This, combined with his poor tactical choices, the weak nature of the force he took with him, and his failure to listen to the criticism and advice of others, suggests that he remained, at least to some degree, reckless.

This speaks to a much larger problem with Wellington's generalship. His inability to accept blame for his mistakes might not in itself have been a great problem, but it suggests an inability, or an unwillingness, to learn from his mistakes. Relatively minor transgressions, such as an insufficiently developed understanding of the merits and limitations of naval power, or more serious offences, such as an inability to stem the spiralling cost of the war despite drastically underestimating it in the first place, are not uncommon flaws in an eighteenth- or nineteenth-century general; they were neither admirals nor economists. However, Wellington seriously erred when it came to logistical planning and learning to rely on intelligence when it did not confirm his own expectations.

Wellington has been trumpeted as a true genius in the field of logistics, particularly when it came to assessing the durability and sustainability of his logistics systems. A more impartial critique suggests otherwise. Beginning in India, although he recognised the inherent flaws of the logistics systems that the British used in their campaigns against native powers, his replacements for them were not entirely satisfactory. Although the development of 'Light and Quick' operations was itself a reaction to the logistical difficulties of the Mysore campaign in 1799, it still had its shortcomings when implemented both in 1800 and 1803. On both occasions, food quickly fell into short supply, and during both campaigns, lengthy and unplanned operational pauses needed to be taken to allow supplies to catch up with the army.[4]

It was in the Peninsula, however, that Wellington's reputation as a logistical genius appears to have been confirmed. To be fair, he did expend a great deal of time, energy and treasure attempting to build a sustainable and efficient logistics system. That this frequently failed completely appears to be the fault of incompetent commissaries. However, the fact remains that even at its most efficient, the logistics system in the Peninsula never worked as well as Wellington suggested it did. Men frequently failed to receive adequate sustenance.[5] Small wonder, then, that there was an insurmountable problem with pillaging and looting, as redcoats sought to supplement their meagre and insufficient diet. Rather than looking to the 'scum of the earth' for an explanation for failures of discipline, who at their best alienated the Spanish population and at their worst precipitated a comprehensive breakdown in the cohesion of the British force, one must turn instead to the commanding officer, Wellington, for somewhere to pin the blame.

Similarly, Wellington has attained a reputation as a user of intelligence that can be compared with few of his peers. True, Wellington's understanding of the importance of intelligence, and his use of it, is one of the pillars of his military genius. In India, Wellesley adapted a pre-existing intelligence collection system to suit his needs.[6] It did not work all the time, and, when it did, it supplied sometimes suspect information. The key problem, though, was not the intelligence system, but Wellesley's analysis, based as it was on inaccurate assumptions about his enemy's force.[7] This, combined with his aggressive stance while in India, led to avoidable mistakes and unnecessary losses on the battlefield.[8] Reflecting on the campaign, Wellesley learned lessons related to the collection and analysis of information, but did not recognise his own errors of judgement. This appears to be a problem he never surmounted; throughout the Peninsular War and the Waterloo Campaign, Wellington continued to consider his intuitive judgement to be more reliable than the intelligence at his disposal. This problem should not be exaggerated. For the most part, the intelligence received supported Wellington's viewpoints, and it frequently helped Wellington reach a decision when he was otherwise uncertain. But if the intelligence flatly contradicted his assumptions, he chose to trust his intuitive judgement instead. This was a significant factor leading to the disaster at Burgos, and nearly cost Wellington the Waterloo Campaign.

Intimately linked with these decisions, however, were political constraints and requirements. Wellington's true genius lay in the consummate balancing, throughout his career, of contradictory political objectives. As with 'Light and Quick' operations and intelligence, he learned this skill in India, but, likewise, he also picked up some unfortunate bad habits. Unquestionably, he learned the art of dealing with allies in India, allies he knew he would eventually betray. He also learned the art of managing the expectations of government. This was a theme that continued in the Peninsula, where Portugal and Spain replaced Indian chieftains as problematic and frequently unwilling and unhelpful allies. Managing the expectations, contributions, demands and suspicion of his allies was, by then, second nature to Wellington, even if his correspondence suggested otherwise.

Throughout the Peninsular War, Wellington faced a range of contradictory political objectives. In descending order of importance, the first was the safety and security of the British Army; the second, the defence of Portugal; third, the liberation of Spain; and fourth, the military defeat of the French. Inevitably, achieving one objective led directly to the next, but for much of the war these objectives were, as a whole, contradictory. Before 1812, the British Army could not be used to liberate Spain without posing a significant threat to its security, for example. It was the balancing of political requirement with military risk that ultimately enabled him to achieve these goals. Yet, the process had been long – some five years before he was able to achieve them – and during this time he was vulnerable to political pressure from a number of sources. This aspect of his career was one of the defining aspects of his personality and his command technique, yet it is frequently overlooked. The Waterloo Campaign posed similar challenges, and, in attempting to balance the military need to defeat Napoleon with the political requirement to constrain the Prussians, Wellington's political generalship, or military statesmanship, nearly came unstuck. If it did so, it was for no less a reason than the future peace of Europe.[9]

When it came to managing the expectations and demands of his own government, Wellington expended time and energy negotiating, harassing, manipulating and coercing his political masters into giving him what he wanted. The process might not always have been pleasant, but the product almost always suited Wellington's requirements. Here, though, was where Wellington came closest to failing as a political general. Faced with money shortages that prohibited his operations on more than one occasion,

Wellington's response was to alienate the holders of the purse strings in a series of vitriolic and ill-considered rants. Only the presence of friends and allies in the government prevented more serious censure, and even they did not escape the wrath of his pen. Even after a regular supply of money was established in the autumn of 1812, Wellington sought to keep the pressure on, refusing to accept the diverging responsibilities and priorities of the government, and blaming ministers for every inconvenience that befell his army. In some ways, maintaining pressure was a reasonable strategy to adopt. Wellington was concerned that a lack of constant pressure bred complacency. Yet, in retrospect, the sarcasm and rudeness that imbued his letters can only be considered detrimental to a functional working relationship.

If ministers in London felt the sharp end of Wellington's scorn, it was as nothing compared to what his Spanish allies sustained. From the outset, Wellington placed his Iberian allies in the same class as the allies he had had in India. In so doing, he failed to recognise or understand the wider political revolution taking place in Spain as a result of Napoleon's invasion. His patronising and, at times, insincere attitude to his allies, both political and military, did nothing to ensure a harmonious working relationship. True, he was confronted with varying levels of incompetence in his dealings with the Spanish, but his refusal to acknowledge Spanish successes, or the contributions of Spanish troops to British successes, alienated his allies, and ultimately made many hostile to his appointment as Commander-in-Chief of the Spanish armies in the autumn of 1812. Wellington blamed the Spanish for his ills and gave them credit for none of their successes. This failure only undermined the credibility of his political strategy during the Peninsular War.

It may seem banal to return to the theme of contradiction and inconsistency in Wellington's military career, but this is what a close analysis of his actions reveals. On the one hand, he was a meticulously professional officer, capable of some of the most dynamic and innovative military thinking of the age; a true pioneer in the history of military intelligence development; and a sophisticated, if discordant, political operator, able quickly and accurately to understand the true nature of a situation, and the political ramifications of the actions he took. Perhaps his greatest political accomplishment was persuading the British government to alter its grand strategy in 1809 and commit to a sustained campaign on the continent; a campaign which, to the surprise of all, reaped enormous political benefits by 1814. On the other hand, we have a vain, aloof, arrogant and difficult figure, impulsive and reckless in the early stages of his career, unwilling to accept criticism or blame later on. His arrogance and imperfect judgement on more than one occasion caused near disaster for the British Army, as he ignored the intelligence he laboured so hard to collect. It is, perhaps, a further reflection of his military skill that he extracted his army from these situations relatively unscathed. Most confusing of all, though, is the egregious political misjudgements he made throughout his career. Here was a man with a rare understanding of the relationship between politics and war who ranted and raved like a petulant child, both publicly and privately, about the incompetence, inability and inexperience of his political masters, his allies, his men and his officers. It is impossible to keep count of the number of separate occasions he threatened to resign his command. Perhaps this is a reflection of the difficulties he faced; perhaps it is a reflection of his shortcomings. Ultimately, though, it is a mark of a true military genius that he was able to achieve astonishing success with such limited resources, and in so doing overcome these very human flaws.

Abbreviations

Add. MS	Additional Manuscript
Adv. MS	Advocate Manuscript
AHM	Arquivo Histórico Militar, Lisbon
APAC	Asia, Pacific and Africa Collection
BD	C. K. Webster (ed.), *British Diplomacy, 1813–1815* (London, 1921)
BL	British Library
BSOAS	*Bulletin of the School of Oriental and African Studies*
CC	Viscount Castlereagh (Robert Stewart, 2nd Marquess of Londonderry), *The Memoranda and Correspondence of Robert Stewart, Viscount Castlereagh* (12 vols, London, 1848–54)
Croker Papers	L. J. Jennings (ed.), *The Croker Papers: The Correspondence and Diaries of John Wilson Croker, From 1809–1830* (3 vols, London, 1884)
EHR	*English Historical Review*
FO	Foreign Office
GRO	Gwent Record Office
HMC Dropmore	Historical Manuscripts Commission, *Report on the Manuscripts of J. B. Fortescue, Esq. Preserved at Dropmore* (10 vols, London, 1892–1927)
IHR	*International History Review*
JBC	J. Bonaparte, *The Confidential Correspondence of Napoleon Bonaparte with his Brother Joseph ... Selected and Translated, with Explanatory Notes,*

	from the 'Memoires du Roi Joseph' (2 vols, London, 1855)
JMH	*Journal of Military History*
LCG	A. Aspinall (ed.), *The Later Correspondence of King George III* (5 vols, Cambridge, 1962–70)
LCM	J. W. Kaye, *Life and Correspondence of Major General Sir John Malcolm* (2 vols, London, 1854)
LME	T. E. Colebrook, *Life of the Hon. Mountstuart Elphinstone* (2 vols, London, 1884)
MC	Military Consultations
MD	Arthur, Duke of Wellington, *The Mysore Letters and Dispatches of the Duke of Wellington, 1799–1805* (Bangalore, 1862)
MSA	Maharashtra State Archives, Mumbai, India
NAI	National Archives of India, New Delhi
NAM	National Army Museum
NLS	National Library of Scotland
Parliamentary Debates	*Parliamentary Debates* (London, T. C. Hansard, 1808–12)
PRC	*Poona Residency Correspondence*, vols 6–10
RD	R. Wellesley (First Marquess), *The Dispatches, Minutes, and Correspondence of the Marquess Wellesley, K.G., during his Administration in India* (London, 1836–7)
RP	Raglan Papers
SD	2nd Duke of Wellington (ed.), *Supplementary Dispatches and Memoranda of Field Marshal Arthur Duke of Wellington, 1797–1818* (14 vols, London, 1858)
SPD	Secret Political Department
TNA	The National Archives
TNSA	Tamil Nadu State Archives, Chennai
WD	J. Gurwood, *The Dispatches of Field Marshal the Duke of Wellington during His Various Campaigns in India, Denmark, Portugal, Spain, The Low Countries and France* (13 vols, London, 1852)
WO	War Office
WP	Wellington Papers, University of Southampton Library

Notes

Preface

1. Gwent Record Office (hereafter GRO), Raglan Papers (hereafter RP), MS A/56, Wellington to Wellesley-Pole, 3 August 1813.
2. Karl von Clausewitz, *On War* (ed. and trans. M. Howard and P. Paret), (Princeton, 1989).
3. M. Duffy, 'A Particular Service: the British Government and The Dunkirk Expedition of 1793', *English Historical Review* (hereafter *EHR*), Vol. 91 (1976), p. 536.
4. J. Ferris and M. Handel, 'Clausewitz, Intelligence, Uncertainty and the Art of Command in Military Operations', *Intelligence and Art of Command*, Vol. 10, No. 1 (January 1995), pp. 4–5.
5. Clausewitz, *On War*, p. 119.
6. C. Hibbert, *Waterloo* (London, 1998), pp. 140–1.
7. Cited in J. B. Fortescue, *A History of the British Army* (19 vols, London, 1906–20), ix, pp. 255–6.

1 An Introduction to War and Politics

1. R. Bayly, *Diary of Colonel Bayly, 12th Regt, 1796–1830* (London: Army and Navy Cooperative Society, 1896), pp. 81–8.
2. British Library (hereafter BL) Additional Manuscript (hereafter Add. MS) 13664, Colonel John Malcolm during the Campaign Against Tipu Sultan, f. 45.
3. BL Add. MS 13663, Journal of Remarks and Observations made on the March from Hyderabad to Seringapatam and during the Mysore Campaign along with the Subsidiary Forces Serving with the Nizam in 1798 & 1799, by Captain Colin MacKenzie, ff. 70–5.
4. See Bayly, *Diary*, p. 88; and G. G. Leveson-Gower and A. D. J. Monson (eds), *Memoirs of George Elers: Captain in the 12th Regiment of Foot (1777–1842)* (London, 1903), pp. 100–3.
5. Bayly, *Diary*, p. 91.
6. See BL Add. MS 13725, Letters of Lieutenant-Colonel Barry Close to Lord Mornington, 1799–1802.
7. Leveson-Gower and Monson (eds), *Memoirs of George Elers*, pp. 100–3.
8. 2nd Duke of Wellington (ed.), *Supplementary Dispatches and Memoranda of Field Marshal Arthur Duke of Wellington, 1797–1818* (14 vols, London, 1858) (hereafter *SD*), i, Wellesley to Mornington, Camp before Seringapatam, 18 April 1799, p. 209.

9. Anon, *An Accurate and Impartial Narrative of the War, by an officer of the Guards in Two Volumes Comprising of the Campaigns of 1793, 1794 and the Retreat Through Holland to Westphalia, in 1795* (London, 1796), pp. 86–90.

10. Earl Stanhope, *Notes of Conversation with the Duke of Wellington, 1831–1851* (London, 1888), p. 181.

11. Wellington Papers (hereafter WP) 1/2, 19 November 1794.

12. BL Add. MS 46702, Beckwith to Don, British HQ, Apeldoorn, 7 January 1795.

13. Stanhope, *Notes*, p. 182.

14. L. J. Jennings (ed.), *The Croker Papers: The Correspondence and Diaries of John Wilson Croker, From 1809–1830* (3 vols, London, 1884), (hereafter *Croker Papers*), I, p. 337.

15. Stanhope, *Notes*, p. 182.

16. BL Add. MS 46702.

17. R. Brown, *An Impartial Journal of a Detachment from the Brigade of Foot Guards Commencing 25th February 1793 and Ending 9 May 1795 by Robert Brown, Corporal in the Coldstream Guards* (London, 1795), pp. 203–6.

18. Stanhope, *Notes*, p. 182.

19. R. Glover, *Peninsular Preparation: The Reform of the British Army, 1795–1809* (Cambridge, 1963), pp. 111–61.

20. J. Black, *Warfare in the Nineteenth Century* (London, 2009).

21. A. Aspinall (ed.), *The Later Correspondence of King George III* (5 vols, Cambridge, 1962–70), (hereafter *LCG*), iii, p. 203.

22. Brown, *An Impartial Journal*, p. 206.

23. Ibid., pp. 197–9.

24. See, for example, National Army Museum (hereafter NAM) MS 7607/45, The Diary of Lieut. Thomas Powell 14th Foot.

25. P. Barua, *The State at War in South Asia* (Lincoln, Nebr., 2005), pp. 23–51.

26. G. J. Bryant, 'Asymmetric Warfare: The British Experience in Eighteenth-Century India', *Journal of Military History* (hereafter *JMH*), Vol. 68, No. 2 (April 2004), p. 446.

27. For more details on the Maratha Confederacy see R. G. S. Cooper, *The Anglo-Maratha Campaigns and the Contest for India: The Struggle for Control of the South Asian Military Economy* (Cambridge, 2003), particularly Chapters 1–3. For more details on the geopolitics of India see P. Barua, 'Military Developments in India, 1750–1850', *JMH*, Vol. 58, No. 4 (October 1994), pp. 599–616.

28. *SD*, i, Draft of Observations upon Mornington's Minute, 28 June 1798, pp. 52–4.

29. Ibid.

30. See R. Mackenzie, *A Sketch of the War with Tipu Sultan* (2 vols, Calcutta, 1792).

31. *SD*, i, Memorandum Respecting Collecting an Army in the Baramahal, July 1798, pp. 55–8.

32. Tamil Nadu State Archives, Chennai, India (hereafter TNSA) Military Consultations (hereafter MC) 246/1703, ff. 7628–7634, Minutes of Military Consulations, Fort St George, 7 December 1798.

33. See L. James, *The Iron Duke: A Military Biography of Wellington* (London, 2002), pp. 72–3.

34. R. Wellesley (First Marquess), *The Dispatches, Minutes, and Correspondence of the Marquess Wellesley, KG, during his Administration in India*, (5 vols, London, 1836–7), (hereafter *RD*), i, Harris to Richard Wellesley, Camp before Seringapatam, 5 April 1799, pp. 514–17.

35. Bayly, *Diary*, p. 72.

36. See BL Add. MS 13664, Malcolm's Journal, ff. 36–7.

37. NAM MS 6810/46, Letter from Lt Patrick Brown, 1st Regiment, Madras NI, to his father, dated Camp at Hyderabad, 20 February 1800, describing fighting against Tipu Sultan.

38. *SD*, i, Arthur Wellesley to Richard Wellesley, Camp, 2 miles west of Seringapatam, 5 April 1799, p. 208.

39. Bayly, *Diary*, p. 73.

40. BL Add. MS 13664, Malcolm's Journal, f. 38.

41. Malcolm acknowledges the importance of the contribution of the Nizam's cavalry in his journal. See ibid.
42. See NAM MS 6810/46, Brown to his father, dated Camp at Hyderabad, 20 February 1800, describing fighting against Tipu Sultan.
43. *SD*, i, Arthur Wellesley to Richard Wellesley, Camp, 2 miles west of Seringapatam, 5 April 1799, p. 208.
44. BL Add. MS 13664, Malcolm's Journal, ff. 36–7.
45. *RD*, i, Harris to Richard Wellesley, Camp before Seringapatam, 4 April 1799, pp. 514–17.
46. Bayly, *Diary*, p. 76.
47. Ibid., pp. 77–9.
48. See *RD*, i, Harris to RW, Seringapatam, 7 May 1799, p. 569; Bayly, *Diary*, p. 92; and 'Letter from Lt Alexander Campbell, 74th Foot, to his brother Lt Frederick Campbell, RA, dated Seringapatam, 20 June 1799, describing the battle there', *Journal of the Royal Highland Fusiliers*, Vol. 6, No. 1 (June 1969), p. 80.
49. *RD*, i, General Return of Killed, Wounded and Missing, of Corps composing the Army before Seringapatam, from 4 April to 4 May 1799 inclusive, Seringapatam, 5 May 1799, p. 707.
50. Bayly, *Diary*, p. 93.
51. Leveson-Gower and Monson, *Memoirs of George Elers*, pp. 100–3.
52. Ibid.
53. TNSA MC246/1725, ff. 7811–7821, Minutes of Military Consultation, Letter to the Military Board, Fort St George, 12 December 1798.
54. Ibid.
55. TNSA Public Consultations 231/1723 ff. 4404–4013, Minutes of Public Consultation, Fort St George, 12 December 1798.
56. TNSA MC246/1741, ff. 7831–7838, Minutes of Military Consultation, Letter to the Military Board, Fort St George, 15 December 1798
57. TNSA Military Miscellaneous Book 63/1742/110, ff. 423–578, Letter to Colonel Sale, Fort St George, 15–31 December 1798.
58. TNSA Secret Consultations 6/1727, ff. 401–2, Minutes of Secret Consultation, Despatch to Government of Bombay, Fort St George, 12 December 1798.
59. *SD*, i, Wellesley to Sydenham, Seringapatam, 16 January 1800, p. 433.
60. For pointers on the comparison see Raghubir Sinh (ed.), *English Records of Maratha History (Poona Residency Correspondence): Volume 10: The Treaty of Bassein and the Anglo-Maratha War in the Deccan, 1802–1804* (Bombay, 1951) (hereafter *PRC*), X, Close to Webbe, Poona, 6 October 1803, pp. 151–3.
61. *SD*, i, Wellesley to Doveton, Seringapatam, 19 January 1800, pp. 440–1.
62. BL Add. MS 13664, Malcolm's Journal, ff. 36–7.
63. BL Add. MS 13725, Close to Richard Wellesley, Mysore, 31 March 1800.
64. *SD*, i, Arthur Wellesley to Richard Wellesley, 23 June 1799, p. 250.
65. J. Severn, *Architects of Empire: The Duke of Wellington and his Brothers* (Norman, Okla., 2007), pp. 119–38.
66. BL Add. MS 13725, Close to Richard Wellesley, Camp at Batmungulum, 11 July 1799.
67. National Archives of India, New Delhi, India (hereafter NAI) Foreign Political, MS15(31/12/1799), From Poornea, Received 20 December 1799.
68. BL Add. MS 13725, Close to Richard Wellesley, Camp at Mulgottah, 3 July 1799.

2 Command Apprenticeship

1. BL Add. MSS 39892, 'A Sketch of a Plan for the Attack of a Mountainous Country in India', ff. 22–4 no date but probably written in the 1780s. This chapter is adapted from an earlier article. See Huw J. Davies, 'Wellington's First Command: The Political and Military Campaign Against Dhoondiah Vagh, May–September 1800' in *Modern Asian Studies*, Vol. 33, No. 3, (September 2010).

2. Arthur, Duke of Wellington, *The Mysore Letters and Dispatches of the Duke of Wellington, 1799–1805* (Bangalore, 1862), (hereafter *MD*), Wellesley to Close, Cannanore, 5 April 1800, p. 54.
3. *MD*, MacFarlane to Wellesley, Hulliall, 7 February 1800, p. 40.
4. *MD*, Wellesley to Close, Seringapatam, 14 February 1800, pp. 38–9.
5. *MD*, Wellesley to Close, Camp at Beloor, 27 May 1800, p. 79.
6. *RD*, ii, Mornington to the Court of Directors, Fort St George, 3 September 1800, pp. 114–17.
7. See *MD*, Wellesley to Close, 3 February 1800, p. 29.
8. See G. J. Bryant, 'Pacification in the Early British Raj, 1755–85', *Journal of Imperial and Commonwealth History*, Vol. 14, No. 1 (October 1985), pp. 3–19; and 'Asymmetric Warfare', pp. 431–69. See also E. Ingram, 'Wellington and India', in N. Gash (ed.), *Wellington: Studies in the Military and Political Career of the First Duke of Wellington* (Manchester, 1990), pp. 11–33.
9. WP 1/42, Montressor to A. Wellesley, 2 May 1800.
10. Ibid.
11. Cited in D. G. Boyce, 'From Assaye to the *Assaye*: Reflections on British Government, Force and Moral Authority in India', *JMH*, Vol. 63, No. 3 (July 1999), p. 648.
12. Cited ibid., p. 646.
13. See ibid., pp. 643–68.
14. See J. Gurwood, *The Dispatches of Field Marshal the Duke of Wellington during His Various Campaigns in India, Denmark, Portugal, Spain, The Low Countries and France* (13 Vols, London, 1852), (hereafter *WD*), i, Wellesley to Munro, Camp at Hoobly, 20 August 1800, pp. 65–6.
15. Indeed, even those nominally allied to the Marathas, in particular, Sindhia, were considered too dangerous to negotiate a formal alliance. See WP 1/44, Close to Wellesley, 2 June 1800. See also NAI Foreign Political MS32(28/08/1800), Webbe to Wellesley, Fort St George, 5 August 1800.
16. See WP 1/44, Close to Wellesley, 2 June 1800.
17. For evidence of Wellesley's sometimes fraught negotiations with local chieftains and rajahs to secure supplies and transportation, see *MD*, Wellesley to Close, Camp at Hurihur, 16 June 1800, pp. 94–5.
18. Ibid., p. 95.
19. *MD*, Wellesley to Close, Camp at Eyamungalum, 7 June 1800, pp. 89–90.
20. *MD*, Wellesley to Close, Camp at Hurihur, 16 June 1800, pp. 94–5.
21. J. Sarkar and G. S. Sardesai (eds), *PRC (English Records of Maratha History): Poona Affairs 1797–1801 (Palmer's Embassy)* (Bombay, 1939), vi, Palmer to R. Wellesley, Poona, 19 July 1806, p. 575.
22. Indeed, in 1799 Dhoondiah had taken refuge in Maratha territory after being defeated by 'a body of troops sent to oppose him'. In 1799, Dhoondiah's force lacked coherence and loyalty, so was easily broken up, although his return with a stronger force in 1800 indicates he was not defeated decisively. See NAI Foreign Political MS20(03/07/1800), Wellesley to Ball Kishen Bhow, Chittledroog, 18 June 1800.
23. Ibid.
24. *PRC*, vi, Palmer to Governor-General Wellesley, Poona, 17 July 1800, p. 574.
25. *PRC*, vi, Palmer to Governor-General Wellesley, Poona, 19 July 1800, p. 575.
26. Ibid. The Rajah of Kolapore and Dhoondiah Punt Goklah were minor *jagirdars* in the south of the Maratha Confederacy.
27. NAI Foreign Political MS31(28/08/1800), Wellesley to Webbe, Camp at Gudduck, 27 July 1800.
28. *PRC*, vi, Palmer to Governor-General Wellesley, Poona, 29 July 1800, p. 581.
29. Ibid.
30. NAI Foreign Political MS20(03/07/1800), Wellesley to Ball Kishen Bhow, Chittledroog, 18 June 1800.
31. NAI Foreign Political MS31(28/08/1800), Wellesley to Webbe, Camp at Gudduck, 27 July 1800.

32. NAI Foreign Political MS20(03/07/1800), Wellesley to Ball Kishen Bhow, Chittledroog, 18 June 1800.
33. NAI Foreign Political MS31(28/08/00), Wellesley to Webbe, Camp at Gudduck, 27 July 1800.
34. NAI Foreign Political MS32(28/08/00), Webbe to Wellesley, Fort St George, 5 August 1800.
35. BL Asia, Pacific and Africa Collection (hereafter APAC) H/564A, ff. 714–22, J. Kirkpatrick to Close, Hyderabad, 27 July 1800; and *PRC*, vi, Translation of a report made to the Resident by Meer Kukiruddin of his conference with the Peshwa on 16 July 1800, Poona.
36. *MD*, Wellesley to Close, Camp at Kanny Bednore, 30 June 1800, p. 108.
37. *MD*, Wellesley to Close, Camp left bank of the Werdah, 10 July 1800, p. 112.
38. *MD*, Wellesley to Close, Camp at Savanore, 13 July 1800, p. 113.
39. BL APAC H/564A, ff. 186–93, Copy of a report of two sepoys of the 11th Native Regiment who arrived in Dhoondiah's camp on 10 April and remained there two days.
40. BL APAC H/564A, ff. 714–22, J. Kirkpatrick to Close, Hyderabad, 27 July 1800.
41. BL APAC H/564A, Translation of a letter from *harkarrah*, dated 17 April, received at Hyderabad, 25 April 1800.
42. BL APAC H/460, ff. 257–8; and APAC H/564A, ff. 371–8, Substance of a report made by three sepoys of the 11th Native Regiment, dated 7 June 1800.
43. BL APAC H/564A, ff. 371–8, Substance of a report made by three sepoys of the 11th Native Regiment, dated 7 June 1800.
44. See *MD*, Wellesley to Close, Camp left bank of the Tungabadra, 26 June 1800, pp. 104–5; and Wellesley to Close, Camp on the right bank of the Werdah, 6 July 1800, pp. 108–9.
45. BL APAC H/564A, ff. 714–22, J. Kirkpatrick to Close, Hyderabad, 27 July 1800.
46. *MD*, Wellesley to Close, Camp on the right bank of the Werdah, 6 July 1800, pp. 108–9.
47. BL APAC H/564A, ff. 714–22, J. Kirkpatrick to Close, Hyderabad, 27 July 1800.
48. *MD*, Wellesley to Close, Camp left bank of the Tungabadra, 26 June 1800, p. 98.
49. *MD*, Wellesley to Close, Camp at Kanny Bednore, 30 June 1800, p. 107.
50. *MD*, Wellesley to Close, Camp right bank of the Werdah, 8 July 1800, p. 110.
51. *MD*, Wellesley to Close, Camp at Soundetty, 3 August 1800, pp. 126–8.
52. See *MD*, Wellesley to Close, Camp at Savanoor, 19 July 1800, p. 119.
53. See *MD*, Wellesley to Close, Camp left bank of the Werdah, 10 July 1800, p. 111.
54. *MD*, Wellesley to Close, Camp 5 miles south of Savanoor, 11 July 1800, p. 113.
55. *MD*, Wellesley to Close, Camp at Sirhetty, 16 July 1800, p. 116.
56. See *MD*, Wellesley to Close, Camp at Dummul, 26 July 1800, p. 124.
57. *PRC*, vi, Palmer to A. Wellesley, Poona, 11 August 1800, p. 586.
58. *MD*, Wellesley to Close, Camp right of the Malprabha, opposite Manowly, 31 July 1800, pp. 124–5.
59. *MD*, Wellesley to Close, Camp at Soundetty, 3 August 1800, p. 127.
60. *MD*, Wellesley to Close, Camp at Kittoor, 8 August 1800, p. 130.
61. *MD*, Wellesley to Close, Camp at Soundetty, 3 August 1800, p. 126.
62. See *MD*, Wellesley to Close, 25 August 1800, p. 137.
63. See *MD*, Wellesley to Close, Camp at Kerry Kerrah, 28 August 1800, p. 138.
64. *MD*, Wellesley to Close, Camp at Yepalpurry, 11 September 1800, p. 143.
65. *WD*, i, Wellesley to Munro, Camp at Yepalpurry, 11 September 1800, p. 229.
66. *MD*, Wellesley to Bowser, Camp at Yepalpurry, 10 September 1800, p. 142.
67. *WD*, i, Wellesley to Close, Camp at Dummel, 27 September 1800, p. 240.
68. *WD*, i, Memorandum upon Operations in the Maratha Territory, December 1800, updated January 1801, pp. 357–65.
69. Cooper, *Anglo-Maratha Campaigns*, p. 71

3 Learning the Wrong Lessons

1. *WD*, i, Wellesley to Close, Camp at Dummel, 27 September 1800, p. 240.
2. See, for example, *SD*, iii, Wellesley to Malcolm, Seringapatam, 11 December 1802, p. 461.

3. E. Longford, *Wellington: Years of the Sword* (London, 1970), p. 79.
4. Severn, *Architects of Empire*, pp. 160–94.
5. *WD*, i, Wellesley to Close, Camp at Dummel, 27 September 1800, p. 240.
6. *SD*, i, A. Wellesley to J. Kirkpatrick, Camp at Mayoondie, 10 November 1800, pp. 254–6.
7. *SD*, ii, Wellesley to Mornington, Trincomalee, 8 January 1801, pp. 323–5.
8. *WD*, i, Wellesley to Close, Bombay, 11 April 1801, p. 321.
9. *WD*, i, Wellesley to Munro, Hoobly, 20 August 1800, pp. 207–10.
10. *WD*, i, Wellesley to Stuart, Erroor on the Kistna, 1 April 1803, p. 457; and *PRC*, x, Arthur Wellesley to Richard Wellesley, Camp at Karijigy, upon the Warda, 13 March 1803, pp. 84–5.
11. Severn, *Architects of Empire*, p. 162.
12. *WD*, i, Wellesley to Close, Hoobly, 15 October 1800, pp. 261–2.
13. *PRC*, x, p. vi.
14. *PRC*, x, Close to Richard Wellesley, Poona, 29 July 1802, pp. 17–18.
15. See *PRC*, x, Close to Richard Wellesley, Poona, 10 October 1802, pp. 23–5.
16. *PRC*, x, Close to Richard Wellesley, Poona, 25 October 1802, pp. 31–2.
17. *PRC*, x, Close to Richard Wellesley, Bassein, 2 January 1803, pp. 59–60.
18. *SD*, iii, Wellesley to Malcolm, Seringapatam, 11 December 1802, p. 461.
19. *PRC*, x, Arthur Wellesley to Richard Wellesley, Poona, 21 April 1803, pp. 95–7.
20. WP 1/143, Arthur Wellesley to Richard Wellesley, Akluj, 15 April 1803.
21. *PRC*, x, Arthur Wellesley to Richard Wellesley, Poona, 21 April 1803, pp. 95–7.
22. WP 3/3/87, Stuart to Wellesley, Myaconda, 3 March 1803.
23. *WD*, i, Stuart to Wellesley, Hurihur, 9 March 1803, p. 423.
24. *SD*, iii, Wellesley to Webbe, Seringapatam, 12 November 1802, p. 381.
25. WP 3/3/87, Stuart to Wellesley, Myaconda, 3 March 1803, p. 49.
26. *WD*, i, Memorandum upon Operations in the Maratha Territory, December 1800, updated January 1801, pp. 357–65.
27. *SD*, iii, Wellesley to Stuart, Seringapatam, 27 November 1802, pp. 431–6.
28. *WD*, i, Wellesley to Stuart, Erroor on the Kistna, 1 April 1803, p. 457. See also BL Add. MS 13746, Malcolm to Richard Wellesley, 3 April 1803, ff. 209–90.
29. *PRC*, x, Malcolm to Clive, Camp near Miraj, 3, April 1803, pp. 89–92.
30. Ibid.
31. *WD*, i, Wellesley to Stuart, Erroor on the Kistna, 1 April 1803, p. 457.
32. J. W. Kaye, *Life and Correspondence of Major General Sir John Malcolm* (2 vols, London, 1854), (hereafter *LCM*), i, Malcolm to Edmonstone, n.d., p. 215.
33. WP 1/143, Arthur Wellesley to Richard Wellesley, Akluj, 15 April 1803.
34. R. Blakiston, *12 Years Military Adventure in three-quarters of the globe ...* (London: Henry Coulburn, 1840), p. 102.
35. See WP 3/3/45, Close to Wellesley, Bassein, 9 April 1803 (received by Wellesley on the 16th); and Maharashtra State Archives, Mumbai, India (hereafter MSA) Secret Political Department (hereafter SPD) No. 140, ff. 2154–7, Close to Governor-General (GG), Bassein, 10 April 1803.
36. WP 3/3/45, Close to Wellesley, Bassein, 11 April 1803.
37. Blakiston, *12 Years Military Adventure*, p. 109.
38. MSA Military Board Diary MBD/61/1724, April 1803. See also *LCM*, i, Malcolm to Edmonstone, Camp, Poona, 21 April 1803, pp. 215–16.
39. *PRC*, x, Arthur Wellesley to Richard Wellesley, Poona, 21 April 1803, pp. 95–7.
40. *LCM*, i, Malcolm to Edmonstone, Camp, Poona, 21 April 1803, pp. 215–16.
41. *PRC*, x, Arthur Wellesley to Richard Wellesley, Poona, 21 April 1803, pp. 95–7.
42. *LCM*, i, Malcolm to Captain Merrick Shawe, Poona, 5 June 1803, pp. 221–2.
43. *LCM*, i, Malcolm to Edmonstone, Camp, Purnaleah, 1 May 1803, pp. 216–17.
44. NAI (Secret Political) MS 25 (11/08/03), Collins to Richard Wellesley, 6 July 1803.
45. MSA SPD No. 147, ff. 5640–52, Bombay Government Proceedings, Bombay Castle, 9 September 1803.

46. *PRC*, x, Translation of Papers of Intelligence, Poona, 3 January 1803, pp. 60–3.
47. See BL Add. MS 13746, Wellesley to Malcolm, Poona, 18 June 1803.
48. Ibid.
49. *SD*, iv, Wellesley to Collins, 29 June 1803, p. 123.
50. *RD*, iii, Richard Wellesley to Arthur Wellesley, Most Secret, Fort William, 27 June 1803, pp. 155–9.
51. NAI Secret Department, Secret Proceedings 28 July–11 August 1803, Collins to R. Wellesley, 2 July 1803, ff. 8613–21.
52. *RD*, iii, Richard Wellesley to Arthur Wellesley, Fort William, 26 June 1803, pp. 149–54.
53. *RD*, iii, Richard Wellesley to Arthur Wellesley, Most Secret, Fort William, 27 June 1803, pp. 155–9.
54. Ibid.
55. See Cooper, *Anglo-Maratha Campaigns*, pp. 74–6.
56. *RD*, iii, Richard Wellesley to Arthur Wellesley, Most Secret, Fort William, 27 June 1803, pp. 155–9.
57. *WD*, ii, Wellesley to Sindhia, 6 August 1803, p. 178.
58. *WD*, ii, Wellesley to Close, 18 June 1803, p. 12.
59. *WD*, i, Memorandum upon Operations in the Maratha Territory, December 1800, updated January 1801, pp. 357–65.
60. WP 3/3/47, Close to Wellesley, Poona, 9 August 1803.
61. *WD*, ii, Stuart to Richard Wellesley, Cuddapa, 8 August 1803, pp. 189–92.
62. *WD*, i, Memorandum upon Operations in the Maratha Territory, December 1800, updated January 1801, pp. 357–65.
63. *PRC*, x, Arthur Wellesley to Collins, Camp at Ahmednagar, 15 August 1803, pp. 126–7.
64. See Cooper, *Anglo-Maratha Campaigns*, Chapter 1.
65. See ibid., pp. 62–3. Also see J. H. Grose, *A Voyage to the East Indies* ii (2 vols, London, 1766), pp. 91–222; and J. Biddulph, *Stringer Lawrence: The Father of the Indian Army* (London, 1901).
66. A. Dirom, *A Narrative of the Campaign in India which Terminated the War with Tippoo Sultan in 1792* (London, 1793), p. 11. See also Cooper, *Anglo-Maratha Campaigns*, pp. 64–8.
67. Dirom, *Narrative of the Campaign*, pp. 103–4.
68. NAI (Secret Political) MS 90 (25/08/03), Collins to Wellesley, 25 July 1803, ff. 9354–5.
69. Blakiston, *12 Years Military Adventure*, p. 145.
70. Ibid.
71. T. E. Colebrook, *Life of the Hon. Mountstuart Elphinstone* (2 vols, London, 1884), i, (hereafter *LME*) Elphinstone to Strachey, Camp on the Godavery, 40 miles S.S.E of Aurangabad, 3 September 1803, p. 55.
72. Blakiston, *12 Years Military Adventure*, p. 106.
73. See WP 3/3/47, Close to Wellesley, Poona, 8 August 1803; BL Add. MS 13599, Message from a Newswriter in Holkar's camp, f. 56; Add. MS 13746, Malcolm to Webbe, 20 June 1803; and BL APAC H/469(4), Intelligence from Holkar's camp by Colonel Stevenson's *harkarrah*.
74. WP 3/3/84, Stevenson to Wellesley, four miles north of Aurangabad, 9 August 1803.
75. Blakiston, *12 Years Military Adventure*, p. 106.
76. *LME*, Elphinstone to Strachey, Camp at Ahmednuggur, 10 August 1803, p. 51.
77. *LME*, Elphinstone to Strachey, Camp at Paloor, 13 miles south of Adjuntee, 9 October 1803, pp. 75–8.
78. *LME*, Elphinstone to Strachey, Camp at Paloor, 3 October 1803, p. 77.
79. For more on the impact of ethnicity and *harkarrah* networks in India at the beginning of the nineteenth century, see C. A. Bayly, *Empire and Information: Intelligence Gathering and Social Communication in India, 1780–1870* (Cambridge, 1996), p. 68.

80. NAI (Secret Political) MS 203 (02/11/03), Collins to Richard Wellesley, 31 August 1803.
81. *PRC*, x, Arthur Wellesley to Collins, Camp at Ahmednagar, 15 August 1803, pp. 126–7.
82. *PRC*, x, Close to Webbe, Poona, 6 October 1803, pp. 151–3.
83. *SD*, iv, Wellesley to Munro, Camp at Cheedkair, 1 November 1803, pp. 210–11.
84. *LME*, Elphinstone to Strachey, Camp at Midgaon (the old place), 16 September 1803, pp. 61–2.
85. *LME*, Elphinstone to Strachey, Camp, 12 miles from Midgaon, 22 September 1803, p. 62.
86. *SD*, iv, Wellesley to Clarke, Camp, 7 November 1803, p. 219.
87. *LME*, Elphinstone to Strachey, Camp near Peepulgaon, 11 September 1803, p. 59.
88. Ibid., pp. 59–60.
89. *SD*, iv, Wellesley to Malcolm, Camp, 9 September 1803, p. 173.
90. J. Welsh, *Military Reminiscences: Extracted from a Journal of Nearly Forty Years Active Service in the East Indies* (2 vols, London, 1830), i, p. 157.
91. *LME*, Elphinstone to Strachey, Camp at Ahmednuggur, 17 August 1803, p. 51. Also, Elphinstone to Strachey, Camp, 7 September 1803, p. 58.
92. *LME*, Elphinstone to Strachey, Camp on the Godavery, 22 August 1803, p. 53. 'Ducks' here refers to the slang expression for the Bombay Army, which was composed of a lower caste of sepoy.
93. *PRC*, x, Close to Webbe, Poona, 6 October 1803, pp. 151–3.
94. Blakiston, *12 Years Military Adventure*, pp. 150–1.
95. *PRC*, x, Close to Webbe, Poona, 6 October 1803, pp. 151–3.
96. *SD*, iv, Wellesley to Munro, Camp at Cheedkair, 1 November 1803, pp. 210–11.
97. Blakiston, *12 Years Military Adventure*, p. 154.
98. *LME*, Elphinstone to Strachey, Camp 12 miles from Midgaon, 22 September 1803, p. 63.
99. Welsh, *Military Reminiscences*, p. 171.
100. Blakiston, *12 Years Military Adventure*, pp. 154–5.
101. NAM MS 8207/64, Account of the Battle of Assaye by Sgt Thomas Swarbrook, 19th Dragoons.
102. Cooper, *Anglo-Maratha Campaigns*, pp. 103–5.
103. Blakiston, *12 Years Military Adventure*, p. 160.
104. Ibid., p. 161.
105. Ibid., p. 162.
106. See *SD*, iv, Letter by Lieutenant Campbell relative to the Battle of Assaye, written at the time of the transaction, p. 185; and BL APAC MS Eur F128/227, Elphinstone to Strachey, Camp near Assaye, 27 September 1803.
107. *SD*, iv, Wellesley to Malcolm, Assaye, 26 September 1803, pp. 180–1.
108. See NAM MS 8207/64.
109. Blakiston, *12 Years Military Adventure*, p. 165.
110. Ibid.
111. *SD*, iv, Letter by Lieutenant Campbell relative to the Battle of Assaye, written at the time of the transaction, pp. 184–7.
112. *LME*, p. 71.
113. Cooper, *Anglo-Maratha Campaigns*, p. 116.
114. *LME*, Elphinstone to Strachey, Camp at Paloor, 13 miles south of Adjuntee, 9 October 1803, p. 76.
115. BL APAC MS Eur F128/227, Elphinstone to Strachey, Camp near Assaye, 27 September 1803.
116. *LME*, Elphinstone to Strachey, Camp at Assaye, 3 October 1803, p. 74.
117. *PRC*, x, Close to Webbe, Poona, 6 October 1803, pp. 151–3.
118. *WD*, ii, Wellesley to Stevenson, Phulambri, 28 October 1803, p. 459.
119. *PRC*, x, Close to Webbe, Poona, 6 October 1803, pp. 151–3.

120. WP 3/3/84, S. Johnstone Persian Interpreter to the Subsidiary Force, Intelligence from the enemy's camp by Colonel Stevenson's Camp, 1 October 1803, f. 427.
121. J. G. Duff, *A History of the Marathas* (3 vols, London, 1826), iii, p. 238.
122. *SD*, iv, Arthur Wellesley – Conference with Jaswant Rao Goorparah and Naru Pant Nana, 10 November 1803, p. 221; and Arthur Wellesley – Conference with Appah Dessaye, 11 November 1803, p. 224.
123. WP 3/3/84, Stevenson to Wellesley, north-east of Mulkapur, 14 November 1803, f. 475.
124. WP 3/3/84, Stevenson to Wellesley, Camp at Agndae, 17 November 1803, f. 480.
125. *WD*, ii, Wellesley to Shawe, Rajura, 23 November 1803, p. 535.
126. *SD*, iv, Armistice proposed between the Company and its allies and the agents of Daulut Rao Sindhia, p. 234.
127. WP 3/3/84, Stevenson to Wellesley, Asirghar, 23 October 1803, f. 467.
128. WP 3/3/84, Stevenson to Wellesley, Asirghar, 19 October 1803, f. 461.
129. *WD*, ii, Wellesley to Shawe, 6 November 1803, p. 481.
130. Welsh, *Military Reminiscences*, p. 188.
131. Blakiston, *12 Years Military Adventure*, p. 195.
132. WP 3/3/2, Arthur Wellesley to Richard Wellesley, Camp at Paterli, 30 November 1803.
133. Cooper, *Anglo-Maratha Campaigns*, p. 127.
134. Blakiston, *12 Years Military Adventure*, p. 197.
135. Ibid., pp. 197–8.
136. *WD*, ii, Wellesley to Shawe, Camp at Akote, 2 December 1803, p. 561.
137. Cooper, *Anglo-Maratha Campaigns*, p. 128.
138. *WD*, ii, Wellesley to Shawe, Camp at Akote, 2 December 1803, p. 561.
139. Welsh, *Military Reminiscences*, p. 191.
140. Ibid.
141. *LME*, Visit to the Field, 30 November 1803, p. 90.
142. *WD*, ii, Arthur Wellesley to Richard Wellesley, Camp at Deogaon, 15 December 1803, p. 583.
143. Blakiston, *12 Years Military Adventure*, pp. 230–1.
144. Ibid.
145. National Library of Scotland (hereafter NLS), MS 13631, Letter from an unknown officer, Gawilghur, 16 December 1803, f. 238.
146. *WD*, ii, Arthur Wellesley to Richard Wellesley, Camp at Deogaun, 15 December 1803, p. 583.
147. Cooper, *Anglo-Maratha Campaigns*, p. 136.
148. *WD*, iii, Wellesley to Shawe, 27 December 1804, p. 582.
149. *SD*, iv, Arthur Wellesley to Richard Wellesley, 15 March 1804, pp. 355–60.
150. Ibid.
151. *WD*, ii, Arthur Wellesley to Richard Wellesley, 7 January 1804, p. 631. See also A. Bennell, 'Factors in the Marquis Wellesley's Failure against Holkar, 1804', *Bulletin of the School of Oriental and African Studies* (hereafter *BSOAS*), Vol. 28, No. 3 (1965), p. 556.
152. *SD*, iv, Arthur Wellesley to Richard Wellesley, 15 March 1804, pp. 355–60.
153. Bennell, 'Wellesley's Failure against Holkar', p. 564.
154. *SD*, iv, Arthur Wellesley to Richard Wellesley, Camp, 31 January 1804, pp. 334–8.
155. See BL Add. MS 13747, Malcolm to Arthur Wellesley, 1 March 1804. See also Bennell, 'Wellesley's Failure against Holkar', p. 563.
156. *SD*, iv, Arthur Wellesley to Richard Wellesley, 15 March 1804, pp. 355–60.
157. *SD*, iv, Arthur Wellesley to Webbe, Fort William, 11 September 1804, pp. 464–5.
158. *SD*, iv, Arthur Wellesley to Elphinstone, Fort William, 12 September 1804, p. 466.
159. *SD*, iv, Arthur Wellesley to Richard Wellesley, 15 March 1804, pp. 355–60.
160. *SD*, iv, Arthur Wellesley to Richard Wellesley, Camp, 31 January 1804, pp. 334–8.
161. *SD*, iv, Arthur Wellesley to Richard Wellelsey, St Helena, 3 July 1805, pp. 507–9.
162. Stanhope, *Notes*, p. 130.

163. *SD*, II, Memorandum on the system of regulating the intelligence department in the Army under the command of Major General the Hon. A. Wellesley, November 1804, pp. 464–5.
164. *LME*, Elphinstone to Strachey, Camp at Firdapoor, 23 October 1803, pp. 83–4.
165. Cooper, *Anglo-Maratha Campaigns*, p. 371, f. 89.
166. Cooper, *Anglo-Maratha Campaigns*, argues that this tipped the balance in Wellesley's favour in the South Asian military economy. See pp. 137–40.

4 From India to the Peninsula

1. *Parliamentary Debates* (London, T. C. Hansard, 1808–12), (hereafter *Parliamentary Debates*) xxxiv, p. 203
2. *Croker Papers*, ii, p. 233.
3. O. Warner, 'The Meeting of Wellington and Nelson', *History Today* (1968).
4. *Croker Papers*, ii, p. 233.
5. *SD*, vi, Arthur Wellesley to Richard Wellesley, Deal, 21 December 1805, pp. 533–41.
6. Severn, *Architects of Empire*, pp. 195–222.
7. *LCG*, iii, Windham to the King, 13 September 1806, pp. 469–70.
8. Black, *Warfare in the Nineteenth Century*, p. 221.
9. See P. Mackesy, *British Victory in Egypt: The End of Napoleon's Conquest* (London, 2010).
10. C. Hall, *British Strategy in the Napoleonic War* (Manchester, 1992), p. 87.
11. P. Mackesy, *Statesmen at War: The Strategy of Overthrow, 1798–99* (London, 1974), p. 3.
12. See ibid.; Hall, *British Strategy*.
13. Cited in Mackesy, *Strategy of Overthrow*, p. 6.
14. C. Esdaile, *Napoleon's Wars: An International History* (London, 2008), pp. 15–71.
15. P. W. Schroeder, *The Transformation of European Politics, 1763–1848* (Oxford, 1994), p. 200.
16. See Mackesy, *Strategy of Overthrow*.
17. N. A. M. Rodger, *The Command of the Ocean: A Naval History of Britain, 1649–1815* (London, 2004), p. 549.
18. See, for a good overview of these operations, J. Black, *Britain as a Military Power, 1688–1815* (London, 1999).
19. See D. A. Baugh, 'Great Britain's "Blue-Water" Policy, 1689–1815', *International History Review*, (hereafter *IHR*), Vol. 10 (1988), pp. 33–58.
20. Schroeder, *Transformation of European Politics*, pp. 177–230.
21. Hall, *British Strategy*, p. 95.
22. Ibid., p. 97.
23. M. Robson, *Britain, Portugal and South America in the Napoleonic Wars: Alliance and Diplomacy in Economic Maritime Conflict* (London 2010), pp. 1–21.
24. Historical Manuscripts Commission. *Report on the Manuscripts of J. B. Fortescue, Esq. Preserved at Dropmore* (10 Vols, London, 1892–1927), (hereafter HMC Dropmore), viii, pp. 386–7.
25. *SD*, vi, Memorandum, 2 November 1806, pp. 35–8.
26. WP 1/165, Memorandum upon the plan of operations proposed 2 November 1806.
27. WP 1/165, Frazer to Windham, 22 October 1806.
28. *SD*, vi, Memorandum, 20 November 1806, pp. 40–7. See also WP 1/165, Undated Memorandum.
29. *SD*, vi, Wellesley to Grenville, 17 February 1807, pp. 56–61.
30. See Robson, *Britain, Portugal and South America*, pp. 83–101.
31. *SD*, vi, Wellesley to Grenville, 17 February 1807, pp. 56–61.
32. See J. Gurney, *The Trial of General Whitelocke* (London, 1807).
33. Viscount Castlereagh (Robert Stewart, 2nd Marquess of Londonderry), *The Memoranda and Correspondence of Robert Stewart, Viscount Castlereagh* (12 vols, London, 1848–54), (hereafter *CC*), vii, Memorandum for the Cabinet relative to South America, 1 May 1807, pp. 314–23.

34. *CC*, viii, Memorandum for Cabinet Measure suggested respecting South America, 21 December 1807; Portland to Castlereagh, 21 December 1807; and Camden to Castlereagh, 22 December 1807, pp. 96–101.
35. *SD*, vi, Memorandum, 8 February 1808, pp. 61–7.
36. *SD*, vi, Memorandum, June 1808, pp. 74–9.
37. The National Archives, Kew (hereafter TNA) War Office (hereafter WO) 1/228, Castlereagh to Wellesley, 20 June 1808. See also R. Muir, *Britain and the Defeat of Napoleon, 1806–1815* (London, 1996), pp. 42–3.
38. Hall, *British Strategy*, pp. 81–2.
39. For a full account of the diplomacy leading to the attack on Copenhagen, see J. H. Rose, 'Canning and Denmark in 1807', *EHR*, Vol. 11, No. 41 (January 1896), pp. 82–92; and for the same author's theories on the agent at Tilsit, see 'A British Agent at Tilsit', *EHR*, Vol. 16, No. 64 (October 1901), pp. 712–18. See also, Muir, *Britain and the Defeat of Napoleon*, p. 23.
40. *LCG*, iv, Castlereagh to the King, St James's Square, 17 July 1807, pp. 606–7.
41. *WD*, iv, Arthur Wellesley to Lord Cathcart, Kiøge, 19 August 1807, pp. 2–4.
42. Muir, *Britain and the Defeat of Napoleon*, pp. 23–5.
43. Cited in Rodger, *Command of the Ocean*, p. 549.
44. Cited in *LCG*, iv, Canning to his wife, 1 August 1807, p. 613.
45. *SD*, vi, Memorandum by Wellesley, June 1808, pp. 80–2.
46. *WD*, iv, York to Wellesley, Horse Guards, 14 June 1808, p. 10.
47. Cited in C. Esdaile, *The Peninsular War: A New History* (London, 2002), p. 30.
48. Ibid., p. 89.
49. Robson, *Britain, Portugal and South America*, p. 222. TNA WO 1/228, Castlereagh to Wellesley, 15 July 1808, pp. 33–40.
50. *LCG*, v, Castlereagh to the King, 14 July 1808, pp. 103–4.
51. *Croker Papers*, i, p. 342.
52. *WD*, iv, Wellesley to Castlereagh, HMS *Donegal*, 1 August 1808, p. 55.
53. *SD*, vi, Wellesley to the Duke of Richmond, 1 August 1808, p. 95.
54. *WD*, iv, Wellesley to Castlereagh, Corunna, 21 July 1808, p. 39.
55. *WD*, iv, Wellesley to Castlereagh, 8 August 1808, pp. 72–3.
56. *WD*, iv, Wellesley to Castlereagh, Caldas, 16 August 1808, pp. 91–3.
57. *WD*, iv, Wellesley to Trant, Alcobaça, 13 August 1808, pp. 87–8.
58. *WD*, iv, Wellesley to Burrard, Lavaos, 8 August 1808, pp. 66–71.
59. See, for example, Devon Record Office MS49/33 Letterbook of Lt-Col. (Later Lt-Gen.) Guard 1808–9, for early efforts at intelligence collection in Portugal.
60. J. Leach, *Rough Sketches of an Old Soldier* (London, 1831), p. 42.
61. *WD*, iv, Wellesley to Castlereagh, Caldas, 16 August 1808, pp. 91–3.
62. *WD*, iv, Wellesley to Castlereagh, Villa Verde, 17 August 1808, pp. 96–9.
63. G. R. Gleig (ed.), *The Hussar: The Story of Sergeant Norbert Landsheit* (Philadelphia, 1845), p. 143.
64. A. Hamilton, *Hamilton's Campaign with Moore and Wellington during the Peninsular War* (New York, 1847), pp. 10–11.
65. Leach, *Rough Sketches*, pp. 50–1.
66. Hamilton, *Campaign with Moore and Wellington*, p. 14.
67. Fortescue, *History of the British Army*, vi, p. 231.
68. Leach, *Rough Sketches*, pp. 55–6.
69. GRO RP MS A/7, Wellesley to Wellesley-Pole, Vimeiro, 24 August 1808.
70. *SD*, vi, Wellesley to Castlereagh, 23 August 1808, pp. 123–4.
71. *Morning Chronicle*, 21 and 29 September 1808.
72. *WD*, iv, Proceedings of the Court of Inquiry, p. 167.
73. J. Sturgis (ed.), *A Boy in the Peninsular War: The Services, Adventures and Experiences of Robert Blakeney, Subaltern of the Twenty-Eighth Regiment* (London, 1899), pp. 49–50.

74. H. Wylly (ed.), *A Cavalry Officer in the Corunna Campaign: The Journal of Captain Gordon of the Fifteenth Hussars* (London, 1913), p. 149.
75. *The Times*, 2 February 1809.

5 The Search for a Strategy

1. *WD*, iv, Memorandum on the Defence of Portugal, London, 7 March 1809, pp. 261–3.
2. For an excellent appraisal of Wellington's political relations with the governments, see J. Moon, *Wellington's Two-Front War: The Peninsular Campaigns at Home and Abroad, 1808–1814* (Norman, Okla., 2010).
3. *WD*, iv, Memorandum on the Defence of Portugal, London, 7 March 1809, pp. 261–3.
4. TNA Foreign Office (hereafter FO) 7/89, Diplomatic Correspondence with Vienna, 2 December 1808.
5. BL Add. MS 37416, Huskisson, Memorandum on War Finance, 13 August 1809.
6. *SD*, vi, Castlereagh to Wellesley, 2 April 1809, pp. 210–12.
7. Ibid.
8. *CC*, vii, Castlereagh to Wellesley, 3 April 1809, pp. 49–50.
9. *WD*, iv, Wellesley to Castlereagh, Lisbon, 24 April 1809, pp. 269–70.
10. A. Ludovici (ed.), *On the Road with Wellington: The Diary of a War Commissary* (London, 1924), pp. 185–6.
11. *WD*, iv, Wellesley to Villiers, 31 May 1809, p. 374.
12. *WD*, iv, Wellesley to Huskisson, 5 May 1809, p. 302.
13. *WD*, iv, Wellesley to Villiers, 31 May 1809, p. 374.
14. *WD*, iv, Wellesley to Villiers, 1 June 1809, p. 382–3.
15. *WD*, iv, Wellesley to Castlereagh, 11 June 1809, pp. 413–14.
16. *WD*, iv, Wellesley to Bourke, Abrantes, 13 June 1809, pp. 419–21.
17. *CC*, vii, Castlereagh to Wellesley, 11 July 1809, pp. 95–6.
18. *SD*, vi, General Order, Abrantes, 18 June 1809, pp. 288–9.
19. *WD*, iv, Wellesley to Frere, Talavera de la Reina, 24 July 1809, pp. 526–7.
20. BL Add. MS 37286, Wellesley to Frere, 24 July 1809.
21. *WD*, iv, Wellesley to Castlereagh, Talavera de la Reina, 24 July 1809, pp. 527–9.
22. A. Haley (ed.), *The Soldier who Walked Away: Autobiography of Andrew Pearson, a Peninsular War Veteran* (Liverpool, n.d.), pp. 67–8.
23. NAM MS 9406/1, Diary of Captain Francis Hood, 3rd Foot Guards.
24. *WD*, iv, Wellesley to Frere, Talavera de la Reina, 30 July 1809, pp. 514–15.
25. *WD*, iv, Wellesley to Frere, Oropesa, 3 August 1809, pp. 529–30.
26. *WD*, iv, Wellesley to Frere, Puerto de Arzobispo, 4 August 1809, pp. 531–3.
27. Ibid.
28. *WD*, iv, Wellesley to Frere, Abrantes, 13 June 1809, p. 422.
29. *WD*, iv, Wellesley to Castlereagh, Talavera de la Reina, 24 July 1809, pp. 527–9.
30. *WD*, v, Wellesley to Castlereagh, Trujillo, 21 August 1809, pp. 69–72.
31. WP 1/273, Arthur Wellesley to Richard Wellesley, 24 August 1809.
32. *WD*, v, Wellesley to Castlereagh, Trujillo, 21 August 1809, pp. 69–72.
33. BL Add. MS 37286, Canning to Richard Wellesley, 12 August 1809.
34. *Parliamentary Debates*, xv, 1 February 1810, p. 280.
35. *The Times*, 3 August 1809.
36. See H. J. Davies, 'Diplomats as Spymasters: A Case Study of the Peninsular War', *JMH*, Vol. 76, No. 1 (January 2012).
37. TNA FO 63/90, Stuart to Wellesley, Lisbon, 29 April 1810.
38. HMC Dropmore, ix, Grey to Grenville, 25 May 1809, p. 308.
39. J. Bonaparte, *The Confidential Correspondence of Napoleon Bonaparte with his Brother Joseph ... Selected and Translated, with Explanatory Notes, from the 'Memoires du Roi Joseph'* (2 vols, London, 1855), (hereafter *JBC*), ii, Napoleon to Clarke, 7 October 1809, pp. 72–3.
40. Ibid., Napoleon to Berthier, Harve, 29 May 1810, pp. 121–3.

41. *WD*, vi, Wellington to Henry Wellesley (Direct from the text), Celorico, 11 June 1810, pp. 181–2.
42. *WD*, v, Memorandum for Lieut. Colonel Fletcher Commanding Royal Engineers, Lisbon, 20 October 1809, pp. 234–9.
43. *WD*, v, Wellington to Liverpool, Badajoz, 28 November 1809, p. 317.
44. *WD*, v, Wellington to Liverpool, Badajoz, 21 November 1809, pp. 305–6.
45. See BL Add. MS 31237, Notes on the Finance of the War by George Rose.
46. *Parliamentary Debates*, xvi, 9 March 1810, p. 16.
47. BL Add. MS 38325, Liverpool to Wellington, 15 December 1809.
48. WP 1/300, Liverpool to Wellington, Downing Street, 3 January 1810.
49. BL Add. MS 38325, Liverpool to Wellington, 13 March 1810.
50. BL Add. MS 38233, Taylor to Bunbury, November 1809.
51. BL MS Loan 72/20, Liverpool to Wellington, 13 February 1810.
52. *WD*, vi, Wellington to Liverpool, 2 April 1810, p. 6.
53. GRO RP MS B/102, Wellesley-Pole to Wellington, 5 April 1810.
54. *WD*, vi, Wellington to Liverpool, Viseu, 2 April 1810, pp. 5–10.
55. BL Add. MS 38325, Liverpool to Wellington, 15 December 1809.
56. BL Add. MS 38325, Liverpool to Wellington, n.d. [May 1810].
57. *WD*, vi, Wellington to Liverpool, Viseu, 2 April 1810, pp. 5–10.
58. Ibid.
59. NLS MS 3606, Hill to Graham, Portalegre, 12 June 1810.
60. *WD*, vi, Wellington to Henry Wellesley, Alverca, 19 July 1810, pp. 270–1.
61. *WD*, vi, Wellington to Henry Wellesley, Celorico, 20 June 1810, p. 206.
62. NAM MS 6807/461, Diary of Lieutenant Richard Brunton, 43rd Regiment.
63. NAM MS 6309/138, Correspondence of Lieutenant-Colonel John Elley, Assistant Adjutant-General of Cavalry, Lisbon, 28 July 1810.
64. *WD*, vi, Wellington to Stuart, Cortiço, 18 September 1810, p. 427.
65. See M. Romans, 'Eyes in the Hills: Intelligence and the Events at Alcántara', in C. M. Woolgar (ed.), *Wellington Studies I* (Southampton, 1996), pp. 164–81.
66. *WD*, vi, Wellington to Cotton, Buçaco, 21 September 1810, pp. 459–60.
67. J. Hale, *Journal of a Late Sergeant of the 9th Regiment of Foot* (London, 1826), p. 51.
68. Leach, *Rough Sketches*, p. 166.
69. Glover, *Peninsular Preparation*, pp. 111–42.
70. GRO RP MS A/34, Wellington to Wellesley-Pole, 5 September 1810.
71. GRO RP MS B/93, Wellesley-Pole to Wellington, 22 August 1809.
72. S. Monick (ed.), *Douglas's Tale of the Peninsula and Waterloo* (London, 1997), pp. 21–2.
73. Ludovici, *On the Road with Wellington*, p. 261.
74. Leach, *Rough Sketches*, pp. 175–6.
75. BL Add. MS 38325, Liverpool to Wellington, 10 September 1810.
76. *Parliamentary Debates*, ixx, Ponsonby to House of Commons, 18 March 1811, pp. 394–8.
77. GRO RP MS A/39, Wellington to Wellesley-Pole, 11 January 1811.
78. WP 1/324, Liverpool to Wellington, 20 February 1811.

6 England's Oldest Ally

1. *WD*, vii, Wellington to Liverpool, Villa Formosa, 7 May 1811, pp. 521–6.
2. F. A. De la Fuente, 'Dom Miguel Pereira Forjaz: His Early Career and Role in the Mobilization and Defense of Portugal during the Peninsular War' (Unpublished PhD Thesis, Florida State University, 1980), pp. 1–23.
3. E. Warre (ed.), *Letters from the Peninsula, 1808–1812 by Lieutenant General Sir William Warre* (London, 1909), p. 78.
4. W. Grattan, *Adventures with the Connaught Rangers from 1808 to 1814* (London, 1847), p. 37.
5. *SD*, vi, Wellington to Wellesley-Pole, Leiria, 4 October 1810, pp. 606–7.

6. The history of the Anglo-Portuguese alliance is complicated, to say the least. The best and most detailed history of it is de la Fuente's PhD thesis on Dom Miguel Pereira Forjaz.

7. See de la Fuente, 'Forjaz', pp. 132–3.

8. *WD*, vi, Wellington to Stuart, Gouvea, 6 October 1810, pp. 494–5.

9. *WD*, vii, Wellington to Prince Regent of Portugal, Cartaxo, 30 November 1810, pp. 15–18

10. TNA FO 63/102, Linhares to Strangford, Rio de Janeiro, 7 February 1811.

11. TNA FO 63/102, Prince João to Wellington, Rio de Janeiro, 11 February 1811.

12. *WD*, vii, Wellington to Stuart, Villa Formosa, 6 May 1811, pp. 518–19.

13. *WD*, viii, Wellington to Stuart, 11 September 1811, p. 265.

14. Arquivo Histórico Militar, Lisbon (hereafter AHM) MS 1/14/186, Wellington to the Prince Regent of Portugal, Villa Formosa, 7 May 1811.

15. *WD*, vii, Wellington to Liverpool, Villa Formosa, 7 May 1811, pp. 521–6.

16. AHM, MS 1/14/186, Prince Regent of Portugal to Wellington, Rio de Janeiro, 24 July 1811.

17. De la Fuente, 'Forjaz', pp. 176–8.

18. *WD*, vii, Wellington to R. Wellesley, Cartaxo, 26 January 1811, pp. 191–6.

19. I. Rousseau (ed.), *The Peninsular War Journal of Major General Sir Benjamin D'Urban, 1808–1817* (London, 1930), p. 103.

20. *WD*, vii, Wellington to R. Wellesley, Cartaxo, 26 January 1811, pp. 191–6.

21. *SD*, vii, Liverpool to Wellington, Downing Street, 20 February 1811, pp. 68–70.

22. *WD*, vii, Wellington to R. Wellesley, Cartaxo, 26 January 1811, pp. 191–6.

23. Historical Manuscripts Commission, *Report on the Manuscripts of Reginald Rawdon Hastings* (22 vols, London, 1928), iii, J. H. Doyle to Sir Charles Hastings, 9 April 1811, pp. 288–9.

24. WP 1/327, Liverpool to Wellington, Downing Street, 11 April 1811.

25. *WD*, vii, Wellington to Liverpool, Villa Formosa, 8 May 1811, pp. 528–37.

26. T. Howell (ed.), *Journal of a Soldier of the 71st, 1806–1815* (London, 1828), p. 78.

27. *WD*, vii, Wellington to Liverpool, Villa Formosa, 8 May 1811, pp. 528–37.

28. NAM MS 7409/12, Diary of John Insley, 1st Dragoons.

29. E. Costello, *Adventures of a Soldier, or Memoirs of Edward Costello, KSF, formerly a Non–Commissioned Officer in the Rifle Brigade and Late Captain in the British Legion comprising Narratives of the Campaigns in the Peninsular War under the Duke of Wellington and the recent Civil Wars in Spain* (London, 1841), p. 95.

30. *WD*, vii, Wellington to Liverpool, Villa Formosa, 8 May 1811, pp. 528–37.

31. Costello, *Adventures of a Soldier*, pp. 122–3.

32. J. Dobbs, *Gentlemen in Red: Recollections of an Old 52nd Man* (London, 1863), p. 25.

33. J. Kincaid, *Adventures in the Rifle Brigade in the Peninsula, France and the Netherlands from 1809 to 1815* (London, 1830), pp. 75–6.

34. Grattan, *Adventures*, i, pp. 97–8.

35. Ludovici, *On the Road with Wellington*, pp. 311–13.

36. *SD*, vii, Wellington to Wellesley-Pole, 23 May 1811, p. 123.

37. *WD*, vii, Wellington to Liverpool, Freneda, 15 May 1811, p. 565.

38. C. Leslie, *Military Journal of Colonel Leslie, KH, of Balquhain, while serving with the Twenty-Ninth Regiment in the Peninsula and the Sixtieth Rifles in Canada, 1807–1832* (Aberdeen, 1887), pp. 219–20.

39. Ibid., p. 220.

40. Ibid., pp. 220–1.

41. J. Sherer, *Recollections of the Peninsula* (London, 1823), p. 159.

42. J. S. Cooper, *Rough Notes of Seven Campaigns in Portugal, Spain, France and America during the Years 1809–15* (London, 1869), pp. 59–61.

43. NAM MS 6807/219, Correspondence and Diary of Brigadier-General Robert Long, Long to his brother, Camp outside Badajoz, 22 May 1811.

44. GRO RP MS A/43, Wellington to Wellesley-Pole, Freneda, 2 July 1811.

45. WP 1/330, Beresford to Wellington, Albuera, 17 May 1811.

46. Stanhope, *Notes*, p. 67.
47. GRO RP MS B/114, Wellesley-Pole to Wellington, 16 June 1811.
48. See WP 1/332, Wellington to H. Wellesley, 22 May 1811; WP 1/332, Wellington to Cooke, 23 May 1811; and WP 1/344, Wellington to Liverpool, 23 May 1811.
49. TNA WO 1/252, Graham to Liverpool, 27 May 1811.
50. *SD*, vii, Liverpool to Wellington, Downing Street, 29 May 1811, pp. 144–5.
51. *WD*, viii, Wellington to Liverpool, Quinta de Granicha, 13 June 1811, pp. 12–17.
52. *WD*, vii, Wellington to Spencer, Quinta de Granicha, 2 June 1811, p. 618.
53. *WD*, viii, Wellington to Liverpool, Memorandum of Operations in 1811, Freneda, 28 December 1811, pp. 474–99.
54. NAM MS 7409/67, E. Pakenham to T. Longford, Pedroga, 20 August 1811.
55. TNA FO 63/113, Stuart to Wellesley, Lisbon, 5 October 1811.
56. *WD*, viii, Wellington to Liverpool, Memorandum of Operations in 1811, Freneda, 28 December 1811, pp. 474–99.
57. HMC Dropmore, x, Grenville to Grey, 28 January 1812, p. 199; and Grey to Grenville, 1 September 1811, p. 168.
58. TNA FO 63/127, Stuart to Wellesley, Lisbon, 18 January 1812.
59. TNA FO 63/130, Stuart to Castlereagh, Lisbon, 23 May 1812, enclosing Diary of Madrid Correspondent.
60. *WD*, v, Wellington to Liverpool, Freneda, 4 December 1811, pp. 389–90.
61. TNA FO 63/114, Stuart to Wellesley, Lisbon, 19 October 1811.
62. Kincaid, *Adventures in the Rifle Brigade*, pp. 115–16.
63. J. McCarthy, *Recollections of the Storming of the Castle of Burgos by the Third Division under the Command of Lieut. Gen. Sir Thomas Picton, GCB, on the Sixth of April 1812* (London, 1836), pp. 15–29.
64. G. N. Bankes (ed.), *The Autobiography of Sergeant William Lawrence, a Hero of the Peninsular and Waterloo Campaigns* (London, 1886), pp. 112–13.
65. W. Verner (ed.), *A British Rifleman: Journals and Correspondence during the Peninsular War and the Campaign of Waterloo* (London, 1899), p. 229.
66. J. Donaldson, *Recollections of the Eventful Life of a Soldier* (Edinburgh, 1852), pp. 156–7.
67. Sturgis, *Boy in the Peninsular War*, pp. 273–4.
68. F. Bamford (ed.), *Journal of Mrs Arbuthnot 1820–1832* (2 vols, London, 1950), i, p. 143.

7 England's Essential Ally

1. WP 1/351, Wellington to Cooke, 25 November 1812.
2. TNA FO 63/129, Stuart to Castlereagh, Lisbon, 25 April 1812, enclosing Diary of Madrid Correspondent.
3. *WD*, ix, Wellington to Liverpool, Fuente Guinaldo, 26 May 1812, p. 175.
4. *WD*, ix, Wellington to Graham, Fuente Guinaldo, 4 May 1812, pp. 117–18.
5. NLS MS 3610, Graham to Wellington, Portalegre, 17 April 1812.
6. WP 1/347, Wellington to Roche, 5 August 1812.
7. *WD*, ix, Wellington to Hill, Rueda, 10 June 1812, p. 226.
8. *WD*, ix, Wellington to Graham, Cabrillas, 14 June 1812, p. 238.
9. *WD*, ix, Wellington to Liverpool, Salamanca, 1 June 1812, p. 241.
10. *WD*, ix, Wellington to Liverpool, Salamanca, 25 June 1812, p. 255.
11. Cited in I. Fletcher (ed.), *For King and Country: Letters and Diaries of John Mills, Coldstream Guards, 1811–14* (London, 1995), pp. 178–9.
12. C. Greville, *The Greville Memoirs: A Journal of the Reigns of King George IV and William IV, and Queen Victoria* (ed. H. Reeve, 8 vols, London, 1888), iv, p. 141, 18 November 1838.
13. R. Muir, *Salamanca 1812* (London, 2001), pp. 68–9.
14. Grattan, *Adventures*, pp. 182–3. Wallace's brigade, of course, did not encounter the whole of Thomières's division, and its numbers were certainly not 5,000. Probably fewer than a third of Thomières's leading brigade – numbering approximately 2,000 – were able to bring their weapons to bear. See Muir, *Salamanca*, pp. 92–3.

15. Monick, *Douglas's Tale*, p. 45.
16. A. Leith-Hay, *A Narrative of the Peninsular War* (London, 1839), pp. 259–60; NAM MS 7912/21, Anonymous Memoirs of a Private Soldier in 1/38th; Hale, *Journal*, p. 86.
17. G. Wrottesley (ed.), *The Life and Correspondence of Field Marshal Sir John Burgoyne* (2 vols, London, 1873), i, Burgoyne to his Sister, 25 July 1812, p. 204.
18. Cited in H. A. Bruce, *The Life of General Sir William Napier, KCB* (2 vols, London, 1864), i, p. 279.
19. T. Hamilton, 'Letters from the Peninsula, No. IV: The Battle of Salamanca', *Blackwood's Edinburgh Magazine*, Vol. 23, No. 138 (May 1828), p. 548.
20. NLS Advocate Manuscript (hereafter Adv. MS) 46.2.15/38, De Lancey to Murray, 4 August 1812.
21. H. Ross-Lewin, *With the 'Thirty-Second' in the Peninsula* (Dublin, 1904), pp. 184–5.
22. HMC Dropmore, x, Grey to Grenville, 8 May 1812, p. 243.
23. GRO RP MS A/47, Wellington to Wellesley-Pole, 29 June 1812.
24. Severn, *Architects of Empire*, pp. 328–58.
25. *SD*, vii, Wellington to Liverpool, 22 April 1812, pp. 318–19.
26. *SD*, vii, Bathurst to Wellington, Downing Street, 31 August 1812, pp. 412–13; Bathurst to Wellington, Downing Street, 9 September 1812, pp. 457–8.
27. Historical Manuscripts Commission, *Report on the Manuscripts of Earl Bathurst* (London, 1923), Bathurst to Harrowby, 16 September 1812, pp. 231–4.
28. B. H. Liddell Hart, *The Letters of Private Wheeler, 1809–1828* (London, 1951), pp. 90–1.
29. TNA WO 1/250, Wellington to Liverpool, 11 July 1811.
30. *WD*, v, Wellington to B. Frere, 6 December 1809.
31. WP 12/1/2, Wellington to H. Wellesley, 23 December 1810.
32. T. McGuffie (ed.), *Peninsular Cavalry General (1811–13): The Correspondence of Lieutenant General Robert Ballard Long* (London, 1951), p. 96.
33. *WD*, vii, Wellington to H. Wellesley, Cartaxo, 23 February 1811, pp. 286–7.
34. WP 1/341, H. Wellesley to R. Wellesley, 25 March 1811.
35. *SD*, vii, H. Wellesley to Wellington, Isla de Leon, 25 January 1811, pp. 47–8.
36. *WD*, vii, Wellington to Liverpool, Cartaxo, 2 February 1811, pp. 224–5.
37. See WP 1/351, Wellington to H. Wellesley, 11 September 1812, and WP 12/23sh3, H. Wellesley to Wellington, 30 August 1812.
38. WP 1/361, Sydenham to H. Wellesley, 28 September 1812.
39. C. Esdaile, *The Duke of Wellington and the Command of the Spanish Army, 1812–14* (London, 1990), pp. 53–8.
40. WP 1/346, Wellington to Liverpool, Elvas, 12 March 1812.
41. WP 1/351, Wellington to Bathurst, Madrid, 5 October 1812.
42. *WD*, ix, Wellington to Bathurst, Madrid, 18 August 1812, p. 363.
43. NAM MS 7409/67, Edward Pakenham to Thomas Longford, Madrid, 18 October 1812.
44. R. Muir (ed.), *At Wellington's Right Hand: The Letters of Lieutenant-Colonel Sir Alexander Gordon, 1808–1815* (Stroud, 2003), Alexander Gordon to Charles Gordon, Villa de Toro, 3 October 1812, p. 325.
45. *SD*, vii, Thomas Sydenham to Henry Wellesley, Villa Toro, 10 October 1812, pp. 447–54.
46. *WD*, ix, Wellington to Bathurst, Madrid, 18 August 1812, p. 363.
47. See BL Add. MS 35060, Wellington to Hill, Villa de Toro, 12 October 1812.
48. See National Maritime Museum (hereafter NMM) MS 77/109, Popham to Keith, HMS *Venerable*, Castro, 17 September 1812.
49. BL Add. MS 35060, Wellington to Hill, Madrid, 24 and 25 August 1812.
50. BL Add. MS 35060, Wellington to Hill, Villa de Toro near Burgos, 21 September 1812.
51. BL Add. MS 35060, Wellington to Hill, Villa de Toro, 9 October 1812. See also TNA FO 63/135, Stuart to Wellesley, Lisbon, 17 October 1812.

52. BL Add. MS 35060, Wellington to Hill, Villa de Toro, 2 October 1812.
53. Anon., *The Personal Narrative of a Private Soldier who served in the Forty-Second Highlanders for Twelve Years during the Late War* (London, 1821), pp. 141–2.
54. Cited in Fletcher, *For King and Country*, p. 229.
55. W. Thomson (ed.), *An Ensign in the Peninsular War: The Letters of John Aitchison* (London, 1981), p. 206.
56. Cited in Fletcher, *For King and Country*, p. 243.
57. Thomson, *An Ensign in the Peninsular War*, p. 208.
58. BL Add. MS 35060, Wellington to Hill, Villa de Toro, 12 October 1812.
59. Ibid.
60. See TNA FO 63/135, Stuart to Wellesley, Lisbon, 31 October 1812 and 7 November 1812.
61. *WD*, ix, Wellington to Henry Wellesley, Rueda, 1 November 1812, p. 524.
62. WP 1/361, Sydenham to H. Wellesley, 12 September 1812.
63. WP 1/355, Wellington to Carvajal, 4 December 1812.
64. WP 1/365, Wellington to Bathurst, 27 January 1813.
65. WP 1/355, Wellington to Carvajal, 27 December 1812.
66. WP 1/355, Wellington to Carvajal, 4 December 1812.
67. *Suplmento al Tribuno del Pueblo Español*, 1 January 1813, cited in Esdaile, *Wellington and the Command of the Spanish Army*, p. 99.
68. WP 1/355, Wellington to Carvajal, 25 December 1812.
69. WP 1/365, Wellington to Bathurst, 27 January 1813.
70. TNA FO 72/143, H. Wellesley to Castlereagh, 20 January 1813.
71. *Suplmento al Tribuno del Pueblo Español*, 1 January 1813, cited in Esdaile, *Wellington and the Command of the Spanish Army*, p. 100.

8 'I Will Beat Them Out, and with Great Ease'

1. H. G. W. Smith, *Autobiography of Sir Harry Smith, 1787–1819* (London, 1910), Chapter 15.
2. Ibid.
3. See WP 1/364, Hill to Wellington, Coria, 19 January 1813; *WD*, x, Wellington to Bathurst, Freneda, 17 February 1813, p. 125; and TNA FO 63/152, Stuart to Castlereagh, Lisbon, 6 March 1813.
4. TNA FO 63/151, Stuart to Castlereagh, Lisbon, 3 January 1813.
5. WP 1/365, Wellington to Bathurst, 27 January 1813.
6. NAM MS 7409/67, Pakenham to Longford, Momenta de Beira, 5 January 1813.
7. WP 1/370, Wellington to O'Donoju, 4 June 1813.
8. Esdaile, *Wellington and the Command of the Spanish Army*, p. 124.
9. One culprit was the temporary Quartermaster-General, James Willoughby Gorden. See University of Durham Library UDL GRE/B19/123, Gordon to York, Cordovilla, 14 September 1812.
10. NAM MS 6702/33, Correspondence of Lieutenant Henry Booth, 43rd Regiment, Booth to his sister, 20 June 1813.
11. *SD*, vii, General Order, 1 March 1813, pp. 562–4.
12. NAM MS 6807/267, Diary of Lieutenant George Woodberry, 18th Hussars, 15 June 1813.
13. See E. J. Coss, *All for the King's Shilling: The British Soldier under Wellington, 1808–1814* (Norman, Okla., 2010). For an example of a British historian on the subject, see I. Robertson, *A Commanding Presence: Wellington in the Peninsula, 1808–1814* (London, 2008).
14. *WD*, x, Wellington to Fisher, Freneda, 4 May 1813, pp. 346–7.
15. *SD*, vii, General Order, Freneda, 21 April 1813, pp. 607–8.
16. *SD*, vii, General Order, Freneda, 21 May 1813, p. 622.
17. *WD*, x, Wellington to Martin, Freneda, 28 April 1813, p. 334.

18. *WD*, x, Wellington to Bathurst, Irurzun, 24 June 1813, p. 458.
19. *WD*, x, Wellington to Bathurst, Freneda, 7 April 1813, p. 273.
20. C. Hall, *Wellington's Navy: Sea Power and the Peninsular War, 1807–1814* (London, 2004), p. 210.
21. *SD*, viii, Melville to Wellington, Wimbledon, 28 July 1813, pp. 144–7.
22. *WD*, x, Wellington to Bathurst, Freneda, 11 May 1813, p. 372.
23. NAM MS 6807/163/3, Bingham to Gundry, Sandio, 12 June 1813.
24. *WD*, x, Wellington to Graham, Castromonte, 5 June 1813, p. 417.
25. *WD*, x, Wellington to Graham, Freneda, 18 May 1813, p. 387.
26. NLS Adv. MS 46.2.18, Arrangements for the Movements of Army on 3 June 1813.
27. NAM MS 6807/267, Diary of Lieutenant George Woodberry, June 1813.
28. NLS Adv. MS 46.2.18, Matthews to Ponsonby, Santayo, 8 June 1813.
29. See NLS Adv. MS 46.2.18, Arrangements for the Movements of the army on 10 June, 9 June 1813.
30. NAM MS 7510/27, Diary of Brigadier-General Charles Ashworth, June 1813.
31. NLS Adv. MS 46.2.18, Murray to Graham, Valladiego, 13 June 1813.
32. NAM MS 6807/345, Wellington to Cole, 12.30, 19 June 1813; Wellington to Cole, 13.45, 19 June 1813; Wellington to Cole, 14.00, 19 June 1813.
33. Sherer, *Recollections of the Peninsula*, pp. 237–8.
34. NAM MS 7104/45, Andrew Hay to Mary Hay (daughter), 8.30p.m., 21 June 1813; Andrew Hay to Mary Hay, 23 June 1813.
35. H. B. Robinson, *Memoirs of Sir Thomas Picton* (2 vols, London, 1836), ii, pp. 195–6.
36. C. Oman, *A History of the Peninsular War* (7 vols, Oxford, 1902), vi, p. 411.
37. NAM MS 7510/27, Diary of Ashworth, June 1813.
38. Leach, *Rough Sketches*, p. 319.
39. G. Wood, *The Subaltern Officer: A Narrative* (London, 1826), pp. 183–4.
40. J. Green, *The Vicissitudes of a Soldier's Life, or a Series of Occurrences from 1806 to 1815* (Louth, 1827), pp. 163–4.
41. NAM MS 9204/182, Diary of Captain John Duffy, 43rd Regiment.
42. Cited in Oman, *History*, vi, p. 444.
43. *WD*, x, Wellington to Bathurst, 29 June 1813, pp. 472–3.
44. Leith-Hay, *Narrative*, ii, pp. 203–8.
45. NAM MS 7510/27, Diary of Ashworth, June 1813.
46. *WD*, x, Wellington to Bathurst, 9 July 1813, p. 519.
47. *WD*, x, Wellington to Bathurst, 2 July 1813, pp. 495–6.
48. *SD*, vii, Liverpool to Wellington, 27 October 1812, pp. 462–3.
49. *WD*, ix, Wellington to Bathurst, 7 November 1812, pp. 541–2.
50. WP 1/372, Bathurst to Wellington, 14 July 1813.
51. WP 1/372, Prince of Wales to Wellington, 3 July 1813.
52. *WD*, x, Wellington to Bathurst, 24 June 1813, pp. 458–9.
53. *WD*, x, Wellington to Bathurst, 8 August 1813, p. 615.
54. *WD*, x, Wellington to Collier, 22 July 1813, pp. 561–2.
55. *WD*, x, Wellington to Bathurst, 10 July 1813, pp. 522–3.
56. C. Lloyd (ed.), *The Keith Papers* (3 vols, London, 1955), iii, Melville to Keith, 24 August 1813, pp. 300–1.
57. WP 1/372, Melville to Wellington, 28 July 1813.
58. R. V. Hamilton (ed.), *Letters and Papers of Admiral of the Fleet Sir T. Byam Martin* (2 vols, London, 1898), ii, Melville to Keith, 3 September 1813, p. 365.
59. *SD*, viii, Melville to Wellington, 3 September 1813, pp. 223–6.
60. *WD*, xi, Wellington to Bathurst, 1 November 1813, pp. 238–41.
61. GRO RP MS A/56, Wellington to Wellesley-Pole, 3 August 1813.
62. *WD*, xi, Wellington to Bathurst, 23 August 1813, pp. 34–5.
63. Smith, *Autobiography*, Chapter 13.
64. *WD*, xi, Wellington to Bathurst, 19 September 1813, pp. 123–4.

65. *WD*, xi, Wellington to Bentinck, 15 September 1813, pp. 85–7.
66. *WD*, xi, Wellington to Bathurst, 19 September 1813, pp. 123–4.
67. NAM MS 8807/52, Correspondence of Ensign John Blackman, Blackman to his parents, 9 October 1813.
68. Smith, *Autobiography*, Chapter 14.
69. *SD*, viii, Quartermaster-General (QMG) to Alten, Vera, 11 October 1813, p. 305.
70. *SD*, viii, Arrangement for a Forward Movement of the Army, on the Surrender of Pamplona, Vera, 27 October 1813, pp. 325–9.
71. Ibid.
72. Smith, *Autobiography*, Chapter 15.
73. Ibid.
74. Ibid.
75. Oman, *History*, vii, pp. 193–4.
76. W. Leeke, *History of Lord Seaton's 52nd Regiment* (2 vols, London, 1866), ii, p. 365.
77. F. S. Larpent, *The Journal of F. Seymour Larpent* (3 vols, London, 1853), iii, p. 41.
78. *WD*, xi, Wellington to Stuart, 28 January 1814, pp. 485–6.
79. WP 1/381, Wellington to Stuart, 8 November 1813.
80. BL Add. MS 38255, Wellington to Bathurst, 21 November 1813.
81. WP 1/396, Wellington to Beresford, 28 January 1814.
82. WP 1/381, Wellington to Freire, 14 November 1813.
83. Cited in Esdaile, *Wellington and the Command of the Spanish Army*, p. 160.
84. Ibid., p. 273.
85. WP 1/381, Wellington to Bathurst, 27 November 1813.
86. WP 1/380, Bathurst to Wellington, 10 January 1814.
87. *WD*, ix, Wellington to Bathurst, 8 January 1814, pp. 425–6.
88. *WD*, ix, Wellington to Liverpool, 4 March 1814, pp. 546–7.
89. See, for more details, Esdaile, *Napoleon's Wars*, pp. 499–531; D. Lieven, *Russia against Napoleon* (London, 2010), pp. 460–520; and M. V. Leggiere, *The Fall of Napoleon: The Allied Invasion of France, 1813–1814* (Cambridge, 2007).
90. *Parliamentary Debates*, xxvii, Bathurst to the Lords, 8 November 1813, p. 47.

9 Wellington's Waterloo

1. *WD*, xii, Wellington to Bathurst, Brussels, 19 June 1815, p. 484.
2. Schroeder, *Transformation of European Politics*, p. 567.
3. P. Mansell, 'Wellington and the French Restoration', *IHR*, Vol. 11, No. 1 (February 1989), p. 79.
4. WP 1/417, Wellington to San Carlos, 21 May 1814.
5. Esdaile, *Wellington and the Command of the Spanish Army*, pp. 179–80.
6. *WD*, xii, Wellington to Bathurst, Memorandum on the Defence of the Frontier of the Netherlands, Paris, 22 September 1814, pp. 125–9.
7. BL Add. MS 52441, Sir James Mackintosh to Lady Mackintosh, 12 and 25 November 1814.
8. BL Add. MS 52441, Sir James Mackintosh to Lady Mackintosh, 28 November 1814.
9. Cited in A. Zamoyski, *Rites of Peace: The Fall of Napoleon and the Congress of Vienna* (London, 2007), p. 71.
10. Cited ibid., p. 202.
11. *CC*, x, Castlereagh to Wellington, Vienna, 1 October 1814, p. 142.
12. *SD*, ix, Castlereagh to Wellington, Vienna, 25 October 1814, p. 372.
13. *SD*, ix, Liverpool to Wellington, Fife House, 23 December 1814, p. 494.
14. *CC*, x, Wellington to Castlereagh, Mons, 18 August 1814, p. 93.
15. *SD*, ix, Castlereagh to Liverpool, Vienna, 21 November 1814, p. 447.
16. *SD*, ix, Castlereagh to Wellington, Vienna, 25 October 1814, p. 372.
17. C. K. Webster (ed.), *British Diplomacy, 1813–1815* (London, 1921), (hereafter *BD*), Castlereagh to Liverpool, Vienna, 11 November 1814, p. 233.

18. See *BD*, Castlereagh to Liverpool, Vienna, 21 November 1814, pp. 238–40.
19. *SD*, ix, Liverpool to Castlereagh, Fife House, 18 November 1814, p. 438.
20. *SD*, ix, Castlereagh to Liverpool, Vienna, 5 December 1814, p. 462.
21. *SD*, ix, Liverpool to Wellington, Fife House, 23 December 1814, p. 494.
22. *SD*, ix, Castlereagh to Liverpool, Vienna, 5 January 1815, p. 527.
23. *BD*, Castlereagh to Liverpool, 6 February 1815, p. 302.
24. See E. E. Kraehe, *Metternich's German Policy: The Congress of Vienna, 1814–1815* (Princeton, 1983).
25. *BD*, Wellington to Castlereagh, 12 March 1815, p. 312.
26. George Herbert, Count Münster, *Political Sketches of the State of Europe from 1814–1867* (Edinburgh, 1868), p. 231.
27. *WD*, xii, Wellington to Clancarty, Brussels, 3 May 1815, p. 346. See also Kraehe, *Metternich's German Policy*.
28. TNA FO 92/13, Castlereagh to Wellington, 8 April 1815.
29. *WD*, xii, Wellington to Stewart, Brussels, 8 May 1815, p. 358.
30. *WD*, xii, Wellington to Cole, Brussels, 2 June 1815, p. 435.
31. *SD*, x, Memorandum by Gneisenau, n.d. pp. 196–7.
32. *WD*, xii, Memorandum by Wellington, 12 April 1815, p. 304.
33. *WD*, xii, Wellington to the Prince of Orange, Brussels, 11 May 1815, p. 375.
34. *SD*, x, Röder to Wellington, Brussels, 9 April 1815, p. 52.
35. *WD*, xii, Secret Memorandum from Wellington to Prince of Orange, Uxbridge, Hill, and the Quartermaster General (QMG), Brussels, 1815, pp. 337–8.
36. P. Hofschröer, *1815 The Waterloo Campaign: Wellington, his German Allies and the Battles of Ligny and Quatre Bras* (London, 1998), pp. 115–16.
37. *WD*, xii, Wellington to Stewart, Brussels, 8 May 1815, p. 359.
38. *WD*, xii, Wellington to Schwarzenberg, Brussels, 2 June 1815, p. 437.
39. See Leggiere, *Fall of Napoleon*, pp. 534–54.
40. *WD*, xii, Wellington to Hardinge, Brussels, 14 May 1815, pp. 384–5.
41. *WD*, xii, Wellington to Stewart, Brussels, 8 May 1815, p. 359.
42. *WD*, xii, Wellington to Hardinge, Brussels, 14 May 1815, pp. 384–5.
43. *WD*, xii, Wellington to Metternich, Brussels, 20 May 1815, p. 409.
44. C. F. von Müffling, *Passages from my Life, together with Memoirs of the Campaign of 1813 and 1814* (London, 1853), p. 221.
45. *WD*, xii, Wellington to Bathurst, Brussels, 22 May 1815, p. 416.
46. J. Haswell, *The First Respectable Spy: The Life and Times of Colquhoun Grant, Wellington's Head of Intelligence* (London, 1969), p. 224.
47. *WD*, xii, Wellington to Torrens, Brussels, 29 April 1815, p. 336.
48. *WD*, xii, Wellington to Hardinge, Brussels, 7 May 1815, p. 356.
49. *WD*, xii, Wellington to Hardinge, Brussels, 11 May 1815, p. 372.
50. *WD*, xii, Wellington to Hardinge, Brussels, 16 May 1815, p. 394.
51. *SD*, x, Dörnberg to Somerset, Mons, 6 June 1815, p. 421.
52. Hofschröer, *1815*, pp. 148–9.
53. *SD*, x, Dörnberg to Somerset, Mons, 8 June 1815, p. 432.
54. *WD*, xii, Wellington to Hardinge, Brussels, 10 June 1815, p. 457.
55. *SD*, x, Hardinge to Wellington, Namur, 14 June 1815, p. 476.
56. Cited in Hofschröer, *1815*, p. 159.
57. Ibid., p. 156.
58. Ibid., pp. 161–209.
59. J. H. Malmesbury, *Letters of the First Earl of Malmesbury, 1745–1820* (2 vols, London, 1870), ii, pp. 445–6.
60. Cited in Hofschröer, *1815*, p. 232.
61. *SD*, x, Dispositions of the British Army at 7a.m. on 16 June 1815, by W. de Lancey, forwarded by G. de Lacy Evans, p. 496.
62. Hofschröer, *1815*, pp. 357–65.
63. Stanhope, *Notes*, p. 109.

64. Cited in Hofschröer, *1815*, p. 236.
65. See Müffling, *Passages from my Life*.
66. H. T. Siborne, *The Waterloo Letters* (York, 2009), pp. 349–50.
67. NAM MS 6310/36, Correspondence of Captain William Elton, 1st Dragoon Guards, Elton to Anon., 15 July 1815.
68. F. Llewellyn (ed.), *Waterloo Recollections: Rare First Hand Accounts, Letters, Reports and Retellings from the Campaign of 1815* (York, 2007), p. 84.
69. Cited in J. C. Herold, *Battle of Waterloo* (London, 1967), p. 124.
70. NAM MS 6807/209/1, Diary of Ensign Edward Macready, 30th Regiment of Foot.
71. R. H. Gronow, *Reminiscences of Captain Gronow, Formerly of the Grenadier Guards: Being Anecdotes of the Camp, the Court, and the Clubs, at the Close of the Last War with France* (London, 1862), p. 46.
72. Müffling, *Passages from my Life*.
73. J. S. Kennedy, *Notes on the Battle of Waterloo: With a Memoir of the Author's Service during the Peninsular War and at Waterloo, 1815* (York, 2010), pp. 128–9.
74. Hibbert, *Waterloo*, p. 227.
75. A. Uffindell and M. Corum, *On the Fields of Glory: The Battlefields of the 1815 Campaign* (London, 2002), p. 41.
76. See J. Black, *The Battle of Waterloo* (New York, 2010), pp. 112–51.
77. Müffling, *Passages from my Life*.
78. E. Cotton, *A Voice from Waterloo: A History of the Battle Fought on the 18th June 1815* (London, 2009), p. 138.
79. *CC*, x, Castlereagh to Liverpool, Paris, 8 July 1815, p. 419.
80. *WD*, xii, Wellington to Castlereagh, 14 July 1815, p. 558.
81. *WD*, xii, Wellington to Castlereagh, Paris, 11 August 1815, p. 596.
82. Schroeder, *Transformation of European Politics*, pp. 551–3.

Conclusion

1. For an erudite appraisal of Nelson's status as a national hero, see A. Lambert, *Nelson: Britannia's God of War* (London, 2004).
2. See C. Esdaile, 'Waterloo', in Jeremy Black (ed.), *The Seventy Great Battles of All Time* (London, 2005), p. 197.
3. See Black, *Waterloo*, pp. 190–200.
4. See R. G. S. Cooper, 'Beyond Beasts and Bullion: Economic Considerations in Bombay's Military Logistics', *Modern Asian Studies*, Vol. 33, No. 1 (1999).
5. Coss, *All for the King's Shilling*, pp. 91–101. A Roman soldier received 6,348 kcal; a Spanish galley slave, 2,618; and a redcoat in the Peninsula, 2,350.
6. For more on the intelligence systems available to the British in India, see Bayly, *Empire and Information*.
7. For more on Western archetypes of Indian warfare, see, among others, P. Barua, *The State at War in South Asia* (Lincoln, Nebr., 2005).
8. See Cooper, *Anglo-Maratha Campaigns*, pp. 82–141.
9. The best analysis of the balance of power debate in Europe in the eighteenth and nineteenth centuries can be found in Schroeder, *Transformation of European Politics*.

Bibliography

Manuscript Sources

United Kingdom

<u>British Library, London</u>

Asia, Pacific and Africa Collection

European Manuscripts
MS Eur F128/227

Home Series
H/469(4); H/564A

Manuscripts

Add. MS 13599
Add. MS 13663
Add. MS 13664
Add. MS 13725
Add. MS 13746
Add. MS 13747
Add. MS 31237
Add. MS 35060
Add. MS 37286
Add. MS 37416
Add. MS 38233
Add. MS 38255
Add. MS 38325
Add. MS 39892
Add. MS 46702
Add. MS 52441
MS Loan 72/20

<u>Devon Record Office, Exeter</u>

MS 49/33

Gwent Record Office, Cwmbran (now moved to Pontypool)

Raglan Papers
MS A/7; MS A/34; MS A/39; MS A/43; MS A/47; MS A/56; MS B/93; MS B/102; MS
    B/114

The National Archives, Kew

Foreign Office Series
FO 7/89

Foreign Office Correspondence with Portugal
FO 63/90
FO 63/102
FO 63/113
FO 63/114
FO 63/127
FO 63/129
FO 63/130
FO 63/135
FO 63/151
FO 63/152

Foreign Office Correspondence with Spain
FO 72/143

Foreign Office Correspondence with France
FO 92/13

War Office
WO 1/228
WO 1/250
WO 1/252

National Army Museum, Chelsea

MS 6309/138 Correspondence of Lieutenant Colonel John Elley, Assistant Adjutant
    General of Cavalry
MS 6310/36 Correspondence of Captain William Elton, 1st Dragoon Guards
MS 6702/33 Correspondence of Lieutenant Henry Booth, 43rd Regiment
MS 6807/163/2–3 Correspondence of Colonel George Bingham, 1812–13
MS 6807/209/1 Diary of Ensign Edward Macready, 30th Regiment of Foot
MS 6807/219 Correspondence and Diary of Brigadier-General Robert Long
MS 6807/267 Diary of Lieutenant George Woodberry, 18th Hussars
MS 6807/345 Papers of General Sir Lowry Cole
MS 6807/461 Diary of Lieutenant Richard Brunton, 43rd Regiment
MS 6810/46 Letter from Lt Patrick Brown, 1st Regiment, Madras NI
MS 7104/45 Correspondence of Major-General Andrew Hay
MS 7409/12 Diary of John Insley, 1st Dragoons
MS 7409/67 Correspondence of General Sir Edward Pakenham and Captain Hercules
    Pakenham
MS 7510/27 Diary of Brigadier-General Charles Ashworth
MS 7607/45 The Diary of Lieut. Thomas Powell 14th Foot
MS 7912/21 Anonymous Memoirs of a Private Soldier in 1/38th
MS 8207/64 Account of the Battle of Assaye by Sgt Thomas Swarbrook, 19th Dragoons

MS 8807/52 Correspondence of Ensign John Blackman
MS 9204/182 Diary of Captain John Duffy, 43rd Regiment
MS 9406/1 Diary of Captain Francis Hood, 3rd Foot Guards

National Library of Scotland, Edinburgh

Advocates Manuscripts

Adv. MS 46.2.15; Adv. MS 46.2.18

Manuscripts

MS 3606; MS 3610; MS 13631

National Maritime Museum, Greenwich

Popham Papers
MS 77/109

University of Durham Library

Grey Papers
GRE/B19/123

University of Southampton Library

Wellington Papers
WP 1/2; 1/42; 1/44; 1/143; 1/165; 1/273; 1/300; 1/324; 1/327; 1/330; 1/332; 1/341;
    1/344; 1/346; 1/347; 1/351; 1/355; 1/361; 1/364; 1/365; 1/370; 1/372; 1/380; 1/381;
    1/396; 1/417
WP 3/3/2; 3/3/45; 3/3/47; 3/3/84; 3/3/87
WP 12/1/2; 12/2/3

India

Maharashtra State Archives, Mumbai, India

Military Board Diary
MBD/61/1724

Secret Political Department
SPD No 140
SPD No 147

National Archives of India, New Delhi

Foreign Political
MS15 (31/12/1799); MS 20 (03/07/1800); MS 31 (28/08/1800); MS 32 (28/08/1800)

Secret Political
MS 25 (11/08/03)
MS 90 (25/08/03)
MS 203 (02/11/03)

Tamil Nadu State Archives, Chennai

Military Consultations
246/1703; 246/1725; 246/1741

Military Miscellaneous Book
63/1742/110

Public Consultations
231/1723

Secret Consultations
6/1727

Portugal

Arquivo Histórico Militar, Lisbon

MS 1/14/186
MS 1/14/6/199/14
MS 1/14/6/202/10
MS 1/14/6/37–39

Newspapers and Contemporary Publications

Parliamentary Debates (London, T. C. Hansard, 1808–12)
Morning Chronicle
The Times

Battlefields Studied

Increasingly, the ground on which a battle has been fought is considered a primary source. In the course of writing this book, I have visited several, and this has improved my understanding of both the battles and of Wellington's thinking before, during and after. The battlefields have therefore helped with the writing of the book, and are included here as primary sources.

Shrirangapattana (aka Seringapatam), Mysore, India (May 1799) (12°24'50"N; 76°42'14"E)
Buçaco, Portugal (27 September 1810) (40°20'40"N; 8°20'15"W)
Torres Vedras, Portugal (October–March 1810) (39°05'59"N; 9°15'53"W)
Ciudad Rodrigo, Spain (19 January 1812) (40°36'0"N; 6°32'0"W)
Badajoz, Spain (6 April 1812) (38°52'44"N; 6°58'1"W)
Salamanca, Spain (22 July 1812) (40°57'42"N; 5°40'3"W)
Burgos, Spain (October–November 1812) (42°21'0"N; 3°42'0"W)
Vitoria, Spain (21 June 1813) (42°51'0"N; 2°41'0"W)
San Sebastian, Spain (31 August 1813) (43°19'17"N; 1°59'8"W)
Battle of the Nivelle, La Rhune, France (10 November 1813) (43°18'33"N; 1°38'8"W)
Orthez, France (27 February 1814) (43°29'21'N; 0°46'11"W)

Published Primary Sources

Anon., *An Accurate and Impartial Narrative of the War, by an officer of the Guards in Two Volumes Comprising of the Campaigns of 1793, 1794 and the Retreat Through Holland to Westphalia, in 1795* (London, 1796)

Anon., *The Personal Narrative of a Private Soldier who served in the Forty-Second Highlanders for Twelve Years during the Late War* (London, 1821)

Aspinall, A. (ed.), *The Later Correspondence of King George III* (5 vols, Cambridge, 1962–70)

Badcock, L., 'A Light Dragoon in the Peninsula: Extracts from the Letters of Captain Lovell Badcock, 14th Light Dragoons, 1809–1814', *Journal of the Society for Army Historical Research*, Vol. 34 (1956)

Bamford, F. (ed.), *Journal of Mrs Arbuthnot 1820–1832* (2 vols, London, 1950)

Bankes, G. N. (ed.), *The Autobiography of Sergeant William Lawrence, a Hero of the Peninsular and Waterloo Campaigns* (London, 1886)

Bayly, R. *Diary of Colonel Bayly, 12th Regt, 1796–1830* (London: Army and Navy Cooperative Society, 1896)

Bennell, A. (ed.), *The Maratha War Papers of Arthur Wellesley, January to December 1803* (Stroud, 1998)

Blakiston, R., *12 Years Military Adventure in three-quarters of the globe . . .* (London: Henry Coulburn, 1840)

Bonaparte, J., *The Confidential Correspondence of Napoleon Bonaparte with his Brother Joseph . . . Selected and Translated, with Explanatory Notes, from the 'Memoires du Roi Joseph'* (2 vols, London, 1855)

Brown, R., *An Impartial Journal of a Detachment from the Brigade of Foot Guards Commencing 25th February 1793 and Ending 9 May 1795 by Robert Brown, Corporal in the Coldstream Guards* (London, 1795)

Bruce, H. A., *The Life of General Sir William Napier, KCB* (2 vols, London, 1864)

Campbell, A., 'Letter from Lt Alexander Campbell, 74th Foot, to his brother Lt Frederick Campbell, RA, dated Seringapatam, 20 June 1799, describing the battle there', *Journal of the Royal Highland Fusiliers*, Vol. 6, No. 1 (June 1969)

Castlereagh, Viscount (Robert Stewart, 2nd Marquess of Londonderry), *The Memoranda and Correspondence of Robert Stewart, Viscount Castlereagh* (12 vols, London, 1848–54)

Clausewitz, Karl von, *On War*, ed. and trans. M. Howard and P. Paret (Princeton, 1989)

Colebrook, T. E. (ed.), *Life of the Hon. Mountstuart Elphinstone* (2 vols, London, 1884)

Cooke, J. H., *With the Light Division: The Experiences of an Officer of the 43rd Light Infantry in the Peninsula and South of France during the Napoleonic Wars* (York, 2007)

Cooper, J. S., *Rough Notes of Seven Campaigns in Portugal, Spain, France and America during the Years 1809–15* (London, 1869)

Costello, E., *Adventures of a Soldier, or Memoirs of Edward Costello, KSF, formerly a Non-Commissioned Officer in the Rifle Brigade and Late Captain in the British Legion comprising Narratives of the Campaigns in the Peninsular War under the Duke of Wellington and the recent Civil Wars in Spain* (London, 1841)

Cotton, E., *A Voice from Waterloo: A History of the Battle Fought on the 18th June 1815* (London, 2009)

Dirom, A., *A Narrative of the Campaign in India which Terminated the War with Tippoo Sultan in 1792* (London, 1793)

Dobbs, J., *Gentlemen in Red: Recollections of an Old 52nd Man* (London, 1863)

Donaldson, J., *Recollections of the Eventful Life of a Soldier* (Edinburgh, 1852)

Duff, J. G., *A History of the Marathas* (3 vols, London, 1826)

Elphinstone, M., *The Rise of the British Power in the East* (London, 1887)

Fletcher, I. (ed.), *For King and Country: Letters and Diaries of John Mills, Coldstream Guards, 1811–14*, (London, 1995)

Gleig, G. R. (ed.), *The Hussar: The Story of Sergeant Norbert Landsheit* (Philadelphia, 1845)

——, *The Life of Major-General Sit Thomas Munro, Bart. and KGB, Late Governor of Madras with Extracts from his Correspondence and Private Papers* (2 vols, London, 1831)

Glover, G. (ed.), *The Waterloo Archive* (2 vols, London, 2009–10)

Grattan, W., *Adventures with the Connaught Rangers from 1808 to 1814* (2 vols, London, 1847)

Green, J., *The Vicissitudes of a Soldier's Life, or a Series of Occurrences from 1806 to 1815* (Louth, 1827)

Greville, C., *The Greville Memoirs: A Journal of the Reigns of King George IV and William IV, and Queen Victoria* (ed. H. Reeve, 8 vols, London, 1888)

Gronow, R. H., *Reminiscences of Captain Gronow, Formerly of the Grenadier Guards: Being Anecdotes of the Camp, the Court, and the Clubs, at the Close of the Last War with France* (London, 1862)

Grose, J. H., *A Voyage to the East Indies* (2 vols, London, 1766)

Gurney, J., *The Trial of General Whitelocke* (London, 1807)

Gurwood, J., *The Dispatches of Field Marshal the Duke of Wellington during His Various Campaigns in India, Denmark, Portugal, Spain, The Low Countries and France* (13 vols, London, 1852)

Hale, J., *Journal of a Late Sergeant of the 9th Regiment of Foot* (London, 1826)

Haley, A. (ed.), *The Soldier who Walked Away: Autobiography of Andrew Pearson, a Peninsular War Veteran* (Liverpool, n.d.)

Hamilton, A., *Hamilton's Campaign with Moore and Wellington during the Peninsular War* (New York, 1847)

Hamilton, R. V. (ed.), *Letters and Papers of Admiral of the Fleet Sir T. Byam Martin* (2 vols, London, 1898)

Hamilton, T., 'Letters from the Peninsula, No. IV: The Battle of Salamanca', *Blackwood's Edinburgh Magazine*, Vol. 23, No. 138 (May 1828)

Herbert, George, Count Münster, *Political Sketches of the State of Europe from 1814–1867* (Edinburgh, 1868)

Historical Manuscripts Commission, *Report on the Manuscripts of Earl Bathurst* (London, 1923)

——, *Report on the Manuscripts of J. B. Fortescue, Esq. Preserved at Dropmore* (10 vols, London, 1892–1927)

——, *Report on the Manuscripts of Reginald Rawdon Hastings* (22 vols, London, 1928)

Howell, T. (ed.), *Journal of a Soldier of the 71st, 1806–1815* (London, 1828)

Ingram, E. (ed.), *Two Views of British India: The Private Correspondence of Mr Dundas and Lord Wellesley: 1798–1801* (Bath, 1970)

Jennings, L. J. (ed.), *The Croker Papers: The Correspondence and Diaries of John Wilson Croker, from 1809–1830* (3 vols, London, 1884)

Kaye, J. W., *Life and Correspondence of Major General Sir John Malcolm* (2 vols, London, 1854)

Kennedy, J. S., *Notes on the Battle of Waterloo: With a Memoir of the Author's Service during the Peninsular War and at Waterloo, 1815* (York, 2010)

Kincaid, J., *Adventures in the Rifle Brigade in the Peninsula, France and the Netherlands from 1809 to 1815* (London, 1830)

Larpent, F. S., *The Journal of F. Seymour Larpent* (3 vols, London, 1853)

Leach, J., *Rough Sketches of an Old Soldier* (London, 1831)

Leeke, W., *History of Lord Seaton's 52nd Regiment* (2 vols, London, 1866)

Leith-Hay, A., *A Narrative of the Peninsular War* (2 vols, London, 1839)

Leslie, C., *Military Journal of Colonel Leslie, KH, of Balquhain, while serving with the Twenty-Ninth Regiment in the Peninsula and the Sixtieth Rifles in Canada, 1807–1832* (Aberdeen, 1887)

Leveson-Gower, G. G., and A. D. J. Monson (eds), *Memoirs of George Elers: Captain in the 12th Regiment of Foot (1777–1842)* (London, 1903)

Liddell Hart, B. H., *The Letters of Private Wheeler, 1809–1828* (London, 1951)

Llewellyn, F. (ed.), *Waterloo Recollections: Rare First Hand Accounts, Letters, Reports and Retellings from the Campaign of 1815* (York, 2007)

Lloyd, C. (ed.), *The Keith Papers* (3 vols, London, 1955)

Ludovici, A. (ed.), *On the Road with Wellington: The Diary of a War Commissary* (London, 1924)

McCarthy, J., *Recollections of the Storming of the Castle of Burgos by the Third Division under the Command of Lieut. Gen. Sir Thomas Picton, GCB, on the Sixth of April 1812* (London, 1836)

McGuffie, T. (ed.), *Peninsular Cavalry General (1811–13): The Correspondence of Lieutenant General Robert Ballard Long* (London, 1951)

Mackenzie, R., *A Sketch of the War with Tipu Sultan* (2 vols, Calcutta, 1792)

Malmesbury, J. H., *Letters of the First Earl of Malmesbury, 1745–1820* (2 vols, London, 1870)

Marmont, A., *Mémoires du Maréchal Marmont, duc de Raguse de 1792 au 1841* (9 vols, Paris, 1857)

Monick, S. (ed.), *Douglas's Tale of the Peninsula and Waterloo* (London, 1997)

Müffling, C. F. von, *Passages from my Life, together with Memoirs of the Campaign of 1813 and 1814* (London, 1853)

Muir, R. (ed.), *At Wellington's Right Hand: The Letters of Lieutenant-Colonel Sir Alexander Gordon, 1808–1815* (Stroud, 2003)

Napier, W. F. P., *History of the War in the Peninsula and in the South of France, from 1807 to 1814* (6 vols, London, 1828–40)

Page, J., *Intelligence Officer in the Peninsula: Letters and Diaries of Major the Honourable Edward Charles Cocks, 1786–1812* (Tunbridge Wells, 1986)

Philips, C. H. (ed.), *The Correspondence of David Scot Director and Chairman of the East India Company relating to India Affairs, 1787–1805* (2 vols, London, 1951)

Robinson, H. B., *Memoirs of Sir Thomas Picton* (2 vols, London, 1836)

Ross-Lewin, H., *With the 'Thirty-Second' in the Peninsula* (Dublin, 1904)

Rousseau, I. (ed.), *The Peninsular War Journal of Major General Sir Benjamin D'Urban, 1808–1817* (London, 1930)

Sarkar, J., and G. S. Sardesai (eds), *English Records of Maratha History (Poona Residency Correspondence): Poona Affairs 1797–1801 (Palmer's Embassy)*, (Bombay, 1939)

Sherer, J., *Recollections of the Peninsula* (London, 1823)

Siborne, H. T., *The Waterloo Letters* (York, 2009)

Sinh, Raghubir (ed.), *English Records of Maratha History (Poona Residency Correspondence): Volume 10: The Treaty of Bassein and the Anglo-Maratha War in the Deccan, 1802–1804* (Bombay, 1951)

Smith, H. G. W., *Autobiography of Sir Harry Smith, 1787–1819* (London, 1910)

Stanhope, Earl, *Notes of Conversation with the Duke of Wellington, 1831–1851* (London, 1888)

Sturgis, J. (ed.), *A Boy in the Peninsular War: The Services, Adventures and Experiences of Robert Blakeney, Subaltern of the Twenty-Eighth Regiment* (London, 1899)

Thomson, W. (ed.), *An Ensign in the Peninsular War: The Letters of John Aitchison* (London, 1981)

Thorn, W., *Memoir of the War in India Conducted by General Lord Lake, Commander-in-Chief, and Major-General Sir Arthur Wellesley, Duke of Wellington; from its Commencement in 1803, to its Termination in 1806, on the Banks of the Hyphasis* (London, 1818)

Tomkinson, W., *The Diary of a Cavalry Officer, 1809–1815* (London, 1971)

Verner, W. (ed.), *A British Rifleman: Journals and Correspondence during the Peninsular War and the Campaign of Waterloo* (London, 1899)

Walpole, S., *The Life of the Right Honourable Spencer Perceval, including Correspondence with Many Distinguished Persons* (London, 1874)

Warre, E. (ed.), *Letters from the Peninsula, 1808–1812 by Lieutenant General Sir William Warre* (London, 1909)

Webster, C. K. (ed.), *British Diplomacy, 1813–1815* (London, 1921)

Wellesley, Arthur, Duke of Wellington, *The Mysore Letters and Dispatches of the Duke of Wellington, 1799–1805* (Bangalore, 1862)

Wellesley, Arthur, 2nd Duke of Wellington (ed.), *Supplementary Dispatches and Memoranda of Field Marshal Arthur Duke of Wellington, 1797–1818* (14 vols, London, 1858)

Wellesley, R. (First Marquess), *The Dispatches, Minutes, and Correspondence of the Marquess Wellesley, KG, during his Administration in India* (5 vols, London, 1836–7)

Welsh, J., *Military Reminiscences: Extracted from a Journal of Nearly Forty Years Active Service in the East Indies* (2 vols, London, 1830)

Wood, G., *The Subaltern Officer: A Narrative* (London, 1826)

Wrottesley, G. (ed.), *The Life and Correspondence of Field Marshal Sir John Burgoyne* (2 vols, London, 1873)

Wylly, H. (ed.), *A Cavalry Officer in the Corunna Campaign: The Journal of Captain Gordon of the Fifteenth Hussars* (London, 1913)

Secondary Sources

In writing on a subject as vast as the military career of the Duke of Wellington, I have inevitably found myself leaning on the views and analysis of authors of books focusing on specific aspects of Wellington's life outside my expertise. I owe it to the authors of those books to highlight the contribution of their work to the creation of my own. On India, the must-read text on Wellesley's campaigns is Randolf Cooper's *The Anglo-Maratha Campaigns and the Contest for India*. Cooper's depth of research and innovative thinking were of fundamental importance to the development of my own ideas, and his arguments resonate throughout the present volume. On the period between Wellesley's campaigns in India and the Peninsula, Martin Robson's *Britain, Portugal and South America in the Napoleonic Wars* is a masterful study of the development of British strategy before the Peninsular War began. For in-depth analysis of British policy and strategy during the Peninsular War, I turned to Rory Muir's *Britain and the Defeat of Napoleon*, and Josh Moon's *Wellington's Two Front War*. For unbeatable analyses of Spanish politics and military transformation during the Peninsular War, one cannot do better than Charles Esdaile's *The Peninsular War*, *The Spanish Army in the Peninsular War* and *The Duke of Wellington and the Command of the Spanish Army*. His arguments were most useful when investigating Wellington's relations with his Spanish allies. The best and most critical analysis of Wellington's army and his command of it is Ed Coss's *All for the King's Shilling*. This is described as the most important book ever to have been written about the British Army of the Napoleonic Wars. It is. Charles Webster provided the grounding for British foreign policy towards Europe with his two-volume *The Foreign Policy of Castlereagh*, whilst Paul Schroeder's *The Transformation of European Politics* is a seminal analysis of international relations between 1763 and 1848. I would go so far as to say that the Napoleonic Wars cannot be truly understood without reference to this work. The same can be said of Esdaile's *Napoleon's Wars*. Michael Leggiere's *Napoleon and Berlin* and *The Fall of Napoleon* provide the best analyses of what was going on elsewhere in Europe when Wellington was focused on the Peninsula. Peter Hofschröer's two-volume *1815: Waterloo Campaign* is a great, if controversial, scholarly analysis of Waterloo, and I have leaned heavily on his arguments in coming to my own conclusions, whilst Jeremy Black's *The Battle of Waterloo* provided important new avenues of thought and analysis. For details of Wellington's personal life, his relationship with his brothers, and how this impacted on Wellington's decision-making, I always reached for John Severn's *Architects of Empire*.

Alawi, S., *The Sepoys and the Company: Tradition and Transition in Northern India, 1770–1830* (Oxford, 1995)

Alexander, D. W., 'French Replacement Methods during the Peninsular War, 1808–1814', *Military Affairs*, Vol. 44, No. 4 (December 1980)

——, *Rod of Iron: French Counter-Insurgency Policy in Aragón during the Peninsular War* (Wilmington, Del., 1985)

Andrews, T. J., 'Massena's Lines of March in Portugal and French Routes in Northern Spain', *EHR*, Vol. 16, No. 63 (July 1901)

Asprey, R. B., *The Rise and Fall of Napoleon Bonaparte* (2 vols, London, 2000–1)

Barbero, A., *The Battle: A History of the Battle of Waterloo* (London, 2005)

Barnett, C., *Britain and her Army, 1509–1970: A Military, Political and Social Survey* (London, 1970)

Bartlett, C., *Castlereagh* (London, 1966)

Barua, P., 'Military Developments in India, 1750–1850', *JMH*, Vol. 58, No. 4 (October 1994)

——, *The State at War in South Asia* (Lincoln, Nebr., 2005)

Baugh, D. A., 'Great Britain's "Blue-Water" Policy, 1689–1815', *IHR*, Vol. 10 (1988)

Bayly, C. A., *Empire and Information: Intelligence Gathering and Social Communication in India, 1780–1870* (Cambridge, 1996)

Bell, D., *The First Total War: Napoleon's Europe and the Birth of Modern Warfare* (London, 2007)

Bennell, A., 'Factors in the Marquis Wellesley's Failure against Holkar, 1804', *BSOAS*, Vol. 28, No. 3 (1965)

——, *The Making of Arthur Wellesley* (London, 1997)

Berkeley, A. (ed.), *New Lights on the Peninsular War: International Congress on the Iberian Peninsula, 1780–1840* (Lisbon, 1991)

Biddulph, J., *Stringer Lawrence: The Father of the Indian Army* (London, 1901)

Bird, W.D., 'The Assaye Campaign', *Journal of the United Services Institute of India*, Vol. 41, No. 187 (1912)

——, 'Examples of Wellington's Strategy: The Vitoria Campaign, 1813', *Army Quarterly*, Vol. 19 (1930)

Black, F. H., 'Diplomatic Struggles: British Support in Spain and Portugal, 1800–1810' (Unpublished PhD Thesis, Florida State University, 2005)

Black, J. *The Battle of Waterloo* (New York, 2010)

——, *Britain as a Military Power, 1688–1815* (London, 1999)

——, *British Diplomats and Diplomacy, 1680–1800* (Exeter, 2001)

——, *A Military Revolution? Military Change and European Society 1550–1800* (London, 1991)

——, *War and the World: Military Power and the Fate of Continents, 1450–2000* (London, 2000)

——, *War: Past, Present and Future* (Stroud, 2001)

——, *Warfare in the Nineteenth Century* (London, 2009)

Bowen, H. V., *The Business of Empire: The East India Company and Imperial Britain, 1756–1833* (Cambridge, 2006)

Boyce, D. G., 'From Assaye to the *Assaye*: Reflections on British Government, Force and Moral Authority in India', *JMH*, Vol. 63, No. 3 (July 1999)

Broers, M., *Europe under Napoleon, 1799–1815* (London, 1996)

——, *Napoleon's Other War: Bandits, Rebels and their Pursuers in the Age of Revolutions* (London, 2010)

Brown, D., *Palmerston: A Biography* (London, 2010)

Brumwell, S., *Redcoats: The British Soldier and War in the Americas, 1755–1763* (Cambridge, 2002)

Bryant, A., *The Age of Elegance, 1812–22* (London, 1950)

——, *The Great Duke or the Invincible General* (London, 1971)

——, *The Years of Endurance, 1793–1802* (London, 1942)

——, *Years of Victory, 1802–1812* (London, 1944)

Bryant, G. J., 'Asymmetric Warfare: The British Experience in Eighteenth-Century India', *JMH*, Vol. 68, No. 2 (April 2004)

——, 'Pacification in the Early British Raj, 1755–85', *Journal of Imperial and Commonwealth History*, Vol. 14, No. 1 (October 1985)

Burton, R. G., *Wellington's Campaigns in India* (Calcutta, 1908)

Butler, I., *The Eldest Brother: The Marquess Wellesley, 1760–1842* (London, 1973)

Carver, M., 'Wellington and his Brothers', Wellington Lectures, University of Southampton (Southampton, 1989)

Chakravorty, U. N., *Anglo-Maratha Relations and Malcolm, 1798–1830* (New Delhi, 1979)

Chancey, M. K., 'In the Company's Secret Service: Neil Benjamin Edmonstone and the First Indian Imperialists, 1780–1820' (4 vols, Unpublished PhD Thesis, Florida State University, 2003)

Chandler, D., *The Campaigns of Napoleon* (London, 1995)

Clark, C., *Iron Kingdom: The Rise and Downfall of Prussia, 1600–1947* (London, 2006)

Clarke, J., *British Diplomacy and Foreign Policy, 1782–1865: The National Interest* (London, 1989)

Coen, T. C., *The Indian Political Service* (London, 1971)

Collins, B., *War and Empire: The Expansion of Britain, 1790–1830* (London, 2010)

Connelly, O., *Blundering to Glory: Napoleon's Military Campaigns* (Wilmington, Del., 1987)

——, *The Gentle Bonaparte: Biography of Joseph, Napoleon's Elder Brother* (New York, 1968)

——, 'Joseph Bonaparte as Military Commander: The Talavera Campaign, 1809', in *Consortium on Revolutionary Europe, 1750–1850: Selected Papers* (Auburn, Ala., 1992).

Cooper, R. G. S., *The Anglo-Maratha Campaigns and the Contest for India: The Struggle for Control of the South Asian Military Economy* (Cambridge, 2003)

——, 'Beyond Beasts and Bullion: Economic Considerations in Bombay's Military Logistics', *Modern Asian Studies*, Vol. 33, No. 1 (1999)

——, 'Indian Army Logistics 1757–1857: Arthur Wellesley's Role Reconsidered', in A. J. Guy and P. B. Boyden (eds), *Soldiers of the Raj: The Indian Army 1600–1947* (London, 1997)

——, 'New Light on Arthur Wellesley's Command Apprenticeship in India: The Dhoondiah Waugh Campaign of 1800 Reconsidered', in A. J. Guy (ed.), *The Road to Waterloo* (London, 1990)

——, 'Wellington and the Marathas', *IHR*, Vol. 11, No. 1 (February 1989)

Coss, E. J., *All for the King's Shilling: The British Soldier under Wellington, 1808–1814* (Norman, Okla., 2010)

Creveld, M. van, *Command in War* (London, 1985)

——, *Supplying War: Logistics from Wallenstein to Patton* (Cambridge, 1977)

Croxton, D., '"The Prosperity of Arms is Never Continual": Military Intelligence, Surprise and Diplomacy in 1640s' Germany', in *JMH*, Vol. 64, No. 4 (October 2000)

Dallas, G., *1815: The Roads to Waterloo* (London, 1996)

Dalrymple, W., *White Mughals: Love and Betrayal in Eighteenth-Century India* (London, 2002)

Davies, D., *Sir John Moore's Peninsular Campaign, 1808–9* (The Hague, 1974)

Davies, G., *Wellington and his Army* (Oxford, 1954)

Davies, H. J., 'Diplomats as Spymasters: A Case Study of the Peninsular War', *JMH*, Vol. 76, No. 1 (January 2012)

Davis Hanson, V., *Carnage and Culture: Landmark Battles in the Rise of Western Power* (New York, 2002)

De la Fuente, F. A., 'Dom Miguel Pereira Forjaz: His Early Career and Role in the Mobilization and Defense of Portugal during the Peninsular War' (Unpublished PhD Thesis, Florida State University, 1980)

DeToy, B., 'Wellington's Admiral: The Life and Career of George Berkeley, 1753–1818' (2 vols, Unpublished PhD Dissertation, Florida State University, 1997)

Dighe, V. G., *Peshwa Bajirao I and Maratha Expansion* (Bombay, 1944)

Dixon, P., *Canning: Politician and Statesman* (London, 1976)

Duffy, M., 'A Particular Service: The British Government and the Dunkirk Expedition of 1793', *EHR* Vol. 91 (1976)

——, 'British Naval Intelligence and Bonaparte's Egyptian Expedition of 1798', *Mariner's Mirror*, Vol. 84, No. 3 (August 1998)

Ehrman, J., *The Younger Pitt* (4 vols, London, 1969)

Ellis, G., *The Napoleonic Empire* (London, 1991)

Elting, J. R., *Swords around a Throne: Napoleon's Grand Armée* (New York, 1997)

Emsley, C., *British Society and the French Wars, 1793–1815* (London, 1979)

Englund, S., *Napoleon: A Political Life* (New York, 2004)

Epstein, R., *Napoleon's Last Victory and the Emergence of Modern Warfare* (Lawrence, Kans., 1995)

Esdaile, C. *The Duke of Wellington and the Command of the Spanish Army, 1812–14* (London, 1990)

——, *Fighting Napoleon: Guerrillas, Bandits and Adventurers in Spain, 1808–1814* (London, 2004)

——, *Napoleon's Wars: An International History* (London, 2008)

——, *Peninsular Eyewitness: The Experiences of War in Spain and Portugal, 1808–1813* (Barnsley, 2008)

——, *The Peninsular War: A New History* (London, 2002)

——, 'Waterloo', in Jeremy Black (ed.), *The Seventy Great Battles of All Time* (London, 2005)

——, 'Wellington and the Military Eclipse of Spain', *IHR*, Vol. 11 (1989)

Ferris, J., and M. Handel, 'Clausewitz, Intelligence, Uncertainty and the Art of Command in Military Operations', *Intelligence and Art of Command*, Vol. 10, No. 1 (January 1995)

Fortescue, J. B., *A History of the British Army* (19 vols, London, 1906–20)

Franklin, R., *Lord Stuart de Rothesay* (Upton-upon-Severn, 1993)

Fryman, M., 'Charles Stuart and the Common Cause: The Anglo-Portuguese Alliance, 1810–1814' (Unpublished PhD Dissertation, Florida State University, 1974)

Gash, N., *Lord Liverpool: The Life and Political Career of Robert Bankes Jenkinson, Second Earl of Liverpool, 1770–1828* (London, 1984)

—— (ed.), *Wellington: Studies in the Military and Political Career of the First Duke of Wellington* (Manchester, 1990)

Gates, D., *The British Light Infantry Arm, c. 1790–1815: Its Creation, Training and Operational Role* (London, 1987)

——, *The Spanish Ulcer: A History of the Peninsular War* (London, 1986)

Gerges, M., 'Command and Control in the Peninsula: The Role of the British Cavalry, 1808–1814' (Unpublished PhD Thesis, Florida State University, 2005)

Gill, J. H., *1809 Thunder on the Danube: Napoleon's Defeat of the Habsburgs* (3 vols, London, 2006–10)

Glover, M., *Britannia Sickens: Sir Arthur Wellesley and the Convention of Cintra* (London, 1970)

——, *Peninsular War, 1807–1814: A Concise Military History* (London, 1974)

——, *Wellington as Military Commander* (London, 1968)

——, *Wellington's Peninsular Victories* (London, 1963)

Glover, R., 'Arms and the British Diplomat in the French Revolutionary Era', *Journal of Modern History*, Vol. 29, No. 3 (September 1957)

——, *Britain at Bay: Defence against Bonaparte, 1803–14* (London, 1973)

——, *Peninsular Preparation: The Reform of the British Army, 1795–1809* (Cambridge, 1963)

Gordon, S., *Marathas, Marauders, and State Formation in Eighteenth-Century India* (Oxford, 1994)

Graceffo, J., 'Making of a Marshal: Bertrand Cluazel Takes Command of the Army of Portugal, 1812' (Unpublished PhD Thesis, Florida State University, 2005)

Grainger, J. D., *The Amiens Truce: Britain and Bonaparte, 1801–1803* (Woodbridge, 2004)

Grammer, T. G., 'The Peninsula Reassessed: A Critical Analysis of Wellington's Peninsular Campaign in Light of his Operational Intentions', in *Consortium on Revolutionary Europe, 1750–1850: Selected Papers* (Tallahassee, Fla., 1990)

Graves, D. E., *Fix Bayonets! A Royal Welch Fusilier at War, 1795–1815* (London, 2006)

Grehan, J., *The Lines of Torres Vedras: The Cornerstone of Wellington's Strategy in the Peninsular War 1809–1812* (London, 2004)

Griffith, P. (ed.), *A History of the Peninsular War, IX: Modern Studies of the War in Spain and Portugal, 1808–1814* (London, 1999)

——, *Wellington – Commander: The Iron Duke's Generalship* (Chichester, 1986)

Guedalla, P., *The Duke* (London, 1931)

Hall, C., *British Strategy in the Napoleonic War, 1803–1815* (Manchester, 1992)

——, 'The Royal Navy and the Peninsular War', *Mariner's Mirror*, Vol. 79, No. 4 (November 1993)

——, *Wellington's Navy: Sea Power and the Peninsular War, 1807–1814* (London, 2004)

Hamilton-Williams, D., *Waterloo: New Perspectives: The Great Battle Reappraised* (London, 1993)

Harvey, A. D., 'The Ministry of All the Talents: The Whigs in Office, February 1806 to March 1807', *Historical Journal*, Vol. 15, No. 4 (December 1972)

Harvey, R., *Mavericks: The Maverick Genius of Great Military Leaders* (London, 2008)

Haswell, J., *The First Respectable Spy: The Life and Times of Colquhoun Grant, Wellington's Head of Intelligence* (London, 1969)

Hay, W. A., *The Whig Revival, 1808–1830* (New York, 2005)

Hayman, P., *Soult: Napoleon's Maligned Marshal* (London, 1990)

Haythornthwaite, P., *The Armies of Wellington* (London, 1994)

Headrick, D. R., *The Tools of Empire: Technology and European Imperialism in the Nineteenth Century* (Oxford, 1981)

Herold, J. C., *Battle of Waterloo* (London, 1967)

Hibbert, C., *Waterloo* (London, 1998)

Hill, J., *Wellington's Right Hand: Rowland, Viscount Hill* (London, 2011)

Hofschröer, P., *1815 The Waterloo Campaign: Wellington, his German Allies and the Battles of Ligny and Quatre Bras* (London, 1998)

——, *1815 The Waterloo Campaign: The German Victory* (London, 2004)

—— (ed.), *On Wellington: A Critique of Waterloo by Karl von Clausewitz* (Norman, Okla., 2010)

Holmes, R., *Redcoat: The British Soldier in the Age of Horse and Musket* (London, 2002)

——, *Sahib: The British Soldier in India, 1750–1914* (London, 2006)

——, *Wellington: The Iron Duke* (London, 2003)

Hopton, R., *The Battle of Maida, 1806: Fifteen Minutes of Glory* (Barnsley, 2002)

Horward, D. D., *The Battle of Bussaco: Massena vs Wellington, 1810* (Tallahassee, Fla., 1965)

——, 'Logistics and Strategy in the Peninsula: A Case Study, 1810–11', *Consortium on Revolutionary Europe Proceedings* (Charleston, SC, 1999)

——, *Napoleon and Iberia: The Twin Sieges of Ciudad Rodrigo and Almeida, 1810* (London, 1994)

——, 'Wellington and the Defence of Portugal', *IHR*, Vol. 11, No. 1 (February 1989)

——, 'Wellington as a Strategist, 1808–1814' in N. Gash (ed.), *Wellington: Studies in the Military and Political Career of the First Duke of Wellington* (Manchester, 1990)

——, 'Wellington, Berkeley, and the Royal Navy: Sea Power and the Defence of Portugal (1808–1812)', in *British Historical Society of Portugal Annual Report*, No. 18 (1991)

Houlding, J. A., *Fit for Service: The Training of the British Army, 1715–1795* (Oxford, 1981)

Houssaye, H., *1815 Waterloo* (London, 1900)

Hyden, J. S., 'The Sources, Organisation and Uses of Intelligence in the Anglo-Portuguese Army, 1808–1814', *Journal for the Society of Army Historical Research*, Vol. 62 (1984)

Ingram, E., 'Wellington and India', in N. Gash (ed.), *Wellington: Studies in the Military and Political Career of the First Duke of Wellington* (Manchester, 1990)

James, L., *The Iron Duke: A Military Biography of Wellington* (London, 2002)

Johnson, O. W., 'British Espionage and Prussian Politics in the Age of Napoleon', *Intelligence and National Security*, Vol. 2, No. 2 (April 1987)

Jupp, P., *Lord Grenville, 1759–1834* (Oxford, 1995)

Kantak, M. R., *The First Anglo-Maratha War 1774–1783: A Military Study of Major Battles* (Bombay, 1993)

Keay, J., *A History of India* (London, 2000)

Keegan, J., *Face of Battle: A Study of Agincourt, Waterloo and the Somme* (London, 2004)

——, *A History of Warfare* (London, 1993)

——, *The Mask of Command* (New York, 1987)

Kennedy, P., *The Rise and Fall of British Naval Mastery* (London, 1976)

——, *The Rise and Fall of the Great Powers: Economic Change and Military Conflict from 1500 to 2000* (New York, 1987)

Kissinger, H., *A World Restored: Metternich, Castlereagh and the Problems of Peace, 1812–22* (London, 2000)

Knight, G., 'Lord Liverpool and the Peninsular Struggle, 1809–1812,' *Consortium on Revolutionary Europe Proceedings*, Vol. 20 (Tallahassee, Fla., 1990)

——, 'Lord Liverpool and the Peninsular War, 1809–1812' (Unpublished PhD Thesis, Florida State University, 1976)

Knight, R., *The Pursuit of Victory: The Life and Achievements of Horatio Nelson* (London, 2005)

Knox, M., and M. Williamson (eds), *The Dynamics of Military Revolution 1300–2050*, (Cambridge, 2001)

Kolff, D. H., *Naukar, Rajput & Sepoy: The Ethnohistory of the Military Labour Market in Hindustan, 1450–1850* (Cambridge, 1990)

Kraehe, E. E., *Metternich's German Policy: The Congress of Vienna, 1814–1815* (Princeton, 1983)

——, 'Wellington and the Reconstruction of the Allied Armies during the Hundred Days', *IHR*, Vol. 11, No. 1 (February 1989)

Krajeski, P., 'British Amphibious Operations during the Peninsular War, 1808–1814', (Unpublished Master's Thesis, Florida State University, 1995)

——, *In the Shadow of Nelson: The Naval Leadership of Admiral Sir Charles Cotton, 1753–1812* (Westport, Conn., 2000)

Lambert, A., *Nelson: Britannia's God of War* (London, 2004)

Latimer, J., *1812: War with America* (London, 2007)

Leggiere, M. V., *The Fall of Napoleon: The Allied Invasion of France, 1813–1814* (Cambridge, 2007)

——, *Napoleon & Berlin: The Franco-Prussian War in North Germany, 1813* (Norman, Okla., 2002)

Lieven, D., *Russia against Napoleon* (London, 2010)

Lipscombe, N., *The Peninsular War Atlas* (London, 2010)

Longford, E., *Wellington: Years of the Sword* (London, 1970)

Lorge, P. A., *The Asian Military Revolution: From Gunpowder to the Bomb* (Cambridge, 2008)

Lynn, J. A., *Battle: A History of Combat and Culture from Ancient Greece to Modern America* (Philadelphia, 2003)

—— (ed.), *Tools of War: Instruments, Ideas and Institutions of Warfare, 1445–1871* (Urbana, Ill., 1990)

McCranie, K. D., *Admiral Lord Keith and the Naval War against Napoleon* (Gainesville, Fla., 2006)

McGrigor, M., *Wellington's Spies* (Barnsley, 2005)

Mackesy, P., *British Victory in Egypt: The End of Napoleon's Conquest* (London, 2010)

——, *Statesmen at War: The Strategy of Overthrow, 1798–99* (London, 1974)

McNeill, W. H., *The Pursuit of Power* (Chicago, 1982)

Malbon Jr, A., 'Knowing What Was on the Other Side of the Hill: A Survey of the Duke of Wellington and Intelligence in the Peninsular War, 1808–1814', in *Consortium on Revolutionary Europe, 1750–1850: Selected Papers* (Shreveport, Calif., 1995).

Mallinson, A., *The Making of the British Army: From the English Civil War to the War on Terror* (London, 2009)

Mansell, P., 'Wellington and the French Restoration', *IHR*, Vol. 11, No. 1 (February 1989)

Meyer, J. A., 'Wellington in the Talavera Campaign', in *Consortium on Revolutionary Europe, 1750–1850: Selected Papers* (1992), pp. 130–41.

Middleton, C. R., *The Administration of British Foreign Policy, 1782–1846* (Durham, NC, 1977)

Moon, J., *Wellington's Two-Front War: The Peninsular Campaigns at Home and Abroad, 1808–1814* (Norman, Okla., 2010)

Moon, P., *The British Conquest and Dominion of India* (London, 1989)

Moore Smith, G., *The Life of John Colborne, Field Marshal Lord Seaton* (London, 1903)

Muir, R., *Britain and the Defeat of Napoleon, 1806–1815* (London, 1996)

——, *Salamanca 1812* (London, 2001)

——, *Tactics and the Experience of Battle in the Age of Napoleon* (London, 1998)

——, R. Burnham, H. Muir, and R. McGuigan, *Inside Wellington's Peninsular Army, 1808–1814* (Barnsley, 2006)

——, and C. Esdaile, 'Strategic Planning in a Time of Small Government: The Wars against Revolutionary and Napoleonic France, 1793–1815', in C. Woolgar, *Wellington Studies I* (Southampton, 1996), pp. 1–90

Musteen, J. R., 'Becoming Nelson's Refuge and Wellington's Rock: The Ascendancy of Gibraltar during the Age of Napoleon (1793–1815)' (Unpublished PhD Thesis, Florida State University, 2005)

Norris, A. H., *The Lines of Torres Vedras: The First Three Lines and Fortifications South of the Tagus* (Torres Vedras, 2001)

Nosworthy, B., *Battle Tactics of Napoleon and his Enemies* (London, 1995)

Oman, C., *A History of the Peninsular War* (7 vols, Oxford, 1902)

——, *Wellington's Army* (London, 1912)

Pagden, A., *Worlds at War: The 2,500-Year Struggle between East and West* (Oxford, 2008)

Paget, J., *Wellington's Peninsular War: Battles and Battlefields* (London, 1990)

Parker, G., *The Military Revolution: Military Innovation and the Rise of the West, 1500–1800* (Cambridge, 1988)

Peers, D. M., *Between Mars and Mammon: Colonial Armies and the Garrison State in Early Nineteenth-Century India* (London, 1995)

Pemble, J., 'Resources and Techniques in the Second Maratha War', *Historical Journal*, Vol. 19, No. 2 (1976)

Philips, C. H., *The East India Company, 1784–1834* (Manchester, 1940)

Popham, H., *A Damned Cunning Fellow: The Eventful Life of Rear-Admiral Sir Home Popham, KCB, KCH, KM, FRS, 1762–1820* (Tywardreath, 1991)

Porter, A. (ed.), *The Oxford History of the British Empire: The Nineteenth Century* (Oxford, 2009)

Ralston, D. B., *Importing the European Army: The Introduction of European Military Techniques and Institutions into the Extra-European World, 1600–1914* (Chicago, 1990)

Read, J., *War in the Peninsula* (London, 1977)

Redgrave, T. M. O., 'Wellington's Logistical Arrangements in the Peninsular War, 1809–1814' (Unpublished PhD Thesis, University of London, n.d.)

Roberts, A., *Napoleon & Wellington* (London, 2001)

——, *Waterloo: Napoleon's Last Gamble* (London, 2005)

Roberts, M., 'The Ministerial Crisis of May–June 1812', *EHR*, Vol. 51, No. 203 (July 1936)

Roberts, P. E., *India under Wellesley* (London, 1929)

Robertson, I., *A Commanding Presence: Wellington in the Peninsula, 1808–1814* (London, 2008)

——, *Wellington at War in the Peninsula, 1808–1814: An Overview and Guide* (London, 2000)

——, *Wellington Invades France: The Final Phase of the Peninsular War, 1813–14* (London, 2003)

——, and M. Brown, *An Atlas of the Peninsular War* (London, 2010)

Robson, M., *Britain, Portugal and South America in the Napoleonic Wars: Alliance and Diplomacy in Economic Maritime Conflict* (London, 2010)

Rodger, N. A. M., *The Admiralty* (Lavenham, 1979)

——, *The Command of the Ocean: A Naval History of Britain, 1649–1815* (London, 2004)

——, *The Safeguard of the Sea: A Naval History of Britain, 660–1649* (London, 1997)

Rogers, C. J. (ed.), *The Military Revolution Debate: Readings on the Military Transformation of Early Modern Europe* (Boulder, Col., 1995)

Rogers, H., *Wellington's Army* (London, 1979)

Romans, M., 'Eyes in the Hills: Intelligence and the Events at Alcántara', in C. M. Woolgar (ed.), *Wellington Studies I* (Southampton, 1996)

Rose, J. H., 'A British Agent at Tilsit', *EHR*, Vol. 16, No. 64 (October 1901)

——, 'Canning and Denmark in 1807' *EHR*, Vol. 11, No. 41 (January 1896)

——, 'The Political Reactions of Bonaparte's Eastern Expedition', *EHR*, Vol. 44, No. 173 (January 1929)

Rothenburg, G. E. *The Art of Warfare in the Age of Napoleon* (Bloomington, Ind., 1980)

——, *The Emperor's Last Victory: Napoleon and the Battle of Wagram* (London, 2004)

Roy, K., *From Hydadpes to Kargil: A History of Warfare in India from 326BC to AD 1999* (New Delhi, 2004)

Rydjord, J., 'British Mediation between Spain and her Colonies, 1811–1813', *Hispanic American Historical Review*, Vol. 21, No. 1 (February 1941)

Sack, J. J., *From Jacobite to Conservative: Reaction and Orthodoxy in Britain, c. 1760–1832* (Cambridge, 2004)

Sarkar, J., *Military History of India* (Calcutta, 1996)

Schneid, F. C., 'The Dynamics of Defeat: French Army Leadership, December 1812–March 1813,' *JMH*, Vol. 63, No. 1 (January 1999).

——, *Napoleon's Conquest of Europe: The War of the Third Coalition* (Oxford, 2005)

Schroeder, P. W., *The Transformation of European Politics, 1763–1848* (Oxford, 1994)

Severn, J., *Architects of Empire: The Duke of Wellington and his Brothers* (Norman, Okla., 2007)

——, 'The Peninsular War and the Ministerial Crisis of 1812', in *Consortium on Revolutionary Europe, 1750–1850: Selected Papers* (Norman, Okla., 1992)

——, 'The Retaming of Bellona: Prussia and the Institutionalisation of the Napoleonic Legacy, 1815–1876', in *Military Affairs*, Vol. 44, No. 2 (April 1980)

——, *A Wellesley Affair: Richard, Marquess Wellesley and the Conduct of Spanish Diplomacy, 1809–1812* (Tallahassee, Fla., 1981)

Sherwig, J. W., *Guineas and Gunpowder: British Foreign Aid in the Wars with France, 1793–1815* (London, 1969)

Sigler, J. L., 'General Paul Thiébault: His Life and Legacy' (Unpublished PhD Thesis, Florida State University, 2006)

Smith, E. A., *Lord Grey, 1764–1845* (Oxford, 1990)

Snow, P., *To War with Wellington: From the Peninsula to Waterloo* (London, 2010)

Sparrow, E., 'The Alien Office, 1792–1806', *Historical Journal*, Vol. 33 No. 2, (1990)

——, *Secret Service: British Agents in France, 1792–1815* (Woodbridge, 1999)

Springer, W. H., 'The Military Apprenticeship of Arthur Wellesley in India, 1797–1805' (Unpublished PhD Thesis, Yale University, 1965)

Stein, B., *Thomas Munro: The Origins of the Colonial State and his Vision of Empire* (New Delhi and Oxford, 1989)

Strachan, H., *The Politics of the British Army* (Oxford, 1997)

Strathern, P., *Napoleon in Egypt* (London, 2007)

Teffeteller, G., *The Surpriser: The Life of Sir Rowland Hill* (Brunswick, NJ, 1983)

——, 'Wellington and Sir Rowland Hill', *IHR*, Vol. 11 (1989)

Thompson, N., *Earl Bathurst and the British Empire, 1762–1834* (Barnsley, 1999)

Tone, J., *The Fatal Knot: The Guerrilla War in Navarre and the Defeat of Napoleon* (Chapel Hill, NC, 1994)

Uffindell, A., *The National Army Museum Book of Wellington's Armies: Britain's Campaigns in the Peninsula and at Waterloo, 1808–1815* (London, 2003)

—— (ed.), *On Wellington: The Duke and his Art of War by Jac Weller* (London, 1998)

——, and M. Corum, *On the Fields of Glory: The Battlefields of the 1815 Campaign* (London, 2002)

Urban, M., *The Man Who Broke Napoleon's Codes: The Story of George Scovell* (London, 2001)

——, *Rifles: Six Years with Wellington's Legendary Sharpshooters* (London, 2003)

Vichness, S. E., 'Marshal of Portugal: The Military Career of William Carr Baresford, 1785–1814' (Unpublished PhD Thesis, Florida State University, 1976)

Ward, S. G. P., *Wellington's Headquarters: A Study of the Administrative Problems in the Peninsula, 1809–1814* (Oxford, 1957)

Warner, O., 'The Meeting of Wellington and Nelson', *History Today* (1968)

Webster, C. K., *The Foreign Policy of Castlereagh, 1812–1815* (London, 1931)

Weigley, R. F., *The Age of Battles: The Quest for Decisive Warfare from Breitenfeld to Waterloo* (Bloomington, Ind., 1991)

Weller, J., *Wellington in India* (London, 1972)

—, *Wellington in the Peninsula* (London, 1962)

—, *Wellington at Waterloo* (London, 1967)

Woolgar, C. M., 'Writing the Dispatch: Wellington and Official Communication', in C. M. Woolgar (ed.), *Wellington Studies II* (Southampton, 1999)

Young, P., and J. P. Lawford, *Wellington's Masterpiece: The Battle and Campaign of Salamanca* (London, 1973)

Yule, H., and A. C. Burnell, *Hobson-Jobson: A Glossary of Colloquial Anglo-Indian Words and Phrases, and of Kindred Terms, Etymological, Historical, Geographical, and Discursive* (London, 1985)

Zamoyski, A., *Rites of Peace: The Fall of Napoleon and the Congress of Vienna* (London, 2007)

Index